EQUALITY AT THE BALLOT BOX

EQUALITY

VOTES FOR WOMEN ON THE

AT THE

NORTHERN GREAT PLAINS

BALLOT BOX

Edited by Lori Ann Lahlum & Molly P. Rozum

To my dear friend Ellen,
"And the Women Persisted!"
Ruth Page Jones

SOUTH DAKOTA HISTORICAL SOCIETY PRESS PIERRE

The South Dakota Historical Society Press gratefully acknowledges
generous support for this special woman suffrage anthology from the
Presentation Sisters of Aberdeen, S.Dak., and other donors who have
helped sponsor our woman suffrage publications through
the South Dakota Historical Society Foundation.

Library of Congress Cataloging-in-Publication Data
Names: Lahlum, Lori Ann, 1962– editor. | Rozum, Molly Patrick, editor.
Title: Equality at the ballot box : votes for women on the Northern Great Plains /
Edited by Lori Ann Lahlum and Molly P. Rozum.
Identifiers: LCCN 2019026169 | ISBN 9781941813263 (hardcover)
Subjects: LCSH: Women—Suffrage—Montana—History. | Women—Suffrage—
North Dakota—History. | Women—Suffrage—South Dakota—History. |
Suffragists—Montana—Biography. | Suffragists—North Dakota—Biography. |
Suffragists—South Dakota—Biography.
Classification: LCC JK1911.M85 E86 2019 | DDC 324.6/230978—dc23
LC record available at https://lccn.loc.gov/2019026169
The paper in this book meets the guidelines for permanence and
durability of the Committee on Production Guidelines for Book Longevity
of the Council on Library Resources.

The paper in this book meets the guidelines for
permanence and durability of the Committee on Production Guidelines
for Book Longevity of the Council on Library Resources.

Cover and Frontispiece: Women and children gather outside a tent
sponsored by the Votes for Women League and the Woman's Christian
Temperance Union at a county fair in Bottineau, North Dakota, in 1914.
State Historical Society of North Dakota

Designed by Rich Hendel
Typeset in Monotype Walbaum

Please visit our website at sdhspress.com
Printed in the United States of America

20 19 18 17 16   1 2 3 4 5

Dedicated to our Grandmothers,
who were born when women did not have
full suffrage rights and witnessed ratification
of the Nineteenth Amendment in 1920:
Mary Bonertz Dugan (1886–1972)
Ruth Chilson Holte (1897–1966)
Anna Anderson Lahlum (1908–1994)
Elsie Naeve Rozum (1877–1951)

CONTENTS

ACKNOWLEDGEMENTS

A project like *Equality at the Ballot Box* involves many people. First and foremost, we would like to thank Nancy Tystad Koupal, director of the South Dakota Historical Society Press, for trusting us with this important work. What we had envisioned as a special issue of *South Dakota History* commemorating the one-hundredth anniversary of woman suffrage in South Dakota became a book project when Koupal and Jeanne Kilen Ode, managing editor of *South Dakota History*, approached us at the 2015 Northern Great Plains History Conference in Bismarck and suggested that a book would be better than a special issue of the journal. While we conceived of a book on the Dakotas, Nancy pushed us to think more broadly, and regionally, about the Northern Great Plains states and woman suffrage. Her expansive vision has made this collection of essays much stronger. We also thank Jennifer McIntyre and Cody Ewert at the press for guidance and careful editing, as well as two anonymous readers for feedback that made the book stronger.

When we started talking about this project in the fall of 2015, we knew of a few people working on suffrage topics connected to the region because of an ongoing series of woman suffrage round-tables and paper sessions at the Northern Great Plains History Conference. These sessions, begun in 2012, sought to promote suffrage centennials in various states. In many ways, the Northern Great Plains History Conference shaped this book and reinforced the importance of woman suffrage in the region. While many of the authors in this collection participated in one or more of these conference sessions, far too many gaps remained to complete our vision of a four-state regional history. We issued a call for proposals targeted to scholars we thought might be interested in contributing to the volume and curated a few pieces from additional scholars. We asked some people to change their topics fundamentally. Graciously, they agreed. All of the contributors have been generous with us as we asked them to reimagine pieces they submitted. It has been rewarding to work with all of the contributors, each of whom brought insight, knowledge, and enthusiasm about votes for women.

Many professionals helped with sources and material culture: Liz Almlie (South Dakota State Historical Society Office of Historic Preservation); Wes Anderson (Barnes County Historical Society); Sara Casper, Matthew T. Reitzel, and Ken Stewart (South Dakota State Historical Society Archives); Jessica Rockeman and Danielle Stuckle (State Historical Society of North Dakota); and Jeff Sauve (Norwegian-American Historical Association). Sarah Carter (University of Alberta) shared her unpublished manuscript on woman suffrage in the Canadian Prairie Provinces with us. Susan Wefald put us in touch with Darrell Dorgan, who allowed us to photograph his women's ballot box.

A number of people supported us in this endeavor, becoming cheerleaders for the project: Liz Almlie, Mary Anderson, Anne Bailey, Elise Boxer, Angela Jill Cooley, Anthony Dutton, Kent K. B. Hanson, Tom Isern (who introduced us to each other many years ago), Elizabeth Jameson, Audrey Lahlum, Howard Lahlum, Kirsten Lahlum, Michael Lansing, Sara Lampert, Carol Leibiger, Jim Naylor, Agnes Odinga-Oluoch, Martha Pfeifle, Jennifer Ritterhouse, and Alan Stern. We wish to thank members of the Historians of MNSU writing group (Angela Jill Cooley, Rachael Hanel, Laura Harrison, and Chad McCutchen) and Jim Naylor for reading the introduction and asking questions that made it stronger. Minnesota State University, Mankato, provided Lori Lahlum with a sabbatical in 2017-2018 that allowed her time to work on this project. Grants from the Allene R. Chiesman Fund at the University of South Dakota and the South Dakota Humanities Council supported the research of Molly Rozum.

As daughters of the Northern Great Plains and historians of women, we found this project rewarding.

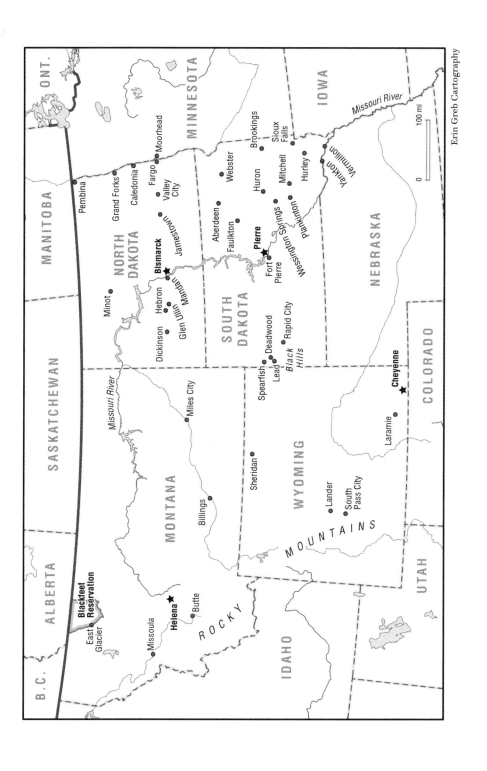

Erin Greb Cartography

INTRODUCTION
"WE WILL NEVER HALT TILL THE PRIZE IS WON"
Suffrage on the Northern Great Plains

MOLLY P. ROZUM & LORI ANN LAHLUM

"No, No! Suffragists arouse! Let us consecrate ourselves
fully to a pure devotion to our holy cause of human justice, and
press fearlessly on, well knowing that the right must prevail."
—Emma Smith DeVoe[1]

The summer and early fall of 1889 was an exhilarating time for suffragists on the Northern Great Plains. In that year, North Dakota, South Dakota, Montana, and Wyoming all petitioned the United States Congress for statehood, and spirited debates over the enfranchisement of women took place at all of the state constitutional conventions as suffrage supporters tried to secure the measure in the state constitutions. National suffragists hoped the new states would enter the Union with full voting rights for women. Opponents of woman suffrage throughout the region, and even some supporters, warned that including it in the new state constitutions could give Congress a reason not to admit the petitioning states or offer voters a reason to reject the constitution. Even in Wyoming, which enacted woman suffrage in 1869, some statehood boosters feared that Congress would not admit a state that enfranchised women. Thanks in part to its long history of voting rights for women and support from Governor Francis E. Warren and Congressional Delegate Joseph M. Carey, however, Wyoming carried full woman suffrage into statehood.[2]

While delegates at the Wyoming constitutional convention debated whether to continue full suffrage rights for women, south-

[1]

ern Dakota Territory, northern Dakota Territory, and Montana Territory grappled with expanding women's previously established right to vote in school elections into full enfranchisement. Though activists had high hopes, by the start of the summer, the *Woman's Journal*, a suffrage newspaper edited by Bostonians Lucy Stone and Henry Blackwell, conceded that securing full franchise rights for women would be difficult in Montana. At the close of the North Dakota, South Dakota, and Montana constitutional conventions, women retained the right to vote on certain school matters. Montana women, however, could neither vote for state superintendent of public instruction nor run for the position.[3]

Suffragists had hoped that if the state constitutions did not include full suffrage rights, alternative provisions would allow the state legislatures to enfranchise women following statehood. Instead, the three conventions attempted to adopt a requirement to amend the constitutions by submitting the issue to male voters. The South Dakota state constitution explicitly stated that male residents, including foreign-born men who were not citizens but had begun the naturalization process, could vote on removing the word "male" in the article addressing voting rights in the year following statehood. Montana and North Dakota also allowed foreign-born men to vote in elections, but Wyoming rejected such a provision, even though the territory's enabling act had given them the vote. North Dakota allowed for a referendum on woman suffrage, but the language of the authorization made its success unlikely. Montana, meanwhile, rejected a proposal that its male population vote on the proposed constitution and woman suffrage separately.[4] Voters in all of the new states approved their new constitutions—Wyoming by a large margin.

When national suffrage advocate Henry Blackwell appeared before the North Dakota constitutional convention in the midst of drought in 1889, he commented on the "bleak prairies."[5] When Blackwell canvassed for woman suffrage in Kansas, Colorado, and Nebraska, he had enthused over the sunshine and this "wonderful wild new country." Even as he railroaded west to Montana's convention, Blackwell took pleasure in "small patches of verdure on the low flats."[6] Several weeks later, geologist John

Wesley Powell appeared at the conventions of North Dakota and Montana (he also went on to Wyoming) to suggest that drought would be a common occurrence in any state that included part of the physiographic "plains" province.[7] Similar to woman suffragists, Powell recognized regional state-making as a chance to enhance democracy. He toured with a United States Senate irrigation study committee and urged convention delegates to turn their attention to the effects of climate on unaided agriculture in a broad transitional plains area. Powell had long warned the United States Congress of the need to change land and water laws in a fluctuating "arid region."[8] A year later, national suffragist Susan B. Anthony recognized that the continuing drought caused financial distress that affected South Dakota's campaign for women's voting rights. She spoke for woman suffrage, but Anthony also gave her opinion that Congress should have appropriated money for artesian well development, rather than fund a congressional commission to investigate irrigation.[9]

The drought-prone plains of North Dakota, South Dakota, Montana, and Wyoming proved a key point of connection among these states as they developed.[10] Variable climate, cold temperatures, cyclical drought, and the "transitional character of the physical environment," if not entirely clear to convention delegates or settler society generally when Powell spoke, helped forge the region's identity during the long era of woman suffrage campaigning. Shared climate and topography, along with similar histories and demographics, bound the Northern Great Plains states into a coherent region.[11]

Their respective constitutional conventions provide insight into how the Northern Great Plains states differed on the question of woman suffrage. By the time the United States ratified the Nineteenth Amendment in 1920, settlers in the region had debated suffrage for over fifty years while engaged in a broader effort to advance the nation's westward expansion. Like settler society itself, the woman suffrage movement rippled across the Northern Great Plains at a continuous but irregular pace. A brief overview of some of the major events, issues, and personalities important to the many legislative votes and referenda on woman suffrage in North Dakota, South Dakota, Montana, and Wyoming suggests how these states help us better understand woman suffrage in the region and nation.

Wyoming is often viewed as an outlier among the Northern Great Plains states because it enacted woman suffrage in 1869—the first territory and the first state in the United States to do so. As the events of 1889 demonstrate, however, these states have much in common when it comes to suffrage. All the territorial legislative assemblies debated the issue. Suffrage supporters understood the advantages of securing electoral rights for women under the territorial system because Congress did not have to approve such legislation.[12] In most cases, a successful vote in the legislative assembly and the governor's signature enacted woman suffrage. A state constitution, however, required the approval of male voters and Congress, which made the process inherently more challenging. National suffragists focused on states, not territories, because territorial residents did not vote for president or send representatives and senators to Congress. Nonetheless, the prolonged territorial discussion of woman suffrage in the Northern Great Plains states became important precursors for post-statehood efforts to secure voting rights.

The Civil War, Reconstruction, westward expansion, and early debates over women's rights in eastern states shaped how settlers on the Northern Great Plains discussed suffrage, including the vote for African Americans. To clear extensive tracts of northern plains land for settlement, the United States fought wars, signed treaties and agreements, and, ultimately, removed American Indians to restricted reservations in the region, exemplifying the ideology that recent scholars have called settler colonialism.[13] Congress organized Dakota Territory in 1861 from parts of Minnesota and Nebraska territories, originally including what became Montana Territory and a portion of Wyoming Territory. By the time Congress created Montana (1864) and Wyoming (1868) territories, the question of suffrage for African American men had become part of the debate. The organic acts that created Dakota and Montana territories limited voting rights to white men. In early 1867, Congress modified territorial organic acts as part of its Reconstruction measures, granting African American men suffrage rights three years before ratification of the Fifteenth

Amendment. Hamilton Wilcox, a New York suffragist, proposed including women in the amended organic acts, but his measure failed. Dakota Territory adopted legislation granting African American men the right to vote in 1867. Montana Territory initially resisted, and many African American men experienced violence when they tried to vote. African Americans could vote in Wyoming Territory from its inception.[14] Ignored in this conversation, for the most part, were American Indians.

As territorial legislatures expanded voting rights to African American men, delegates in Dakota Territory and Wyoming Territory began discussing the enfranchisement of women. While scholars have long recognized the suffrage debate in Wyoming Territory, events in Dakota Territory have been overlooked. Indeed, the first legislative discussions on woman suffrage on the Northern Great Plains took place there in December 1868, during the 1868–1869 legislative session. Enos Stutsman, a representative from the northeastern section around Pembina, put forth a bill "to confer upon women elective franchise and the eligibility to office."[15] One newspaper speculated that with its passage, the territory would gain "notoriety" and become a "mecca" for "the strong-minded."[16] The bill passed the house by a vote of fourteen to nine. The council, however, passed a different bill. Delegate Charles Rossteuscher, a brewer from Yankton, introduced language that appears to have mocked the bill's intent. While his resolution failed, the house refused to pass the council's version, and woman suffrage died in early 1869.[17] Suffragist Alice Pickler suspected that the council suffrage bill may have been "a burlesque" because original supporters in the house, like Stutsman, voted against it.[18]

In December 1869, the Wyoming territorial legislature passed, and the governor signed into law, the first woman suffrage bill in the United States. The following year, Dakota Territory again considered removing the word "male" from its constitution, but the bill failed.[19] The *Laramie Sentinel* soon reported the defeat and invited "all" women to Wyoming, where they would be "appreciated."[20] In the fall of 1871, Wyoming's second legislature attempted to repeal women's voting rights, but a gubernatorial veto of the bill stood by one vote. In Dakota Territory, woman suffrage failed again by one vote in the 1872 legislature.[21] This early period may have been suffragists' best opportunity for success. Yet, only one territory on the Northern Great Plains granted women the franchise.

Efforts to enfranchise women continued in Dakota and Montana territories, though not always in a sustained manner. School suffrage had been easier to achieve because people often saw women as playing an important role in educating children. In 1879, some women in Dakota Territory acquired the right to vote on school matters. The legislature made changes to the law in the 1880s, and by 1887, women who had guardianship of children and women taxpayers could vote for school officers and county superintendent. Meanwhile in Montana Territory, the 1883 legislature enacted local school suffrage.[22] Laws regulating school elections in Dakota and Montana territories pushed suffrage conversations forward and raised hope among suffragists that broader enfranchisement would happen soon.

By 1885, Dakota Territory residents had launched a new effort to push assemblymen to vote for full suffrage rights for women. John Pickler of Faulkton, a suffragist from southern Dakota Territory, introduced a bill "granting women the right of suffrage," although it did not allow women to run for elective office. Residents from the southern portion of the territory petitioned the legislative assembly to support Pickler's bill, calling women "as sober, as moral, and as capable as" men and arguing that such a bill would "promot[e] sobriety, peace, morality, education and prosperity." The house and council passed the suffrage bill, but territorial governor Gilbert A. Pierce vetoed it. Pierce's veto highlights obstacles to enacting woman suffrage in the region. According to Pierce, residents with electoral rights, meaning men, should have the right to vote on the measure. Further, he claimed that only Congress should enact such a law and that most women in Dakota Territory did not want the right to vote. Perhaps most importantly, Pierce suspected that enacting woman suffrage would impede the prospect for statehood. The territorial legislature could not override Pierce's veto.[23] In the next territorial assembly, women from the Franchise Department of the Woman's Christian Temperance Union (WCTU) presented, without success, "hundreds of petitions" signed by men and women of Dakota Territory asking for woman suffrage.[24]

While suffrage supporters in Dakota failed to make headway, in 1883, the Montana legislature passed a partial suffrage law that allowed women taxpayers to vote on issues involving taxes. Six years later, the Montana constitutional convention extended the right for women taxpayers to vote "upon all questions submitted to the vote of the taxpayers of the State or any political division thereof." Women who paid property taxes and met "the qualifications of suffrage required of men . . . shall equally, with men, have the right to vote."[25] Among women who could be eligible to vote under Montana's law were women who owned houses used for prostitution. Although the Montana constitution clearly granted voting rights to women taxpayers, debate over whether these eligible voters could cast ballots in city elections occurred in Billings and Bozeman, among other cities. Additionally, some men sought to disenfranchise women taxpayers. In response, women petitioned the legislature not to change the law.[26]

Though Dakota, Montana, and Wyoming all enacted measures allowing women to vote prior to statehood, only in Wyoming did women possess full suffrage rights. The many years of lobbying for territorial suffrage had well prepared women and pro-suffrage legislators for the debates that took place during the 1889 Northern Great Plains statehood conventions. North Dakota, South Dakota, and Montana joined the Union in 1889 and Wyoming in 1890. Suffrage supporters ensured that Wyoming retained women's voting rights, while the other three states continued the fight to extend the franchise to white women. Instead, each state witnessed many failed attempts to push woman suffrage through state legislatures and endured eight referendum campaigns to enfranchise women from 1890 to 1918, six of them in South Dakota.

South Dakota's 1889–1890 campaign, led by both state and national suffrage organizations, failed. A statewide Equal Suffrage Association (ESA) formed in 1889, and the WCTU franchise departments trained many suffragists during the campaign. Susan B. Anthony from the National Woman Suffrage Association (NWSA) toured the state in November 1889 to kick off the campaign and

Rev. Anna Howard Shaw

ADDRESS AT

Opera House, Huron, S. D.

SATURDAY, OCT. 29, '10

At 8 O'clock

Equal Suffrage Amendment

*National suffrage advocates such as Anna Howard
Shaw toured the Northern Great Plains states throughout the
late-nineteenth and early-twentieth centuries.*
Richardson Collection, University of South Dakota

advise the new state organization. She returned the next year, along with Anna Howard Shaw and Henry Blackwell, among others, under the auspices of the newly formed National American Woman Suffrage Association (NAWSA) to canvass the entire state to build support. Key organizations like the Farmers' Alliance and the Knights of Labor supported woman suffrage in principle but failed to provide practical support. Neither the Democratic or Republican Parties, nor the new Independent—later Populist—Party, included it in their platforms. Disappointed supporters pointed to ties between prohibition and woman suffrage and suggested that financial support from liquor interests and anti-temperance ethnic voters were the culprits. The rising activity of the Remonstrants, a Boston-based anti-suffrage group, also played a role. In addition, the heated vote on the location of the state's capital may have distracted voters. Drought also hurt enthusiasm and financial support for the campaign. National suffrage canvassers had taken note of the "forsaken desperate look worn" by those they lobbied.[27] Suffragists also openly feared that "ignorant Sioux Indians" might vote before "intelligent women."[28] After the 1890 vote, observers noted with displeasure that more male voters failed to restrict the vote of American Indian men who maintained tribal affiliation than supported woman suffrage. Finally, tensions between the state ESA, allied with the WCTU, and NAWSA leaders also damaged the campaign.[29]

In the 1890s, while NAWSA fought to separate prohibition from conversations about woman suffrage, the WCTU played a crucial role in suffrage successes on the Northern Great Plains, emerging as a distinguishing feature of the region's movement. Not only was the organization embedded in local communities, it became the only consistent suffrage organization in the region over the long battle to enfranchise women. In all three states, membership in the WCTU far exceeded membership in other suffrage organizations, and the WCTU trained women to speak publicly in favor of woman suffrage. As a result, small towns and villages throughout the region had access to suffrage speakers. Many male voters in the Northern Great Plains states supported temperance and prohibition, and WCTU speakers frequently found audiences open to their message. The power of prohibition was clear when North Dakota and South Dakota both entered the Union as dry states in 1889. Activists in national suffrage organizations often failed to recognize that this linkage could be an asset in the region. To be sure, suffragists like Mary ("Mamie") Shields Pyle of South Dakota and Jeannette Rankin of Montana opposed linking these causes as a strategy.[30] Nonetheless, the connection between woman suffrage and prohibition often helped convince men that they should support suffrage. More importantly, tethering prohibition to suffrage prompted women to advocate for female enfranchisement.

The large number of European immigrants in the Northern

Great Plains states also influenced suffrage debates in the region. Much of the strategizing for suffrage campaigns concerned how to win the vote in predominantly foreign-language-speaking ethnic communities. Although much of the settler population had migrated from nearby states, the Northeast, and Canada, the region had significant foreign-born populations from Germany, Bohemia, England, Ireland, Norway, and Sweden, as well as large numbers of Russian-born Germans in the Dakotas. In 1890, 42.7 percent of the North Dakota population identified as foreign-born; in Montana, South Dakota, and Wyoming, the figures were 30.2 percent, 26.1 percent, and 23.8 percent, respectively. By 1900, the percentage of foreign-born residents in each state had fallen, but they all possessed high numbers of second-generation immigrants fully embedded in ethnic communities.[31] Local suffragists and national leaders often disagreed over the potential of immigrant voters. As Sara Egge contends, far too many eastern suffragists saw immigrants as impediments, while local workers, though often frustrated in their ability to reach into these ethnic enclaves, viewed them as opportunities for suffrage success. With so many immigrants and children of immigrants on the Northern Great Plains, they would clearly play a role in suffrage votes, and debates about immigrants remained a persistent feature of woman suffrage in the region.[32]

A few years after the unsuccessful 1890 suffrage campaign in South Dakota, the North Dakota legislature passed a bill granting white women suffrage rights in 1893. With the governor poised to sign the bill, however, it disappeared through legislative subterfuge. Throughout the 1890s, women in Montana, who could vote as taxpayers and in school elections, met regular resistance as some men questioned even partial suffrage. In 1895, the Montana house of representatives passed a suffrage amendment, but it lost in the senate. In the wake of this defeat, Emma Smith DeVoe, prominent in the 1890 South Dakota campaign and now an organizer for NAWSA, came to Montana to organize suffrage clubs. By 1896, more than two hundred fifty women had joined. White suffragists reached out to African American women in Helena, encouraging them to become engaged in the movement. Both the 1895 and 1897 Montana legislatures considered a woman suf-

Photographed by the Suffrage Daily News *of Helena,*
these suffragists toured four counties ahead of Montana's 1914 election.
Montana Historical Society Research Center

frage bill, but the requirement for two-thirds of members to support a constitutional amendment proved an impediment. As in
South Dakota by 1900, the WCTU was the most visible suffrage
presence in Montana and North Dakota.[33]

Amid efforts to achieve full enfranchisement throughout the
Northern Great Plains, South Dakota held a lackluster school
suffrage campaign that would have allowed women to vote for
county superintendents and state superintendent of public instruction in 1894 and a referendum campaign for full suffrage
in 1898. Both failed, leaving suffragists in the state dispirited.
Another popular defeat in South Dakota in 1910 brought an end
to the idea that woman suffrage could be won in tandem with
prohibition and prompted a formal reorganization of the state's
primary suffrage association. In Montana, the legislature voted
on suffrage measures every year from 1895 to 1911.[34] In North Dakota, suffrage supporters were eerily silent.

The success of woman suffrage in Washington, California,

Arizona Territory, Kansas, and Oregon between 1910 and 1912 reinvigorated suffragists on the Northern Great Plains. In 1914, Montana, North Dakota, and South Dakota each held major campaigns to enfranchise women. While state organizations in Montana and South Dakota unlinked prohibition and woman suffrage, the causes retained a close association in North Dakota. The Montana campaign succeeded, while those in North Dakota and South Dakota failed. By 1914, Montana had a robust and organized Montana Equal Suffrage Association (MESA). Although MESA, under the leadership of Jeannette Rankin, denounced linking suffrage and prohibition, women like Mary Long Alderson continued to advocate for both causes. To Rankin, making woman suffrage and prohibition "twin sisters" explained why enfranchisement had failed in the past. Yet, Rankin could not separate the twins in the 1914 suffrage campaign. In 1916, Montanans voted on a prohibition measure. For the most part, counties that had the highest levels of support for woman suffrage in 1914 also voted for prohibition with majorities of 60 percent or higher.[35] Unlike in Wyoming, prohibition followed soon after the enfranchisement of Montana women.

In North Dakota, WCTU president and suffrage activist Elizabeth Preston Anderson and Votes for Women League (VWL) president Grace Clendening led the 1914 campaign to enfranchise women. Two years earlier, the VWL had organized as the state's first successful suffrage organization. Members established clubs, campaigned throughout the state during 1913 and 1914, and invited speakers to rally support for woman suffrage. In 1913, Jeannette Rankin traveled to North Dakota and spoke on the necessity of expanding voting rights for women. For suffrage supporters, the electoral loss that followed was devastating. While it appears there were election irregularities, the sizeable German-Russian population influenced the final results. In most German-Russian counties, support for the suffrage amendment typically garnered under 20 percent of the vote, and in McIntosh County (the most German-Russian county in the state), a mere 8.7 percent of male voters cast ballots in its favor. Despite North Dakota being a dry state, some voters, especially German Russians, were deeply concerned about the impediment woman suffrage might pose to repealing prohibition. Women in North Dakota finally acquired voting rights after voters swept the Non-partisan League into power and the 1917 legislature enacted partial suffrage—presidential, county, and municipal.[36]

By the time of the 1914 campaign, South Dakota suffragists had been working under a restructured and renamed state organization, the South Dakota Universal Franchise League (SDUFL), for several years, with Pyle as president. Pyle intended to keep woman suffrage and prohibition issues separate, and SDUFL activists emphasized increased male support for suffrage. They also successfully lobbied within the state capitol and issued a weekly suffrage newspaper called the *South Dakota Messenger*. Yet, the campaign failed. It took two more campaigns for South Dakota women to win the right to vote. Suffragists blamed the votes of Germans and German Russians for the 1916 defeat, noting that, of nineteen counties with a German population over 25 percent, seventeen of them defeated woman suffrage. Higher German-population counties also correlated with lower support for prohibition, which became law once again in 1916. Victory for woman suffrage in South Dakota finally came in 1918, albeit with an unfortunate consequence: it disenfranchised the state's noncitizen immigrants, who had been permitted to vote since territorial days. On the Northern Great Plains, only North Dakota lacked full suffrage rights for white women when the states ratified the Nineteenth Amendment.[37]

When it came time for the Northern Great Plains states to ratify the Nineteenth Amendment in 1919–1920, John Wesley Powell would not have been too surprised to learn that drought and a poor economy actually made it easier for the cost-conscious governors of North Dakota, Montana, and Wyoming to call special legislative sessions. The governors were reticent to authorize special sessions solely for the purpose of ratifying the Susan B. Anthony Amendment. The need to institute economic and environmental relief measures, however, gave additional rationale for the special legislative sessions that successfully ratified the woman suffrage amendment to the United States Constitution.[38]

The Nineteenth Amendment suggested the beginning of a national shift to citizenship as the nation's primary qualification for

The legislative committee of the South Dakota Universal Franchise League—Etta Estey Boyce, Mary Shields Pyle, and Mabel Rewman, seen here on the steps of the state capitol in 1915—successfully lobbied legislators to include a suffrage measure on the 1916 ballot. Private Collection suffrage rights. South Dakota's 1918 woman suffrage victory had reflected this trend. Since at least the passage of the Fourteenth Amendment, national suffragists had asserted that the right to vote stemmed from national citizenship. Even after the ratification of the Nineteenth Amendment, however, not all women who were citizens could vote. A variety of state-level laws, for example, took advantage of "constitutional loopholes" that excluded at least three-fourths of African American women from the vote.[39] Additionally, women who married noncitizens before 1922 lost the right to vote under the concept of "marital unity" except in the few states where aliens and women had the right to vote. The practice would have affected many women on the Northern Great Plains who married noncitizen immigrants without voting rights or men who lost the vote when state naturalization laws tightened. Suffragists soon advocated a new law, passed in 1922, that prevented the denial of citizenship—and voting rights—to women who married aliens.[40] After 1888, some American Indian women qualified to vote if they became United States citizens through marriage to non-Indians. Yet, only in 1924 did a congressional act confer citizenship, and presumably suffrage rights, on all American Indians without requiring a simultaneous disavowal of tribal affiliation. State laws in the Northern Great Plains states, however, also took advantage of loopholes in the United States Constitution to deny American Indian women voting rights.[41]

Equality at the Ballot Box: Votes for Women on the Northern Great Plains is the first volume to explore this long history of woman suffrage in Wyoming, Montana, South Dakota, and North Dakota from a regional perspective. In his classic study of the plains region, historian Walter Prescott Webb wondered why voting rights for women "spread practically all over the Great Plains before it was adopted in the East." He related the success of woman suffrage on the Great Plains and in the West to a general tradition of political radicalism and suggested that finding the reason might reveal some of "the spirit" of the place.[42] Webb, however, paid little attention to women and suggested that they lacked an affinity for the plains environment. Publications such as *Women on the North American Plains*, edited by Renee M. Laegreid and Sandra K. Mathews, have begun to remedy Webb's "casual neglect" of women by exploring diverse plainswomen's experiences over hundreds of years. The essays show how women have "adjusted to the specifics of the environment" with the same variance as men. Building on such regional scholarship and western women's history, the essays in *Equality at the Ballot Box* continue Laegreid and Matthews's project of "connecting specific people and locations to a larger picture," producing a more textured history of woman suffrage in the United States.[43]

In addressing Webb's question about the success of woman suffrage on the Northern Great Plains, historians have looked only through the lens of state history. The earliest suffrage studies —mostly student research papers—placed women's voices and experiences into the historical record using extensive primary research in state newspapers, government documents, periodicals, and personal interviews. They also engaged with the six-volume *History of Woman Suffrage*, written from the perspective of participants in the United States movement and edited by Susan B. Anthony, Elizabeth Cady Stanton, Matilda Joslyn Gage, and Ida Husted Harper. Early works on Northern Great Plains woman suffrage laid out the basic chronology, major issues, and key participants in respective state suffrage movements.[44]

Each state's movement had a unique trajectory. With Wyoming's prime role as the first territory and the first state to grant women suffrage rights, historians have asked why woman suffrage succeeded there. In South Dakota, with many territorial legislative attempts to pass woman suffrage and six referenda for full women's voting rights, historians have focused on organizations and asked why woman suffrage failed. In Montana, full woman suffrage passed with only one referendum, making it the second northern plains state to support full woman suffrage. Even so, women's voting rights came only after decades of suffrage lobbying. Observers also identified the nature of the woman suffrage in North Dakota, seemingly rooted in complex political party and business machinations. Newspaper coverage and family and community connections spread discussions about woman suffrage across settler society in the long era between statehood and the Nineteenth Amendment, but each state had a unique rhythm.

State suffrage histories exhibit some common themes. Regional scholarship has addressed national figures such as Susan B. Anthony, Henry Blackwell, and Carrie Chapman Catt, who provided common points of connection and sources of financial support while highlighting cultural friction. Much of the state scholarship addresses key persons in the state movements, such as Jeannette Rankin and Ella L. Knowles in Montana; Marietta Bones, Emma Smith DeVoe, and Mary Shields Pyle in South Dakota; Elizabeth Preston Anderson, Laura J. Eisenhuth, and Linda Slaughter in North Dakota; and Julia Bright and Ester Morris in Wyoming. These individuals often represented particular organizations that have received scholarly attention, such as the Woman's Christian Temperance Union, religious groups, the Populists, and the Nonpartisan League. More recent perspectives on woman suffrage have focused on "Domestic Feminism," "New Women," and settler colonialism. Recent scholarship has also examined popular memory surrounding suffrage and efforts to commemorate activists and key events.[45] The new research and interpretations presented in this collection deepen this literature while highlighting the significance of the region in the national suffrage movement.

Equality at the Ballot Box also seeks to re-center our understanding of place and suffrage. This volume is not a comprehensive study of woman suffrage in the Northern Great Plains states. Instead, the essays highlight key aspects of woman suffrage in the region, while recognizing differences among and within the states and pointing to regional connections. The essays in Part 1 provide overviews of suffrage politics in each of the states. Jennifer Helton examines Wyoming's 1869 territorial suffrage victory in the context of Reconstruction-era politics and the Radical Republican vision of the West. Helton also argues that the state's achievement should be seen as part of a national movement rather than as an inexplicable surprise. Barbara Handy-Marchello's comprehensive essay on North Dakota argues that boss politics and powerful railroads impeded reform measures such as woman suffrage during the early years of statehood. Boss Alexander McKenzie dictated the failure of woman suffrage in order to keep German-Russian voters in the Republican Party fold and to ensure legislative support for the Northern Pacific Railway. Jennifer Hill explores how various forms of public activism shaped the suffrage experiences of three Montana women, Clara McAdow, Mary Long Alderson, and Maria Dean. Their commitment to civic engagement provided opportunities for other women in public spaces and helped them develop leadership skills they would later put to use for woman suffrage. Hill's essay reminds us that the Montana suffrage story extends beyond Jeannette Rankin, as McAdow, Alderson, and Dean each began their suffrage work decades earlier. Paula M. Nelson provides a close look at anti-suffrage women from the territorial period to the adoption of suffrage almost three decades after South Dakota statehood. Nelson challenges assumptions about the forces of opposition emphasized in the literature on South Dakota's long woman suffrage struggle, highlighting instead women's perceptions of their social roles and reassessing the part that liquor interests played in defeating the state's many suffrage campaigns.

Part 2 features case studies that focus on important themes in the suffrage movement on the Northern Great Plains. Ruth Page Jones focuses on the understudied topic of school suffrage, examining shifting laws in Dakota Territory and South Dakota. Jones argues that school suffrage helped change the social reality of women in politics while increasing male support for full female suffrage. In the next essay, Sara Egge explores ethnicity in southeastern South Dakota during the 1890 and 1898 suffrage campaigns, highlighting differences between local pro-suffrage activists, who often accepted nearby ethnic enclaves, and the oppositional attitudes of NAWSA leadership toward the state's large ethnic population. Lack of national support for later South Dakota campaigns, Egge argues, stemmed from faulty judgement of the prospects for influencing the state's ethnic minorities. Molly P. Rozum delves into the intersection of citizenship, property, gender, race, and suffrage in South Dakota's 1890 election, when the electorate voted on a referendum to strike the word "male" from its year-old constitution and another that would restrict the voting rights of American Indians. Rozum argues that while property emerged as the leading rationale for voting rights on the Northern Great Plains, racism exhibited through the discourses of educated suffrage and civilization kept suffragists from supporting American Indian suffrage. Amy McKinney examines the celebration of the fiftieth anniversary of woman suffrage, focusing on Wyoming's ratification of the Nineteenth Amendment. National suffragists wanted Wyoming to become the first to ratify, but the state's governor, along with the governors of Montana, North Dakota, and South Dakota, proved reluctant to call a special session.

The essays in Part 3 provide gendered analyses of woman suffrage in the Northern Great Plains states by studying the lives of individual women and their suffrage experiences. Kristin Mapel Bloomberg illuminates Cora Smith Eaton's early suffrage career in northern Dakota Territory and North Dakota. Smith Eaton, a well-known suffragist, grew up in northern Dakota Territory, and her experiences there informed her development as a regional and national suffrage leader. Additionally, Bloomberg shows how male resistance limited women's voting rights. In the next essay, Dee Garceau reveals how racism and the complexity of citizenship laws shaped Helen Piotopowaka Clarke, a Blackfeet woman in Montana, and led her to champion expansive civil and political rights for American Indians. According to Garceau, for Blackfeet women like Clarke and Virginia Billedeaux, support for woman suffrage emerged from a broader agenda of political and human rights. Finally, Ann W. Braaten argues that Kate Selby Wilder embodied the link between woman suffrage and the WCTU through that group's "Do-Everything" policy. Wilder came to support the enfranchisement of women as part of the WCTU and traveled North Dakota delivering addresses in support of the issue on its behalf. Indeed, Wilder, an affluent and connected white woman in Fargo, used her privileged position to gain political rights for non-American Indian women in the state.

Interspersed between the three essay sections are short pieces that we call Suffrage Snapshots, whose authors look at specific problems, persons, turning points, and the material culture of the suffrage movement on the Northern Great Plains. The first group features snapshots of Wyoming statehood, Norwegian-American support for suffrage and prohibition in eastern South Dakota, and attitudes toward woman suffrage revealed in German-language newspapers. The second set of snapshots includes pieces on Martha Symons Boies Atkinson, the first woman bailiff in Wyoming; on Kate Selby Wilder's lingerie dress, the *de facto* uniform of the suffrage movement; on Jeannette Rankin's use of the automobile in suffrage campaigning; and on Mabel Rewman, a suffragist in South Dakota's Black Hills. These Suffrage Snapshots point to further research yet to be done on the Northern Great Plains woman suffrage movement.

While this collection covers a lot of ground, it also makes clear that work remains to be done, such as research into African Americans and woman suffrage on the Northern Great Plains. A region with such a significant American Indian population also requires additional studies of American Indians and woman suffrage. The snapshots on German- and Norwegian-language sources indicate the rich possibilities for using non-English sources to study woman suffrage in the region. Comparative studies between Northern Great Plains states and Canada's three Prairie Provinces, which all passed provincial woman suffrage in 1916, could contribute to understanding regional connections and national political patterns that shaped woman suffrage.[46] More in-depth studies of individual men and male-dominated legislatures in forestalling and fostering woman suffrage may yield further insights into state and regional political culture. Finally, greater exploration of how geography, space, and sense of place shaped woman suffrage is needed for a full understanding of how the movement developed in these states.

The new research presented in *Equality at the Ballot Box*, combined with classic state suffrage scholarship, begins to convey something of the spirit of the Northern Great Plains. These essays offer a view of suffrage politics at the intersection of westward expansion, settler colonialism, and nationalism. Examining the ways that national suffrage organizations and closely linked reform groups like the WCTU responded to the diverse populations of the Northern Great Plains reveals how assumptions about immigrants, American Indians, and rural Americans shaped broader conceptions of democracy. As territorial and state legislatures considered woman suffrage, local activists gained vital political experience that helped advance the national movement. Campaigning for—and in some cases, against—the vote transformed generations of women into experienced political actors. First, however, Northern Great Plains suffragists needed to win the vote.

NOTES

1. DeVoe quoted in *Black Hills Union*, 4 Dec. 1890.

2. *Cheyenne Daily Sun*, 10 Oct. 1889; T. A. Larson, "Woman Suffrage in Wyoming," *Pacific Northwest Quarterly* 56 (Apr. 1965): 63–64; Miriam Gantz Chapman, "The Story of Woman Suffrage in Wyoming, 1869–1890" (master's thesis, University of Wyoming, 1952), pp. 91–100; Michael Malone, Richard R. Roeder, and William L. Lang, *Montana: A History of Two Centuries*, 2d ed. (Seattle: University of Washington Press, 1991), p. 197; Doris Buck Ward, "The Winning of Woman Suffrage in Montana" (master's thesis: Montana State University, 1974), pp. 20, 26–27; Alma Lutz, "Susan B. Anthony in the Dakotas," *North Dakota History* 25 (Oct. 1958): 120. Congress did not authorize Wyoming Territory to organize for statehood, but the territorial governor called for a constitutional convention with the idea that Wyoming could become a state alongside its Northern Great Plains neighbors. What hindered Wyoming statehood in 1889 was not woman suffrage but, rather, its small population.

3. *Cheyenne Daily Sun*, 15 Aug. 1889; Leslie Wheeler, "Woman Suffrage's Gray-Bearded Champion Comes to Montana, 1889," *Montana: The Magazine of Western History* 31 (Summer 1981): 2–13. Blackwell also sent letters from national politicians who supported woman suffrage to Wyoming's governor, who in turn presented them to the 1889 convention. *See* Wyoming, *Journal and Debates of the Constitutional Convention of the State of Wyoming* (Cheyenne, 1893), pp. 29–30, 173–74.

4. Patrick M. Garry, *The South Dakota State Constitution* (New York: Oxford University Press, 2014), p. 158; Kristin Mapel Bloomberg, "Cora Smith Eaton and North Dakota Woman Suffrage, 1888–1897," herein; Barbara Handy-Marchello, "Swashing around in the Sisterhood of States: Statehood for North Dakota in 1889," *North Dakota History* 79 (Dec. 2014): 6–7; Wheeler, "Woman Suffrage's Gray-Bearded Champion," p. 12; T. A. Larson, "Montana Women and the Battle for the Ballot," *Montana: The Magazine of Western History* 23 (Winter 1973): 27–29; Ward, "Winning of Woman Suffrage in Montana," pp. 10, 14–30. North Dakota initially allowed the state legislature to enact woman suffrage but voted one day later to require that male residents decide the issue.

5. Quoted in North Dakota, *Proceedings and Debates of the First Constitutional Convention of North Dakota* (Bismarck, 1889), p. 40.

6. Quoted in Wheeler, "Woman Suffrage's Gray-Bearded Champion," p. 5.

7. Wallace Stegner, *Beyond the Hundredth Meridian: John Wesley Powell and the Second Opening of the West* (1954; repr., New York: Penguin, 1992), pp. 313–16. *See also* Donald Worster, *A River Running West: The Life of John Wesley Powell* (New York: Oxford University Press, 2001), pp. 480–81. Members of the Congressional Irrigation Committee, with whom Powell traveled, visited South Dakota before Powell arrived in the region. South Dakota, *South Dakota Constitutional Convention*, Vol. 2: *Held at Sioux Falls, 1889* (Huron, [1907]), pp. 419–20, 422, 461–62, 466–67. Most geographers and historians have accepted Walter Prescott Webb's definition of "the Plains proper," a landmass between the Rocky Mountains and an uncertain swath around the 98th and 100th meridians. Webb first popularized John Wesley Powell's twenty-inch line of rainfall as the general limit for unaided agriculture. Webb, *The Great Plains* (1931; repr. Lincoln: University of Nebraska Press, 1959), pp. 6–7, 32, and 353.

8. Montana, *Proceedings and Debates of the Constitutional Convention* (Helena, 1921), p. 822. In Montana, Senator William Stewart of Nevada spoke before Powell and explained the boundaries of the arid region: "All that is west of the 100th meridian is certainly a portion of it, and some that is east of the 100th meridian" (p. 805). For Montana, Powell proposed a new county organization with boundaries shaped by natural drainage basins. In North Dakota, Powell admonished: "Don't let these streams get out of possession of the people. If you fail in making a Constitution in any respect, fail not in this one" (*First Constitutional Convention of North Dakota*, p. 412). *See also* Worster, *River Running West*, pp. 354–60.

9. Ida Husted Harper, *The Life and Work of Susan B. Anthony* (Indianapolis: Bowen-Merrill Company, 1898), p. 690.

10. Plains historian Frederick Luebke suggested that scholars "speak, not of the Great Plains *region*, but of the Great Plains *states*," each of which contains part of the physiographic plains (Luebke, Introduction to *Ethnicity on the Great Plains*, ed. Luebke [Lincoln: University of Nebraska Press, 1980]: p. xiii [emphasis in original]).

11. David J. Wishart, "The Great Plains Region," in *Encyclopedia of the Great Plains*, ed. Wishart (Lincoln: University of Nebraska Press, 2004), pp. xiii–xiv. *See also* Gilbert C. Fite, "Regionalism: The Historical Perspective —Northern Plains," *South Dakota Review* 18 (Winter 1981): 17–38; James C. Malin, *The Grassland of North America: Prolegomena to Its History* (Gloucester, Mass.: Peter Smith, 1967), pp. 75, 80; James R. Shortridge, *The Middle West: Its Meaning in American Culture* (Lawrence: University Press

of Kansas, 1989), pp. 5–10, 14–26, 97–133, and "The Expectations of Others: Struggles toward a Sense of Place in the Northern Great Plains," in *Many Wests: Place, Culture, and Regional Identity*, ed. David M. Wrobel and Michael C. Steiner (Lawrence: University Press of Kansas, 1997), p. 116; Sonja Rossum and Stephen Lavin, "Where are the Great Plains? A Cartographic Analysis," *Professional Geographer* 52 (Aug. 2000): 543–52. The historical development of Northern Great Plains territories distinguishes them from neighboring states in the modern Pacific Northwest, the Middle West, and the Central and Southern Great Plains. Iowa achieved statehood in 1846, Minnesota in 1858, Kansas in 1861, Nebraska in 1867, and Colorado in 1876. These earlier states developed in a political atmosphere of national territorial expansion and slavery debates that led to a transformative Civil War. Central plains states of Nebraska and Colorado developed in relation to extensive settler travel across the central plains and on the Overland Trail to California and Oregon from the 1840s to the 1860s. While Idaho and Washington might be seen in the same historical development model, as they were admitted to the United States with the four key northern plains states in 1890 and 1889, respectively, they did not develop with "plains proper" land within their borders. For distinctions within the Great Plains states, *see* Renee M. Laegreid and Sandra J. Mathews, eds., *Women on the North American Plains* (Lubbock: Texas Tech University Press, 2011).

12. In Utah Territory, however, the federal government reasserted its broad power over the territories, disenfranchising women. Utah reinstated woman suffrage shortly after it gained statehood in 1896. Allison L. Sneider, *Suffragists in an Imperial Age: U. S. Expansion and the Woman Question, 1870–1929* (New York: Oxford University Press, 2008), pp. 73–80.

13. Lorenzo Veracini, *Settler Colonialism: A Theoretical Overview* (New York: Palgrave Macmillan, 2010); Virginia Scharff, "Broadening the Battlefield: Conflict, Contingency, and the Mystery of Woman Suffrage in Wyoming, 1869," in *Civil War Wests: Testing the Limits of the United States*, ed. Adam Arenson and Andrew R. Graybill (Berkeley: University of California Press, 2015), pp. 205–6, 208, 215–16; Ward, "Winning of Woman Suffrage in Montana," p. 102. Lakotas, Nakotas, Dakotas, Mandans, Hidatsas, Arikaras, Blackfeet, Flatheads, Cheyennes, Crows, Shoshonis, and Arapaos are some of the major American Indian landholders on the northern plains. On securing the land for settlers, *see* Jeffrey Ostler, *The Plains Sioux and U. S. Colonialism from Lewis and Clark to Wounded Knee* (Cambridge: Cambridge University Press, 2004); Hana Samek, *The Blackfoot Confederacy, 1880–1920: A Comparative Study of Canada and U. S. Indian Policy* (Albuquerque: University of New Mexico Press, 1987); Roy W. Meyer, *The Village Indians of the Upper Missouri: The Mandans, Hidatsas, and Arikaras* (Lincoln: University

of Nebraska Press, 1977). Both Wishart, "Great Plains Region," p. xvi, and Shortridge, "Expectations of Others," pp. 118, 121, 132, argue that the persistence of American Indians is a distinguishing feature of Northern Great Plains culture.

14. Dakota Territory Organic Act, sec. 5, in Dakota Territory, *General Laws and Memorials and Resolutions of the Territory of Dakota Passed at the First Session of the Legislative Assembly* (Yankton, 1862), p. 23; "Organic Act of the Territory of Montana," p. 9; Montana Territory, *Acts, Resolutions and Memorials, of the Territory of Montana, Passed by the First Legislative Assembly* (Virginia City, 1866), p. 375; Rebecca J. Mead, *How the Vote Was Won: Woman Suffrage in the Western United States, 1868–1914* (New York: New York University Press, 2004), p. 36; T. A. Larson, "Emancipating the West's Dolls, Vassals and Hopeless Drudges: The Origins of Woman Suffrage in the West," in *Essays in Western History in Honor of Professor T. A. Larson*, ed. Roger Daniels (Laramie: University of Wyoming Publications, 1971), pp. 1–16; Barbara Carol Behan, "Forgotten Heritage: African Americans in the Montana Territory, 1864–1889," *Journal of African American History* 91 (Winter 2006): 25–26; Montana Territory, *General Laws, and Memorials and Resolutions of the Territory of Montana, Passed at the Fourth Session of the Legislative Assembly* (Virginia City, 1868), p. 96; Jennifer Helton, "So Great An Innovation," herein. The organic act establishing Montana Territory did not restrict voting rights to white men. The first Montana territorial legislature, however, did. *See* Stanley R. Davison and Dale Tash, "Confederate Backwash in Montana Territory," *Montana: The Magazine of Western History* 17 (Autumn 1967): 50–58. In 1861, the act creating Dakota Territory granted suffrage rights to "every free white male," but Congress modified it in early 1867 to prevent territories from denying male citizens the right to vote based upon their "race, creed, or previous condition of servitude" (Dakota Territory, *House Journal of the Seventh Session of the Legislative Assembly of the Territory of Dakota* [Yankton, 1867–1868], p. 31 [hereafter cited as *House Journal*]).

15. *House Journal*, p. 78.

16. *Union and Dakotian* (Yankton), 26 Dec. 1868, quoted in Dale Gibson with Lee Gibson and Cameron Harvey, *Attorney for the Frontier: Enos Stutsman* (Winnipeg: University of Manitoba Press, 1983), p. 74.

17. *House Journal*, pp. 95, 195; Dakota Territory, *Council Journal of the Eighth Session of the Legislative Assembly of the Territory of Dakota* (Yankton, 1869), pp. 73, 160, 170, 218 (hereafter cited as *Council Journal*); Ken Stewart, "'Dakota's Finest': A Sampler of Early South Dakota Brewing History," *South Dakota History* 42 (Dec. 2012): 291–92.

18. Mrs. John A. Pickler [Alice Alt Pickler] to Doane Robinson, n.d., in

"Excerpts from Correspondence," *South Dakota Historical Collections* 2 (1904): 28.

19. Chapman, "Woman Suffrage in Wyoming," p. 7-8; *House Journal*, 1870, pp. 29, 44, 46, 53, 86–88, 90–91; *Council Journal*, 1870, pp. 143, 146, 156; Handy-Marchello, "Quiet Voices in the Prairie Wind," herein.

20. *Laramie Sentinel*, 21 Jan. 1871, quoted in Chapman, "Woman Suffrage in Wyoming," p. 42.

21. Larson, "Woman Suffrage in Wyoming," pp. 62–63; Chapman, "Woman Suffrage in Wyoming," pp. 69–79; Susan B. Anthony and Ida Husted Harper, eds. *History of Woman Suffrage*, Vol. 4 (Rochester, N.Y.: Susan B. Anthony, 1902), p. 543. In the late 1860s and early 1870s, Montana legislators referenced forthcoming woman suffrage bills, but none materialized. *See* Larson, "Montana Women and the Battle for the Ballot," p. 26.

22. Jones, "'The Women Voted,'" herein; Ward, "Winning of Woman Suffrage in Montana," pp. 4, 6.

23. *House Journal*, 1885, pp. 139, 162, 187–88, 227, 939–41. Governor Pierce also noted that because the 1885 suffrage bill did not remove the word "male," women in many cities would have been denied suffrage rights because of municipal law—something the legislature had not addressed. Some members of the house who voted in favor of woman suffrage cast ballots against overriding Pierce's veto. The *Bismarck Weekly Tribune* ridiculed pro-suffrage house members V. V. Barnes (De Smet), J. T. Blakemore (Highmore), and Pickler (Faulkton), dubbing them Miss Belva Barnes, Elizabeth Cady Blakemore, and Miss Susan B. Pickler (13 Feb. 1885). Years later, after learning of Pierce's death in 1901, Susan B. Anthony wrote to Alice Pickler and asked her how "Susan Pickler" was doing, noting that Pierce "cheated us out of suffrage for women in both the Dakotas" (Anthony to Pickler, in *The Selected Papers of Elizabeth Cady Stanton and Susan B. Anthony: An Awful Hush, 1895–1906*, ed. Ann D. Gordon [Rutgers, N. J.: Rutgers University Press, 2013], p. 176).

24. Dorinda Riessen Reed, *The Woman Suffrage Movement in South Dakota*, 2d ed. (Pierre: South Dakota Commission on the Status of Women, 1975), p. 16. Although the bill failed in both houses, the women succeeded in getting the legislature to pass a "local option" law to allow prohibition on the county level.

25. Montana, *Constitution*, 1889, art. 9, sec. 12, pp. 37–38. *See also* Ward, "Winning of Woman Suffrage in Montana," p. 18. Like men, women had to be twenty-one, citizens (a noncitizen eligible to vote under the territorial constitution could vote for five years until that privilege would disappear), not convicted of a felony, and have resided in the state for at least one year.

26. *Billings Herald*, 31 Jan. 1885; *Bozeman Weekly Chronicle*, 7, 14 Sept. 1887. Historian Paula Petrik found madams who owned more than one-

hundred-thousand-dollars-worth of property and paid more than one thousand dollars in city taxes (property and personal). Petrik, "Capitalists with Rooms: Prostitution in Helena, 1865–1900," *Montana: The Magazine of Western History* 31 (Spring 1981): 38.

27. Anna Howard Shaw, quoted in Cecelia M. Wittmayer, "The 1889–1890 Woman Suffrage Campaign: A Need to Organize," *South Dakota History* 11 (Summer 1981): 220. On Remonstrants, *see* Nelson, "Anti-Suffrage Women in South Dakota Suffrage Campaigns," herein. The National Woman Suffrage Association (NWSA) and the American Woman Suffrage Association (AWSA) merged in February 1890 to become the National American Woman Suffrage Association (NAWSA).

28. Helen Gougar, June 1890, quoted in Mary Kay Jennings, "Lake County Woman Suffrage Campaign in 1890," *South Dakota History* 4 (Fall 1975): 401–2. Suffragists took note of the attention political parties paid to American Indians. Patricia O'Keefe Easton, "Opposition to Woman Suffrage in South Dakota" (master's thesis, University of South Dakota, 1982), p. 36–37; Jennifer M. Ross-Nazzal, *Winning the West for Women: The Life of Suffragist Emma Smith DeVoe* (Seattle: University of Washington Press, 2001), p. 66. According to the results of the 1890 referenda, 45 percent of male voters supported the exclusion of American Indian men who did not give up tribal affiliations from voting, while only 33 percent voted for woman suffrage. Alan L. Clem, *South Dakota Political Almanac*, 2d ed. (Vermillion, S.Dak.: Dakota Press, 1969), p. 33.

29. Easton, "Opposition to Woman Suffrage," pp. 24, 28–29, 31–32, 37–38, 44; Wittmayer, "1889–1890 Woman Suffrage Campaign," pp. 202–3, 205–8, 216–17, 220.

30. *See*, for example, Ross-Nazzal, *Winning the West for Women*; Nancy Tystad Koupal, "Marietta Bones: Personality and Politics in the South Dakota Suffrage Movement," in *Feminist Frontiers: Women Who Shaped the Midwest*, ed. Yvonne J. Johnson (Kirksville, Missouri: Truman State University Press, 2010), pp. 69–82; Jennifer J. Hill, "The Marathon of Montana Suffrage," herein; Ward, "Winning of Woman Suffrage in Montana," pp. 45–72, 126–32; Bill G. Reid, "Elizabeth Preston Anderson and the Politics of Social Reform," in *The North Dakota Political Tradition*, ed. Thomas W. Howard (Ames: Iowa State University Press, 1981), pp. 197–98; Ann B. Braaten, "Kate Selby Wilder: Clubwoman, Suffragist, Temperance Activist, and City Commissioner," herein; Lutz, "Susan B. Anthony in the Dakotas," p. 120; Sara Egge, *Woman Suffrage and Citizenship in the Midwest, 1870–1920* (Iowa City: University of Iowa Press, 2018), pp. 66–67, 70, 76–109, 148–51. For a statistical analysis that links WCTU engagement and woman suffrage, *see* Holly J. McCammon, "Stirring up Suffrage Sentiment: The Formation of the

State Woman Suffrage Organizations, 1866–1914," *Social Forces* 80 (Dec. 2001): 467–68. On the WCTU in Wyoming, *see* Chapman, "Woman Suffrage in Wyoming," pp. 88–89.

31. Shortridge, "Expectations of Others," pp. 115–16, 124. Different streams of European, African, and American Indian immigrant peoples originating largely in the southern United States populated the plains states of Oklahoma and Texas, with the latter also having a large Mexican-American population. *See also* Wishart, "Great Plains Region," p. xiv; Luebke, "Introduction," pp. xviii–xix, xxi; Luebke, "Ethnic Group Settlement on the Great Plains" *Western Historical Quarterly* 8 (Oct. 1977): 405–30.

32. Egge, "Ethnicity and Woman Suffrage on the South Dakota Plains," herein; Ward, "Winning of Woman Suffrage in Montana," pp. 134–36.

33. Handy-Marchello, "Quiet Voices in the Prairie Wind," herein; *Helena Daily Independent*, 3, 7 Oct. 1890; *Fergus County Argus* (Lewistown, Mont.), 11, 25 Apr. 1895; *Ravalli Republican* (Stevensville, Mont.), 9 Jun. 1897; *Anaconda (Mont.) Standard*, 9 Sept. 1899; Larson, "Montana Women and the Battle for the Ballot," pp. 30–33; Ward, "Winning of Woman Suffrage in Montana," pp. 42–63. The Saint James AME Church in Helena became a cultural hub for African Americans in Helena and engaged in suffrage debates. *See* St. James AME Church, Montana Historic Property Record, Montana Memory Project, mtmemory.org.

34. Reed, *Woman Suffrage Movement in South Dakota*, pp. 51–53, 56, 117; Ward, "Winning of Woman Suffrage in Montana," passim.

35. Ward, "Winning of Woman Suffrage in Montana," pp. 117–50; Larson, "Montana Women and the Battle for the Ballot," pp. 36–41. For an overview of suffrage campaigns in Washington, California, Arizona Territory, Kansas, and Oregon, *see* Mead, *How the Vote Was Won*.

36. Handy-Marchello, "Quiet Voices in the Prairie Wind," herein; Reid, "Elizabeth Preston Anderson," pp. 197–98; Braaten, "Kate Selby Wilder," herein; North Dakota, *Legislative Manual* (Bismarck, 1919), p. 220; U.S., Department of Commerce, Bureau of the Census, *Fourteenth Census of the United States, State Compendium: North Dakota* (Washington, D.C.: Government Printing Office, 1924), p. 42. In North Dakota after 1917, women could vote in any race not defined in the state constitution.

37. Easton, "Woman Suffrage in South Dakota," pp. 212–15, 218. Although South Dakota entered the Union as a dry state, the legislature became embroiled in vitriolic resubmission debates, eventually sending a repeal amendment to voters that they approved in 1896.

38. McKinney, "Wake Up, Wyoming," herein. South Dakota's governor also called a special session and showed concern about cost, but drought relief does not appear to have been a part of his rationale.

39. Rosalyn Terborg-Penn, *African American Women in the Struggle for the Vote, 1850–1920* (Bloomington: Indiana University Press, 1998), pp. 160, 163. On the shift to citizenship in South Dakota, *see* Nelson, "Anti-Suffrage Women in South Dakota Suffrage Campaigns," herein. The strategy argued that women, as "persons" under the Fourteenth Amendment, had the right to vote. Advocates also contended that women were included in the Fifteenth Amendment as part of the "race" of people authorized to vote. The United States Supreme Court ruled against this interpretation in *Minor v. Happersett* (1875). *See* Lisa Tetrault, *The Myth of Seneca Falls: Memory and the Women's Suffrage Movement, 1848–1898* (Chapel Hill: University of North Carolina Press, 2014), pp. 57–60. *See also* Allison L. Sneider, *Suffragists in an Imperial Age*, pp. 55, 60.

40. The Expatriation Act of 1907 codified a practice of "marital unity" by which a woman who married a foreign man lost her citizenship. The practice dates until at least 1855, when Congress passed an act that allowed citizenship to foreign women who married men with United States citizenship. A 1915 United States Supreme Court case (*MacKenzie v. Hare*) upheld the practice codified in the 1907 law. The law overturning "martial unity" citizenship was the 1922 Cable Act. *See* Tetrault, *Myth of Seneca Falls*, pp. 57–60, 66–68. Allison L. Sneider explains that although the 1917 Jones Act for Puerto Rico granted citizenship to Puerto Ricans and shifted the power of granting woman suffrage to the territorial legislature, the Nineteenth Amendment did not apply to the territory (Sneider, *Suffragists in an Imperial Age*, pp. 57–86, 117, 128). The Territory of Puerto Rico enfranchised "literate women" in 1929 (p. 134). *See also* Linda K. Kerber, *No Constitutional Right to be Ladies: Women and the Obligations of Citizenship* (New York: Hill & Wang, 1998), pp. 37, 41–43, 324n108.

41. Bethany R. Berger, "Red: Racism and the American Indian," *UCLA Law Review* 56, no. 591 (2009): 633; Jeanette Wolfley, "Jim Crow, Indian Style: The Disenfranchisement of Native Americans," *American Indian Law Review* 16, no. 1 (1991): 5–6, 171, 173, 178–81; Daniel McCool, Susan M. Olson, and Jennifer L. Robinson, *Native Vote: American Indians, the Voting Rights Act, and the Right to Vote* (New York: Cambridge University Press, 2007), pp. 1–20.

42. Webb, *Great Plains*, pp. 504–5.

43. Laegreid and Mathews, Introduction to *Women on the North American Plains*, pp. xxi, xxiii–iv.

44. Until Barbara Handy-Marchello's essay in this volume, the only comprehensive look at the movement in North Dakota was undertaken by a University of North Dakota undergraduate student, Jeanne F. Tucker, "The History of the Woman's Suffrage Movement in North Dakota," 1951, pp. 33–34,

folder 12, box 1, Research Papers Written on North Dakota History Collection, OGLMC 263, Chester Fritz Library, University of North Dakota, Grand Forks. Miriam Gantz Chapman wrote a master's thesis on Wyoming woman suffrage in 1952 at the University of Wyoming, and in 1958, Dorinda Riessen Reed chose South Dakota's woman suffrage movement as the topic of her master's thesis at the University of South Dakota. The South Dakota Commission on the Status of Women reprinted Reed's master's thesis under the same name in 1975. Doris Buck Ward wrote her 1974 master's thesis on Montana's woman suffrage movement at Montana State University. Historian T. A. Larson provided the first, but brief, overview of Montana woman suffrage, "Montana Women and the Battle for the Ballot." On the constructed and sanitized nature of the six-volume *History of Woman Suffrage*, see Tetrault, *Myth of Seneca Falls*, pp. 6–10, 112–44, esp. 133–34.

45. Wittmayer, "1889–1890 Woman Suffrage Campaign"; Jennings, "Lake County Woman Suffrage Campaign in 1890"; Easton, "Woman Suffrage in South Dakota," pp. 206–26; Wheeler, "Woman Suffrage's Gray-Bearded Champion Comes to Montana"; Judith K. Cole, "A Wide Field for Usefulness: Women's Civil Status and the Evolution of Women's Suffrage on the Montana Frontier, 1864–1914," *American Journal of Legal History* 34 (Jul. 1990): 262–94; Jim McMillan, "The Macdonald-Nielson Imbroglio: The Politics of Education in North Dakota, 1918–1921," *North Dakota History* 52 (Fall 1985): 2–11; Reid, "Elizabeth Preston Anderson"; Susan Wefald, "Breaking an 1889 Glass Ceiling: Laura J. Eisenhuth, First Woman Elected to Statewide Office in the United States," *North Dakota History* 79 (Dec. 2014): 13–25; Koupal, "Marietta Bones"; Ross-Nazzal, *Winning the West for Women*; Linda Johnson Wurtz, "Elizabeth Preston Anderson: A Rhetorical Legacy," *North Dakota History* 63, nos. 2 & 3 (1996): 49–58; Kathryn Anderson, "Steps to Political Equality: Woman Suffrage and the Electoral Politics in the Lives of Emily Newell Blair, Anne Henrietta Martin, and Jeannette Rankin," *Frontiers: A Journal of Women Studies* 18 no. 1 (1997): 101–21; Roger D. Hardaway, "Jeannette Rankin: The Early Years," *North Dakota Quarterly* 48 (Winter 1980): 62–68; Richard B. Roeder, "Crossing the Gender Line: Ella L. Knowles, Montana's First Woman Lawyer," *Montana: The Magazine of Western History* 32 (Summer 1982): 64–75; Dennis Norlin, "The Suffrage Movement and South Dakota Churches: Radicals and the Status Quo, 1890," *South Dakota History* 14 (Winter 1984): 308–34; Kim E. Nielson, "'We All Leaguers by Our House': Women, Suffrage, and Red-Baiting in the National Nonpartisan League," *Journal of Women's History* 6, no. 1 (1994): 31–50; Michael J. Lansing, *Insurgent Democracy: The Nonpartisan League in North American Politics* (Chicago: University of Chicago Press, 2015), pp. 165–70; Virginia Scharff, "The Case for Domestic Feminism: Woman Suffrage in Wyoming," *Annals of*

Wyoming 56, no. 2 (1984): 29–37; Virginia Scharff, "Broadening the Battle-field"; Anderson, "Steps to Political Equality"; Katy Morris, "'More reputation than she deserves': Remembering Suffrage in Wyoming," *Rethinking History* 21, no. 1 (2017): 63; Victoria Lamont, "'More Than She Deserves': Suffrage Memorials in the 'Equality State,'" *Canadian Review of American Studies* 36, no. 1 (2006): 17–43.

46. *See* Sarah Carter, *"Ours By Every Law of Right and Justice": Women and Suffrage in the Prairie Provinces to 1918* (forthcoming); Joan Sangster, *One Hundred Years of Struggle: The History of Women and the Vote in Canada* (Vancouver: UBC Press, 2018).

PART ONE

"SO GREAT AN INNOVATION"

Woman Suffrage in Wyoming

JENNIFER HELTON

"Ladies, prepare your ballots."—*Cheyenne Leader*, 6 Dec. 1869

Eva Lambertson emigrated to Lander, Wyoming, from Pennsylvania in the early 1890s. A reform-minded woman, Lambertson soon discovered the local liquor dealers ran the county's politics. She consulted her neighbors and found that many shared her reform sentiments. "Conversations with numbers of women," she reported, "revealed the fact that there was very general dissatisfaction with this condition." So, Lambertson and her friends organized. They attended precinct meetings as the local political parties were preparing for primary elections. At one of these meetings, Lambertson warned that if "saloon men" were nominated for office in the next elections, they would be defeated. "Evidently they did not believe me," she later wrote. Most thought that the liquor dealers "who had dominated affairs so long would continue to do so." According to Lambertson, local women "didn't hold any meeting. We didn't circulate any literature, not even chain letters." Instead, she said, "Every one chose a few women to talk with. These in turn chose others. Our 'chain conversations' covered the county." When the votes were tallied on election day, "all saloon candidates were defeated."[1] Like many women of her generation, Lambertson wanted to implement reforms in her community, but she had one tool at her disposal that few other American women had: Eva Lambertson could vote.

By the time Lambertson and her friends voted the saloon men out of office, Wyoming women had already exercised the franchise for a generation. Wyoming's first territorial legislature granted women suffrage and the right to hold public office. When the territorial governor, John Allen Campbell, signed the measure on 10 December 1869, Wyoming women became the first in the history of the United States with full voting rights. The year 1870 saw many firsts for women. Esther Hobart Morris, the first female justice of the peace, began hearing court cases in South Pass City in mid-February. In March, Laramie women served on juries, and Laramie's sheriff appointed Martha Symons Boies Atkinson bailiff.[2] During the 1870 election season, two women sat on the Laramie County Republican Central Committee, and two more ran for office on the Republican ticket. These women were the first to run for office, but not the last. By the time Wyoming became a state in 1890, dozens had done so, and women's political involvement had become commonplace decades before the Nineteenth Amendment to the United States Constitution barred discrimination in voting on the basis of sex.

How did this radical experiment in democracy come to Wyoming Territory? Those who witnessed it saw it as an expression of the spirit of their age. Reflecting on the September 1870 election, the editor of the *Laramie Daily Sentinel*, Dr. J. H. Hayford, wrote:

> Yesterday, for the first time in the world, Wyoming put into practice the theory of female suffrage. . . . As we viewed this seen [sic] our mind somehow reverted to another incident in our country's history, when an old, grey-headed man was accorded the privilege of firing the first gun upon Fort Sumpter [sic]. What a contrast! But whatever may have been the motive of "Old man Ruffin," that gun . . . sounded the death knell of human bondage in the land of the free. And that first little slip of paper which ever fell from the hand of a woman into the ballot-box . . . may be frought [sic] with interest as momentous as the booming of the first gun in the slaveholders' rebellion.[3]

Hayford's parallel between the start of the Civil War and the first vote of a woman demonstrates that, for him and many of his contemporaries, woman suffrage was part of the same trajectory towards equality that had freed the slaves. In arguing that the

EQUALITY AT THE BALLOT BOX

long-term impact of women voting might eventually be as important as the Civil War itself, Hayford placed woman suffrage as the next step in the movement towards democratic progress in the United States.

Women's political rights in Wyoming grew out of the debates around equality, citizenship, and suffrage that accompanied the end of the Civil War. While many of these debates centered around the rights of freedmen, some activists also hoped to use Reconstruction—the popular term for the federal government's effort to rebuild society, politics, and industry in the wake of the war—to expand the franchise to women of all races. For a generation prior to the war, advocates such as Lucy Stone, Elizabeth Cady Stanton, and Susan B. Anthony had used the language of universal human rights—"all men and women are created equal," in Stanton's rephrasing—to argue for women's economic and political equality.[4] During Reconstruction, when the nation was in the midst of redefining citizenship, some of these advocates pushed for women to take their place at the ballot box. In most of the country, Reconstruction-era efforts to enfranchise women failed. But in Wyoming, they succeeded.

Nothing called Wyoming existed in the West before the 1840s. American Indians, including Shoshones, Lakotas, Crows, Arapahos, Arikaras, Bannocks, Blackfeets, Gros Ventres, Kiowas, Nez Perces, Utes, and Cheyennes, controlled the region.[5] Apart from a few fur traders, virtually no European or American presence existed in the area. This fact changed when emigrants began to journey west on the trails that crossed present-day Wyoming's plains and mountains. By the late 1840s, thousands of people traveled through Wyoming each year on their way to Utah, Oregon, and California on land American Indians had not given them permission to cross. In 1849, the United States military purchased a fur-trading post on the North Platte River and renamed it Fort Laramie. Two years later, the United States government negotiated a treaty with several of the American Indian tribes in the region. The Fort Laramie Treaty of 1851 granted the right of passage to travelers on the trails. In exchange, the treaty set aside land and guaranteed annuities for the signatory tribes. Congress never properly ratified the treaty, and the United States govern-

MRS. F. A. BLAKE.

MRS. MARTHA BOIES.

MRS. ELIZA BOYD.

MRS SARAH W. PEASE.

Suffrage created new paths into public life for many Wyoming women. Martha Boies became Laramie's first woman bailiff in 1870; Sarah Pease served as a juror; Eliza Boyd ran for office in Albany County; and Mrs. F. A. Blake helped found Laramie's Presbyterian church. Wyoming State Archives Photo Collection ment frequently failed to meet the financial and security commitments it specified. Even so, Americans set up regular mail and passenger stagecoach routes across Wyoming in the 1850s. Tensions increased, trust declined, and occasionally bloodshed resulted. The land that would become Wyoming was contested space.[6]

In March 1861, the federal government created Dakota Territory to govern the vast expanse of the Northern Great Plains. From its capital in Yankton, the Dakota territorial government exerted authority over the land that would become Wyoming. Politicians in Yankton, however, were primarily concerned with the needs of settlers on the high, wide prairies of the Dakotas. In remote and inaccessible Wyoming, there was not much American settlement to govern. Meanwhile, the Civil War broke out on 12 April 1861, plunging much of the West into a state of uncertainty that threatened to degenerate into anarchy. After the South seceded, Congress was anxious to ensure the West did not collapse into chaos, or worse, fall under Confederate control. Representative James Ashley, an Ohio Republican and chairman of the House Committee on Territories, spent much of his time thinking about these challenges. An ardent abolitionist, Ashley was first elected to Congress in 1858, gaining his chairmanship in 1861. On 5 January 1865, a few months before the Civil War ended, Ashley attempted to create a separate Territory of Wyoming.[7]

Ashley wrote his Wyoming bill, House Resolution 633, in the standard language that Congress used when creating a new territory. While little in the bill was unusual, the fact that it had been proposed at all raises many questions. Why not simply leave the region under the control of Yankton? At the time, few Americans were present in what is now Wyoming. Soldiers were posted along the Oregon Trail, and some men—and fewer women—ran the stage stops for the overland postal routes. A handful of settlers supplied hay or livestock to the army or trail companies. Most of these residents did not plan to establish permanent settlements in Wyoming. Of course, the possibility of change hung in the air as telegraph workers strung line across Wyoming in 1861, and passage of the Pacific Railroad Act in 1862 meant the Iron Horse might soon steam across the plains. But in early 1865, the final route of the railroad had not yet been determined, and influential Coloradans lobbied hard for a route over Berthoud Pass. It was not clear the railroad would cross Wyoming at all.[8] Furthermore, the 1851 Fort Laramie Treaty, shaky as it was, did make it clear that much of the land of the proposed territory of Wyoming was off limits for American development. Given the miniscule American population, no compelling economic interests, and an unclear title to the land, why was Ashley in a rush to create a territory there?

The answer can be found in another bill that Ashley supported. On 6 January 1865, the day after he introduced the bill to create Wyoming, he rose to ask the House to consider a bill that he had brought to members' attention several times the previous year. This measure eventually became the Thirteenth Amendment to the Constitution of the United States, abolishing slavery. The two bills may seem unrelated, but they were two sides of the same coin. The sixth article of Ashley's Wyoming bill would have outlawed slavery in the new territory. The bill also attempted to limit any Confederate attempts to undermine federal authority in the region with its fifth article: "No person who has served in the rebel army, or has in any manner aided the rebellion . . . shall be a voter at the first election."[9] Ashley had pushed unsuccessfully for the Thirteenth Amendment for years. At the beginning of 1865, before the war was over, it was not clear that it would even pass Congress, let alone be ratified by the states. After a month of tough negotiation, the House finally passed the Thirteenth Amendment to a "tumult of joy that was vast, thundering and uncontrollable."[10] Because the Senate had approved it in 1864, the amendment now went to the states for ratification. By the end of 1865, it had become law. Ashley's Wyoming bill, although it would die in committee, represented an insurance policy of sorts. Had the Thirteenth Amendment failed to pass, Ashley reasoned that his Wyoming bill would still have prohibited slavery in a large section of the West and prevented Confederates from establishing a government there. Ashley supported similar bills for Colorado, Nebraska, Montana, and Nevada.[11]

Such provisions were indicative of the Republican vision of the West. Republicans sought to build a free-soil, free-labor West.

　　　EQUALITY AT THE BALLOT BOX

These values had guided the creation of the party in 1854, when leaders imagined hard-working yeoman farmers living with their wives and children on 160-acre plots, growing a cash crop that would be exported via a railroad yet to be built. Republicans took it for granted that somehow—whether through force or forced assimilation—American Indians in the West would make way for the arrival of this vision. The Homestead Act, the Pacific Railroad Act, and the Morrill Act all passed Congress in 1862 to make this ideal a reality.[12] To secure their vision, however, Republicans needed to control the territories. While the outcome of the war was still uncertain, Republicans passed laws to ensure that slaveholders and Confederate sympathizers would not find a friendly reception—or be able to vote themselves into power—in the West. The attempt to create Wyoming Territory served as a preemptive effort to secure these objectives, even though there were not yet enough Americans there to establish settlement patterns.

On 13 February 1868, Senator Richard Yates—who, like Ashley, was a Radical Republican, advocating abolition and the expansion of black civil rights without compromise—proposed Senate Bill 357. This Wyoming bill was almost identical to Ashley's, with two exceptions. First, since the Thirteenth Amendment was now law, the bill did not mention slavery. Second, the wording of section five, concerning the franchise, had been revised to prohibit the legislature from denying "the right of suffrage, or to hold office, on account of the race, color or previous condition of servitude of any resident of the Territory."[13] Tellingly, Congress would pass the Fifteenth Amendment, which used nearly identical language in prohibiting efforts to restrict voting rights on the basis of race, in February 1869, a year after Yates put his bill forward. Once again, Wyoming served as a testing ground for the implementation of the Republican vision of the West, which now included the extension of voting rights to African Americans. In 1868, however, it was far from certain that Congress could pass a federal voting rights amendment, given the widespread opposition to black suffrage. Moreover, some activists wanted to include voting rights for women in the proposed amendment.

A number of Congressmen, including James Ashley, supported woman suffrage. Ashley's wife, Emma Ashley, would become the founding president of the Toledo, Ohio, Woman Suffrage Society in 1869. During the Congressional debates over the Fourteenth Amendment, which granted citizenship to any person born in the United States, Ashley proposed changes to its language that, if accepted, would have enfranchised women. In a speech on the floor of Congress on 1 June 1868, Ashley declared, "I want citizenship and suffrage to be synonymous. . . . For this purpose I have added to the proposed amendment for the election of president a section on suffrage, to which I invite special attention."[14] Ashley's section used the words "inhabitants" and "citizens" to define who could vote and specified that suffrage "shall be impartial."[15] In the end, Congress rejected Ashley's language and inserted the word "male" into the Fourteenth Amendment. Frustrated, national suffrage leaders pushed for the inclusion of women in the proposed Fifteenth Amendment. Many, however, argued that fighting for suffrage for both women and African American men was too radical and would destroy the amendment's chances. These debates raged on throughout 1868 and 1869, but ultimately the amendment omitted woman suffrage.[16]

In July 1868, Congress passed a revised version of Yates's bill and created the Territory of Wyoming. The final law removed the provision excluding Confederate soldiers from the vote but kept the provision prohibiting the abridgement of the right to vote on the basis of race or previous condition of servitude.[17] Thus, a version of the Fifteenth Amendment existed as law in Wyoming for more than a year before the states ratified it, putting this scantily populated territory at the vanguard of civil rights from the day of its creation.

Yet, much of the land included in the new territory belonged—by treaty—to American Indians. The construction of the transcontinental railroad as well as the gold rushes of 1863 in Montana and 1867 in central Wyoming's South Pass region lured American settlers to the area. Travelers and settlers frequently encroached on tribal lands guaranteed under the Fort Laramie Treaty of 1851. Many tribes resisted these incursions, most famously in the Red Cloud War of 1866–1868, following which the entities negotiated two new treaties. The Fort Laramie Treaty of 1868 confirmed American Indians' ownership of vast portions of the Wyoming plains. The same year, the Shoshone and Bannock tribes signed the Treaty of Fort Bridger, guaranteeing them rights to land in central Wyoming.[18] Despite the new treaties, American settlers pushed into Indian lands. Though it had achieved territorial status, Wyoming still remained contested ground.

After President Andrew Johnson signed the law that created Wyoming—known as the Wyoming Territorial Organic Act—on 25 July 1868, he appointed officials to govern the territory. Relations between the president and Congress were frosty in the wake of Johnson's 1868 impeachment, however, and Congress refused to confirm the appointments. Indeed, Representative Ashley voted against the Wyoming Territorial Organic Act precisely because it gave Johnson the opportunity to appoint opponents of the Republican vision of the West to territorial offices.[19] Ulysses S. Grant's victory in the 1868 presidential election gave Republicans the chance to appoint territorial officials, many of whom were Union Army veterans he trusted to help construct a Republican West. These officials would play key roles in the passage and implementation of woman suffrage in Wyoming.

Grant chose John Allen Campbell for territorial governor. Born in Salem, Ohio, in 1835, Campbell and his five brothers had been raised by his mother and eldest sister following his father's early death. At the time, women's educational and economic opportunities were limited, so his mother took in boarders while his sister Susan taught school to support the family and ensure that the Campbell boys received strong educations. Campbell became a printer and joined the Union Army at the beginning of the war. He quickly rose in the ranks, becoming aide-de-camp to Lieutenant General John Schofield, one of William Tecumseh Sherman's key commanders. After Schofield's appointment as secretary of war in June of 1868, Campbell followed him to Washington, D.C., and served as his undersecretary. Campbell was in Virginia during the debate around the Fourteenth Amendment, working with Schofield's army to implement the federal government's Reconstruction policies. His responsibilities included setting up voting districts, ensuring that African Americans were able to vote, and investigating the activities of the Ku Klux Klan and other white supremacist organizations. By the time he came to Wyoming,

Campbell had spent years implementing controversial federal civil rights policies in a hostile environment.[20] Having worked to bring the Republican vision to the South, he was a logical candidate to do the same in the West.

An incident from early in his term as territorial governor demonstrates Campbell's support for legal equality. Wyoming's first legislature passed an anti-miscegenation bill that prohibited marriage between whites and Asians or African Americans, which Campbell vetoed. In his message, Campbell wrote, "In its present shape the bill appears to partake of the nature of legislation for or against particular classes, and as in my opinion, class legislation is opposed to the spirit of our Organic Act, the genius of Republican Institutions, and the progress of the age, I cannot approve the bill."[21] Unimpressed by Campbell's argument, the Democratic legislature overrode his veto. While he was not always successful in imposing the Republican vision of equality on the territory, Campbell retained his personal commitment to equal protection under the law.[22]

Edward Merwin Lee, the new territory's secretary of state, assisted Campbell in these efforts. Like the governor, Lee was deeply committed to African American voting rights. He was also a seasoned advocate for woman suffrage. Born in 1835 in Guilford, Connecticut, Lee served in the Fifth Michigan Cavalry. Captured in October 1863, he survived Libby, Andersonville, and other Confederate prisons until his release in December 1864.[23] Emaciated and half-starved, Lee reportedly gave a Fourth of July speech while imprisoned in which, according to the *Weekly Rocky Mountain Star,* he exclaimed, "He hoped the war would never close, no never, until the doctrine of man's equality before the law should be unchangeably engrafted on the Constitution."[24] Lee mustered out of the army at the close of the war and spent the remainder of 1865 giving speeches on behalf of the Union cause.[25] In 1866, Lee was elected to the Connecticut State Assembly.

In 1867, the Connecticut assembly took up the question of woman suffrage. Frances Ellen Burr, a longtime women's rights activist, had collected many petitions demanding that Connecticut women receive the vote. Lee guided the bill through the legislature, where, on 11 July 1867, the assembly debated whether they

EQUALITY AT THE BALLOT BOX

would become the first state to grant women the right to vote.[26] The *Hartford Courant* reported, "The hall was crowded—seats, platform, gallery and aisles—with an enlightened and discriminating audience." Lucy Stone, one of the most famous female orators of the day, rose to state the case for women's rights. "In this hour of national reconstruction," Stone argued, "let no man dream that national peace and prosperity can be secured while one-half of the entire people are excluded from political power." Shed added, "Put this great principle of impartial suffrage, irrespective of sex or color, beneath the foundation of our temple of liberty, and it will rise in fair and beautiful proportions, wanting nothing."[27] The committee on constitutional amendments voted in favor of woman suffrage, and on 27 July, Lee rose to call for a vote in the full assembly, where it failed, 111–93.[28]

On 15 March 1869, Radical Republican George Julian introduced a draft constitutional amendment in Congress: "The Right of Suffrage in the United States shall be based on citizenship, and shall be regulated by Congress; and all citizens of the United States, whether native or naturalized, shall enjoy this right equally without any distinction or discrimination whatever founded on sex."[29] Like most of the other woman suffrage efforts of the 1860s, Julian's amendment failed. By then, Campbell and Lee were on their way to Wyoming Territory, traveling with fellow appointee Chief Justice John H. Howe. They arrived in Cheyenne on 7 May 1869. The construction of the transcontinental railroad had transformed Wyoming Territory into a booming frontier. In June of 1867, railroad engineer Grenville Dodge began to plat out a city on the plains near Crow Creek. Soon, settlers rushed to the new community of Cheyenne. Towns such as Laramie, Rawlins, Rock Springs, Green River, Bryan, and Evanston followed as the track inched west. Governor Campbell spent the summer of 1869 familiarizing himself with these communities.[30]

In late June, Campbell made a trip to the mining region around South Pass. While there, he met E. A. Slack, who worked under Justice John W. Kingman as clerk of the Third District Court. Slack's mother, Esther Morris, would figure prominently in Wyoming's suffrage story. Born Esther Mae Hobart McQuigg near Spencer, New York, in 1814, Morris was the eighth of eleven children. Orphaned at an early age, she earned her living as a milliner and dressmaker. Upstate New York in the mid-nineteenth century was a hotbed of both abolitionist and women's rights activism. The first women's rights convention was held in Seneca Falls, New York, not far from Spencer, in 1848.[31] One possibly apocryphal tale relates that at the age of about twenty, Esther McQuigg attended an abolition meeting at her local Baptist church. Proslavery forces tried to break up the gathering, warning the attendees, "If the ladies would leave the church, they would tear it down." McQuigg refused to leave, saying, "If it is proposed to burn it down, I will stay here and see who does it."[32]

Esther McQuigg married Artemus Slack, a civil engineer, in 1841. He died just three years after their marriage, leaving her alone with a young son, Edward Archibald ("E. A.") Slack. Morris traveled with her child to Illinois to take possession of land that her husband owned there. Laws that made it difficult for widowed women to claim property owned by their husbands complicated her efforts. Morris again went into business as a milliner and settled in Peru, Illinois. In 1845, she married merchant John Morris, a Jewish Polish immigrant. The couple had three children, two of whom, twins Edward and Robert, survived to adulthood. During the war, E. A. Slack served in the Union Army, and in the summer of 1868, John Morris and Slack moved to Wyoming, searching for a fresh start for the family. Esther Morris followed with her twin sons the next summer, shortly before Campbell met Slack in South Pass.[33]

A forceful personality, Morris stood "almost six feet tall and . . . would attract attention in any company," a contemporary said. "She had a head and face that indicated strong character, positive will, dominating spirit."[34] Even with her determined personality, Morris keenly felt the social limitations imposed upon her. In 1864, she wrote to her niece, "I am a larger *woman* although I am often called a great *girl*." In the same letter, she lamented being unable to vote in the 1864 presidential election.[35] She regularly read local Republican papers as well as the abolitionist magazine the *Atlantic Monthly* and the *Banner of Light*, a spiritualist periodical that debated reform issues. She was particularly interested

EQUALITY AT THE BALLOT BOX

in what she called "the woman question." In 1866, she reported reading the works of Gail Hamilton, Isabella Beecher, and Harriet Beecher Stowe, the author of *Uncle Tom's Cabin,* the famous anti-slavery novel. Isabella Beecher, Stowe's sister, was a leader in the woman suffrage movement, and Gail Hamilton's work focused on the themes of economic independence and marriage.[36] Morris advised her niece, Frances McQuigg, to "feel strong in the magnetism of self-reliance," one of the virtues Hamilton advocated.[37]

Morris belonged to a family of suffrage activists. She corresponded regularly with McQuigg, whose mother served as the president of a suffrage organization in Los Angeles. Another niece, Elizabeth Browne Chatfield, worked as Susan B. Anthony's private secretary in the late 1860s and early 1870s. She and her sister Julia Browne also worked on the newspaper Anthony founded in 1868, the *Revolution.* In the spring and summer of 1868, Robert Morris and Esther Morris were living in New York City, where the paper was published, and saw "Cousins Libbie and Julia" frequently. Their letters do not record if they met the sisters' employer, Susan B. Anthony.[38] Whether or not Morris personally knew Anthony, she had strong connections to the woman suffrage movement. When Morris arrived in South Pass, Wyoming, in June of 1869, she brought radical ideas, an extensive network, and apparently suffrage pamphlets. She wrote to her niece, "I gave your Mother's Circular to Mr. Morris and I will write you the result."[39]

Morris's network of friends included radicals of many types. In the fall of 1869, she hosted her "old friend" Seth Paine, a well-known radical social reformer, in her log cabin in South Pass. Paine had founded a communal utopian farming community in the 1840s. After that, he started the Bank of Chicago, a Christian bank that operated on principles explained in his newspaper, the *Christian Banker.* More recently, he had founded the Working Women's Home in Chicago, which provided affordable lodging to "friendless women." While he stayed with Morris, he also acted as a special correspondent for the *Chicago Tribune.* Graciously, he had all the liberal papers delivered to Morris's home in South

Pass.[40] Paine stayed in the mining region of Wyoming for several months, during which time both he and his wife involved themselves in the community, including the promotion of woman suffrage.[41]

It is unclear whether Campbell met Morris when he came to South Pass as part of his tour of Wyoming Territory in June of 1869. He did, however, spend a long afternoon with Slack and Kingman, riding out to inspect the mines.[42] Whether Campbell spoke with Kingman and Slack about woman suffrage, he certainly heard about it when he returned to Cheyenne. Indeed, woman suffrage seems to have been a constant subject of public discussion in the city. Soon after Cheyenne was founded, the question of woman suffrage arose in the city's papers. Commenting on the 1867 Kansas woman suffrage campaign, the *Cheyenne Leader* noted, "[We] give the event to our readers as one of the curious movements of this progressive age, that must be discussed and disposed of by the press and platform, and finally by the votes at the ballot box."[43] Little did the editor realize the issue would be disposed of in his own city in just two years.

Such snippets of suffrage news frequently appeared in the paper. In January 1869, the *Leader* reported Wyoming's neighbor on the Great Plains, Dakota Territory, had considered a woman suffrage bill. The territorial council had passed it, but the house rejected it. By doing so, the *Leader* suggested, "the members of the Dakota Legislature . . . have thrown away the only chance they ever had to distinguish themselves." The writer warned that the territory's inaction meant, "Kansas, Iowa or some other State, will have gained the honor of having been the first to recognize what will soon be universally considered women's political rights."[44] Many in Wyoming seemed to consider woman suffrage inevitable, believing it would be adopted somewhere on the Great Plains in the near future.

Several prominent woman suffrage advocates traveled through Cheyenne that summer and fall. In June, the newly appointed governor of Colorado, Edward McCook, and his wife spent three days there. Campbell and McCook had served together under General Schofield. In 1870, a few months after staying with Campbell, McCook advocated for woman suffrage in his annual address to the

EQUALITY AT THE BALLOT BOX

Colorado legislature. Both he and his "beautiful, accomplished and gracefully aggressive wife" participated in an unsuccessful suffrage campaign in Colorado soon afterwards.[45] In June, former Ohio senator Benjamin Wade, one of the most radical of the Radical Republicans, and a vocal supporter of woman suffrage, traveled through Wyoming on his way to San Francisco. Campbell spent an afternoon with him in Laramie, and they spent another day together in July on the senator's return trip. Another prominent advocate, Samuel Bowles, the nationally known editor of the *Springfield Republican*, visited Cheyenne in July and again in August. Campbell recorded speaking with him.[46] We do not know if Campbell discussed woman suffrage with McCook, Wade, or Bowles, but their visits do illustrate that Campbell knew some of the movement's most vocal male advocates.

Wyoming held its first territorial election on 2 September 1869, and Campbell's experience with protecting voting rights in the Reconstruction South stood him in good stead when Democrats in South Pass City opposed African American suffrage. In the 1868 election, the national Democratic Party had run on a platform of white supremacy, particularly with respect to voting, a position the local Democrats supported. Anticipating trouble, Campbell sent United States Marshal Church Howe to South Pass.[47] On election day, a mob attempted to prevent African American community members from voting. According to Justice Kingman, who was in charge of the judicial district that included South Pass, Howe dealt with the situation effectively:

Some drunken fellows with large knives and loaded revolvers swaggered around the polls, and swore that no negro should vote. One man remarked quietly that he thought the negroes had as good a right to vote as any of them had. He was immediately knocked down, jumped on, kicked and pounded without mercy, and would have been killed, had not his friends rushed into the brutal crowed and dragged him out, bloody and insensible. . . . There were quite a number of colored men who wanted to vote but did not dare approach the polls until the United States Marshal placed himself at their head and with revolver in hand escorted them through the crowd, saying he would shoot the first man that interfered with them. There was much quarreling and tumult, but the negroes voted.[48]

In sending Howe to South Pass, Campbell signaled that the Fourteenth Amendment and federal authority would be respected in the territory. Despite these efforts to bring the Republican spirit of equal protection to the territory, Democrats won every seat in the legislature. "Beaten at election," wrote Campbell in his diary.[49]

Before the Democrats took charge, a sensational voice for the Republican cause graced the platform in Cheyenne. Anna Dickinson, whom the *Leader* called "the brilliant advocate of woman's cause everywhere," spoke to an audience of about two hundred and fifty people on 24 September.[50] One of the most famous lecturers in the United States, Dickinson was a fierce abolitionist and advocate of equal rights for both African Americans and women. In 1864, she had spoken on the floor of the House of Representatives to an audience that included President Abraham Lincoln and First Lady Mary Todd Lincoln. Her passionate lectures in support of the Union led some to call her "America's Joan of Arc." A friend to Susan B. Anthony and Frederick Douglass, she was well known as a powerful voice for equality.[51]

Secretary Lee introduced Dickinson in Cheyenne, and Governor Campbell attended.[52] The *Cheyenne Daily Leader* grudgingly admitted, "her lecture exhibited marked ability and was gracefully rendered" before denouncing it as containing too many "sweeping assertions" and a "spirit of exaggeration."[53] Of the actual content of her arguments, the writer said little. Typically, Dickinson's lectures at this stage in her career addressed questions of women's economic rights, equal pay for equal work, and suffrage.[54]

Esther Morris may also have lobbied for women's rights that fall. Grace Raymond Hebard, an early historian of Wyoming, claimed that prior to the September 1869 election, Morris held a tea party at her house and pressed candidates for the territorial legislature to introduce a suffrage bill. The evidence supporting Hebard's claim has been the subject of much controversy. Regardless, Morris belonged to a family active in suffrage causes and likely recognized that this first legislature presented a unique political opportunity. Indeed, the first legislature passed several bills related to women's rights. Democratic representatives from South Pass introduced all these measures, even though the national Democratic Party did not include women's rights in its platform. When Susan B. Anthony appeared at the 1868 national Democratic convention, the audience had literally laughed at her. Given the disdain of the national party for women's rights, it seems likely that someone sparked Wyoming Democrats' interest in women's issues. The well-connected and well-informed Esther Morris may have done so, tea party or not.[55] In any case, she expected the legislature to act on women's issues. On 13 October, as the legislative session began in Cheyenne, Morris wrote to her niece that she would keep her "well posted of the women's question."[56]

Amalia Post also had an interest in women's issues. Like Morris, Post's life experiences had shaped her views. She had come west to Elk Horn, Nebraska, from Vermont with her first husband in 1858. The marriage ended in divorce in Denver after their only child died and her husband abandoned her for his mistress. Post found herself alone, destitute, and devasted by the loss of her child. Refusing to be beaten, she started various enterprises and became a successful businesswoman. She married Morton E. Post, and the couple settled in Cheyenne, where he established one of the largest banks in the territory. By 1869, the Posts were one of the wealthiest and most politically influential couples in Cheyenne, where their social position gave them access to politicians of both parties.[57]

Perhaps, members of the legislature had the words of Dickinson, Morris, or Post ringing in their ears when the first territorial legislative assembly began its proceedings on 12 October 1869. It consisted of two bodies, the council and the house. From the first, members showed interest in issues concerning women. On 16 October, for instance, the house adopted a resolution that read, "*Resolved,* That the sergeant-at-arms be directed to assign seats within the bar of the house to ladies who may desire to attend the deliberations of this body."[58] On 1 November, Council Member

William S. Rockwell announced he would introduce "a bill for an act protecting married women in the enjoyment of their property and the fruits of their labor." Rockwell, a Democratic lawyer from South Pass City, proposed a bill that attacked the long-standing legal institution of coverture, which held that a husband could legally control his wife's property, wages, and other aspects of her legal existence. Some of the women's rights movement's earliest legislative successes, the 1845 and 1860 Married Women's Property Acts of the New York legislature, had also targeted coverture. Rockwell's bill gave married women full control over their property, business, and income, and guaranteed women the right to make a will and to sue and be sued.[59] Justice Kingman, writing later about the Wyoming law for *The History of Woman Suffrage*, explained, "to a person who has grown up under the common law and the usages of English-speaking people, [the marriage and inheritance laws] undoubtedly appear extravagant if not revolutionary, and well-calculated to disturb or overthrow the very foundations of social order." He added, "Experience has not, however, justified any such apprehensions."[60]

On 4 November, Louis Miller, a member of the house of representatives from Albany County, requested that Redelia Bates of Saint Louis be allowed to use the house chamber to deliver a lecture.[61] The next day, the *Leader* announced the arrival of "the beautiful and talented lecturer," who that evening would address the citizens of Cheyenne on "The Question of the Hour," embracing "the subject of female suffrage in all its bearings."[62] No record of Bates's lecture survives, though the *Leader* commented that she drew a strong crowd. Whether many members of the legislature watched is unclear, but inviting a female suffrage lecturer to speak in the house chamber during the legislative session was certainly intended to make a point.

Exactly one week after Bates's appearance, William Bright, president of the territorial council, announced that he would "introduce a bill for woman's rights."[63] Bright, a Virginian, made his way west after the Civil War and in the summer of 1867, began speculating in mining claims around South Pass City. After giving birth to their son, his wife joined him there the following year, and they opened a saloon.[64] Few direct statements from Bright survive, so the reasoning that led him to propose a woman suffrage bill is unknown. Several of his contemporaries believed his wife inspired him. Fellow legislator Ben Sheeks described Julia Bright as "a very womanly suffragist. And I always understood . . . that it was through her influence that the bill was introduced."[65] Justice Kingman, who also knew Bright, agreed: "He had an excellent, well-informed wife, and he was a kind, indulgent husband. In fact, he venerated his wife, and submitted to her judgement and influence more willingly than one could have supposed; and she was in favor of woman suffrage."[66] Bright's few surviving statements suggest that Esther Morris influenced his decision to introduce the bill. In an 1876 letter to the *Denver Post*, Bright named Morris, Mrs. Seth Paine—the wife of Morris's radical houseguest—and Amalia Post as being "proverbial for their earnestness in the [woman suffrage] matter and they advocated the cause with great zeal."[67] In 1902, at the annual conference of the National American Woman's Suffrage Association, Bright told Susan B. Anthony that his wife Julia and Esther Morris had influenced him to present the bill.[68]

Racism was also a factor in Bright's and other Democrats' support of woman suffrage. A Southerner and a Democrat, Bright represented the forces that opposed the Republican vision of the West, particularly with respect to African American voting rights. On 30 May 1868, South Pass Democrats issued a call for a "Grand Democratic Mass Meeting. . . . All good and true men, who repudiate the Reconstruction policy of Congress, negro suffrage, and the principles espoused by the Radical Republican party . . . are respectfully invited to participate." Bright chaired the meeting, which resolved, "we enter an earnest protest against the Radicals in Congress, for forcing negro suffrage upon the Territories and the Southern States."[69]

Many white suffrage activists, both male and female, embraced racism and nativism. Arguments for woman suffrage often reflected the language of universal rights: all citizens, regardless of race or gender, should have the vote as one of the fundamental rights of citizenship. As the women's movement faced defeat after defeat in the 1860s, however, some leaders began to argue that educated white women had a stronger claim on the vote than uneducated freedmen or immigrants. In the 1867 Kansas suffrage campaign, Stanton and Anthony toured with George Francis Train, a virulent racist who spoke out against black suffrage even as Stanton and Anthony argued for woman suffrage.[70] Henry Blackwell, the husband of Lucy Stone, also argued that black suffrage necessitated enfranchising white women. Writing to southern legislatures in 1867, he argued, "Your four millions of Southern white women will counterbalance your four millions of negro men and women and thus the political supremacy of your white race will remain unchanged."[71]

Bright and other white settlers in the region also felt threatened by the American Indians whose territories lay close to mining settlements. When Grant became president in 1868, he hoped to steer a new course with respect to the Great Plains tribes and pursue peace. Grant had visited Wyoming in July, before his election.[72] During the early years of his administration, Republican Indian policy focused on restricting the tribes to reservations, where they would be, as Campbell said, "taught the arts of civilization, and instructed in the cultivation of the soil."[73] In other words, they would be assimilated into the Republican vision of the West, whether they wanted to be or not. Few Americans, Republican or Democrat, saw the situation from the tribes' points of view.

South Pass Democrats detested Grant's Peace Policy almost as much as they despised the Reconstruction Amendments. Shortly after the Fort Laramie Treaty was signed, the editor of the *Sweetwater Mines,* a South Pass newspaper, called for genocide, urging the government to "kill off the Indians" and pay fifty dollars to each American man who brought in a scalp.[74] The first Wyoming territorial legislature urged Grant to abandon peace and instead adopt a "hostile and offensive policy" against the "murderously inclined savages."[75] Governor Campbell, who generally avoided such extreme racism, supported the Peace Policy. He too, however, considered the 1868 treaties overly generous, suggesting that much of the Indians' land should be "given up to civilization."[76] Some woman suffrage advocates believed that enfranchising women would increase the number of white voters who supported this position. Further, giving more rights to women could encourage them to emigrate to Wyoming, speeding the spread of "civilization."

Bright, who was not a lawyer and may not have written the actual bill, presented the woman suffrage measure to the territorial council on 27 November 1869. Clearly, Bright had secured the votes before introducing the bill, and it passed easily. Kingman claimed that the wives of a few men in the legislature influenced their support for the bill, and Bright rounded up the rest of the votes by pointing out that passage of such a bill would bring "a great deal of talk, and attract attention to the legislature, and the territory." Edward Lee agreed that many members supported it for the sake of publicity rather than out of principle. Kingman was clear, though, that Bright "was himself fully and firmly convinced of the justice and policy of his bill and gave his whole energy to secure its passage."[77] In his own account, Bright emphasized that woman suffrage had his "sympathies and hearty support."[78] The bill received its third hearing on 30 November and passed the council, 6–2.[79]

Just a few hours after passing the suffrage bill, the council considered yet another bill that concerned women's rights. On 26 November, Rockwell had introduced a school bill that, during debate, acquired a provision stating, "All teachers shall be paid according to their ability, and the work done by them, and no discrimination, shall be made on account of their sex."[80] A version with similar language would eventually make it into law, becoming an early example of equal-pay legislation. Later in the session, representative Ben Sheeks from South Pass introduced a divorce bill in the house that allowed either husbands or wives to sue for divorce and protected women's property rights in the case of divorce. Back in the council, Rockwell introduced a bill on descents and distributions.[81] Kingman described the measure as "peculiar and unusual" by the standards of the day, for in the final version, "the wife is treated exactly as the husband is; each having the same right in the estate of the other."[82] This legislative body passed laws considerably more equitable to women than those common in the rest of the country to the point of being radical.

Despite this warm embrace of women's economic rights, the suffrage bill met opposition in the house, which first took it up on 30 November, immediately after the council passed it. The bill was sent to committee, which recommended passage on 4 December. At this point, Ben Sheeks and J. C. Strong attempted various procedural maneuvers to kill it. Sheeks had supported the other women's rights measures but balked at the idea of women voting. The house rejected his attempts to shut down the bill. Recognizing defeat, Sheeks settled for amending the bill to raise the voting age to twenty-one. When the final vote was taken, the bill passed 7–4. The amended bill then returned to the council, which quickly passed it with a vote of 7–3 and sent it to the governor's desk.[83]

The decision was now Campbell's to make. The bill sat on his desk until 10 December. Justices Kingman and Howe discussed the legislation with the governor and, according to Kingman, "urged him to sign it with all the arguments we could command." Amalia Post and another prominent Cheyenne woman, Mrs. M. H. Arnold, also lobbied Campbell, and Kingman noted, "many letters were written from different parts of the territory, and particularly by the women, to members of the legislature, urging its passage and approving its object."[84] Campbell's diary does not record any of his thinking around his decision. He signed the bill on the evening of 10 December 1869. For the first time in United States history, women had equal political rights with men.

Who deserves credit for the passage of woman suffrage in Wyoming? Bright introduced the law, but why he did so has been extensively debated. Was he persuaded by his wife? By Esther Morris? By Edward Lee? By his fear of enfranchised African Americans? By his hope that expanding the pool of white voters would ensure white domination over American Indian nations?[85] In the absence of new sources, we will likely never have a definitive answer. Debating the question of who gets credit for the bill, however, misses the forest for the trees. Radical social and political change does not occur simply because one man introduces a bill or because one woman lobbies for it. Social change occurs over time. When Esther Morris wrote about women's issues to her niece and discussed those issues with her neighbors in South Pass City, for instance, she laid the groundwork for change. Writing about his mother, E. A. Slack argued that she was striving for more than "the mere privilege of putting a piece of paper in the ballot box." Rather, he added: "It has been well said that all reforms are crude and bungling at the outset. They are little more than a protest against existing conditions. Yet people then begin to think, and the work broadens out and assumes a different phase."[86]

By 1869, the issue of woman suffrage had already been in the public eye for some time, and it had been defeated nearly everywhere it was attempted. In the fight to enfranchise women in the Fourteenth and Fifteenth Amendments, in the legislature in Connecticut, at the ballot box in Kansas, on the Northern Great Plains of Dakota, woman suffrage had always lost. In Wyoming, however, a preponderance of people thought that it might work. No formal suffrage organization existed in Wyoming, but women and men who had read and thought about women's issues and the meaning of equality acted. A critical mass of people agreed to try a new idea.

Of course, their reasons for supporting woman suffrage differed. Esther Morris, Amalia Post, Mrs. Paine, and Mrs. Arnold— at least three of whom were staunch Republicans—likely supported the law because their experiences as women led them to agree with the arguments of suffrage leaders and writers. Republican leaders such as Campbell, Lee, and Kingman supported it because they believed in the doctrine of equality they fought for during the Civil War. Bright and other Democrats, meanwhile, likely espoused woman suffrage because they sought to limit the power of African Americans, American Indians, and Asian immigrant voters by enfranchising white women. Just as crucially, there was no organized opposition to woman suffrage in Wyoming. A few weeks after the suffrage bill passed, Robert C. Morris, Esther Morris's son, explained to the *Revolution,* "It is a fact that all great reforms take place not where they are most needed, but in places where the opposition is weakest; and then they spread until they take up all in one great principle of right and become universal; just so it will be with Woman Suffrage."[87]

The successful implementation of the new law demonstrates the political and public support it enjoyed. After the legislative session ended, Campbell headed east for the holidays, and Edward Lee became acting governor of the territory. Lee knew that merely passing a law was not sufficient to ensure lasting change in the status of a disenfranchised population. The day after the legislature passed the woman suffrage bill, J. C. Strong proposed "an act to provide that women who exercise the rights of the elective franchise should perform all other duties of citizens."[88] The bill was tabled, but it illustrated the attitude that many opponents of woman suffrage held, that is, women did not deserve the vote because they were not capable of meeting all of the responsibilities associated with suffrage. Lee gave women a concrete opportunity to prove this assumption wrong. In early February, he sent letters to Esther Morris and Caroline Neil, offering them positions as justices of the peace for Sweetwater County. He also sent a letter to Frances Gallagher of South Pass, offering her a position as constable.[89] Morris's son, E. A. Slack, knew Campbell and Kingman through his work at the district court, and another of her sons, Robert, also worked for the courts. Kingman and other members of the South Pass community had recommended Morris to Lee.[90] The county commissioners approved her application, and afterwards the commission's chair ordered that telegrams be sent out to the world that Wyoming "gave equal rights to women in actions as well as words."[91] Morris, whose term began on 14 February 1870, served through November. She had no formal legal training, but that was not unheard of in frontier towns. All sources agree that her successful term proved women could hold such a position.[92]

Justice Morris was not the only woman to take up judicial responsibilities that spring. In March 1870, women served on juries in Laramie. According to Kingman, opponents of woman suffrage made the decision to call women as jurors in hopes that the sight of women on juries would be so horrifying as to turn public opinion against the concept of women's rights. The women chosen endured taunts before Judge Howe issued a statement "to make it known to those ladies who have been summoned on the juries, that they will be received, protected and treated with all the respect and courtesy due, and ever paid, by true American gentlemen to true American ladies."[93] Backed by the courts, women served on juries throughout 1870 and 1871. Amalia Post, who acted as a jury forewoman, was proud to serve but found it grim work. In March 1871, she wrote her sister Ann: "I am serving on the jury now have not much time to write. . . . I was Foreman of the Jury & the man was condemed [sic] & sentenced to be hung . . . . There is no fun sitting on a jury where there is murder cases to be tried. . . . there is annother [sic] murder case to be tried on Monday."[94]

Wyoming women had their first chance to exercise the right to vote on 6 September 1870. Though they had not initiated it, Republicans embraced the new reform. As election season came around in the late summer of 1870, two women sat on the Laramie County Republican Central Committee—Mrs. W. D. Pease and Amalia Post. The committee nominated two women as candidates on the Republican ticket for Laramie County: Phoebe Pickett for the office of county clerk, and Mrs. M. H. Arnold for superintendent of county schools.[95]

Anticipation ran high as election day dawned. "Upon the occasion of so great an innovation," reported the *Laramie Daily Sentinel*, "our election was conducted with the utmost quiet and good order."[96] Secretary of the Territory Edward Lee recorded that a "vast assemblage of men, with uncovered heads, respectfully contemplated the scene."[97] As the polls opened in Laramie, "Mrs. Louisa A. Swain, a lady seventy years of age, walked up and deposited her vote, it being the first here, and probably the first ever deposited in the world by a lady at a general election." The editor of the *Sentinel* described Swain as "an old lady of the highest social standing in our community, universally beloved and respected, and the scene was in the highest degree interesting and impressive."[98] After Swain voted, "An aisleway was opened through the crowd, and three tremendous cheers were given as the aged grandam retired homeward."[99]

Neither of the two women who ran for office in Laramie County won her race, but both performed respectably. Arnold polled 40.5 percent of the vote, while Pickett pulled in 46.7 percent, proving that a substantial percentage of the electorate was willing to vote for women. In the biggest news of the election, women largely voted Republican, contrary to the hopes of the Democrats.[100] The *Cheyenne Leader* headlined its coverage, "Wyoming Redeemed!

Rousing Republican Victory!" In contrast to the Democrats' blowout victory in 1869, Republicans won several offices, including the critical position of delegate to Congress.[101] The editor of the *Laramie Daily Sentinel* credited this shift to the fact that women now possessed the franchise: "There is not a person in our territory who does not know we owe it to the Ladies of this Territory that we have been able to elect Judge Wm. T. Jones [the Republican candidate, originally a federally appointed territorial judge] to Congress. . . . We prophesy that his position in Congress will be none the less honorable, and his influence none the less potent, that he is the first legislator in the world, who owes his position to woman."[102]

The events of 1870 demonstrate that the success of suffrage stemmed from broad-based public support. At the level of government, Lee appointed women to office, and Howe ensured they were welcome in his court. The Republicans of Laramie County brought women into their organization. Several newspapers supported suffrage. At the polls, voters did not interfere with women voting, and many voters cast ballots for women. Nevertheless, when the second legislative assembly met in November 1871, the Democrats, led by Ben Sheeks, attempted to repeal the suffrage law. Bright did not run for reelection, and while the second legislature contained Republican members, a preponderance of the Democrats opposed woman suffrage, or at least opposed women voting Republican. After a lengthy debate, the legislature passed a bill to repeal the suffrage law. Governor Campbell immediately vetoed the measure. Campbell, who saw the extension of voting rights to women as the natural next step after the Reconstruction Amendments, explained his reasoning in supporting women's rights: "I was driven to the application of principles which through the whole course of our national history have been more powerfully and beneficially operative in making our institutions more and more popular, in framing laws more and more just, and in securing amendments to our Federal Constitution . . . what is there but conjecture, prejudice and conservatism opposing this reform?"[103] The legislature failed to override his veto. No other serious attempt to eliminate woman suffrage was ever made in Wyoming.[104]

*Organized in 1881, Johnson County, Wyoming, held its
first election on 19 April of that year. Delilah S. Sonnesberger of
Sheridan, a physician, rancher, and mother of seven children,
cast the first vote.* Wyoming State Archives Photo Collection

Once enfranchised, Wyoming women played a significant role
in territorial politics. After 1870, they ran for local office in almost every election year during the territorial period. Electoral
records indicate that at least ninety women ran for a county election in the years between 1870 and 1906. Women most commonly
ran for the office of county superintendent of schools. Mrs. M. H.
Arnold of Laramie County was the first woman to do so in 1870.
In 1872, the Republicans of Albany County nominated Eliza Boyd
as their candidate. Boyd lost the election with 47.9 percent of the

vote, just thirty-eight votes shy of the winning candidate. The first woman to win this office, based on available sources, was Lizzie W. Smith, elected in Carbon County in 1882. Every county in Wyoming except Uinta elected a woman as superintendent of schools at some point during the territorial period, and four counties elected only women.[105]

Women also followed in Esther Morris's footsteps and ran for the offices of justice of the peace, constable, and county clerk. At least five women seem to have been elected justice of the peace in Wyoming's early years: in Sweetwater County, Mrs. W. V. Clark in 1882, Jennie S. Holden in 1884, and Mrs. W. M. Moss in 1892; in Albany County, Maggie Gillespie of Lookout in 1898 and Mary Garrett of Rock Creek in 1902. Justice Garrett served, according to one source, for twenty years. These women lived in small, remote ranching communities and performed a number of other public duties. Justice Gillespie ran a ranch and raised seven children on her own after the death of her husband. She also served on her local election board for twenty-four years, was a deputy game warden for two years, and managed to squeeze in service on the district school board.[106] Justice Garrett helped her husband run their ranch, operated a mercantile business, served as postmaster, and took in homeless or orphaned children in addition to raising her own family of seven. Further, like many a Wyoming woman before and since, Garrett was "a marvelous 'shot' and a fearless and intrepid rider. She was well able to hold her own in any situation."[107]

Some Wyoming women served at the state and national levels. Republican Estelle Reel ran for state superintendent of public instruction in 1894 and became the second woman in the United States elected to a statewide office. In 1898, President William McKinley appointed Reel national superintendent of Indian schools, making her the first woman to receive a federal appointment. Democrat Mary Bellamy was elected to the Wyoming state legislature in 1910, the first woman elected to that office. In 1917, Bellamy served as Wyoming's representative in Washington, D.C., during the campaign for the Nineteenth Amendment, illustrating again how significant Wyoming was to the national movement.[108]

As early as 1871, Post had attended a convention of the National Women's Rights Association in Washington, D.C., reporting, "I was made more of than any other Lady in Convention." Isabella Beecher Hooker even offered to pay her expenses if Post would help her to "besiege congress."[109] Along with Esther Morris, William Bright, and Governor John Hoyt, Post was honored with a lifetime vice-presidency of the National American Woman Suffrage Association (NAWSA). Wyoming women regularly attended NAWSA conventions and served on its committees, including the congressional committee that lobbied Congress on suffrage issues. Wyoming Congressman Clarence Clark introduced an unsuccessful female suffrage bill in the fifty-second Congress in 1891.[110]

Wyoming women also participated in regional suffrage campaigns up and down the Great Plains. The most important of these leaders was Theresa Jenkins, who had arrived in Wyoming in 1877. In 1883, after hearing a speech by Frances Willard in Cheyenne, Jenkins helped found the Wyoming chapter of the Woman's Christian Temperance Union (WCTU). She lobbied the 1889 Wyoming Constitutional Convention to ensure that the territory entered the Union as a suffrage state, and in 1890, Jenkins was the featured speaker at the statehood celebration. Jenkins also worked on suffrage and WCTU efforts across the West.[111] She helped in the successful 1893 Colorado suffrage campaign, where "her testimony to the good effects of the ballot were simply invaluable. . . . She always carried conviction with her, yet never failed to leave it behind her."[112] Jenkins participated in twelve campaigns, but she was not the only Wyoming woman active in spreading suffrage. In 1894, the South Dakota chapter of NAWSA reported, "A good club has been newly organized at Waterto[w]n and also one at Yankton, of which Margaret E. Peel, a former voter in Wyoming, is President."[113]

Wyoming women used their political rights to influence the development of the territory, region, and nation, particularly in the areas of education and suffrage advocacy. Still, remarkable as it was, the expansion of rights in Wyoming had limits. Women's officeholding and political influence in Wyoming politics was far more extensive than in the rest of the country, but men still controlled most levers of power. Women officeholders mostly stayed in the traditional female realm of education. When they strayed too far, they faced barriers. For example, though women served successfully on juries in 1870 and 1871, the courts did not again call women to service. Justice Howe retired in 1871, and apparently his replacements were uncomfortable with women jurors. Women did not return to juries in Wyoming until 1950.[114]

Wyoming's example also illustrates that the expansion of women's rights, like Reconstruction itself, failed to live up to the notions of universal equality that had originally motivated its adherents. Some suffrage supporters both nationally and locally held racist and elitist views. The passage of the anti-miscegenation law over the veto of Governor Campbell shows that the same people who voted for woman suffrage were not in support of full racial equality. Few immigrants to 1860s Wyoming, whether male or female, Democrat or Republican, espoused expanding citizenship or equal rights to American Indians. Most American Indian women and men would not gain the right to vote until the passage of the Indian Citizenship Act in 1924. Even while fighting against some prejudices, suffrage advocates embraced others. Although not a full revolution, woman suffrage in Wyoming was a major step forward in the expansion of political rights in the United States. At the edge of the Great Plains, Wyoming was one of the few places in which at least some of the Reconstruction dreams of a more equal society came to fruition.

NOTES

The author would like to thank the staff of the Wyoming State Archives, whose depth of knowledge about the history of the territory and state of Wyoming is an invaluable resource. The staff at the American Heritage Center in Laramie provided much assistance with papers related to Wyoming women. The Connecticut State Library and the Northwest Museum of Arts and Culture in Spokane, Washington, were kind and supportive with my long-distance research requests. And many thanks to Molly Rozum and Lori Lahlum, whose support and feedback did much to bring this work into being.

1. Lambertson, "A Long Trail, 1930," *Annals of Wyoming* 10 (Jan. 1938): 30–31.

2. T. A. Larson, *History of Wyoming* (Lincoln: University of Nebraska

Press, 1965), p. 84; Marcy Lynn Karin, "Esther Morris and Her Equality State: From Council Bill 70 to Life on the Bench," *American Journal of Legal History* 46 (July 2004): 339.

3. *Laramie Daily Sentinel*, 7 Sept. 1870.

4. "Declaration of Sentiments and Resolutions," in *Selected Papers of Elizabeth Cady Stanton and Susan B. Anthony: In the School of Anti-Slavery, 1840–1866*, Vol. 1, ed. Ann D. Gordon (Rutgers University Press: New Brunswick, N. J., 1997), p. 78.

5. Colin Calloway, *One Vast Winter Count* (Lincoln: University of Nebraska Press, 2003), pp. 267–312.

6. Merrill J. Mattes, *Ft. Laramie Park History, 1834–1977* (Sept. 1980), Rocky Mountain Regional Office, National Park Service, Department of the Interior, www.nps.gov/fola/historyculture/upload/FOLA_history.pdf. For a discussion of the legal complications relating to the ratification and citation of the treaty, *see* Charles D. Bernholz, "Citation Abuse and Legal Writing: A Note on the Treaty of Fort Laramie with Sioux, etc., 1851 and 11 Stat. 749," *Legal Reference Services Quarterly* 29, no. 2 (2010): 133–48.

7. Richard White, *It's Your Misfortune and None of My Own: A New History of the American West* (Norman: University of Oklahoma Press, 1991), pp. 155–78; Robert Horowitz, *The Great Impeacher: A Political Biography of James M. Ashley* (New York: Brooklyn College Press, 1979), pp. 50, 66, 98. During the war, Ashley wrote or shepherded legislation that would eventually create the territories of Arizona and Montana (of which he would one day become governor) and bring statehood to Nevada and Nebraska. Ashley also strove unsuccessfully to gain statehood for Colorado.

8. U.S., H.R. Res. 633, 38th Cong., 2d Sess. (5 Jan. 1865); Grenville M. Dodge, *How We Built the Union Pacific Railway, and Other Railway Papers and Addresses*, S. Doc. No. 447, 61st Cong., 2d sess. (Washington, D.C.: Government Printing Office, 1870), pp. 5, 20–22; Stephen Ambrose, *Nothing Like It in the World* (New York: Simon & Schuster, 2000), pp. 127–28. The Berthoud Pass option was rejected in late 1864, but lobbying around the issue continued. The final route through Wyoming was not approved until late 1866.

9. H.R. Res. 633.

10. *Jeffersonian* (Stroudsburg, Penn.), 9 Feb. 1865.

11. Horowitz, *Great Impeacher*, p. 98.

12. James McPherson, *Battle Cry of Freedom: The Civil War Era* (New York: Ballantine Books, 1988), pp. 193–94.

13. U.S., S. Bill 357, 40th Cong., 2d sess., (14 Feb. 1868); Larson, *History of Wyoming*, p. 65. Larson points out that bills to create Wyoming Territory were also proposed in 1866 and 1867 by another Radical Republican, Congressman William Lawrence of Ohio.

14. Elizabeth Cady Stanton, Susan B. Anthony, Matilda Joslyn Gage, eds., *History of Woman Suffrage, 1876–1885*, Vol. 3 (Rochester, N.Y.: Susan B. Anthony, 1886), p. 495. For information on Emma Ashely, *see* p. 503.

15. Horowitz, *Great Impeacher*, p. 119.

16. Faye Dudden, *Fighting Chance: The Struggle over Woman Suffrage and Black Suffrage in Reconstruction America* (New York: Oxford University Press, 2011), pp. 161–88.

17. Act of 25 July 1868, *U.S. Statutes at Large* 15 (1868): 178–83.

18. "Treaty with the Sioux–Brule, Oglala, Miniconjou, Yanktonai, Hunkpapa, Blackfeet, Cuthead, Two Kettle, San Arcs, and Santee–and Arapaho, 1868" and "Treaty with the Eastern Band Shoshoni and Bannock, 1868," in *Indian Treaties: 1778–1883*, comp. Charles J. Kappler (New York: Interland Publishing, 1975), pp. 998–1007, 1020–24.

19. Lewis L. Gould, *Wyoming from Territory to Statehood* (1969; new ed., Worland, Wyo.: High Plains Publishing Co. 1989), pp. 6–7.

20. "A Noble Woman Gone," *Salem (Ohio) Daily News*, 4 Jan. 1892; John A. Campbell Military Records, Campbell Family Papers, Wyoming State Archives (WSA), Cheyenne; Donald B. Connelly, *John M. Schofield and the Politics of Generalship* (Chapel Hill: University of North Carolina Press, 2006), p. 210; *General Orders, Department of the Missouri*, 1862, *Department of the Ohio*, 1863, and *Department of North Carolina*, 1865, all U.S., War Department, copies in Campbell Family Papers.

21. Campbell to Council of the Legislative Assembly of the Territory of Wyoming, 6 Dec. 1869, House of Representatives Correspondence, 1869–1898, box 5, sub-subseries 2, series 2, Records of the Wyoming Secretary of State, WSA.

22. Wyoming Territory, *Council Journal of the Legislative Assembly of the Territory of Wyoming, 1869* (Cheyenne, 1870), p. 79 (hereafter *Council Journal*).

23. W. A. Croffut and John M. Morris, *The Military and Civil History of Connecticut during the War of 1861–1865* (New York: Ledyard Bill, 1868), pp. 500, 752. One of Lee's brothers died as a result of mistreatment at Andersonville.

24. *Weekly Rocky Mountain Star* (Cheyenne, Wyo.), 26 May 1869.

25. Marcus C. Ward to Edwin M. Stanton, 16 Nov. 1865, File L499–Lee, Edward M., Letters Received, 1863–1870, Records of the Adjutant General's Office, 1762–1984, Record Group 94, National Archives Identifier 300360, NARA, www.fold3.com/image/304956338.

26. Carole Nichols, *Votes and More for Women: Suffrage and After in Connecticut* (New York: Haworth Press, 1983), pp. 5–6.

27. *Hartford (Conn.) Courant*, 12 July 1867.

28. Connecticut, *Journal of the House of Representatives of the State of Connecticut, May Session, 1867* (Hartford, 1867), pp. 777–78.

29. Quoted in Ann D. Gordon, "Woman Suffrage (Not Universal Suffrage) by Federal Amendment," in *Votes for Women! The Woman Suffrage Movement in Tennessee, the South, and the Nation*, ed. Marjorie Spruill Wheeler (Knoxville: University of Tennessee Press, 1995), p. 6. *See also* Alexander Keyssar, *The Right to Vote: The Contested History of Democracy in the United States* (New York: Basic Books. 2000), p. 185; Dudden, *Fighting Chance*, p. 164.

30. Campbell, "Diary, 1869–1875," *Annals of Wyoming* 10 (Jan. 1938): 7; Dodge, *How We Built the Union Pacific Railway*, p. 23.

31. Campbell, "Diary, 1869–1875," *Annals of Wyoming* 10 (Apr. 1938): 60; Michael A. Massie, "Reform Is Where You Find It: The Roots of Woman Suffrage in Wyoming," ibid. 62 (Spring 1990): 11; Lavinia Dobler, *Esther Morris* (Riverton, Wyo.: Big Bend Press, 1993), p. 3; Karin, "Esther Morris and Her Equality State," p. 301.

32. Quoted in Cora Beach, *Women of Wyoming*, Vol. 1 (Casper, Wyo.: n. p., 1927), p. 11.

33. Ibid., p. 13; Karin, "Esther Morris and Her Equality State," p. 302; Wyoming Territory, Census, 1869, volume 1, subseries 11, series 1, Records of the Wyoming Secretary of State; Esther Morris to Frances McQuigg, 24 Nov. 1864, Frances ("Franky") McQuigg Stewart Papers, WSA.

34. W. E. Chapin, "Woman Suffrage Pioneer Recalled," *Laramie Boomerang*, reprinted in *Wyoming Kit and Caboodle Gazette* (Cheyenne: Wyoming Archives, Museums & Historical Dept., Mar. 1981), p. 6.

35. Esther Morris to McQuigg, 24 Nov. 1864, Stewart Papers (emphasis in original).

36. Robert Morris to McQuigg, 8 Jan. 1866, and Esther Morris to McQuigg, 8 Jan. 1866, ibid. Gail Hamilton was the penname of Mary Abigail Dodge. Her works include *A New Atmosphere* (Boston: Ticknor & Fields, 1866); *Stumbling-Blocks* (Boston: Ticknor & Fields, 1864), *Gala–Days* (Boston: Ticknor & Fields, 1863), and *Country Living and Country Thinking* (Boston: Ticknor & Fields, 1862).

37. Esther Morris to McQuigg, 18 May 1866, Stewart Papers.

38. Robert Morris to McQuigg, 28 May 1868, and Esther Morris to McQuigg, 7 Mar. [1870], ibid. [WSA dated this letter 1869, but Morris refers to her service as justice of the peace, which began in Feb. 1870]; J. Matthew Gallman, *America's Joan of Arc: The Life of Anna Elizabeth Dickinson* (New York: Oxford University Press, 2006), p. 118; Ann Gordon, ed., *The Selected Papers of Elizabeth Cady Stanton and Susan B. Anthony: An Awful Hush, 1895 to 1906*, Vol. 6 (New Brunswick: Rutgers University Press, 2018), p. 495.

39. Esther Morris to McQuigg, 22 June 1869, Stewart Papers.

40. Esther Morris to McQuigg, 13 Oct. 1869, ibid. For Paine's biography, *see* Alfred Theodore Andreas, *History of Chicago* (New York: Arno Press, 1975), pp. 408, 540–44.

41. *Wyoming Weekly Leader*, 29 Jan. 1876; *Council Journal*, p. 79.

42. Campbell, "Diary," *Annals of Wyoming* 10 (Apr. 1938): 60.

43. *Cheyenne Leader*, 8 Oct. 1867.

44. *Wyoming Weekly Leader*, 9 Jan. 1869.

45. Stanton et al., eds., *History of Woman Suffrage*, p. 715; Campbell, "Diary," *Annals of Wyoming* 10 (Jan. 1938): 11.

46. Campbell, "Diary," *Annals of Wyoming* 10 (Apr. 1938): 11, 61, and (July 1938): 63; Dudden, *Fighting Chance*, p. 153.

47. Larson, *History of Wyoming*, p. 72.

48. Kingman, "Wyoming," in *History of Woman Suffrage*, ed. Stanton et al., p. 729.

49. Campbell, "Diary," *Annals of Wyoming* 10 (Apr. 1938): 64.

50. *Cheyenne Leader*, 25 Sept. 1869.

51. Gallman, *America's Joan of Arc*, p. 36.

52. Campbell, "Diary," *Annals of Wyoming* 10 (Apr. 1938): 65.

53. *Cheyenne Leader*, 25 Sept. 1869.

54. Gallman, *America's Joan of Arc*, pp. 69, 88. Dickinson may have met Esther or Robert Morris in New York in 1868. She almost certainly met their cousins, Elizabeth Browne and Julia Browne. In later years, Robert Morris and Dickinson were close friends, and on several occasions, Dickinson lived in the home of Elizabeth Browne Chatfield. It is not known who requested Dickinson to speak in Cheyenne or who paid her lecture fee.

55. Hebard's main work on this topic is *How Suffrage Came to Wyoming* (1920; reprint, New York: William Dean Embree, 1940). Massie, "Reform Is Where You Find It," summarizes the controversy and evidence around this issue. *See also* Mike Mackey, *Inventing History in the American West* (Powell, Wyo.: Western History Publications, 2005); Virginia Scharff, *Twenty Thousand Roads* (Berkeley: University of California Press, 2003), pp. 94–114. For the national Democratic convention, *see* Dudden, *Fighting Chance*, p. 153.

56. Esther Morris to McQuigg, 13 Oct. 1869, Stewart Papers.

57. Correspondence of Amalia Post, folders 1–11, box 1, Morton E. Post Family Papers, 1850–1900, American Heritage Center (AHC), University of Wyoming, Laramie.

58. Wyoming Territory, *House Journal of the Legislative Assembly of the Territory of Wyoming, 1869* (Cheyenne, 1870), p. 29 (hereafter *House Journal*).

59. *Council Journal*, p. 50. On coverture, *see* Linda K. Kerber, *Toward an Intellectual History of Women* (Chapel Hill: University of North Carolina Press, 1997), pp. 264–68; Dudden, *Fighting Chance*, p. 28. Susan B. Antony was instrumental in the passage of the 1860 law.

60. Kingman, "Wyoming," p. 728.

61. *House Journal*, p. 59.

62. *Cheyenne Leader*, 5 Nov. 1869.

63. *Council Journal*, p. 66.

64. Massie, "Reform Is Where You Find It," p. 7.

65. Sheeks to Grace Hebard, 20 Aug. 1920, in *Wyoming Kit and Caboodle Gazette*, p. 8.

66. Kingman, "Wyoming," p. 730.

67. Quoted in *Wyoming Weekly Leader*, 29 Jan. 1876.

68. Ida Husted Harper, ed., *The History of Woman Suffrage, 1900–1920*, Vol. 5 (New York: National American Woman Suffrage Association, 1922), p. 34.

69. *Sweetwater Mines*, 30 May, 6 June 1868.

70. Dudden, *Fighting Chance*, pp. 127–32.

71. Blackwell, *What the South Can Do: How the Southern States Can Make Themselves Masters of the Situation* (New York: Henry B. Blackwell, 1867), p. 2. *See also* Jean Baker, *Sisters: The Lives of America's Suffragists* (New York: Hill & Wang, 2005), pp. 34–35.

72. *Cheyenne Leader*, 25 July 1868.

73. Quoted in *Council Journal*, p. 17.

74. *Sweetwater Mines*, 30 May 1868.

75. "Memorial and Joint Resolution of the Legislative Assembly of the Territory of Wyoming, with Reference to Indians," in Wyoming Territory, *Session Laws of the First Legislative Assembly for the Territory of Wyoming* (Cheyenne, 1870), pp. 725–32.

76. Quoted in *Council Journal*, p. 17.

77. Kingman, "Wyoming," p. 730. *See also* Lee, "The Woman Movement in Wyoming," *Galaxy* 13 (June 1872): 755. Justice Kingman believed Bright had a lawyer write it. In a 1952 interview, Sadie Bristol Jensen, the niece of Edward Lee, told historian Miriam Gantz Chapman that Lee had suggested the bill to Bright. She claimed Lee wrote the law, which Bright then introduced. Given that Lee was a lawyer and suffrage advocate, it is a possibility. In his own writings on the subject, however, Lee did not claim credit. Chapman, "The Story of Woman Suffrage in Wyoming" (master's thesis, University of Wyoming, 1952), pp. 63–67.

78. Quoted in *Wyoming Weekly Leader*, 29 Jan. 1876.

79. *Council Journal*, pp. 110, 122.

80. Ibid., p. 123. It is not known who added this language.

81. Ibid., pp. 68, 118.

82. Kingman, "Wyoming," p. 728.

83. *House Journal*, pp. 158, 159, 189, 196, 198, 207; *Council Journal*, p. 58.

84. Kingman, "Wyoming," pp. 730–31.

85. *See* Massie, "Reform Is Where You Find It," for a summary of the debate; *see also* Sidney Howell Fleming's "Solving the Jigsaw Puzzle: One Suffrage Story at a Time," *Annals of Wyoming* 62 (Spring 1990): 23–73, which provides an exhaustive discussion of the evidence. Virginia Scharff's "Broadening the Battlefield: Conflict, Contingency, and the Mystery of Woman Suffrage in Wyoming, 1869," in *Civil War Wests: Testing the Limits of the United States*, ed. Adam Arenson and Andrew R. Graybill (Oakland: University of California Press, 2015), pp. 212–16, contains a discussion of the connection between suffrage and empire.

86. Quoted in *Cheyenne Daily Leader*, 3 Apr. 1902.

87. Morris to the *Revolution*, 37 Dec. 1869, in *Wyoming Kit and Caboodle Gazette*, p. 8.

88. *House Journal*, p. 213.

89. Lee to Esther Morris, Lee to Neil, Lee to Frances Gallagher, all dated 17 Feb. 1870, box 1, sub-subseries 3, subseries 1, series 2, Records of the Wyoming Secretary of State.

90. Massie, "Reform Is Where You Find It," pp. 11–15.

91. Quoted in transcript of "The Female Justice of the Peace," Atlantic City, W.T., 14 Feb. 1870, Correspondence of the *Chicago Times*, 1870, folder 22, box 40, Grace Raymond Hebard Papers, AHC.

92. Massie, "Reform Is Where You Find It," pp. 14–15. It is not known for certain whether Carolyn Neil served; no copy of a court docket listing her as justice has been found, though records do exist showing that she posted a bond in Sweetwater County. Similarly, no records of Frances Gallagher's service as a constable in South Pass have been found.

93. Kingman, "Wyoming," p. 732.

94. Post to Ann Kilbourne, Mar. 1871, folder 11, box 1, Post Papers.

95. *Cheyenne Daily Leader*, 3 Sept. 1870.

96. *Laramie Daily Sentinel*, 7 Sept. 1870.

97. Lee, "Woman Movement in Wyoming," p. 758.

98. *Laramie Daily Sentinel*, 7 Sept. 1870. A limited number of women had voted prior to the passage of suffrage in Wyoming. Some single, propertied women voted legally in New Jersey from 1776 to 1807. In addition, some women in Kentucky (1838), Michigan (1855), and Kansas (1861) had gained school suffrage rights. Utah enfranchised its women in February of 1870;

women there voted in a municipal election that same month. Wyoming is, however, the first case in which women were fully enfranchised, able to hold any elected office, and actually voted for a federal official. Carol Cornwall Madsen, ed., *Battle for the Ballot: Essays on Woman Suffrage in Utah, 1870–1896* (Logan: Utah State University Press, 1997), p. 6; Alice Stone Blackwell, *Women and the School Vote* (New York: National American Woman Suffrage Association, 1913); Marilyn Schultz Blackwell, "The Politics of Motherhood: Clarina Howard Nichols and School Suffrage," *New England Quarterly* 78 (Dec. 2005): 570–98.

99. Lee, "Woman Movement in Wyoming," p. 758.

100. *Wyoming Blue Book*, Vol. 1, ed. Marie Erwin (Cheyenne: Wyoming State Archives & Historical Dept., 1974), pp. 385–86.

101. *Cheyenne Daily Leader*, 7 Sept. 1870.

102. *Laramie Daily Sentinel*, 8 Sept. 1870.

103. Campbell, "Message of Governor Campbell to the Legislature of Wyoming," 4 Dec. 1871, in *Council Journal*, 1871, pp. 79–80.

104. When Wyoming became a state in 1890, some delegates discussed the question of eliminating woman suffrage at the constitutional convention, but the idea was quickly shut down. *See* McKinney, "A Sentiment of Justice," herein.

105. *Wyoming Blue Book*, pp. 342–449; Abstracts of Election 1869, 1883–1906, box 1 and 2, subseries 2, series 2, Records of the Wyoming Secretary of State; *Laramie Daily Sentinel*, 20 Aug. 1872. The *Wyoming Blue Book* notes that Mrs. M. H. Arnold won election as county superintendent of schools in Laramie County in 1872 (p. 354), which seems to be a mistake. Contemporary newspaper accounts record that her husband, M. H. Arnold, won the election.

106. *Wyoming Blue Book*, pp. 342–449; Abstracts of Election 1869, 1883–1906, box 1 and 2, subseries 2, series 2, Records of the Wyoming Secretary of State; Cora Beach, *Women of Wyoming*, 2 vols. (Casper, Wyo.: n.p., 1927), 2: 216–19. Records for this period are scarce, and it is possible that one more woman, Eva Bell, served as justice of the peace in 1906 in Mountain Home.

107. Beach, *Women of Wyoming*, 1: 425–27.

108. Abstracts of Election 1869, 1883–1906; *Wyoming Blue Book*, Vol. 2, pp. 146, 543, 753.; *Laramie Daily Boomerang*, 2 Nov. 1910.

109. Post to Ann Kilbourne, 5 Feb. 1871, Post Papers.

110. Proceedings, *Twenty-Fifth Annual Convention of the National-American Woman Suffrage Association Held in Washington, D.C., January 16–19, 1893* (Philadelphia: By the Association, 1893), pp. 101, 164–65; Proceedings, *Thirty-Second Annual Convention of the National-American Woman Suffrage Association Held in Washington, D.C., February 8–14, 1900*, p. 10;

Proceedings, *Thirty-Fourth Annual Convention of the National-American Woman Suffrage Association Held in Washington, D.C., February 12–18, 1903*, p. 11.

111. Susan B. Anthony and Ida Husted Harper, eds., *History of Woman Suffrage, 1883–1900*, Vol. 4 (Rochester: Susan B. Anthony, 1902), p. 646; "Noted Wyoming Woman Expires Today," *Wyoming State Tribune*, [date Illegible] 1936, clipping in Jenkins, J. F. (Theresa, Mr. and Mrs.) File, WSA.

112. Proceedings, *Twenty-Sixth Annual Convention of the National-American Woman Suffrage Association Held in Washington, D.C., February 15–20, 1894*, pp. 186, 215.

113. Ibid., p. 215.

114. Chapman, "Story of Woman Suffrage in Wyoming," pp. 21–33.

QUIET VOICES IN THE PRAIRIE WIND

The Politics of Woman Suffrage in North Dakota, 1868–1920

BARBARA HANDY-MARCHELLO

In 1874, when Linda Slaughter campaigned for the elected position of Burleigh County superintendent of public instruction, she could not vote. Far from a suffragist, she did not believe that women should vote or have a public voice. She did not publicly campaign for the office, partly because she believed it unladylike and partly because the campaign speeches of other candidates were usually offered in a Bismarck bar. Following one candidate's speech, the voters would move to the other end of the street to a different bar to hear from another candidate. Instead of making a public spectacle of herself in a saloon, Slaughter visited the women of the town and asked them to urge their husbands to vote for her. Throughout her four terms as superintendent, Slaughter consciously clung to the concept of True Womanhood, which, she believed, prescribed limited public engagement for women. Nevertheless, she sought the office because she was educated, experienced, fearless, and committed to seeing Bismarck's children grow up with first-class educations.[1]

Slaughter's experience serves as a symbol of the decades-long suffrage campaign in northern Dakota Territory and eventually North Dakota. Ambivalence characterized the sporadic efforts to secure woman suffrage before 1913. Even after suffragists organized to promote a statewide vote on woman suffrage, the campaign was timid. This ambivalence suggests that woman suffrage in North Dakota was less about women's rights or democracy and equality than it was about the daily, dirty politics of a prohibition state largely controlled by railroads and milling interests.[2]

The United States Congress created Dakota Territory in 1861 as the nation writhed under the distress of disunion and the developing suffrage movement gathered steam.[3] With debates about equality and freedom in the political air, the territory's legislative assembly considered legalizing woman suffrage in its early sessions. Enos Stutsman, a legislator from the far northern part of the territory, introduced a bill in December 1868 that would confer the right of suffrage on women. Though Stutsman was known for his earthy sense of humor and rough frontier ways, he was quite serious about woman suffrage. He knew it was a radical departure from the usually conservative interests of the territorial assembly, but his arguments carried the bill in the lower chamber, known as the house. The upper chamber, or council, however, tabled the bill indefinitely.[4]

In 1870–1871, the territorial assembly considered a bill that proposed to strike the word "male" from election laws. At the time, women made up about one-third of the tiny non-Indian population living in the territory's few organized counties. In the unorganized portion, women constituted less than one-sixth of the non-Indian population. The council, acknowledging that Susan B. Anthony and Lucy Stone were not able to attend the session to "personally defend" their cause, invited the women of Yankton to speak on their interest in suffrage. Nevertheless, both house and council declined to pass the bill.[5]

For a short time in 1874, the focus of the debate about woman suffrage in northern Dakota Territory shifted to the United States Congress. The unwieldy territory lacked systematic and speedy communication between the major towns located on its extreme eastern edge. Senator Alexander Ramsey of Minnesota introduced a bill in Congress that would divide the territory in two, the northern portion to be called Pembina. Before the bill came to a vote, Congress amended it to include woman suffrage. Though the bill passed the House, it failed in the Senate, and the territory of Pembina never came into being.[6] The failure of the bill, according to contemporary regional historian George Kingsbury, was the "unfavorable aspect" of the Republican Party in the territory. Quarrels within the party left the territory vulnerable to the election of "one good democrat."[7]

The *Bismarck Tribune*, however, saw the situation differently.

EQUALITY AT THE BALLOT BOX

It reported on 10 June that, in Senator Ramsey's opinion, the Senate defeated the bill due to the "tedious debate growing out of the proposed women's suffrage amendment."[8] While some residents of the new territory would have welcomed any amendment in order to become independent of the southern portion of the territory, others, including Linda Slaughter, opposed the suffrage amendment. In a lengthy letter to the *Tribune*, she addressed the "stigma and disgrace" of the amendment. This woman, a married mother of three daughters, serving as an elected county official, referred to woman suffrage as "a perfect Pandora box of evils," a "premium to celibacy," and a "wicked and dangerous experiment." She presumed to speak for all Dakotans (or Dakotaians as they called themselves) when she stated, "rather than submit to this absurd amendment, as a humiliating condition of our admission, we prefer to stay out in the cold, forever!" These strong words coming from a woman deeply engaged in electoral politics set the stage for how suffrage issues would be debated for the next decade. An array of voices—few of them women's voices—sparred over what women wanted or what might be the greater social good. From 1874 until 1917, most legislators seemed content to follow the advice Slaughter threw at them in her newspaper article: "Why can't you let the women alone?"[9]

At least superficially, the course of woman suffrage in Dakota Territory appears to have followed the same course as it did in other territories and states. Favored by urban middle-class women, mostly wives of professional and business men, and opposed by large interstate corporations and socially conservative politicians, suffrage made slow progress. Dakota Territory, however, was largely rural, precariously perched on an agricultural economy, dependent on distant markets, and politically in thrall to a powerful transcontinental railroad. The urban middle class formed a small part of the population of its three largest cities, none of which were large even by the standards of the time.[10]

In 1883, the Dakota Territory legislature passed a bill granting women—meaning mothers and those with school-age children—the vote in school elections. This right applied only to elections concerning local and county superintendents, school bond issues, school board members, and other school issues. Women could also sit on the school board. Passing a school suffrage bill put the territory in league with the many states and territories that had passed school-suffrage bills in the 1870s. While school suffrage was important, it did not resolve the major concerns of suffragists —in particular, it did not offer women equality before the law. Indeed, school suffrage tended to reinforce many of the arguments employed to exclude women from the right and privilege of full suffrage. School suffrage was closely allied with women's "proper" role as a mother and teacher of children. All legislators could support this bill, for it was both progressive and socially conservative. It reinforced women's power to create a home that nourished children physically and mentally while setting them on the road to civic responsibility.[11]

Historians have debated the exact date of this small step toward suffrage. The confusion lies in the wording and intent of two different laws. In 1879, the territorial legislature allowed women to vote in school meetings. Under this law, if a woman attended a school meeting where an issue, perhaps the choice of textbooks, was to be decided, a woman could raise her hand in support of her chosen position and her vote would be counted even if her husband was present and voting. This law, however, served only to clarify women's place in public school meetings and did not in any way confer the right and privilege of suffrage. The legislature granted school suffrage with a separate ballot for women in 1883.[12]

Progress on securing the elective franchise for women in North Dakota stalled until 1917. In the intervening years, woman suffrage bills were often introduced in the legislature, and some came close to passing. More than one suffrage organization forged a political presence but could not sustain it in the face of massive disinterest. Legislators justified their lack of action on woman suffrage by pointing to the absence of local demand.

Citizens of the territory had two opportunities to consider woman suffrage in 1885. The legislature, the first to meet after school suffrage passed, considered a bill to grant women voting rights. John A. Pickler, an ardent suffragist and prohibitionist from Faulkton (now in South Dakota), introduced the bill, which legislators met with comic derision. One wag suggested the bill be referred to the committee on Indian Affairs; another wanted it sent to the military committee.[13] Though legislators had fun with Pickler's bill, it generated serious and largely positive discussion in territorial newspapers. For example, the *Bismarck Tribune* reprinted an editorial from the *Big Stone Herald* which noted that voters "must see that women will elevate the moral and social tone of our politics: drive drunkenness, jobbery and profanity from the polls." It was not sufficient, the editor argued, "to say that woman does nor does not want the ballot. She has the right, but the question is, has she the privilege to protect herself and family against abuses licensed by the votes of men who in nine cases out of ten are less qualified to pass judgments on moral questions than she is."[14]

Though Linda Slaughter was previously opposed to woman suffrage, by 1885, she had become a suffragist. Now divorced and struggling to support her daughters with her own earnings, she wrote to the *Bismarck Weekly Tribune* in support of Pickler's suffrage bill. Women who worked to support their children and paid taxes, she argued, deserved the vote. "It is perfectly safe to assume," she wrote, "that were all men endowed with the angelic attribute of perfection—and . . . all women possessed of ideal homes—the vexed question of women's suffrage would never have arisen to disturb the vexed dreams of legislators."[15] Slaughter's former husband, Benjamin F. ("Frank") Slaughter, also wrote in favor of woman suffrage. Chastising the Republican-dominated legislature for not feeling "the pulse of the people on this important subject," Slaughter, a Democrat, observed that in the "home, in the church and in society woman's influence is ever for good and to enlarge her sphere of action but increases her measure of usefulness."[16]

Newspapers across the territory, even the Republican papers, championed the Pickler bill. In spite of popular support, Pickler had to coax the bill through the legislature. After approval, the bill went to the territorial governor, Gilbert Pierce, who had previously indicated that he would sign it into law. Instead, Pierce, whom President Chester A. Arthur had appointed only six months earlier, vetoed the bill and returned it to the assembly with a long list of his reservations. Among other concerns, he declared that

Linda Slaughter, c. 1880.
State Historical Society of North Dakota

woman suffrage would delay Dakota's claim to statehood and that women did not want to vote. He suggested the bill should be referred to the voters. The assembly failed to override his veto.[17]

The same year, citizens of Dakota Territory elected delegates to a constitutional convention in anticipation of statehood. There were strong advocates for woman suffrage among the delegates, and once again, some citizens expressed their opinion that women should have the privilege of voting. Many newspapers, with the prominent exception of the *Fargo Argus*, supported extending the categories in which women could vote. Nevertheless, the proposed constitution assured women of school suffrage and

EQUALITY AT THE BALLOT BOX

no additional franchise privilege. Women voters lost nothing, then, when Congress refused to act on the territory's request for statehood.[18]

Some opponents of woman suffrage argued that even though women had the right to vote on all school issues, few women actually voted. Early-twentieth century voting records provide a singular but suggestive example. In one township for which voting records are still available, only seven women voted in the 1916 school election. Seventy-one men voted in the same election. In the same township in 1920, after full suffrage, one-third of the voters were women.[19] However few, the women who voted appeared unhampered by public opinion. With humor, an anonymous woman wrote about her first trip to the polls where she and other women had been "permitted to hold in our hand that telling and mighty power, a small piece of white paper called a ballot, and I repeat, permitted yes,—actually permitted by our brothers to deposit the same in a box along with theirs." She concluded: "When we arrived at home after having been away one-half hour, we found our better half in the best of humor with ample time to vote, and the children not gone to ruin and rags. So endeth our first experience with woman suffrage."[20]

In 1889, Congress finally overcame a variety of political objections and passed the Omnibus Bill that granted statehood to Montana, Washington, and Dakota Territory, which was divided into the two large states of North Dakota and South Dakota. On the Fourth of July, amid great celebration, delegates convened in Bismarck, the former territorial capital and now the capital of North Dakota, to write a constitution. The delegates were all male, of course, and of European descent or birth. There were fifty-six Republicans and nineteen Democrats. A few of the delegates were lawyers, some were businessmen, and many were farmers.[21]

Each delegate received a model constitution written by Harvard professor James Thayer at the request of Henry Villard, chairman of the board of the Northern Pacific Railway. The first days of the convention brimmed with speeches from visitors interested in land, water, constitutional law, and woman suffrage. Nationally known suffragist Henry B. Blackwell, who was touring the new states on the Northern Great Plains to speak in favor of woman suffrage, gave one of the first presentations. Blackwell appeared as something of a curiosity to delegates and residents of the state.[22] The *Jamestown Weekly Alert* described him as a "little old gentleman with silver hair . . . who . . . bellows for the suffragists." The *Alert's* editor suspected that the "old man . . . can do the ladies little good in our North Dakota. Some younger gallant, overflowing with strength and romantic enthusiasm, must respond to the bugler's call for a champion. Then will the girls have a chance for success."[23] While this paper supported woman suffrage, it nonetheless confused women's political interests with their sexuality. Blackwell recommended that suffrage be submitted to the people for approval separately from the rest of the constitution, and delegates vigorously debated his proposal. Leaving Bismarck, Blackwell headed to the new state of Montana to address yet another constitutional convention on woman suffrage.

If Blackwell had concerns about the weak presence of suffrage organizations in the state, he did not express them publicly. The dawn of statehood was the perfect moment to organize a strong campaign for suffrage, but the few suffragists, most of whom lived in the cities, seemingly had little connection with one another. The National Woman Suffrage Association (NWSA) could claim at least two members in Dakota Territory: Marietta Bones in the southern portion and Linda Slaughter, NWSA's corresponding secretary for the north. In 1888, Bones remarked in a letter to Slaughter that the two of them were the only NWSA members in the territory.[24] Nevertheless, Susan B. Anthony and Ida Husted Harper reported that a group had organized in Grand Forks in the spring of 1888, and "other local clubs were formed during the following years." Although Anthony and Harper wrote these paragraphs with great enthusiasm, the clubs faded quickly, and with the notable exception of Cora E. Smith (later Dr. Cora Smith Eaton), few of the women whose names were associated with these clubs publicly promoted suffrage. Smith, secretary of the Grand Forks Suffrage Club and later a prominent suffragist in Washington State, traveled to Bismarck and set up an office near the convention hall. These "friends of woman suffrage" invited delegates who had not decided on the suffrage issue to their office, where they received the men with "scrupulous formality and courtesy."[25] The *Fargo Argus,* which opposed woman suffrage, reported that suffragists had come to Bismarck for the convention, but other newspapers did not mention their presence in the capital.[26]

Delegate Henry F. Miller of Cass County introduced Blackwell's plan for a constitutional amendment on suffrage. In committee, however, Sam Moer of LaMoure proposed an amendment that limited full suffrage to males but opened the possibility of achieving woman suffrage through popular vote in the future. The wording of the new amendment foreshadowed a troubled future for woman suffrage: "No law extending or restricting the right of suffrage shall be enforced until adopted by *a majority of the electors of the State voting at a general election.*"[27] Moer argued, "The right of suffrage is a right conferred by the government for the public good. It is not a right inborn in any individual."[28] Moer had a particularly narrow view of political rights; he also opposed suffrage for foreign-born men who had resided in the state for fewer than five years. Moer's argument, as with other arguments both favoring and opposing the franchise for women, stemmed from principle, not a close reading of the United States Constitution.

Judge Robert Pollock, a lawyer and dedicated suffragist, noted that if the constitutional convention adopted the Moer amendment and a future legislature passed a suffrage bill, the electors who would vote on the referred bill would not include women. This bill muted women's voices and left their interests to the care of male voters and legislators. Others argued that there had been no demand for woman suffrage and no "serious discussion of the question" in spite of editorial letters to the newspapers and suffrage bills that had been introduced in sessions of the territorial legislature. John W. Scott, who appeared to have been somewhat ambivalent about woman suffrage, explained, "I should be willing to leave it to the women of the State themselves, provided they would get out to vote."[29] Scott's doubts reflect the absence of statewide suffrage organizations as well as the reluctance of other states on the Northern Great Plains to adopt woman suffrage.

Some delegates brought emotion and sentiment into the debate. Lorenzo Bartlett of Ellendale opposed woman suffrage in any form: "Show me one single individual family that is in favor of woman suffrage—I mean those who make a business of it—and how are their children? Do they raise a family equal to those who don't believe in it? No . . . if the man is a republican . . . the woman will become a democrat. . . . Anything that brings discord and sorrow into the family is not for the best interests of the people."[30] Bartlett's concern about women voting for Democratic candidates may have been the foundation of many legislators' reluctance to advance woman suffrage. Maintaining a Republican majority in the legislature likely mattered more to the delegates than women's rights. On the other side of the debate, delegate Ezra Turner of Bottineau declared that women needed the right to vote because they were "enslaved" and would only be happy if they had "their just rights and privileges."[31] Oddly, however, Turner offered an amendment that granted women the right of suffrage but not the right to hold office. Turner's motion failed; Moer's amendment passed.

The convention debated the right of women to vote in school elections even though territorial legislation had settled the issue and women had been voting in school elections for six years. Nevertheless, Bartlett and several others made their opposition known. Barlett offered an amendment that would limit school suffrage to unmarried women, a peculiar position when school suffrage proponents usually argued that mothers should have a voice in their children's education. In response, Rueben Stevens of Lisbon, a proponent of woman suffrage, used the moment to ridicule Bartlett. He facetiously declared, "I hope this Convention will not offer a premium on old maids . . . I haven't any use for them."[32] The school suffrage measure ultimately passed with a provision for separate and distinct ballots for women.

Another brisk debate concerned the prohibition of the use, manufacture, and sale of alcoholic beverages. North Dakota wrote prohibition into its constitution but planned to present the measure to the voters, as would have been the case if a woman suffrage amendment had been adopted. The delegates did not want the constitution to fail because of a single controversial clause. The prohibition clause passed, though by a smaller margin than the rest of the constitution. North Dakota entered the

EQUALITY AT THE BALLOT BOX

Union "dry" and remained so until the repeal of federal prohibition laws in the 1930s led to the repeal of the state's prohibition clause. Over the next twenty years, prohibition proved to be the most significant influence over the question of woman suffrage.[33]

North Dakota was nearly as ambivalent about prohibition as it was about suffrage. Prohibition sentiment was strong; yet, many cities and small towns, especially in the western counties, had multiple saloons. Even the prohibition-leaning Norwegian Lutheran population tolerated alcoholic beverages for "medicinal" purposes or the occasional celebration. In the legislature and the public arena, prohibition appeared to be a moral issue, but its political power grew out of the influence of the Northern Pacific Railway (NPR) and its representative in Bismarck, Alexander McKenzie. McKenzie used a complex system of legislative control to stall reform measures, including woman suffrage, as a means of protecting the railroad's interests.[34]

Alexander McKenzie had been in the shadows of nearly every political event in the territory and state since his arrival in Bismarck in 1874. He came to Dakota Territory from his birthplace in Canada as an illiterate laborer. Although he eventually learned to read and write, perhaps with the help of his friend Linda Slaughter, he left few letters and records, and he kept his personal life secret. When elected Burleigh County sheriff, he kept order in Bismarck with his powerful physical presence. By 1883, McKenzie represented the interests of the NPR in Dakota Territory and wielded a great deal of control over territorial politics. Using political trickery, he forced the removal of the territorial capital from Yankton to a section of land on a hill just north of Bismarck, the NPR's preferred site. After statehood, he controlled the state legislature, and sometimes the governor, until the Nonpartisan League took control of the state house of representatives in 1917.[35]

Soon after statehood, an important new player entered the North Dakota political arena. Elizabeth Preston, a former schoolteacher, had found her call to service in the Woman's Christian Temperance Union (WCTU). The evangelistic superintendent of the newly created North Dakota chapter of the WCTU served as the assistant organizer at her first national convention in 1889.

Elizabeth Preston Anderson, c. 1893.
State Historical Society of North Dakota

She became state president of the North Dakota WCTU in 1893 and worked in that capacity for another forty years. As president, she attended every legislative session, served as the watchdog for re-submission of the prohibition clause of the constitution, and promoted woman suffrage. She was gentle, an astute political observer, and a formidable check on the power of Alexander McKenzie.[36]

The same year that Elizabeth Preston took the reins of the WCTU, Laura Eisenhuth set out to test, and prove, the suitability of women to hold statewide elected office. Eisenhuth, a resident of Carrington, was elected Foster County's superintendent of schools in 1888 and 1890. In 1890, with the state constitution granting women the right to vote in school elections and to hold elective offices associated with schools, the Independent Party, a coalition of populists, prohibitionists, and the Farmers' Alliance, nominated her for the position of state superintendent of public instruction. She later received the Democratic Party's nomination as well. Though the Independent Party may have been interested in obtaining women's loyalty by nominating a woman for office, the Farmers' Alliance had stood for political equality since statehood. Eisenhuth also had the support of the WCTU. Her opponent, John Ogden, was well qualified, however, and with the support of the powerful Republican Party, he won the election.[37]

Eisenhuth ran for Foster County superintendent again in June 1892 but lost the election by a few votes. She demanded a recount, which the county auditor refused. Undeterred, she took the county to court and successfully forced a recount, which she won by eight votes. Her experience in electoral politics prepared her to run once more for the state superintendency that fall, receiving the Independents' nomination and an endorsement from the Democrats. Eisenhuth won the contest, becoming the first woman in the United States to be elected to state office. She defeated her Republican opponent by more than seventeen-hundred votes out of a total 36,421 votes cast, no small accomplishment in a Republican-dominated state. Eisenhuth lost in her second campaign for superintendent to Emma Bates, a woman who had the support of both the Republican Party and the Prohibition Party.[38]

The year that Eisenhuth upset the political apple cart and became state superintendent of public instruction was momentous for woman suffrage. When the legislature met early in 1893, Elizabeth Preston was present to monitor any bills of interest to the WCTU. Resubmission of the prohibition clause was nearly always on the agenda. "Wets" and the NPR wanted to send the prohibition clause back to the voters, believing that prohibition would not survive another vote. Preston noticed that whenever a resubmission bill came up, prohibitionists who suffered from alcohol addiction would be called out of the chamber and return "under the influence of liquor."[39] She also overheard lobbyists referring to monetary payments to encourage a vote in their favor. Preston's watchful presence not only helped to preserve prohibition in North Dakota, it established a record of corruption in the legislative chambers. The extent to which outside forces used corruption and fraud to control the legislature helps to explain how and why Alexander McKenzie and the NPR opposed woman suffrage.

Senator James W. Stevens of the Independent Party in Dickey County introduced a bill to confer full suffrage on women in the 1893 legislature. Preston and the WCTU supported the bill. By this session, suffrage had become a standing joke in the legislature. As Preston noted in her memoir, "When any question especially obnoxious or ludicrous comes up, there is usually some member, who is not burdened by the amount of brain he carries with him, ready to arise and move to refer the matter to the woman suffrage committee."[40] Nevertheless, the senate passed Stevens's bill and sent it to the house late on the last day of the session. The speaker of the house graciously suspended the session and invited Preston to come to the floor of the chamber to speak for the measure. When the house re-convened, the members passed the suffrage bill. Legislators knew that Governor Eli Shortridge, an Independent, was waiting in his office to sign the bill into law.[41]

Apparently, house leaders had not planned for the bill to pass. The speaker of the house, George H. Walsh, refused to sign the bill and, according to Preston, "a spectacular fight" ensued. Governor Shortridge declared that the speaker's signature was not necessary if the bill passed both houses and received the governor's signature. The bill, however, did not make it to the governor's office. According to Preston, "Men were placed in the halls and outside the doors of the Governor's office."[42] The men were probably agents of McKenzie's Republican-railroad-liquor-interest machine. The bill was "lost" for a time, but someone in the senate retrieved it. Senator Stevens had "ordered the postmaster of the senate . . . to hide the bill in the hope that it would be signed by the governor and become a law."[43] The postmaster put the bill under a floor mat, but a janitor found it. The house requested that the bill be returned to the lower chamber, but the senate, by vote, denied the request. Then, Senator Judson LaMoure moved to bar the president of the senate from signing more house bills

EQUALITY AT THE BALLOT BOX

until the speaker of the house signed Stevens's suffrage bill. According to Preston, "pandemonium reigned" because it was late in the evening of the session's last day. There were so many bills waiting for passage that the senate finally relented and released the bill to the house, where, wishing to disguise its own responsibility for the entire mess, the representatives voted to expunge the record. No official legislative record remains to prove that in 1893 a woman suffrage bill passed both houses of the North Dakota legislature.[44]

It was, surprisingly, Judson LaMoure, McKenzie's lead ally in the state senate, who offered the motion to stall all legislation until the house approved the woman suffrage bill. On this measure, LaMoure slinked away from his usual position of opposition to suffrage. He was seeking revenge against legislators who had not supported his capital-removal bill of the previous session. Revenge may seem a petty action for a leading state senator, but by turning his back on his usual cohorts, he restored his control of the senate. The women of the WCTU and their suffragist allies had no idea of the extent of the deceit, fraud, and corruption they were up against.[45]

As historians struggle to unravel the political threads of suffrage and prohibition, they must address a pertinent question: why did Alex McKenzie or the railroads care about woman suffrage and the liquor trade? Although McKenzie had plenty of vices, he did not drink. The quantity of liquor the railroads transported paled in comparison to the bushels upon bushels of grain that were the lifeblood of the railroads in North Dakota and kept this huge interstate corporation closely linked to every farmer and small town in the state. Other factors, however, shed some light on this political puzzle. First, the Republican Party needed the votes of the German and German-Russian communities in the state. Germans comprised the second largest immigrant group in the state. Beer and wine were important to their cultural traditions, and Germans were, for the most part, loyal Republicans. Opposition to woman suffrage occurred in counties dominated by German-speaking ethnic groups because of the strong political ties between prohibition and suffrage. The WCTU had linked prohibition to suffrage in the public mind. Although

McKenzie did not propose to legalize the sale and manufacture of liquor in German-speaking communities, by deflecting the quest for woman suffrage, the possibility of successful resubmission of prohibition remained viable.[46]

McKenzie's main interest was to ensure that the North Dakota legislature did not place any limitations on the NPR. Whenever a proposed bill threatened greater state control over railroads, one of McKenzie's men would threaten to introduce a bill to resubmit the prohibition clause of the state constitution to the voters. The promise that McKenzie's men would kill the resubmission bill before it got out of the legislature wooed legislators who favored prohibition away from railroad reform. If threats of resubmission did not work, McKenzie used bribery to buy votes against railroad reform. The passage of a woman suffrage bill would give prohibitionists greater assurance that the prohibition clause would stand another vote and release them to vote their conscience on railroad reform. By denying women the right to vote, McKenzie ensured that prohibition would continue to be his most effective and legal tool for controlling the legislature.[47]

The liquor lobby also aided McKenzie's hold on the legislature. A prohibition resubmission bill was introduced in the 1893 legislature. This same legislative session had passed a full suffrage bill, "lost" the bill, prevented another vote, and then expunged the record. It was a busy session for McKenzie. He employed his usual tactics to defeat reform bills, but he also had the aid of the liquor dealers of East Grand Forks and Moorhead, Minnesota. The sale of liquor was legal in these Red River border towns. Minnesota saloons quenched the thirst of North Dakotans and profited from North Dakota's prohibition laws. In addition, saloonkeepers in North Dakota who ran "blind pigs," or illegal saloons, did not want to see the prohibition clause overturned. They made good money on illegal whiskey and did not want to have to pay for a license. When temperance women approached the whiskey interests' lobbyist, Dan Sullivan of East Grand Forks, to thank him for his support in killing the resubmission bill, he replied, "Don't congratulate me, ladies. It was my $5,000 that did it." Sullivan proceeded to supply champagne to his supporters in the legislature until he decided it was in his best interest to get out of town.[48]

If fraud and bribery were not sufficient to sway legislators to vote against woman suffrage, McKenzie's henchmen would employ ethnic prejudice. Ethnic stereotypes prevailed in spite of the great variety of ethnic groups represented in the state and the legislature. One legislator reportedly said of the 1893 suffrage bill, "If that bill becomes a law, every Norwegian woman in the state will vote, and there won't be a white woman in the state that'll vote, and the result will be in a few years not a man can be elected to the Legislature unless he's a Scandinavian."[49] McKenzie also held Scandinavian immigrants in low regard. In one Burleigh County election, he brought Swedish farmers to town, offered them liquor, and gave them marked ballots to cast. The next day, opponents located the farmers and gave them fresh ballots, an act that upended McKenzie's plan and caused his opinion of Swedish farmers to decline even further. Lawmakers steeped in anti-immigrant prejudice believed that voting against the extension of woman suffrage would help Anglo-Americans maintain political power in the state.[50]

During the two decades that followed the corrupt political events of 1893, suffrage bills appeared in the legislature, and supporters started a few suffrage clubs. In 1895, women in several towns, including Jamestown and Grand Forks, organized suffrage clubs and held a statewide woman suffrage convention in Grand Forks. The convention chose Laura Johns of Kansas as its president. Among the women attending were Dr. Cora Smith Eaton, a Grand Forks physician, and Helen deLendrecie, whose husband was a leading Fargo merchant. Although there was no shortage of intelligent and well-connected women at the convention, the organization did not flourish. These were quiet years for North Dakota's suffrage movement. Even in 1906, when the state reined in Alex McKenzie's power through a political turnabout known as "the Revolution of 1906," the progressive Republicans who replaced McKenzie's wing of the party were not ready to support votes for women.[51]

In 1912, North Dakota women responded to the stirrings of suffragists across the nation. Among the national suffrage leaders who had visited since statehood were Susan B. Anthony, Matilda Joslyn Gage, whose daughter lived on a homestead in LaMoure County, and Carrie Chapman Catt. In February, Sylvia Pankhurst, a noted British suffragist, visited Fargo to speak to suffragists at the home of Mary Darrow Weible. "Fired" by Pankhurst's militant feminism, the women in attendance organized the Fargo Votes for Women League. In March, a second league organized in Grand Forks. Finally, in June, a statewide organization formed in Fargo, led by Clara Darrow, mother of Mary Darrow Weible. Many of the members of the two city clubs were married to university professors, but some working women took leading roles in the renewed fight for suffrage. Among them were Kate Wilder, who in 1919 became a Fargo City commissioner holding the police and health portfolios, and Mary Ann Whedon, a journalist.[52]

In June 1912, North Dakota suffragists met at convention in Fargo with Clara D. Darrow presiding. Members decided to support introduction of a woman suffrage bill in the 1913 legislature. The cause had lost strength in the state during its quiescence, however. Some legislators even seem to have thought the subject had become dormant, leading Senator H. E. Lavayea of Grand Forks County to attempt to repeal school suffrage in 1901. His unconstitutional proposal died before it came to a vote. Comments in some newspapers suggested that women's work should focus on home and children and that voting might corrupt women as it had corrupted men. Even the state's progressives appeared to lack enthusiasm for woman suffrage. Governor Louis B. Hanna, a progressive Republican, gave only lukewarm support to the cause when he said, "They [the women] can have my vote anytime."[53]

In spite of indifference, the Votes for Women Leagues persisted, meeting in cities and towns to keep the issue alive through public discussions. The prominence of the leadership—white women who were married to lawyers, professors, and leading merchants—was important in preventing the issue from being swept out of sight by opponents. This organization and publicity paid off with three suffrage bills introduced in the 1913 legislative session. Grand Forks senator H. A. Bronson introduced a full suffrage bill (Senate Bill 8). Representative Victor Wardrope of

Leeds introduced a bill in the house granting women the privilege of voting provided that male voters approved the law in a referral vote. Senator John Cashel of Grafton introduced an amendment to the state constitution conferring the privilege of voting on women that would also require voters' approval. The Bronson bill passed the senate and was sent to the house. Procedural matters delayed Wardrope's bill, so he threw his support behind the Bronson bill.[54]

Suffragists debated which bill to support. Elizabeth Preston Anderson, who had married Rev. James Anderson in 1901, argued that the constitutional amendment was the best option. Bronson's bill would have to be submitted to the voters for approval, and according to the state constitution, it would require a majority of all the voters voting at the election, including those who did not vote on that issue, to pass. Preston Anderson considered this impossible. Cashel's constitutional amendment, on the other hand, would have to be passed by both the 1913 legislature and the 1915 legislature, then go to the voters, where it would require only a simple majority of those voting on that issue. Suffragists understood that the Bronson bill was the least likely path to success. The legislature, however, approved both Bronson's bill and the Cashel amendment. The Bronson bill would go to the voters as a referred measure in November 1914.[55]

Suffragists put great effort into the campaign, organizing clubs in several small towns. Newspapers regularly covered the North Dakota suffrage campaign as well as the status of woman suffrage in other states. Women handed out literature on the streets and published notices in the newspapers. Jeannette Rankin of Montana, who took time away from campaigning for passage of a similar suffrage bill there, and Dr. Anna Howard Shaw, president of the National American Woman Suffrage Association, came to North Dakota to help organize and support the campaign. They gained support from the State Teachers' Association, the State Sunday School Association, the State Nurses' Association, and the Federation of Women's Clubs. Suffrage associations printed literature appealing to rural women's interests and advertised that they had the support of forty-thousand women because of the extensive and probably overlapping membership of these groups. Neither of the major political parties, however, endorsed woman suffrage or supported the campaign.[56]

In 1914, a new opponent appeared in Fargo. The North Dakota Association Opposed to Woman Suffrage (NDAOWS, or simply, "the Antis") was headed by Ida Clarke Young, a well-educated Phi Beta Kappa married to Judge Newton C. Young, a lawyer, former state supreme court justice, and a Republican. Both Youngs were prominent in public affairs in Fargo and in state-wide organizations. Ida Young, who always used Mrs. with her husband's last name in public matters, organized the NDAOWS in 1914 with the help of national anti-suffrage workers, including Carrie E. Markeson, Marjorie Dorman, and Minnie Bronson. Young had served four terms as president of the Federation of Women's Clubs, which endorsed the suffrage bill that would be on the November ballot. She resigned from the federation to, according to historian Paul Hefti, "ready herself for the upcoming contest," but she likely knew the politics of the federation and decided to distance herself from the group's endorsement of woman suffrage.[57]

The NDAOWS challenged suffragists to debates, and the first was held in Fargo on 25 July. Fifteen hundred people showed up to hear the women discuss women's roles and rights. Another debate occurred shortly after in Grand Forks. The NDAOWS put Marjorie Dorman of New York, a journalist and secretary of the National Woman Wage Earners' League Opposed to Suffrage, on the stage. Irma Poppler of Fargo, a social worker, represented the suffragists. The newspapers did not comment on which side had the best arguments.[58]

The Antis published a one-page statement titled "A Woman's Business." It consisted of a list of three reasons to reject suffrage with supporting statements explaining why the "Family is a Woman's Business." The three reasons were: "To give children good sound bodies. . . . To give children good minds. . . . To give children good morals." One of the more curious supporting statements declared that a woman's business was to "keep her own home clean and to see that the Board of Health looks after her unclean neighbor."[59] This statement may have referenced immigrant households, which, in spite of evidence to the contrary, were often considered unclean and rife with alcohol abuse. Although the Antis apparently declined to engage immigrant women, neither suffrage leaders nor their sisters in the temperance movement made much effort to organize immigrant women, probably because of their own deeply embedded prejudices. In addition, they may have wanted to avoid the taint of ignorance associated with immigrants. They were reluctant to air once again the suggestion posed in the 1893 legislature that most women voters would be immigrants. More puzzling, however, the NDAOWS's call for women to utilize a state agency undermined their argument that women should pay attention only to their own families and not to public issues. Oddly, this statement addressed non-voters who lacked a public voice powerful enough to direct the work of state agencies.

The NDAOWS seldom publicized what might have been the strongest argument against granting women the vote. Representative D. R. Streeter of Emmons County, a strong advocate of resubmitting the prohibition clause of the constitution to the voters, argued that the passage of woman suffrage would guarantee that voters would not see prohibition on the ballot again. Adding women, presumed to be temperance voters, to the electorate probably meant that prohibition could not be overturned. The Antis declined to expose the vulnerability of prohibition in their campaign for women's support, even though resubmissionists in the legislature understood that the only possibility for ending prohibition was to prevent women from becoming voters. Had they employed the anti-prohibition argument, the NDAOWS would have lost the support of many women who believed that temperance laws strengthened their place in the home just as they believed that suffrage threatened their role as homemakers and mothers.[60]

It is impossible to know how much influence the Votes for Women Leagues and the North Dakota Association Opposed to Woman Suffrage had on the election because the largest contributing factor in the failure of the measure was the wording of the 1889 constitution. The 1914 vote was officially reported as 49,348 no votes to 40,209 yes votes. The total vote on this issue, 89,557, added up to 251 more votes than were cast for governor. No other measure received so many votes. Voters passed the six other measures on the ballot. The highest number of votes cast on any one measure was 69,990, nearly twenty-thousand votes less than were counted (not cast) on the suffrage issue. The average number of votes cast on the six non-suffrage amendments was 66,591. There is no way to identify the exact source of those extra votes, but it is clear that voters in each precinct who did not vote on the suffrage measure were added to the "no" votes.[61]

Elizabeth Preston Anderson and Clara D. Darrow published a broadside explaining how the suffrage bill failed at the polls. The two suffragists identified the constitutional complication that voters may not have understood in 1914, explaining, "the man who voted at the election, and failed to vote on this question, was counted as voting against it." They added, "Does it seem probable that more men voted upon woman suffrage than voted for governor?" Preston Anderson and Darrow used the average of votes cast on other questions to calculate what the suffrage measure vote might have been if a constitutional requirement constructed by the "wily opponents" of woman suffrage had not hampered it. The two suffrage leaders concluded that the measure would have passed with a majority of twelve thousand votes.[62] Suffragists worried that legislators would see the 1914 vote on the Bronson bill as a mandate to kill the Cashel amendment that was before the legislature for a second approval. In spite of the suffragists' well-argued position, the 1913 constitutional amendment failed to gain the approval of the 1915 legislature.[63]

Suffragists were not the only North Dakotans at odds with the established political powers. Farmers had tried for decades to generate political or economic reform through association. The Farmers' Alliance endorsed politicians and political ideas but was not a political organization. The American Society of Equity focused on agricultural reform through cooperative exchanges. Members of these organizations had become discouraged with statewide political leaders who did not seem attuned to farmers' needs. At the February 1915 meeting of the American Society of Equity, farmers began to talk about forming a new political organization focused on farm issues. Within weeks, a few not-so-well-to-do farmers, some who had been members of the Socialist Party, gathered at Francis B. Wood's farm near Deering in north-central North Dakota where they formed the Nonpartisan League (NPL). With roots in radical agrarian and socialist thought and strong support among farmers who depended on their wives' physical, financial, and social contributions, the NPL gave women full membership status.[64]

The Nonpartisan League organized farmers quickly, particularly in the western and central parts of the state. The league remained unaffiliated with either political party but endorsed candidates nominated by Republicans or Democrats. In the 1916 general election, league-endorsed candidates took a majority of the seats in the state house of representatives, and the new governor, Lynn Frazier, was also a leaguer. While farmers expected that the current legislative session would pass bills to make farming more profitable, many league-backed legislators were also prepared to support woman suffrage.[65]

Senator Oscar Lindstrom introduced into the 1917 legislature a suffrage bill that Robert Pollock, a Valley City lawyer, suffragist, and temperance worker, wrote. Preston Anderson had urged Pollock to model the bill on the Illinois suffrage law, which conferred presidential and municipal suffrage on women. Suffragists indicated that they would settle for extended but limited suffrage, and the Illinois model had a distinct advantage. The North Dakota constitution required a full suffrage bill to be referred to the voters for approval. Limited suffrage did not face the same requirement, meaning the suffrage campaign would not fail once again by the addition of non-votes to the negative column as in 1914. The Tri-State Grain Growers endorsed the bill and included Josephine Sarles Simpson, a Minneapolis suffragist, among the speakers at its convention. This endorsement reveals one of the complicated alliances of the 1917 campaign for suffrage. The grain growers' association was far more politically conservative than the league, though some members were also leaguers, but had always given farm women a fair hearing.[66]

Among those who straddled the developing political divide between farmers and businessmen was Emily K. Sheldon, whom the Fargo Votes for Women League elected president in 1916. She was married to an attorney and businessman and was the daughter of

Godfrey H. Knight, a wealthy Cass County farmer with business and banking interests in Fargo. The Knights and the Sheldons, among the many business-minded Grand Forks and Fargo suffragists, were not likely to see eye-to-eye with the Nonpartisan League on any issue other than woman suffrage. Farmers in the state's easternmost counties tended to be better off financially and did not share the experience of farmers in the state's western counties who had to contend with poor quality soil, recurring drought, and unreliable markets. The Nonpartisan League had strong support in western counties among farmers who struggled to make a living. Businessmen opposed the NPL's plans, which they closely identified with socialism. Yet, their wives had been stalwarts in the suffrage movement for years.[67]

As the NPL-dominated legislature prepared to meet, Elizabeth Preston Anderson and members of the Fargo Votes for Women League traveled to Bismarck for the opening days of the legislative session, bringing their concerns about suffrage and other social issues. Preston Anderson was prepared to lobby for suffrage and against resubmission. She had asked WCTU members around the state to interview candidates for the legislature and determine their positions on issues of interest to the group. Each of these members then sent Preston Anderson the information they had gathered. She arrived in Bismarck in January 1917 with "considerable knowledge of that law-making body" and knew just how to approach key members for support.[68]

Nonpartisan League women were also working to get the suffrage bill passed, along with other league bills. Marion Wickster Lee and other members of her local NPL club sold raffle tickets, sewed quilts, and held picnics to raise money for NPL activities. "They were politically minded around here," Lee remembered.[69] The activities of the NPL women in rural communities near Minot raised money for their causes just as the women of the Fargo Votes for Women League did.

The Illinois-inspired suffrage bill was introduced 16 January 1917. It quickly passed both houses, and after a day's delay caused by a blizzard, Governor Frazier signed it on 23 January. At last, the women of North Dakota could vote for president of the United States and a variety of county and municipal offices. They could

Flanked by activists such as Elizabeth Preston Anderson
(directly to his right) as well as his wife and daughters (to his left),
Governor Lynn Frazier signed North Dakota's 1917 suffrage bill.
State Historical Society of North Dakota

not vote for legislators or governor, but the national suffrage bill was on the horizon. In a bit of political theater that must have been a sight to behold, Speaker of the House Howard R. Wood, a member of the Nonpartisan League, invited Grace Clendenning, president of the Votes for Women League, to the floor of the House and presented her with the yellow quill pen used to sign the bill.[70] Not all league members were so gallant. A few weeks later, A. G. Divet, an NPL legislator who had voted for the suffrage bill, told lobbyists campaigning for some of the other issues of interest to the Votes for Women League to go home. When they protested that they represented the "people back home," Divet replied, "Then you had better go back home and stay there. . . . We don't want you here. Go home and tend to your own business."[71] Apparently, women voters as lobbyists did not have the same appeal as the liquor lobby.

Suffragists had struggled to organize and sustain a conversation about woman suffrage for twenty-eight years. They had stirred a lethargic public into overcoming liquor politics, bossism, and the humdrum objections of the Antis to achieve their goal. In Fargo, the Votes for Women League approved a "rising vote of thanks . . . to Mr. and Mrs. Robert Pollock for their initiative in advocacy and framing the Limited Suffrage Bill."[72] They made no mention of NPL support for woman suffrage. Their next task was to get women out to vote to prove the naysayers wrong. Near Minot, NPL member Rose Bach drove a horse and buggy around her rural neighborhood to urge women to vote. "They didn't know how to vote," she later claimed, adding, "They didn't know what they could do. Some of them were interested and some of them weren't."[73] In advance of the formation of the League of Women Voters, the Fargo Votes for Women League considered re-organizing as the Voting Woman's Club. Soon, in their first turn at the polls under the new law, the women voters made a surprising debut.[74]

The 1918 election returns revealed that the NPL was losing strength and that women voters had entered into their new civic responsibilities fully independent and unpredictable. The Non-partisan League had made major changes in state government, but the league and some of its leaders had also disappointed some of their members. A door had opened for opponents to organize. The most powerful of the league's opponents was the Independent Voters Association (IVA), which had re-organized in December 1918 after a brief but unsuccessful run earlier that year. The IVA challenged league-sponsored laws, petitioned for referral of the most radical of the new legislation, and attacked league leaders as unpatriotic socialists.[75]

Though the IVA had a vigorous start and a good deal of support in cities and towns, only one IVA-approved candidate, Minnie J. Nielson, won election in November 1918. Nielson was elected state superintendent of public instruction over her NPL-endorsed opponent, the incumbent Neil C. Macdonald. Both candidates appeared well qualified for the position. Macdonald had been employed by a former state superintendent to bring education equality to rural schools and had achieved a national reputation for rural-school reform. He was energetic and popular and had been elected state superintendent of public instruction in 1916.[76] Nielson was serving as Barnes County superintendent of schools, and had previously taught science at Valley City High School, where she had been named "one of the most honored high school teachers ever employed in the city."[77]

As the election approached, Neilson had the endorsement of all ten presidents of County School Officers' Associations and served as president of the Federation of Women's Clubs, arguably the most powerful women's organization in the state. She was also a popular and successful fundraiser for World War I causes. Nielson had increased enrollment, lengthened the school term, and overseen an increase in the number of consolidated schools in Barnes County. She claimed, however, to have at least some college education, which was, at best, a distortion. She had not finished any college courses and had not enrolled in the colleges that she claimed to have attended. Macdonald privately called her a "dear, fat, old maid" and complained that she was a poorly educated woman. He also stated that she campaigned on her Scandinavian heritage and opposition to the Nonpartisan League. Macdonald scornfully added that all these points were true except for the last—her parents had been born in Scotland. Nielson attacked Macdonald with equal vigor, calling him a "slavedriver, autocrat, typical Prussian, and unfit in temperament."[78] In formulating a response to Nielson, the NPL had to tread carefully. She was popular, and the NPL had courted women's votes. Nielson, however, had the support of the IVA, which had been attacking the NPL on many counts and implied that socialism invaded the privacy of the home and threatened the safety of women and children. Nevertheless, the NPL urged rural woman voters to "turn out against the wives of city gangsters"—in other words, the suffragists of Fargo and Grand Forks. Newspapers that opposed the NPL promoted Nielson as "pro-family, state, and nation."[79]

In November, Nielson polled 58,324 votes to 52,777 for Macdonald. Macdonald was the only NPL-endorsed candidate in 1918 to lose, and he did not go gracefully. He refused to yield the office to Nielson, so she appealed to Attorney General William Langer, also an NPL officeholder. Langer agreed that the voters had chosen Nielson, and that she was qualified, and he ordered Macdonald to vacate the office so that the duly elected superintendent could move in.[80]

The 1918 voter turnout was relatively low, but significant numbers of women went to the polls and voted for Minnie Nielson. Women did not seem to disapprove of NPL candidates in general; they cast votes for many other NPL candidates, but they favored Minnie Nielson over the NPL-endorsed candidate even though the NPL was responsible for extending their voting rights. Because women still voted on a separate ballot in 1918, it is possible to look at one county's voting pattern to see how women cast their votes. In Barnes County, urban women cast 714 votes for Nielson and 70 for Macdonald. The influence of the NPL is evident in rural women's votes. Though they voted for Nielson, the margin was much smaller—336 to 216. Urban men in Barnes County also supported Nielson. Barnes County was her home, and voters there had supported her for several years. But rural men in Barnes County stuck with the NPL and voted for Macdonald 1,026 to 750. Women voters proved to be independent in choosing a candidate without regard to the voting preferences of their husbands or their perceived political interests.[81]

Congress passed the woman suffrage amendment to the United States Constitution in 1919, and the North Dakota legislature ratified it later that year. North Dakota women had worked hard for decades to achieve full voting rights. Now women could vote as men did on every candidate and issue on the ballot. In celebrating the achievements of the suffragists, it is worth remembering that their years of struggle resulted in a limited victory: only non-Indian women were included in the organizations, the debates, and the final approval of woman suffrage. In order to vote under North Dakota and federal law, women and men belonging to the seven American Indian nations in North Dakota had to prove citizenship through the provisions of the Dawes Act (1887) and separate themselves from their tribes and cultural heritage. Even when they had met all those conditions, they were likely to be denied a ballot until 1924, when Congress granted citizenship to all American Indians.[82]

Dakota men living in Benson County had successfully sued for the right to vote in 1892, but they still faced challenges when they

In 1923, Burleigh County, North Dakota, seated an all-woman jury.
State Historical Society of North Dakota

attempted to vote. The ironic timing of a similar case sheds light on the context of the climax of the suffrage campaigns. In 1916, the right of Lakotas of the Standing Rock Reservation to vote in Sioux County elections was challenged in court. In this case, *Swift v. Leach*, the North Dakota Supreme Court decided in 1920 that American Indians had become citizens through the Dawes Act (1887) and were, indeed, electors. The court's decision notwithstanding, Elizabeth Preston Anderson, Grace Clendenning, Clara Darrow, and the other suffragists were no more likely to view suffrage as a universal right and obligation than were Alex McKenzie, Judson LaMoure, or Lorenzo Bartlett. The power of the white, urban, middle class to make political change was most effective when focused on white, urban, middle-class interests.[83]

The 1921 legislature further clarified women's civic rights and responsibilities when women appeared on the list of citizens who qualified as jurors. Nationally, women's jury service became a difficult next step in the expansion of their citizenship roles. Many states, including those on the Northern Great Plains, slowly accepted women as jurors. North Dakota was among the minority of states that codified women's jury service soon after the Nineteenth Amendment became part of the constitution. Many of the states that allowed women to serve on juries required women to notify the court that they were available for jury service. The reverse was true in North Dakota where women could be excused from jury duty only if they applied to the court in writing at least five days before the court was in session. In a spectacular display of women's newly acquired citizenship rights and obligations, Burleigh County seated an all-woman jury on 26 July 1923. The bailiff was Linnie Lee Hedstrom, Linda Slaughter's daughter and wife of the county sheriff. Some of the women on the jury had once been students in Slaughter's elementary school classes.[84]

Linda Slaughter would have cheered these women as they exercised their civic responsibility. As an elected official and belated suffragist, she had engaged in the rough politics that characterized the road to full citizenship, but her commitment to the cult of True Womanhood hindered her ability to influence a deeply corrupt territorial and state government controlled by Alex McKenzie. The last generation of North Dakota suffragists were reluctant to employ the dramatic tactics used in other states to win approval of legislators and voters, but they found allies in surprising places and stood fast in the face of discouraging political defeats. They savored their victory as quietly as they had pursued their campaign, using the power of full citizenship to vote their conscience and serve their communities.

NOTES

My mother, Carolyn Pickard Handy, was a remarkable woman. Her life and death are intricately wound up in this article, reminding me that there is no better use of the past than to direct us into the future. This article is dedicated to her.

1. Much of Linda Slaughter's personal history can be found in the many articles she published in the *Bismarck Tribune*, the *Dakota Herald*, and the *St. Paul Pioneer*. Her autobiography was published in the *Bismarck Tribune* in

1893 and later published as *Linda Slaughter's Fortress to Farm, or Twenty-three Years on the Frontier*, ed. Hazel Eastman (New York: Exposition Press, 1972). Barbara Welter first developed the historical concept of True Womanhood in "The Cult of True Womanhood, 1820–1860," *American Quarterly* 18 (Summer 1966): 151–74. I am indebted, as are all scholars of North Dakota suffrage, to Jeanne Tucker who, in 1951, wrote "The History of the Woman's Suffrage Movement in North Dakota" as an undergraduate paper at the University of North Dakota. The first and for many years the only paper on the topic, it remained the most widely used reference on the history of suffrage in North Dakota for more than fifty years. *See* Jeanne Tucker, "The History of the Woman's Suffrage Movement in North Dakota," 1951, folder 12, box 1, Research Papers Written on North Dakota History Collection, OGLMC 263, E. B. Robinson Special Collections, Chester Fritz Library, University of North Dakota (UND), Grand Forks.

2. On the history of North Dakota and its politics, *see* Elwyn B. Robinson, *History of North Dakota* (Lincoln: University of Nebraska Press, 1966); Howard Roberts Lamar, *Dakota Territory, 1861–1889: A Study of Frontier Politics* (1956; repr., Fargo: Institute for Regional Studies, 2001).

3. Dakota Territory in 1861 included what is today North Dakota, South Dakota, and part of Wyoming. The capital until 1883 was in Yankton, in the extreme southeast corner of the territory. This paper focuses on suffrage activity in the northern part of the territory and, after statehood in 1889, North Dakota. The territory's legislative matters, however, necessarily include southern Dakota Territory.

4. Dakota Territory, *House Journal of the Eighth Session of the Legislative Assembly of the Territory of Dakota* (Yankton, 1869), pp. 78, 95; Dakota Territory, *Council Journal of the Eighth Session of the Legislative Assembly of the Territory of Dakota* (Yankton, 1869), pp. 87, 90; Dale Gibson, with Lee Gibson and Cameron Harvey, *Attorney for the Frontier: Enos Stutsman* (Winnipeg: University of Manitoba Press, 1983), pp. 74–75. Wyoming Territory was established in 1868, and the Wyoming assembly passed a full woman-suffrage bill in 1869. *See* Alan P. Grimes, *The Puritan Ethic and Woman Suffrage* (New York: Oxford University Press, 1967), pp. 53–59; Michael Massie, "Reform is Where You Find It: The Roots of Woman Suffrage in Wyoming," *Annals of Wyoming* 62 (Spring 1990): 2–22.

5. *House Journal*, 1871, pp. 44, 90; *Council Journal*, 1871, pp. 78, 87, 93; Doane Robinson to L. N. Crill, 4 Feb. 1922, folder 54, box 3360B, Doane Robinson Papers, State Archives Collection, South Dakota State Historical Society, Pierre; U.S., Department of Commerce, *Ninth Census of the United States, 1870*, AncestryLibrary.com.

6. *Bismarck Tribune*, 3, 10 June 1874.

7. George W. Kingsbury, *The History of Dakota Territory*, Vol. 2 (Chicago: S. J. Clarke Publishing Co., 1915), p. 985.

8. *Bismarck Tribune*, 10 June 1874.

9. Slaughter, "Defeat of a Bill to Divide Dakota Territory: Eloquent Speeches and Votes on Woman's Suffrage," ibid., 17 June 1874.

10. Fargo was the largest city in 1910 with a population of 14,331.

11. Dakota Territory, *Laws Passed at the Fifteenth Session of the Legislative Assembly of the Territory of Dakota* (Yankton, 1883), chap. 44, sec. 66 (hereafter cited as *Session Laws*); Edmund B. Thomas, Jr., "School Suffrage and the Campaign for Women Suffrage in Massachusetts, 1879–1920," *Historical Journal of Massachusetts* 25 (Winter 1997): 3. Fifteen states and territories had passed school or full suffrage laws by 1883.

12. *Session Laws*, 1879, chap. 14, sec. 30. The confusion might have begun in the letter Doane Robinson wrote to L. N. Crill in which Robinson refers to the 1879 bill as conferring school suffrage. *See* note 5. This author's interpretation of Dakota Territory school suffrage law is based on an article in the *Emmons County (N.Dak.) Record*, 17 June 1884, and Susan Wefald, *Important Voices: North Dakota's Women Elected State Officials Share Their Stories, 1893–2013* (Fargo: North Dakota State University Press, 2014), p. 173.

13. "The Dear Women," *Bismarck Weekly Tribune*, 30 Jan. 1885.

14. Ibid., 27 Feb. 1885.

15. "A Woman Speaks," ibid., 13 Feb. 1885.

16. "An Opinion," ibid., 20 Feb. 1885. The Slaughters' relationship after 1879 is difficult to describe. They were probably not living together when these letters were written and may have been divorced. Their affection for each other seems to have remained strong in spite of Frank's alcoholism. Over the course of their thirty-year relationship, they married each other three times and divorced twice. The course of their relationship can be traced in the Benjamin F. and Linda Slaughter Papers, Mss 10003, State Historical Society of North Dakota (SHSND), Bismarck.

17. Elizabeth Cady Stanton, Susan B. Anthony, and Matilda Joslyn Gage, eds., *History of Woman Suffrage*, Vol. 3 (Rochester, N.Y.: Susan B. Anthony, 1887), pp. 667–69; Doane Robinson, *History of South Dakota*, Vol. 1 (Indianapolis: B. F. Bowen & Co., 1904), p. 597.

18. On statehood conventions, *see* Robinson, *History of North Dakota*, pp. 197–208. *See also* Bill Reid, "The North Dakota Votes for Women Leagues—Fargo Branch: Vital Reform or Disappointing Failure?," n.d., Bill G. Reid Papers, Accession 2153, Institute for Regional Studies, North Dakota State University, Fargo. On campaigns in the southern portion of the territory, *see*

Nancy Tystad Koupal, "Marietta Bones: Personality and Politics in the South Dakota Suffrage Movement," in *Feminist Frontiers: Women Who Shaped the Midwest*, ed. Yvonne J. Johnson (Kirksville, Missouri: Truman State University Press, 2010), pp. 69–82.

19. "WOMEN General Election Poll and Tally List . . . November 7, 1916," and "General Election Poll and Tally List . . . November 2, 1920," Precinct 28 (Green Township), Poll Books, 1894–1934, series 41132, Barnes County, Local Government Records, SHSND.

20. "My First Experiences in Voting," *Bismarck Daily Tribune*, 18 June 1890.

21. North Dakota, *Official Report of the Proceedings and Debates of the First Constitutional Convention of North Dakota assembled in the City of Bismarck, July 4th to August 17th, 1889* (Bismarck, 1889), pp. 3–4 (hereafter cited as *Constitutional Convention*).

22. *Jamestown Weekly Alert*, 11 July 1889; *Constitutional Convention*, pp. 34–41.

23. *Jamestown Weekly Alert*, 11 July 1889.

24. Bones to Slaughter, 23 Feb. 1888, Slaughter Papers; Tucker, "History of the Woman's Suffrage Movement," pp. 15–16. *See* Koupal, "Marietta Bones," p. 75, on the formation of a South Dakota State Equal Suffrage Society.

25. Susan B. Anthony and Ida Husted Harper, eds., *The History of Woman Suffrage*, Vol. 4 (Rochester, N.Y.: Susan B. Anthony, 1902), pp. 545–46.

26. Tucker, "The History of the Woman Suffrage Movement," p. 16; Kristin Mapel Bloomberg, "Cora Smith Eaton and North Dakota Woman Suffrage, 1888–1897," herein.

27. Anthony and Harper, eds., *History of Woman Suffrage*, p. 546. Jeanne Tucker writes that the final wording of this amendment came about "mysteriously," but it is clear that opponents of woman suffrage dominated the committee's work. Tucker, "History of the Woman's Suffrage Movement," p. 17.

28. *Constitutional Convention*, p. 277.

29. Ibid.

30. Ibid., p. 280.

31. Ibid., p. 283.

32. Ibid., pp. 573–74.

33. Robinson, *History of North Dakota*, pp. 257–59.

34. *Bismarck Weekly Tribune*, 5 July 1889; Carrie Young, *Nothing to Do but Stay: My Pioneer Mother* (Iowa City: University of Iowa Press, 1991), p. 89; Barbara Handy-Marchello, "Land, Liquor, and the Women of Hatton, North Dakota," *North Dakota History* 59 (Fall 1992): 22–29.

35. Robert P. Wilkins, "Alexander McKenzie and the Politics of Bossism," in *The North Dakota Political Tradition*, ed. Thomas W. Howard (Ames:

Iowa State University Press, 1981), pp. 3–39; Slaughter, *Fortress to Farm*, pp. 151–52. Some historians argue that McKenzie was dethroned in 1906 upon the election of "Honest" John Burke to the governorship. Wilkins argues that McKenzie's influence was merely blunted and that he continued to promote NPR interests until 1917. *See* Charles N. Glaab, "John Burke and the Progressive Revolt," in *North Dakota Political Tradition*, ed. Howard, pp. 46–52. Linda Slaughter, a school teacher, often wrote or read letters for the illiterate adventurers who flocked to Bismarck in the 1870s. She was a friend of McKenzie, so it is likely that she helped him learn to read and write. *See* Slaughter, *Fortress to Farm*, p. 151.

36. Bill G. Reid, "Elizabeth Preston Anderson and the Politics of Social Reform," in *North Dakota Political Tradition*, ed. Howard, pp. 183–202; Elizabeth Preston Anderson, "Under the Prairie Winds: An Autobiography," folders 4–8, box 1, Elizabeth Preston Anderson Papers, Mss 653, Institute for Regional Studies. In 1901, Preston married Rev. James Anderson.

37. Susan Wefald, "Breaking an 1889 Glass Ceiling: Laura J. Eisenhuth, First Woman Elected to Statewide Office in the United States," *North Dakota History* 79 (Dec. 2014): 15–16; "The Following is the Platform of the Farmer's Alliance," *Bismarck Weekly Tribune*, 5 July 1889.

38. Wefald, "Breaking an 1889 Glass Ceiling," p. 22.

39. Preston Anderson, "Under the Prairie Winds," pp. 82–83.

40. Ibid., pp. 83–84. Stevens chaired the Woman Suffrage Committee in the senate.

41. Reid, "Elizabeth Preston Anderson," p. 195. Governor Shortridge belonged to the Farmers' Alliance and ran as an Independent.

42. Preston Anderson, "Under the Prairie Winds," pp. 83–84.

43. *Jamestown Weekly Alert*, 9 Mar. 1893.

44. Preston Anderson, "Under the Prairie Winds," p. 84.

45. Ibid.

46. Bill Reid, "Elizabeth Preston Anderson," p. 196, brings up the concerns of various ethnic groups in the state regarding prohibition. I, however, disagree with his claim that German men simply wanted to keep their wives at home. Gaining access to legal sources of liquor was likely more important to German voters. Little effort was made to control the illegal liquor trade in North Dakota until William Langer became attorney general in 1916. *See* Glenn H. Smith, "William Langer and the Art of Personal Politics," in Howard, *North Dakota Political Tradition*, pp. 123–50.

47. Wilkins, "Alexander McKenzie," p. 29.

48. Quoted in "How Resubmission Failed," *Jamestown Weekly Alert*, 9 Mar. 1893. *See also* Wilkins, "Alexander McKenzie," p. 28.

49. Quoted in Reid, "Elizabeth Preston Anderson," p. 196.

50. Wilkins, "Alexander McKenzie," p. 30.

51. *Jamestown Weekly Alert*, 21 Nov. 1895; Glaab, "John Burke and the Progressive Revolt," pp. 4–65.

52. Tucker, "The History of the Woman Suffrage Movement," pp. 28, 32; *Oakes Weekly Republican*, 12 Sept. 1890; *Jamestown Weekly Alert*, 2 Oct. 1890; *Bismarck Weekly Tribune*, 23 September 1898; Julia Gage Carpenter Diary, folder 2, box 1, Julia Gage Carpenter Papers, OGLMC 520, UND; Reid, "North Dakota Votes for Women Leagues," p. 9. On her tours of western states and territories, Gage visited her daughter homesteading in LaMoure County and her other children, including a daughter who had married L. Frank Baum, living in Aberdeen, South Dakota. Susan B. Anthony attended temperance meetings in North Dakota in September and October 1890.

53. Quoted in *Turtle Mountain Star*, 28 Nov. 1912, requoted in Tucker, "History of the Woman Suffrage Movement," pp. 29, 32–33.

54. Tucker, "History of the Woman Suffrage Movement," pp. 33–34; *Williston Graphic*, 20 Feb. 1913; *Grand Forks Evening Times*, 8 Mar. 1913.

55. Tucker, "History of the Woman Suffrage Movement," pp. 33–34; Preston Anderson, "Under the Prairie Winds," p. 85.

56. Tucker, "History of the Woman Suffrage Movement," pp. 34–35; "40,000 North Dakota Women Ask for the Ballot," *Bismarck Daily Tribune*, 1 Nov. 1914.

57. Paul Hefti, "The Pull of Tradition: the North Dakota Association Opposed to Woman Suffrage," in *Day In, Day Out: Women's Lives in North Dakota*, ed. Bjorn Benson, Elizabeth Hampsten, Kathryn Sweney (Grand Forks: University of North Dakota, 1988), pp. 198–99. I have not been able to confirm Jeanne Tucker's claim that Judge Young was an attorney for the Northern Pacific. *See* Tucker, "History of the Woman Suffrage Movement," p. 36.

58. Hefti, "Pull of Tradition," pp. 202–3.

59. "A Woman's Business," Mss 11354, SHSND.

60. *Valley City Weekly Times-Record*, 13 Mar. 1913.

61. Tucker, "History of the Woman Suffrage Movement," p. 35; Preston Anderson, "Under the Prairie Winds," p. 85; "Militant Suffragists Storm Senate Committee Which Has Measure Under Consideration," *Bismarck Daily Tribune*, 23 Jan. 1915; *Vote of the People: Initiated and Referred Measures in North Dakota from Statehood through 1989*, Vol. 2 (Grand Forks: Bureau of Governmental Affairs, University of North Dakota, 1990), p. 9.

62. Preston Anderson and Darrow, "Statement."

63. Tucker, "History of the Woman Suffrage Movement," p. 36.

64. There are many resources for the Nonpartisan League including its own newspaper, the *Nonpartisan Leader*. A good history of the NPL in North Dakota is Robert Morlan, *Political Prairie Fire: The Nonpartisan League* (St.

Paul: Minnesota Historical Society Press, 1985). A more recent book with a broader view of the league's national impact is Michael J. Lansing, *Insurgent Democracy: The Nonpartisan League in North American Politics* (Chicago: University of Chicago Press, 2015). On North Dakota farm women's work, *see* Barbara Handy-Marchello, *Women of the Northern Plains: Gender and Settlement on the Homestead Frontier, 1870–1930* (St. Paul: Minnesota Historical Society Press, 2005).

65. Morlan, *Political Prairie Fire*, p. 105.

66. Herbert E. Gaston, *The Nonpartisan League* (New York: Harcourt Brace & Howe, 1920), p. 150; *Nonpartisan Leader* (Fargo), 25 Jan. 1917; Elizabeth Preston Anderson, *The Story of Fifty Years: North Dakota Woman's Christian Temperance Union* (n.p., 1939), p. 7, copy in Institute for Regional Studies Collection, NDSU; Tucker, "History of the Woman Suffrage Movement," pp. 37–39.

67. Reid, "North Dakota Votes for Women Leagues," p. 10.

68. *Nonpartisan Leader*, 22 Feb. 1917; Preston Anderson, "Under the Prairie Winds," p. 86.

69. Lynn Severson, *Plum Valley Women: Minot's First One-Hundred Years* (Minot: Minot Commission on the Status of Women, 1985), pp. 187–88.

70. *Nonpartisan Leader*, 1 Feb. 1917.

71. Quoted ibid., 22 Feb. 1917.

72. Meeting Minutes, 3 Feb. 1917, folder 3, box 1, Votes for Women League of North Dakota, Fargo Branch Records, Mss 49, Institute for Regional Studies.

73. Quoted in Severson, *Plum Valley Women*, p. 186.

74. Meeting Minutes, 3 Feb. 1917.

75. D. Jerome Tweton, "The Anti-League Movement: The IVA," in *North Dakota Political Tradition*, ed. Howard, pp. 95–97.

76. Robinson, *History of North Dakota*, pp. 304–5; Lansing, *Insurgent Democracy*, pp. 168–69; Jim McMillan, "The Macdonald-Nielson Imbroglio: The Politics of Education in North Dakota, 1918–1921," *North Dakota History* 52 (Fall 1985): 4.

77. McMillan, "Macdonald-Nielson Imbroglio," p. 4.

78. Both quoted ibid., p. 5.

79. Quoted ibid.

80. Tweton, "Anti-League Movement," p. 129.

81. McMillan, "Macdonald-Nielson Imbroglio," p. 5.

82. Frank L. Polk, "Greetings," box 9, Governor, Incoming Letters, Mss 30153, SHSND; North Dakota, *Session Laws* (Bismarck, 1911), chap. 131.

83. Karen V. Hansen, *Encounter on the Great Plains: Scandinavian Settlers and the Dispossession of Dakota Indians, 1890–1930* (New York: Oxford

University Press, 2013), pp. 186–88; *Swift* v *Leach*, 45 N.D. 437, 178 N.W. 437 (1920). *See also*, Jeanette Wolfley, "Jim Crow Indian Style: The Disenfranchisement of Native Americans," *American Indian Law Review* 16, no. 1 (1991): 167. Sioux County is a North Dakota political division that is contiguous with the boundaries of the portion of the Standing Rock Indian Reservation that lies within North Dakota's borders.

84. Linda K. Kerber, *No Constitutional Right to be Ladies: Women and the Obligations of Citizenship* (New York: Hill & Wang, 1998), pp. 136–51; *Session Laws, 1921*, chap. 81; First All-Women Jury in North Dakota, Bismarck, 26 July 1923, Photo 00091-0243, Fannie Dunn Quain Photograph Collection, SHSND.

THE MARATHON OF MONTANA
SUFFRAGE
A Commitment to Civic Activism

JENNIFER J. HILL

In 1889, suffragist Clara McAdow attended the Montana Constitutional Convention with her husband Perry McAdow, a delegate, and perspicaciously applied herself to politicking. Delegates tasked with creating the governing statutes for the newly minted state of Montana found the responsibility both weighty in significance and tedious in its attention to detail. Lacking official delegate credentials and barred from the floor of the convention, Clara McAdow accosted delegates as they went in and out of the building. By sheer force of personality and strength of argument, McAdow extracted individual pledges of support for women's enfranchisement from both sides of the aisle. The *Forsyth Independent* reported that with "39 democrats and 36 republicans among the delegates . . . Mrs. McAdow undertook to obtain an interview with each. . . . For fear the cause might become a partisan issue, she buttonholed a democrat and a republican alternately."[1] Ambitious and driven, McAdow waded into the political furor surrounding woman suffrage, eager to do her part in shaping her adopted state.

McAdow was not alone in the long campaign for woman suffrage. Two noteworthy contemporaries, Mary Long Alderson, a journalist and temperance advocate, and Dr. Maria Dean, a Helena physician, shared McAdow's commitment to public activism, demonstrating superior analytical abilities and speaking eloquently about the suffrage cause from varying points of authority. McAdow leveraged her business success; Alderson participated in the leadership of women's organizations; and Dean called upon her professional expertise, public service, and status

Clara McAdow, c. 1889.
Montana Historical Society Research Center

as an elected official. Together, these three women, each deeply
committed to gaining Montana women the right to vote, stand as
important examples of how women on the Northern Great Plains
used the democratic process to bring about radical social change.

The future Clara McAdow settled in Billings in 1882 with her
then-husband, Dr. C. E. Tomlinson, and convinced the Billings-
area office of the Northern Pacific Railway to take her on as a
clerk.[2] Unlike many youthful transplants to the Northern Great
Plains, she was, according to the *Grass Range Review*, "a woman
who had entered her forties, but was full of vim and energy."[3] She
advanced professionally—unusual at a time when the railroad
employed few women—and when her husband became ill and
eventually died, she stayed in Billings and invested her earnings.
Known to many as "Captain Tom," she opened a real-estate office and tried her hand, with consistent success, at a number of
business ventures.[4] She kept a high public profile, regularly ap-

pearing in local newspapers due to her fame as a "lady real estate boomer." Even when laid up with a broken leg, she made it known that she was "still at the office, ready to transact real estate business."[5] Consistently active in public circles, Clara Tomlinson cultivated well-heeled social connections, attending the celebration marking the completion of the Northern Pacific line with railroad magnate Frederick Billings and his wife, among other local dignitaries.[6]

In January 1884, Tomlinson, described in the local press as "one of the brightest and most intelligent ladies in Montana," married Perry McAdow, a business owner and entrepreneur.[7] Their marital partnership faced an immediate challenge when Perry's sawmill went bankrupt that spring. After the couple relocated to Maiden, Montana, Clara McAdow's real estate income gave them the necessary capital to explore other speculative investments. As Carroll Van West of the Montana Historical Society observed of their relationship, Clara McAdow quickly filled the role of "dominant partner, becoming, in fact, the family business manager." Good fortune—and her astute financial management—brought success, and "the McAdows became rich through Clara's shrewd business dealings."[8]

Based on a hunch, Clara McAdow invested in the Spotted Horse Mine, at that time nothing more than a ninety-foot-wide hole, and transformed it into a highly profitable gold mine. In the absence of engineers, she directed the construction of roads over rough mountain terrain and the placement of bridges to allow for the transportation of construction materials for the mill and housing for the miners. Based on her initial success, McAdow sold the mine at a profit to investors, but they were unable to make the payments. To salvage her investment, she repurchased it from the initial buyers. Amazingly, a new gold seam was discovered under her supervision. McAdow improved and expanded the mine into a thriving industrial complex with its own stamping mill and ore-processing facilities, and she even ventured underground to supervise the digging. After proving the mine's profitability for a second time, she sold it in 1890 to a group of Helena investors at an even higher price.[9]

While she clearly enjoyed making money and building her investment portfolio, McAdow also aspired to public service. Her work at the Montana Constitutional Convention did not spring from a passing interest in suffrage. McAdow had called for a visit to the territory from a national suffrage personality for several years and finally helped bring Henry Blackwell to Helena as the 1889 convention vote approached. Blackwell, husband of Lucy Stone and brother of Elizabeth Blackwell, achieved national renown through regular speaking tours promoting woman suffrage, his leadership role in the American Woman Suffrage Association (AWSA), and his role as coeditor—alongside his wife—of the *Woman's Journal.* No stranger to constitutional conventions, Blackwell campaigned for woman suffrage in Montana in 1889 immediately after his appearance in North Dakota and just prior to his efforts at the Washington Constitutional Convention. He no doubt brought news of other suffrage efforts in the region and buoyed the spirits of the newly organized Montana contingent.[10]

McAdow and Blackwell, like other advocates across the Northern Great Plains, worked to gain the right to vote for women by eliminating the word "male" from the suffrage portion of the proposed state constitution, thereby establishing voting by all persons "without regard to sex."[11] By altering just a few words in state statutes across the region, activists hoped to effect a dramatic change and extend the franchise to western women.[12] Delegates to the Montana convention, anxious for the passage of a constitution, expressed hesitation about embracing any idea that might delay ratification. As Blackwell put it, "The politicians are timid and now aspiring to state and National offices."[13] Skepticism about full enfranchisement hindered Blackwell's work because some viewed suffrage as a "freak" issue.[14] Blackwell dutifully met with a selection of state leaders. Joseph K. Toole, a Democrat who would become Montana's first governor, stated his opposition to enfranchisement. William A. Clark, the president of the convention, had recently returned from a weekend trip and, according to Blackwell, had clearly "been drunk while away."[15]

Blackwell hoped for the endorsement of three Montana newspapers but secured only two. He did, however, address the convention, where he made the case for woman suffrage based on the American heritage of "life, liberty, and the pursuit of happiness," as well as on the "elevating and purifying influence" of women. Allaying concerns that women's votes would support prohibition, Blackwell referenced the neighboring territory of Wyoming, where women had the vote but had made no move to restrict alcohol. At the conclusion of his Montana visit, Blackwell expressed disappointment at the lack of support for woman suffrage among both male delegates and female residents, but he characterized the people of Montana as "generous, extravagant, entertaining, and impulsive."[16]

While Blackwell made an open but unsuccessful push for converts to the suffrage cause, Clara McAdow's covert meetings with delegates at the 1889 convention nearly secured the vote for Montana women. She obtained commitments from half the delegates—both Democrats and Republicans—before party leadership became aware of her burgeoning bloc of supporters. When McAdow's efforts were revealed, delegates swiftly rallied in opposition, and Toole unleashed a diatribe ridiculing woman suffrage. Despite the scorn of leadership, delegates like J. E. Rickards and Perry McAdow spoke in favor of enfranchisement on the floor of the convention, and the body devoted itself to a lengthy discussion of the issue.[17] For her efforts, McAdow was heralded as the "greatest lobbyist in Montana." At the final count, however, universal enfranchisement in Montana narrowly missed passage.[18]

Women remained without a voice in national elections, but the 1889 Montana Constitutional Convention did bring some important advances, such as allowing women to vote in school elections, giving female property owners the right to vote on tax issues, and establishing the right of female attorneys to be licensed in the state. The argument for women voting in matters related to schools and education stemmed from their domestic and maternal roles, while female property owners made a legitimate claim that they should not be taxed without being allowed a voice in the process. In addition, Montana claimed a number of notable female public servants such as Helen P. Clarke, a mixed-blood Piegan Blackfeet woman who won the 1882 election for superintendent of schools for Lewis and Clark County. Women's visibility supported the idea that they were qualified and deserving of involvement at the polls and in positions of leadership, at least on topics related to education.[19]

After losing narrowly at the convention, advocates for suffrage continued to rally women across the state to support full enfranchisement. Unlike some Montanans, Dr. Maria Dean, a recent graduate of the University of Wisconsin, needed no convincing. After completing her medical training in Boston and Germany, she joined her youngest sister, Annie, in Helena and started a general medical practice. Dean quickly made her presence known in town by driving a "spirited team of horses" on her rounds through the streets of Helena.[20] Her sister's husband, Silas Huntley, raised horses, and the local livery stable kept Dean's team ready for her regular high-speed excursions. The doctor had a life-long relationship with Mary Wheeler, a Helena schoolteacher, and the two shared a home in town. Another Dean sister, Adelaide, also relocated to Helena and married a local bachelor. Their mother, Ellen, eventually joined the civic-minded sisters as well.[21]

Buoyed by her supportive relationships, Dean dove into the bustle of Helena life and ran a busy medical practice. At a time when few public services existed, she paid special attention to the needs of women and children and spoke passionately on behalf of those suffering from mental illness. With an intense and professional demeanor, Dean was soon active in suffrage, education, and public health issues, gaining widespread recognition and acclaim from both women and men. For example, Dean chaired the Helena Board of Education and, in the 1880s, led the Helena Department of Health, where she was credited with initiating the life-saving policy of flagging homes of infected residents during a diphtheria outbreak. She worked in the traditionally female sphere of children's health and education, as well as in the male domain of the medical profession and electoral politics. Dean moved smoothly between these gendered realms, accruing accolades along the way.[22]

Similar to Dean, Clara McAdow resided firmly in the traditionally male public sphere, with occasional forays into activities specifically controlled by women. For example, when Lily Toole, wife of Governor Joseph Toole, withdrew as chair of the

*The Montana exhibit at the World's Columbian Exposition in
Chicago featured a statue of Lady Justice that stood atop a solid-gold
plinth donated by Clara McAdow.* Library of Congress

committee organizing the Montana exhibit in the Women's Hall
at the 1893 World's Columbian Exposition in Chicago—a world's
fair marking the four-hundred-year anniversary of Christopher
Columbus's arrival in the western hemisphere—McAdow took
on the position. No mere figurehead, she sent out public appeals
to women across the state to contribute in advance of the event.
In August 1892, she embarked on a state-wide tour, speaking
to groups in Helena, Butte, and even Miles City, where she met
with prominent women and secured participants and support for
Montana's display. When William A. Clark and Samuel Hauser,
who had purchased McAdow's Spotted Horse Mine, decided that
the Montana exhibition needed a solid-silver statue of Lady Justice, they donated the silver for the project to flaunt their wealth.

Inspired by her experience at the World's Columbian Exposition,
Mary Long Alderson (far right), became a leader in Montana's suffrage
movement. Merrill G. Burlingame Special Collections,
Montana State University

The ever-competitive McAdow then provided sufficient ore for the statue to stand on a solid-gold plinth. Valued at five times the worth of Clark and Hauser's silver, McAdow upstaged the magnates, no doubt savoring the public victory.[23]

Mary Long Alderson, who delighted in travel, crowds, and new sights, was part of the Montana delegation with McAdow in Chicago and found herself energized by the experience. At the exposition, she viewed the Montana women's exhibit of pressed flowers, commenting on how the specimens were "scientifically labeled and properly classified." In later years, she went on to direct the State Floral Emblem Society, which chose the bitterroot as Montana's state flower. With her focus on women's civilizing influence, she saw this work as an important contribution. Gratefully characterizing the Columbian Exposition's Montana Board of Commissioners as acting in a "broad, brotherly manner," she noted, "Of the one hundred thousand dollars appropriated for the use of the State Commission, the men turned ten thousand dollars over to the women to spend just as they chose in their department."[24] From her perspective, 10 percent warranted appreciation, not umbrage.

Alderson perceived no conflict between her support for traditional gender roles and woman suffrage and claimed that women had come "into their own at the wonderful time when the Columbian Exposition opened," going on to laud the presence of "women distinguished in letters, art, science." The World's Congress of Representative Women took place in conjunction with the fair, and the experience inspired Alderson, who took in "the beauty of the scenes and the good will that prevailed, as men and women joined hands in the brotherly love and social courtesy which develop civilization." There, too, she heard leading feminist speakers, including Susan B. Anthony, and saw new "sensible" clothes for women that dispensed with confining corsets and awkward hoops.[25] As energetic and decisive as McAdow, Alderson's subsequent organizing efforts remained within the delineated women's sphere and focused on issues of suffrage and temperance. She based her call to public service on the need to incorporate women's beneficial feminine influences into society. Her Chicago experience pushed her to work with other women in pursuit of change, with "organize, organize" as their call to action.[26] By consistently speaking out in favor of women's legitimate involvement in a range of social and political activities, Alderson—even from a platform openly supporting patriarchy—effectively argued for a significant expansion in women's sphere of influence.

After participating in the Columbian Exposition, Clara McAdow relocated to Detroit, where she built an extravagant home and retired to savor her business and civic accomplishments.[27] Her local, state, and national connections, gained through her experiences in Montana and at the fair, would aid the rising generation of activists. As she exited the state's active leadership, other Montana women—Alderson in particular—brought renewed zest to working for the vote at home. After the failure of universal enfranchisement at the Montana Constitutional Convention in 1889 and on the heels of the Columbian Exposition in 1893, Montana suffragists followed Alderson's call and organized. The Montana legislature met only every other year, so suffrage supporters aimed to amend the state constitution during the legislative session of 1895. After "considerable debate" on the amendment, suffrage advocates sustained yet another defeat as legislators voted it down.[28]

Rallying after another loss, Alderson addressed the 1896 Montana suffrage convention and exhorted delegates to "live up to your privileges. Enter every avenue of knowledge and development open to you. Woman's emancipation in all directions will grow out of her universal education." According to Alderson, women had work to do as they sought the vote. They must actively "prepare for citizenship" by educating themselves on matters related to business, economy, and public affairs, as they "cultivate[d] the judicial state of mind."[29] The change that Alderson advocated encompassed all of civic life, including the availability of liquor, the importance of women's contributions to public dialogue, and the need for prospective female voters to be adequately educated about the democratic process.

Invigorated by the suffrage convention, women returned to lobby the legislature in 1897, in a move that national suffrage leaders fully expected to result in the passage of a Montana suffrage amendment.[30] Under the leadership of Ella Haskell, the first woman to become a licensed attorney in the state, suffrage supporters presented the signatures of about three thousand residents in support of amending the state constitution. After vigorous floor debate in the house, the male representatives defeated the measure by only five votes, another agonizingly close loss.[31] As the defeats mounted up, a pattern of organizing emerged. For many Montana women, suffrage had inherent value, but it also served as a "step to Prohibition."[32] Increasingly, however, suffrage devotees worked to bring women with varied ideological leanings and institutional affiliations across the state together. Like many of her contemporaries, Alderson issued calls to the "right-minded people of Montana," gave lecture after lecture at Woman's Christian Temperance Union (WCTU) and suffrage events, and regularly appeared in newspapers across the state. Delegates to suffrage meetings and conventions often covered long distances in inclement weather.[33]

Working in conjunction with women like Alderson, Dr. Maria Dean also helped organize suffrage clubs, volunteered for committee work, and served as the state suffrage president.[34] Suffrage forces once again returned to the state legislature during the 1899 session. Dean testified in front of this generally friendly crowd, where "the discussion of the question [of the vote for women] consumed nearly the entire afternoon, and the interest was so great that the audience remained till the last gun was fired."[35] Despite this enthusiasm, the suffrage amendment lost yet again.[36] With so many near victories, the loss in 1899 must have been hard to bear, but suffrage leaders remained determined to promote the cause and regrouped.

Nationally known suffragist Carrie Chapman Catt visited the state in 1902 to muster support. That same year, Dean's leadership proved critical. She made consistently favorable impressions as suffrage delegates converged on the capitol city for their convention.[37] Addressing the crowd, Dean epitomized the women supporting suffrage: well educated, informed, and "refine[d]." In an era when activist women regularly saw themselves caricatured as unpleasant, meddling busybodies, Dean's performance led the *Butte Inter Mountain* to report, "There was nothing of the cartoon suffragist about any of the members. Nothing of the hard-faced, bespectacled woman who, with shrill voice and manifest gesticulation, points out the promised disaster of the republic, while its destinies are controlled by men only."[38] Avoiding the impression of a doomsayer, Dean cultivated the image of Montana suffrage advocates as professional, moderate, and disciplined, although, after so many years of legislative refusal, disgust and anger might have been more appropriate.

Dean's hard work helped shape the suffrage supporters into an organization with clear aims. In commenting on the suffragists' intent, the *Butte Inter Mountain* stated, "It is understood that an active program has been prepared that will be carried out to the letter, and the ladies attending the convention believe that they

Dr. Maria Dean (left) examines a portfolio alongside Helena artist Mary Wheeler, c. 1890s. Montana Historical Society Research Center

will succeed in placing Montana alongside the other four free states in the union."[39] The state legislature, however, once again opposed the amendment, refusing even to consider the suffrage measure during the 1903 session.[40] While the consistent legislative losses were undoubtedly tortuous for the women who had fought session after session, many suffragists garnered influence, acclaim, and experience that aided their efforts and helped them train new recruits. Yet, opponents also honed their strategies, and attempts to pass a suffrage amendment failed in 1905 and 1907.

Suffrage advocates often found liquor interests to be their most vocal opponents, but resistance to full enfranchisement ran much deeper.[41] In many eastern states, elite women argued that suffrage would "coarsen the gentle female character and endanger the family," arguments that male officeholders in Montana echoed.[42] As prominent and well-connected Montana residents,

Alderson, McAdow, and Dean were able to lean on their social standing to counteract this opposition. It is possible that they encountered less organized resistance from women than their colleagues in the East, but they still had to contend with the notion that giving women the vote would be abnormal and potentially dangerous. For example, New Jersey extended the vote to property-holding women as early as 1797 but rescinded it just ten years later based on the proposition that woman's suffrage was unseemly.[43] Anti-suffragists had offered similar arguments on the Northern Great Plains since 1869, with some in Wyoming proclaiming women's inherent "incompetency for places of great public trust."[44] Common during Montana's early statehood, arguments of this sort emphasized propriety and alleged that women simply did not belong in the mess of politics.

Despite the resiliency of this negative narrative, the suffrage community continued to attract new and vocal members, including Jeannette Rankin, who would go on to represent Montana as the first female member of the United States Congress.[45] As a fresh voice, Rankin spoke on behalf of woman suffrage to a joint session of the Montana house and senate during the 1911 session. As Alderson explained, the Montana legislature "gave [Rankin] violets, but not the votes we wanted." Reeling from yet another close loss and understandably indignant about years of seemingly wasted investment, suffrage organizers placed Rankin at the head of the 1913 legislative effort.[46]

Suffrage organizers sensed the potential for victory in 1913. They had a charismatic leader in Rankin, the newly elected state suffrage chair. She provided the state organization with renewed energy, canvassing Montana communities from the eastern plains to the mountains of Missoula. Along with vibrancy at the top of the organizational pyramid, woman suffrage supporters had effective local organizations in place. Leading up to the 1913 legislative session, they held rallies, made speeches, and traveled the state. With years of experience honing their message, suffragists made a two-pronged, yet inherently contradictory claim: that women deserved the vote as equals to men and that women offered uniquely maternal insight into public matters. This time the strategy proved successful. After twenty-five years of con-

EQUALITY AT THE BALLOT BOX

stant effort, Montana became the tenth state in the country to give women the right to vote in all elections with the passage of a state constitutional amendment in 1913 and statewide ratification in 1914.[47]

Years of activism and the personal influence of notable women such as McAdow, Alderson, and Dean had finally succeeded in making woman suffrage a reality in the state. Through the years, women gained experience and knowledge from this activist tradition. After enfranchisement—the result of a quarter century of organizing, public speaking, letter writing, testifying, fundraising, and travel—Montana's suffragists could finally rest. Many, however, continued in public service. The veterans of Montana's suffrage movement emerged as some of the state's most educated, public-minded, and respected citizens. Their victory in the long suffrage fight made Montana women some of the most enduring political faces in the state.

Leaders like Dean and Alderson received recognition for their dedication and accomplishments in the press. Upon Alderson's death, the *Bozeman Daily Chronicle* raved that she was "Montana's foremost woman lobbyist at the state capital" as well as a well-known journalist and "one of the few women members of the Montana State Press association for many years."[48] Dean's reputation was no less legendary. She often traveled to Washington, D.C., to work on national issues. When she became seriously ill while visiting the capitol on one trip, President Woodrow Wilson offered his personal railcar for her return to Montana. In 1916, Dean's prominence resulted in an invitation to run for Montana's seat in the United States House of Representatives. Dean demurred, but her suffrage colleague Jeannette Rankin accepted. Rankin won the statewide election and took her place as the first congresswoman in the United States House of Representatives.[49]

Dean, simultaneous with her suffrage work, maintained a medical practice, advocated for the mentally ill, and served on school boards. During one of the many legislative sessions, and despite a commonly held sense that suffrage would be defeated yet again, the *Fergus County Argus* observed, "Dr. Maria Dean and a host of other well-known suffragists are moving heaven and earth to secure the submission of the question to the voters of the state in the shape of a constitutional amendment."[50] In later years, Dean spoke out about the need for female police officers to safeguard female prisoners and served on a Montana commission working to standardize child labor laws. As a respected physician, she maintained professional connections across the state while working on local, state, and national concerns.[51] Upon her death in 1919, the *Helena Independent* hailed her as one of the "first women doctors in Montana," calling her "highly regarded" and respected "not only by the members of her profession but also by many friends throughout the state and women prominent in national politics."[52]

Beginning with her involvement in the World's Columbian Exposition, Alderson spoke, wrote, and lectured widely on suffrage issues and as part of the WCTU. Even after the passage of suffrage, Alderson debated—and encouraged other women to consider—the relative merits and positions of candidates running for office, often holding forth on political strategy. Alderson continued to speak out and agitate for progressive aims until her death at the age of seventy-nine in 1940. McAdow, for her part, maintained vocal support of woman suffrage up until her passing in 1896, in addition to her storied career as a mine owner and service as chair of the committee that created Montana's exhibit for the Women's Hall at the Columbian Exposition.[53]

Why did these women, and so many others, sacrifice themselves on the altar of public service? Why did they devote hours, days, weeks, and lifetimes to uncompensated, thanklessly repetitive trips to the legislature, to suffrage conventions, or to campaign in isolated Montana towns? Given their expansive individual portfolios, they did not agitate out of boredom or the need for a cause, nor did they organize simply for the opportunity to socialize. Instead, they looked to the public sphere to advocate for change on behalf of women like themselves. They made the case that women deserved full entry into public life and civic discourse. Long before they gained the vote, they created a female body politic of suffrage supporters that recognized their voices as legitimate. Analysis of Dean's, McAdow's, and Alderson's activities reveals their intense commitment to public service. These three individuals seemingly possessed marathon

EQUALITY AT THE BALLOT BOX

stamina, working on a variety of campaigns over the decades. Their sustained level of activism in numerous arenas indicates that personal ambition, a less-acknowledged motivation, also drove their actions.[54]

For Maria Dean, Mary Long Alderson, and Clara McAdow, suffrage formed an essential part of personal identity. McAdow, even with her wide-ranging business interests, continued to identify as a suffrage supporter, "actively interested in the enfranchisement of women, of which she herself [was] the living exponent."[55] Eminently proud of her suffrage accomplishments, she went so far as to send a copy of a speech to Bertha Palmer, the leading Chicago socialite with whom she had become acquainted in organizing the Women's Exhibit at the Columbian Exposition. Palmer credited McAdow with being the "sensation of the session," an homage that McAdow no doubt found gratifying.[56] Hailed as heroes by their contemporaries, Dean, Alderson, and McAdow gained prominence as public figures in a time that denied women equal participation in civic life and full benefits of citizenship. Their efforts over a quarter of a century stand as a testament to the value they placed in themselves and their desire to gain full inclusion in the affairs of state. History often views women like these as niche activists dedicated to a boutique issue. Rather, given their long and productive public careers, Dean, Alderson, and McAdow embodied the characteristics of democratic civic culture and personal ambition at its most uplifting and shaped the face and future of the Northern Great Plains and the American West.

NOTES

1. "Greatest Lobbyist in Montana's History Was Woman Who Sought Right to Vote," *Forsyth (Mont.) Independent*, 27 Mar. 1941.

2. "Mrs. P. W. McAdow," *River Press* (Fort Benton, Mont.), 29 Jan, 1896.

3. W. H. Banfill, "Mrs. Tomlinson," *Grass Range (Mont.) Review*, 4 Mar. 1929.

4. "Clever Woman Almost Wrote Equal Suffrage into State Constitution," *Grass Range Review*, 22 Jan. 1923.

5. Banfill, "Mrs. Tomlinson."

6. "Clever Woman."

7. Banfill, "Mrs. Tomlinson."

8. Van West to Anne Pawlik, 14 Oct. 1982, Clara McAdow Vertical File, Montana Historical Society Research Center (MHSRC), Helena.

9. "The Spotted Horse," *Anaconda (Mont.) Standard*, 25 Apr. 1893; Banfill, "Mrs. Tomlinson"; "Mrs. P. W. McAdow;" West to Pawlik; "A Half Century of Progress for Women," pp. 2-5, folder 1, SC122, Mary Long Alderson Collection, MHSRC. McAdow's mine was located near Maiden, Montana, about twenty miles from present-day Lewistown.

10. Leslie Wheeler, "Woman Suffrage's Gray-Bearded Champion Comes to Montana, 1889," *Montana: The Magazine of Western History* 31 (Summer 1981): 6.

11. "Greatest Lobbyist."

12. Elizabeth Cady Stanton, Susan B. Anthony, Matilda Joslyn Gage, eds., *History of Woman Suffrage, 1876–1885*, Vol. 3 (Rochester, N. Y.: Susan B. Anthony, 1886) chronicles state and territorial efforts to procure woman suffrage. The section on the Dakotas is particularly useful in understanding state strategy on the Northern Great Plains. *See* pp. 662–69.

13. Wheeler, "Woman Suffrage's Gray-Bearded Champion," p. 6.

14. "Clever Woman."

15. Wheeler, "Woman Suffrage's Gray-Bearded Champion," p. 7.

16. Ibid., pp. 8–9.

17. "Greatest Lobbyist"; "Half Century of Progress for Women," p. 8.

18. "Greatest Lobbyist"; Wheeler, "Woman Suffrage's Gray-Bearded Champion Comes to Montana," p. 8.

19. Wheeler, "Woman Suffrage's Gray-Bearded Champion," p. 12; "Half Century of Progress for Women," pp. 8–9. Doris Buck Ward offered a more detailed exploration of these voting issues in "The Winning of Woman Suffrage in Montana" (master's thesis, Montana State University, 1974), pp. 14–30.

20. "The Dean Sisters," p. 1, Maria M. Dean Vertical File, MHSRC.

21. Ibid., pp. 1–2; Marcella Walter, "St. Peter's New Dean Center," *Independent Record* (Helena), 17 Dec. 1978.

22. "Dean Sisters," pp. 1-6; Walter, "St. Peter's New Dean Center."

23. "Women's Work at the World's Fair," *Daily Yellowstone Journal* (Miles City), 24 Aug. 1892; "Local Layout," *Livingston Enterprise*, 30 July 1892; "Women's Department," ibid., 6 Aug. 1892; "Juttings about Town," *Helena Independent*, 28 July 1893; "To Women of Montana," *Anaconda Standard*, 24 July 1892; "Beautiful Bozeman," ibid., 7 Aug. 1892; Larry Hoffman, "Clara McAdow—The Amazing Lady Mine Owner," p. 5, Clara McAdow Vertical File.

24. Quoted in "Half Century of Progress for Women," p. 21.

25. Ibid., pp. 22–23.

26. Gail Schontzler, "Mary Long Alderson Fought for Women's Freedom,"

Bozeman Daily Chronicle, 12 June 2011. Alderson's involvement in multiple causes exemplifies the behavior historian Karen J. Blair characterizes as a "natural outgrowth of the efforts of countless women of the early nineteenth century to embody the spreading ideal of ladydom" (Blair, *The Clubwoman as Feminist: True Womanhood Redefined, 1868-1914* [New York: Holmes & Meier Publishers, 1980], p. 117).

27. West to Pawlik, p. 2.

28. "Half Century of Progress for Women," p. 15.

29. "Plead Their Cause," *Anaconda Standard*, 19 Nov. 1896.

30. Louise R. Noun, *Strong-Minded Women: The Emergence of the Woman-Suffrage Movement in Iowa* (Ames: Iowa State University Press, 1969), p. 242. Susan B. Anthony confidently predicted suffrage victories in Montana, Nevada, California, Washington, and Oregon.

31. "Half Century of Progress for Women," pp. 15-16.

32. "A Call to Prayer," *Yellowstone Monitor* (Glendive), 14 Jan. 1915.

33. "W.C.T.U. Convention," *Anaconda Standard*, 22 Oct. 1896; "Ladies Attention," *Yellowstone Monitor*, 6 Nov. 1913; "Additional Local," *Wibaux (Mont.) Pioneer*, 7 Nov. 1913; "Meeting of Women," *Anaconda Standard*, 18 Nov. 1896.

34. "Helena Women Organizing," *Helena Independent*, 12 Nov. 1899.

35. "Without Recommendation: The Bill for Woman Suffrage Given a Hearing in Committee," *Anaconda Standard*, 26 Jan. 1899.

36. "Half Century of Progress for Women," p. 15.

37. Ward, "Winning of Woman Suffrage in Montana," pp. 80-81; "Half Century of Progress for Women," p. 16; "Women Suffragists Appoint Committees and Hear Theses on Their Rights to Vote," *Butte Inter Mountain*, 17 Sept. 1902.

38. "Know What They Want, All Right," *Butte Inter Mountain*, 17 Sept. 1902.

39. "Women Suffragists Appoint Committees."

40. "Half Century of Progress for Women," p. 16.

41. Ibid.; Barbara Handy-Marchello, "Swashing around the Sisterhood of States," *North Dakota History* 79 (Dec. 2014): 4-12.

42. Susan E. Marshall, *Splintered Sisterhood: Gender and Class in the Campaign against Woman Suffrage* (Madison: University of Wisconsin Press, 1997), p. 4. *See also* Wheeler, "Woman Suffrage's Gray-Bearded Champion," p. 12. Marshall demonstrates that some upper-class women opposed suffrage because it threatened their positions of power.

43. Ward, "Winning of Woman Suffrage in Montana," p. 141; Jan Ellen Lewis, "Rethinking Women's Suffrage in New Jersey, 1776-1807," *Rutgers Law Review* 63 (Spring 2011): 1017-35. Ward notes that anti-suffragists "were

slow to organize for an opposition campaign. Resistance to the suffrage amendment in Montana was weak and sporadic until September 1914" (p. 141).

44. Sidney Howell Fleming, "Solving the Jigsaw Puzzle: One Suffrage Story at a Time," *Annals of Wyoming* 62 (Spring 1990): 29.

45. James J. Lopach and Jean A. Luckowski, *Jeannette Rankin: A Political Woman* (Boulder: University Press of Colorado, 2005), pp. 79–100. Just as women across the Northern Great Plains collaborated on suffrage strategy, Rankin had gained experience through activism with other women in New York, Ohio, California, and Washington. Lopach and Luckowski point out that, like Dean, Alderson, and McAdow, Rankin satisfied her ambitions through political involvement. Rankin has been the subject of a number of academic texts—*see also* Norma Smith, *Jeannette Rankin: America's Conscience* (Helena: Montana Historical Society Press, 2002).

46. Quoted in "Half Century of Progress for Women," p. 17.

47. Ibid.; Kathryn Anderson, "Steps to Political Equality: Woman Suffrage and Electoral Politics in the Lives of Emily Newell Blair, Anne Henrietta Martin, and Jeannette Rankin," *Frontiers: A Journal of Women Studies* 18, no. 1 (1997): 101–21; "Centuries of Citizenship: A Constitutional Timeline," National Constitution Center, constitutioncenter.org/timeline, accessed 25 Feb. 2017; "Votes for Women," *Suffrage Daily News*, 25 Sept. 1914. Historian Rebecca Mead credits Rankin with much of the success of the Montana effort in 1913, explaining, "Rankin effectively energized and mobilized like-minded 'New Women' in these final years of the suffrage movement, prodding older colleagues into action and convincing the opposition that they would not behave or rest until their goal was achieved" (Mead, *How the Vote Was Won: Woman Suffrage in the Western United States, 1868–1914* [New York: New York University Press, 2004], p. 152). Lopach and Luckowski also discussed Rankin's savvy political use of maternalism in *Jeannette Rankin*, pp. 96–98. Support for and opposition to women's enfranchisement in 1914 followed a general pattern. The northwestern part of the state with its timber and mining interests supported suffrage, as did rural areas to the east with an expanding homesteading population. In contrast, some urban enclaves and established communities in places like southwest Montana voted against suffrage. *See* Ward, "Winning of Woman Suffrage in Montana," pp. 145–50.

48. "Prominent State Feminist Passes in City Monday," *Bozeman Daily Chronicle*, 9 Jan. 1940.

49. "Dr. Maria M. Dean Dies from Illness," *Helena Independent*, 24 May 1919; Walter, "St. Peter's New Dean Center."

50. "Busy Week in Legislature," *Fergus County Argus*, 15 Feb. 1905.

51. "Women Want Police Matron for the City," *Suffrage Daily News*, 25

Sept. 1914; "Commission Appointed," *Ekalaka Eagle*, 29 Sept. 1916; "Dr. Maria M. Dean Dies from Illness," *Helena Independent*, 24 May 1919.

52. "Well Known in Montana." *Helena Independent*, 24 May 1919.

53. "Members of W.C.T.U. Discuss Candidate," *Great Falls Daily Tribune*, 27 Oct. 1920; "Prominent State Feminist Passes in City Monday," *Bozeman Daily Chronicle*, 9 Jan. 1940.

54. Historian Carol DuBois explains that while a woman's social position had traditionally been defined by her maternal role, the diminishment of the family as the primary economic unit reduced women's overall influence (DuBois, *Feminism and Suffrage: The Emergence of an Independent Women's Movement in America, 1848–1869* [Ithaca, New York: Cornell University Press, 1978], pp. 15–16). Dean, McAdow, and Alderson, as activists and public figures, found satisfaction and acclaim in public life. Gayle Gullett shows that suffragists elsewhere had a similar motivation: "California women pursued citizenship to make themselves powerful. As they struggled to make their voices heard in the public arena, they changed their lives and created new definitions of the appropriate relationship between women and power" (Gullett, *Becoming Citizens: The Emergence and Development of the California Women's Movement, 1880–1911* [Urbana: University of Illinois Press, 2000], p. 201).

55. "Mrs. Clara McAdow," *Helena Independent*, 1 Feb. 1893.

56. Bertha Honore Palmer to Clara McAdow, 15 June 1894, p. 1, Chicago–World's Columbian Exposition, 1893, Vols. 17 and 17a, Chicago History Museum Research Center, Chicago.

DEFENDING SEPARATE SPHERES
Anti-Suffrage Women in South Dakota Suffrage Campaigns

PAULA M. NELSON

In 1890, as the new state of South Dakota prepared to vote on whether to allow full woman suffrage, women in Boston published volume one of the *Remonstrance*, a four-page anti-woman suffrage pamphlet, with the subtitle "Special South Dakota Edition." The arrival of this volume indicated that anti-suffrage activists in the New England states and New York intended to spread their message nationwide. The Remonstrants introduced themselves on page one, declaring, "The Remonstrance is addressed to the voters of South Dakota by Women Remonstrants against the extension of the suffrage to women." The authors claimed support from Remonstrants in Maine, Massachusetts, Illinois, and other states who shared the belief "that the great majority of their sex does not want the ballot, and that to force it upon them would not only be an injustice to women but could lessen their influence for good and imperil the community."[1] In South Dakota, the message resonated, especially with the editor of the *Yankton Press and Dakotan* who quoted a portion of the statement above as a reflection of his point of view on the subject.[2]

Contributors to the Special South Dakota Edition of the *Remonstrance* included Goldwin Smith, former professor of history at Oxford, who supported woman suffrage in Britain in the 1860s but now spoke in opposition. Smith, arguing that since "government is force" it was necessarily male, asked a key question: can women have both equality and privilege? The privileges he referred to included male protection and defense, exclusion from military service and jury duty, and the special social respect that demanded women and children be saved first in times of crisis.

THE REMONSTRANCE.

SPECIAL SOUTH DAKOTA EDITION.

The Remonstrance is addressed to the voters of South Dakota by Women Remonstrants against the extension of the suffrage to women. It expresses the views of such Remonstrants in Massachusetts, Maine, Illinois, and other States who believe that the great majority of their sex do not want the ballot, and that to force it upon them would not only be an injustice to women but would lessen their influence for good and imperil the community. The Remonstrants ask a thoughtful consideration of their views in the interest of fair discussion; and they especially ask the officers of Farmers' Alliances who may receive the paper to do them the favor of distributing copies among the members.

GOLDWIN SMITH ON SUFFRAGE.

PROFESSOR GOLDWIN SMITH's clear and vigorous statement of the case against woman suffrage, in The Forum for January, derives special interest from the fact that the writer, thirty years ago, in company with John Bright, signed John Stuart Mill's petition for the political enfranchisement of women. Both afterward changed their minds; Mr. Bright became the most powerful opponent of woman suffrage, and Professor Smith, influenced in part by the fact that the best representatives of the sex among his acquaintances were opposed to the change, has come to regard the suffrage movement with strong disapproval.

Professor Smith reviews, in a very caustic and effective way, the favorable report of the Senate Committee on Woman Suffrage. To the declaration that suffrage is a natural right he replies that what is essential to the republican form of government can be gathered only by induction from a survey of such republics as have existed; and of all the republics which have existed not one has given a share of the sovereign power or a part in government to women. If government requires a masculine understanding or temperament, and if the practical character by which political questions are likely to be best settled resides in the man whose sphere is the world, rather than in the woman whose sphere is home, there is a reason for preferring such government and legislation, quite independent of any invidious

comparisons, whether intellectual or moral. Why has the male sex alone made the laws? Because law, with whatever majesty we may invest it, is will, which, to give it effect, must be backed by force; and the force of the community is male. That the tendency of a state governed by women would be to arbitrary and sentimental legislation can hardly be doubted. The women of France some years ago would probably have voted a war for the support of the

RECENT DEFEATS OF WOMAN SUFFRAGE.

RESULTS IN 1889.

In **Vermont,** where two years before a municipal suffrage bill passed the House, a similar bill was defeated at the last session: yeas, 391; nays, 192.

In **Maine,** a municipal suffrage bill was defeated in the House, February 28; yeas, 42; nays 90. The Senate rejected the bill by a vote of yeas, 9; nays, 17.

In **New Hampshire,** the Constitutional Convention gave the suffragists "leave to withdraw."

In **Dakota,** where two years before a municipal suffrage bill passed both branches of the Legislature, and was vetoed by the Governor, a similar bill was twice voted down in the Legislature of 1889. Introduced again in a modified form, limiting the privilege to tax-paying women, the measure met with a third and final defeat, February 27.

In **Ohio,** a municipal suffrage bill was defeated in the House, and a proposition for a suffrage constitutional amendment also failed of adoption.

In **Nebraska,** the Legislature voted to "indefinitely postpone" a municipal suffrage bill.

In **Nevada,** a proposed amendment to the Constitution, admitting women to the suffrage, was voted down.

In **Massachusetts,** a municipal suffrage bill was defeated in the House, March 12: yeas, 78; nays, 127. A license suffrage bill which had been engrossed by the Senate, May 16: yeas, 15; nays, 12, reached the House May 24, and was referred to the next General Court by a vote of 101 to 42.

In **Connecticut,** a woman's suffrage amendment to the Constitution was rejected: yeas, 44; nays, 90. Four other suffrage measures were defeated, namely: a municipal suffrage bill, a license suffrage bill, a school suffrage bill, and a bill exempting women from taxation until such time as they are given the ballot.

In **Michigan,** a municipal suffrage bill, which passed the House: 58 yeas; 33 nays, was defeated the same day in the Senate: 10 yeas, 16 nays.

In **Minnesota,** a municipal suffrage bill was killed in the House by the acceptance of an adverse report of the Committee.

In **New York,** the Assembly, March 25, defeated the bill conferring municipal suffrage upon women.

In the new State of **Washington,** October 1, a woman suffrage article in the Constitution was submitted to the people, and rejected by a vote of about two to one.

In **Montana,** the Constitutional Convention voted down propositions to empower the Legislature to confer the suffrage upon women, to submit the question to the vote of the people every four years, and to submit a separate suffrage article at the same time with the Constitution.

In **North Dakota,** the Constitutional Convention rejected a proposition to remit the whole question to the Legislature, and adopt a clause requiring a vote of the people to ratify any act of the Legislature conferring suffrage upon women.

RESULTS IN 1890.

In **North Dakota,** March 4, a Senate bill submitting to a vote of the people a constitutional amendment giving women the right to vote, was defeated in the House after an animated debate.

In **New York,** April 28, the Assembly rejected a municipal woman suffrage bill: yeas, 48; nays, 60. The adverse vote was considerably heavier than in 1889.

In **Massachusetts,** April 17, the House rejected a municipal woman suffrage bill: 73 yeas; nays, 141, including pairs. In 1889, the vote on a similar bill was 90 yeas; 139 nays, including pairs. The vote of 1890, therefore, shows a net loss of 19 for the bill.

temporal power of the Pope. The women of England might have voted intervention in favor of the Queen of Naples. In both cases the men would have refused to march or act, and government would have succumbed. As to the supposed elevating influence of women upon politics, Professor Smith says:—

"The belief that women will impart their tenderness and purity to politics is surely somewhat simple. They are tender and pure, because their sphere has

---

The Remonstrance, *a Boston-based anti-suffrage publication, released a South Dakota edition in 1890.*
South Dakota State Historical Society

He asked, "When woman has lost her privilege, what will she be but a weaker man?"[3]

The anti-suffrage publication also included portions of a letter from Rev. Henry Blanchard, president of the Maine Woman's Suffrage Association, to the *Portland Press*, where he admitted the suffrage campaign had a struggle ahead. "I tell the gentlemen of the [Maine] legislature," he wrote, "that the majority of women are opposed to woman suffrage." Suffragists, he explained, were not "women as a sex, but a clamorous minority of women whom they represent." Blanchard argued it was not right to force women to vote when a "large majority" were not interested and were "averse to having the burden placed on them."[4] *Remonstrance* editors noted with dignified glee that Blanchard's letter appeared "under his own signature" and thus verified his statements. Finally, the editors asked a question of South Dakotans: why not try the school suffrage vote for women for a longer period to see the response over time? The editors suggested that the low turnout of women voters in a June 1890 school board election did not indicate any widespread desire for the ballot.[5]

The Boston anti-suffragists mailed packets of the *Remonstrance* to Farmers' Alliance leaders in South Dakota. John Goodspeed, an alliance secretary in Bangor Township, Brookings County, returned his packet to the editor of the *Dakota Ruralist*. "I enclose to you a copy of a sheet entitled 'The Remonstrance,'" Goodspeed explained. "The wrapper had the postmark of Boston, Mass." Goodspeed was not interested. "They were sent to me for distribution," he continued, "but being an equal suffragist and not in sympathy with its declarations, etc., thought it best to take care of them."[6]

The first edition of the *Remonstrance* addressed ideas that would appear again and again in anti-suffragist literature: men and women were different and fulfilled different obligations in society. Men were political actors. Women played a vital role not only in the private world of domesticity, but also in voluntary associations. Women's organizations provided charity, uplift, and care for the sick, supported churches and schools, and shaped civil society in important ways. Votes for women would place unwanted burdens upon them, requiring them to follow political news and candidates and attend political speeches and local conventions. The vote would also inject partisanship, and therefore conflict, into women's organizations. Anti-suffrage women would defend their existing place in society with vigor for the next three decades, but the rise of progressive politics in the early twentieth century, characterized by an emphasis on organizational structures and the necessity of reform, boosted the suffragists' cause. New campaign and outreach techniques allowed them to reach voters in active, dynamic ways that anti-suffragists rejected as unladylike. America's entrance into World War I in 1917 also changed the tone and direction of the South Dakota suffrage campaign. The state government's focus on citizenship, not sex, as the guarantor of voting eligibility helped suffragists win the day in 1918. Anti-suffrage women, meanwhile, retreated from the field. Many chose to vote out of duty to home and country or to counter the votes of women with whom they disagreed. Their vision of nonpartisan womanhood as a cultural force disappeared, although voluntary associations dedicated to traditional notions of a separate women's sphere continued.

South Dakotans may have discussed and voted on woman suffrage more often than residents of any other Northern Great Plains state. During the territorial period, 1861–1889, the territorial legislature debated woman suffrage in 1868, 1870, and 1872, when they failed to enact it by just one vote. In 1885, the territorial legislature passed a suffrage bill, but Governor Gilbert Pierce vetoed it because he feared Congress would refuse to approve Dakota with woman suffrage in its constitution. In 1887, the territorial legislature rejected it again. South Dakota entered the union on 2 November 1889 without votes for women but with a requirement that the first state legislature put woman suffrage on the ballot. In 1890, the men of South Dakota rejected woman suffrage. In 1898, the electorate again voted no. The new century brought four more efforts, in 1910, 1914, 1916, and finally in 1918. On 6 November 1918, the men of South Dakota voted 49,318 to 28,934 to grant women voting rights equal to their own. After twenty-eight years of statehood and a series of grueling, contentious campaigns, woman suffrage prevailed.[7] The following year, the United States Congress submitted the Nineteenth Amendment to the United States Constitution to the states for ratification. The prospective amendment stated: "The right of citizens of the United States to vote shall not be denied or abridged by the United States or by any State on account of sex." South Dakota ratified the amendment in a special session held on 4 December 1919, ending a decades-long battle over women's right to vote. Within a year, three-quarters of the states had followed suit.[8]

The 1890 campaign, the first in which anti-suffragists played a significant role, was particularly contentious. The arrival of major rail lines across the territory in 1879 brought a rush of mass migration into South Dakota. Drought and attendant hard times followed less than a decade later. Settlers fled recently built towns and farms, and those who stayed struggled to make a living. Some farmers revolted against their circumstances and the entrenched political parties that offered no solutions. The powerful Farmers' Alliance vied for attention and votes as the state's politics grew increasingly fluid and unpredictable. Few political leaders saw woman suffrage as a priority. Suffragist lecturers and organizers nonetheless traveled in farm wagons over frozen prairies, hoping to find receptive audiences. At the same time, state suffrage volunteers warred with national organizers. Susan B. Anthony, technically in charge of the South Dakota campaign, faced revolt from locals over money and the outsized role of the Woman's Christian Temperance Union (WCTU) in the campaign, which many South Dakotans welcomed but Anthony opposed. Though the campaign was disorganized, even chaotic, suffragists remained optimistic about victory.[9]

By the end of the summer, suffrage organizers recognized that the cause was lost. Their opponents were too many, and the drought-stricken, politically riven state faced several pressing crises. The vote tally indicated the depth of the voters' rejection of or distraction from the suffrage question: of the 68,804 votes cast, 45,632 were no.[10] In Day County, Irene Adams of Webster, a temperance and suffrage activist, assessed the result. "It has got to come to a matter of *you must* [vote for woman suffrage] in the majority of homes before we shall win the ballot," Adams wrote. "Women must feel the need of it an hundred fold more than they do now before we shall win equality."[11] In the years to come, suffragists worked to insure that women felt the "need of it," just as anti-suffragists worked to see that the need did not materialize.

Those who opposed woman suffrage in South Dakota included experienced campaigners from earlier suffrage fights, most of the religious denominations in the state, recent immigrants from cultures opposed to progressive notions of family, and organized anti-suffrage women from eastern states, known first as "Remonstrants" and then simply "Antis," who became a force with whom to be reckoned. Their numbers were never large, but their pamphlets and circulars arrived in great quantities before elections. They also sent speakers to spread their message, especially after they organized a national association in 1911. Antis provided local newspapers with material to fill their columns and purchased advertisement space in larger papers. Their influential writings encouraged South Dakota women to speak out and organize against suffrage.[12] To suffragists, opposition seemed to be everywhere. Why, they wondered, would women reject the right to participate in politics?

The campaign for woman suffrage across the United States challenged many social conventions as well as deeply held principles about women's nature and their roles in the family and in society. That men and women had different roles and obligations was an ancient idea. Beginning in the 1960s, scholars in the new field of women's history labeled this system of distinct roles "separate spheres." The middle classes most closely fulfilled this design, but families in wealth or poverty, native-born or immigrant also maintained some definition of women's work and women's place. In the nineteenth century, men were the primary public actors. They voted, spoke publicly on matters of public policy, ran for office, and purported to represent their female family members on the political battlefields of the time. In wartime, they fought on real battlefields, defending the state and their families. Men were the primary providers for their families, and society held them legally and socially accountable. Community opprobrium toward men perceived as lazy, poor providers, drunks, abusers, and other kinds of miscreants aimed to keep men on the proper path. Women, in contrast, maintained home and family and bore children, a potentially life-threatening act. These domestic tasks required a range of skills that relatives, neighbors, and the community also judged. Women nursed the sick, prepared the dead for burial, taught their children, and inculcated values and customs that helped society succeed and flourish. They cooked, cooked again, and cooked some more, every day.

By the mid-nineteenth century, many middle-class women participated in a growing number of volunteer church, school, community, charity, and reform organizations. In so doing, they expanded definitions of home and family responsibilities. Farm families founded churches or Sunday schools, organized local country schools, and provided support in a variety of ways. Town women visited schools to assess teachers' skills and gauge their own children's progress. Town and country women alike eagerly raised funds for their churches. Some even became reformers in groups such as the Woman's Christian Temperance Union. Others enjoyed the readings and discussions at women's club meetings. Through such engagements, women created a vital civil community, all within the constraints of "women's sphere."[13]

By the last decades of the nineteenth century, separate spheres had developed an increasingly flexible definition. Women often worked outside their homes milking cows, raising poultry and eggs, and growing gardens on farms, as well as in small towns. For farm families, the demands of haying and harvest brought daughters and wives into the fields, even among groups that normally rejected the idea of fieldwork for women. The wives of small-town merchants worked behind the counter, especially on busy Saturdays when farmers came to town to trade. Married women's work outside the home in most cases aided the family enterprise. The ideology of separate spheres remained, although real-life activities challenged the tradition. Historian Karen Lystra argues that in the middle classes, couples "maintained outward conformity to sex role ideas while actually being quite flexible in their behavior."[14]

The progressive movement of the first two decades of the twentieth century reshaped nearly every aspect of life, including politics, social organization, and education and altered the ways men and women thought about separate spheres. Progressivism professionalized work that had been part of women's roles from time immemorial. Nursing the sick and caring for the poor became the work of trained, credentialed professionals, often carried out in institutions, not in private homes. As governments formed agencies and bureaus to monitor or manage problems like child labor and juvenile crime, women became social workers, child-welfare agents, investigators, and administrative staff. With women increasingly out of the home and visible in public positions, employed in private business, or earning college degrees, woman suffrage seemed logical to many. Some suffrage advocates, however, relied on notions of innate difference between men and women to support this change. Women's moral character, in this view, would improve American society, cleaning up corruption and injustice, and protecting working women and children. Fighting en masse for the common good, women would enlighten and purify the nation. The farming communities that dominated South Dakota, however, favored personal, less professionalized methods for addressing social problems. Women's roles on farms continued to demand intensive daily labor. Urban cultural values filtered in through the movies, books, and magazines, but social and institutional change occurred more slowly. Antis spoke for many when they advocated for traditional roles, broadly defined, for men and women.[15]

One North Dakota Anti's social and cultural work provides an example of how broadly defined women's roles had become. Ida Clarke Young of Fargo, who was married to lawyer and one-time state supreme court justice Newton C. Young, became the president of the North Dakota Association Opposed to Woman Suffrage, organized in June 1914. Young, a mother of three, served as state president of the Federated Women's Club of North Dakota for four years, retiring in 1912; served on the board of directors for Fargo Associated Charities from its inception in 1909; sat on the board of the Florence Crittenden Home, a refuge for unwed mothers; was a member of the Round Table Club, a history study group, and the Writers' Group of the Fine Arts Club, a philanthropic and enrichment organization. When the United States entered World War I, Ida Young became field secretary for the Red Cross in North Dakota. Though she was active in women's organizations, Young chose "Back to the Home" as the anti-suffrage club's campaign motto. Home in this sense was not just a place for a family to live and a woman to toil; instead, it was a symbol of the group's primary focus on serving family and neighborhood. To do for others, without the self-aggrandizement and striving they attributed to men, was the mission. The Antis' greatest fear was that the sacred and foundational relationships of home and family would become just another job.[16] Suffragists, however, often took the Antis use of "home" quite literally, portraying them as home-bound, even trapped, and reduced to spying on their neighbors for stimulation.[17]

Many women who opposed votes for their sex did so out of deep concern for families and society. Most believed God created men and women with distinctive natures, with different but equally important duties. Most American churches supported this notion, and for many members, the idea reflected God's plan. In South Dakota during the 1890 suffrage campaign, churches either opposed votes for women or avoided the issue. Notable suffrage supporters, such as Matilda Joslyn Gage, who spent time in southern Dakota Territory in the 1880s, criticized churches and declared Christianity a "rotten thing." Suffrage groups passed resolutions asking women "to absent themselves from churches" and to "withdraw from any organization" teaching that wives were subordinate to husbands or that women were punished for the downfall of mankind in Eden by their suffering "in maternity."[18]

The hostility of some suffrage reformers towards Christianity did not encourage South Dakota churches to endorse their program. German and Scandinavian Lutherans generally did not support suffrage, nor did Catholics. Of course, there were some exceptions, such as Father Haire of Aberdeen, who spoke up for the reform. As a result, Bishop Martin Marty of the Diocese of Sioux Falls, which encompassed the entire state, silenced Haire. Lutherans and Catholics made up 58 percent of all church members in South Dakota. Congregational and Presbyterian churches in the state similarly urged women to continue fundraising for missions and advocated for other reforms but not suffrage. Methodists and Baptists endorsed prohibition, and Methodists recognized the connection between prohibition and votes for women, but they chose to endorse the activities of the Woman's Christian Temperance Union, with the exception of suffrage. For women who understood the Bible to be the word of God, suffrage was a violation of God's plan.[19] Mrs. W. A. Woolege of White Lake, writing in 1918, twenty-eight years after the first state vote on suffrage, and dreading the sixth vote to come, explained this adherence to Biblical doctrine: "The fight for suffrage is against the women, not men, who have accepted the Gospel of Christ." God's plan "in no way allows us to teach or escape the authority of men . . . . God gave us our place. We are God's conception of women. His laws will hold."[20]

Most anti-suffrage advocates, however, focused on social roles not specific Biblical precepts in fighting for the status quo. According to historian Thomas J. Jablonsky, Antis promoted "duty, nature, and stability" in a time of massive economic and social change. Rooted in tradition, they resisted what they saw as an attempt to redefine the roles of women and rush them into public life against their will. After all, women could and did participate in reform efforts without the ballot. Many Antis sponsored or worked with charities, schools, orphanages, and many other social-welfare groups. In their eyes, public opinion drove all reform, and legislators were but the tools of implementation, so "the power to choose those public instruments was much less significant than the power to mold the public mind." Women drove and shaped legislation without the vote. Antis also feared the partisan commitments and loyalties that the vote would bring. As a nonpartisan group, women reached all factions. Those they tried to influence did not have to worry that their political affiliation shaped their arguments.[21]

The prospect of votes for women generated opposition from other quarters as well. Liquor interests feared women's prohibitionist tendencies. Factory owners feared child-labor laws and limits on women's hours. In the South, fears of upending the disenfranchisement of African American men and halting Jim Crow legislation fueled opposition. In these cases, objections to women voting reflected deep concern over reform that might undermine or destroy existing systems. In South Dakota, the liquor question was crucial, especially among ethnic Germans and other immi-

grant cultures for whom alcohol was ingrained custom. Similarly, immigrant Lutheran and Roman Catholic churches, rooted
in customs and ideals carried over from Europe, were not as feminized as many American Protestant churches and rejected votes
for women.[22]

The last two South Dakotan campaigns for suffrage in the
1890s ran without much assistance from the National American
Woman Suffrage Association (NAWSA). Officers there believed
the state was too thinly settled and its economic problems too
overwhelming to make full effort and financial support worth-
while. In 1894, the state campaign focused solely on school suffrage through two amendments and received almost no publicity.
Instead, the editor of the *Sioux Falls Argus-Leader* emphasized
women's perceived indifference toward ballot rights already
achieved. He urged female suffrage supporters to turn out for
the school elections in Sioux Falls in June of 1894. If they did not
vote on school issues, which he believed were "closer to the average woman's heart," why would anyone think they wanted to vote
on city, state, or national candidates?[23] If Antis sent literature, it
received little publicity. Reflecting the general air of disinterest,
fewer men voted on the issue in November than previously, and
suffrage lost, 17,010 to 22,682.[24]

The election of 1898 attracted much more attention. Suffrage
speakers traveled the state; clubs organized in several towns; and
optimism among advocates grew. The NAWSA sent an organizer
and one-hundred-dollars-worth of literature. By this time, the
Antis had organized both the Massachusetts Association Opposed to the Further Extension of Suffrage to Women in 1895 and
the New York State Association Opposed to Woman Suffrage in
1894. Antis in both states worked to prevent suffrage from passing their legislatures, but they also worked to defeat suffrage
drives in western states. Wyoming Territory had granted women
the right to vote in 1869 and had been admitted as a state in 1890
with woman suffrage intact. In 1893, Colorado instituted votes
for women, and Idaho and Utah followed suit in 1896. Additional
victories for suffrage anywhere, the eastern Antis feared, would
encourage even more state suffrage campaigns and ultimately a
national suffrage amendment to the United States Constitution.

EQUALITY AT THE BALLOT BOX

The New York and Massachusetts organizations worked together to halt the advancing tide. While these groups had the greatest impact, the Illinois Association Opposed to the Extension of Suffrage to Women also organized. Antis had been active in Illinois since 1886, when strikes, marches, and the Haymarket bombing stirred anti-socialist and anti-radical sentiments in the state. In 1897, visits to the state by suffrage leaders provided renewed stimulus for organization.[25]

During the 1898 suffrage campaign in South Dakota, the Antis from Albany, New York, organized in 1895 as the Anti-suffragists of Albany and Vicinity, played an important role, as did one of their members, Elizabeth S. Crannell. She had become an effective speaker, attending both the Republican and Democratic national conventions in 1896, for which several eastern Anti groups financed her travels. Her speech to the Democrats circulated to Antis in Brookings, South Dakota, where a member cited it in the local newspaper. Crannell was forty-nine years old when she began her work for the anti-suffrage cause. Born in modest circumstances on a small farm in Sharon Springs, New York, at twenty-three, she married William Winslow Crannell, an Albany attorney who worked for the United States Civil Service. They had three sons, the youngest of whom was sixteen in 1896. When the Albany Antis organized, Crannell became chairman of the executive committee. She wrote clear, concise letters to the editors of various New York City newspapers with such titles as "Why Suffrage Would Not Help Women," "Women and the Liquor Traffic," and "The Failures of Woman Suffrage." Crannell also dissected the impact of woman suffrage in Wyoming, a popular tactic among Antis as time went on. States with woman suffrage, Crannell argued, had not become the reformers' paradise suffrage advocates had promised.[26]

In her speech at the Democratic convention, Crannell posed pointed rhetorical questions: would you want your wife or daughter to wait at the polls or attend crowded conventions? Who would care for the home? Who would do the charitable work? Instead of voting, women should "build up homes, not break down the walls and quench the light on the hearthstone." Crannell marshaled figures from states where suffrage-group membership lists had circulated to indicate the limited number of women who favored the vote. In New York State, for example, sixteen hundred women out of a population of seven million people belonged to suffrage organizations. She moved through state after state to illustrate the limited support for the suffrage cause. The remainder of her speech refuted the suffragists' main arguments for having the vote: adopting temperance, raising women's wages, and ending taxation without representation. Temperance was not guaranteed, she argued, because there were woman suffrage states without it. Wages depended on supply and demand. Economics, not politics, ruled on that question. Citizens paid taxes for protection of life, property, and nation. Men who owned property in several jurisdictions voted only in their home communities but paid taxes in all cities, counties, or states where they owned property. Pro-suffrage women, she concluded, wanted to keep the privileges that women have and assume those of men as well.[27]

Crannell came to South Dakota at the request of Marietta Bones, a former suffrage advocate who had turned strongly against woman suffrage and may have played a major role in its defeat in the state.[28] Bones, one of the most complex characters in South Dakota history, held strong opinions and did not respond well to those who crossed her. Julia Ward Howe, prominent suffragist, poet, and author of the "Battle Hymn of the Republic," once said, "There is no monster like an exaggerated personality," a condition that Bones appeared to embody.[29] Bones fought publicly and at length with Susan B. Anthony over the role of the WCTU, finances, and local control when Anthony was in charge of the 1890 suffrage campaign. When her former friends in the Webster, South Dakota, WCTU threw her out of their organization with a public denunciation because of her sharp words to Anthony and her general combativeness, Bones turned against woman suffrage.[30] She filed suit against the *Aberdeen News* for libel, requesting fifty-thousand dollars in damages because of the editors' remarks about her and added "thirty ladies" of Webster as defendants.[31] She eventually lowered her damage request and then dropped the suit entirely. Her greatest revenge was her anti-suffrage work. It is not clear if Crannell knew of this history when she accepted Bones's invitation to South Dakota. Bones credited

Marietta Bones, c. 1893. Private Collection

"the beautiful and accomplished Mrs. W. Winslow Crannell" for increasing anti-suffrage votes. "Her argument was not only convincing as to the wrong suffrage would do to women," Bones wrote, "but it was unanswerable."[32]

Crannell maintained a busy schedule in South Dakota. She came first to Yankton in late September 1898, then traveled to Sioux Falls, where she was feted at a reception, then left for Mitchell. After that, she spoke in Huron, then Aberdeen, and returned to Sioux Falls on 17 October. Suffrage organizers' correspondence indicates other stops on her tours.[33] Crannell's efforts, and the arrival of Anti literature from Albany, raised great concern among suffrage organizers. "About the 'Anti' movement at Aberdeen," wrote Laura A. Gregg, a NAWSA speaker, "the New York Remonstrants are back of it. I don't know whether they've gotten any woman in Aberdeen to take hold or not." Gregg promised to ask around when she arrived in Aberdeen.[34] The Vermillion Equal Suffrage Association secretary wrote to say that Crannell would speak in town the next night and lamented, "Our *Congregational* minister entertains her and is working against us." Congregational churches and ministers nationally often supported woman suffrage, so this defection stung.[35]

In Sturgis, the *Record* published Anti literature, and suffrage supporters there asked Lena Morrow, a socialist political organizer and suffragist, to help counter its influence. Morrow asked Clare Williams, secretary of the South Dakota Equal Suffrage Association, for valid facts to use against the Anti articles.[36] One suffrage speaker thought Crannell's presence might actually stimulate strong pro-suffrage reaction, and workers planned a big "rallie" when Crannell spoke in Milbank.[37] Catherine Waugh McCulloch of Chicago, an auditor for the national organization, wrote Clare Williams that hearing of Crannell's arrival "almost made me sick. How can women work against us so?" McCulloch described Crannell as "a large, voluptuous, handsome woman," whose looks caught men's attention and made them listen. In a letter a week later, however, McCulloch reassured Williams about Crannell's impact. "She is not a good speaker and I don't think she's democratic enough to look at a Pole or a [German] Russian. If you had seen her in white satin evening dress in dirty, tobacco smelling hotel corridors at National Conventions, you would not expect her and the Russian to find much in common."[38]

As the campaign drew to a close, Jane Breeden, an organizer for the South Dakota Equal Suffrage Association, told Williams that a local editor had stopped by with more anti-suffrage literature from Albany, adding, "so no doubt the whole state has been again flooded with it."[39] Suffrage workers also worried that the Antis would critique their methods and behaviors. Laura A. Gregg, for example, wrote Williams about being "the maddest mortal you ever saw" when she arrived at Britton to find local workers planned to send her around the county alone, the only woman with six male Populist office candidates. Gregg feared

Antis "making up a story about me," but she decided to go rather than risk losing the entire Populist vote of the county. As it turned out, all but one of the candidates spoke for suffrage as part of their own stump speeches, and all were cordial and courteous.[40] The Antis apparently found nothing to record, as Gregg did not mention any negative stories.

Brookings, South Dakota, became a laboratory of sorts for the 1898 suffrage campaign. In December 1897, before formal organization of the Anti group in town, local suffragist Anna Hyde wrote to NAWSA in New York City requesting suffrage publications, song leaflets, and an "Equal Suf stickpin" for her own Christmas present. In her letter she noted: "There are a number of intelligent women here who have no sympathy with the subject. We wish we might reach them as they have considerable influence." When asked to host pro-suffrage parlor meetings in their homes, two of these influential women had declined "on the above grounds—lack of sympathy."[41]

As 1898 began, Brookings residents organized a large Equal Suffrage Association (ESA) club, with a long list of members and endorsers, including twenty-eight men. Anne Hyde would serve as president.[42] Clare Williams, at this point the hard-working corresponding secretary for the state ESA, also lived in Brookings and wrote to the *Brookings Press* to challenge the paper's anti-suffrage coverage. Her letter was a spirited defense of female equality and natural rights. While it is true, she wrote, that "men are not rushing the platform to support Woman suffrage," they are discussing the issue. "Intelligent men are saying . . . as they go about their daily duties and as they meet together, that women are their equals, intellectually, morally, and spiritually." Men who valued their own votes could see how women would value theirs. They saw that women "are individuals, with individual interests, and individual responsibilities, they should have the legal right to exercise their God-given right of citizenship." Williams concluded, "Woman suffrage is not a question of expediency, . . . it is a question of abstract right. . . . Right is right, truth is truth and must prevail."[43]

The Brookings anti-suffrage group, in contrast, began with twenty-seven women, with others joining after the list was pub-

lished, according to the editor of the *Brookings Press*, whose wife
was a member of the anti-suffrage group. The Anti women provided a statement of their goals: "to counteract the opinion that
some may have, that all woman [*sic*] want to vote." The *Press*'s
managing editor explained further, "The members of the club
declare that they have all the rights they desire, and do not ask
for suffrage."[44] Most women in the group were married, but some
were single, widowed, or separated. The list included the wives
of a doctor, two lawyers, two lumberyard agents, a bank cashier,
a jeweler, a salesman at a flour mill, the owner of the flour mill,
a furniture dealer, a railroad worker, a clergyman, two farmers,
and the foreman of the railroad water supply. One woman was
separated from her husband, another was a widow who worked
as a saleswoman in a store and kept boarders. Nine of the women
listed no longer lived in Brookings just two years later when the
1900 census was taken. Americans, especially in recently settled
areas, were mobile. This turnover may also reflect the hard times
South Dakota endured in the 1890s. Indeed, the economic position of many of these women and their husbands changed over
time.[45]

 Although the 1898 Brookings anti-suffrage club was small, its
membership list suggests that anti-suffrage women in smaller
towns were not acting out of class-based self-interest. In contrast,
most eastern Antis were women of wealth and status. Scholars
sometimes describe their interests as strictly class-based. Certainly, their social positions allowed them time and resources to
engage in charity and humanitarian work. It also gave them connections to powerful men who could fund their work. Yet, they
did not act in lock step, as class-based analysis often suggests.[46]
Class structures in smaller towns and rural areas were less rigid
than those on the East Coast. Middle-class status often reflected
values and behaviors, not money. Churches or lodge activities
allowed families to maintain their status even if they lost their
businesses or if friends had to fund raise for them in time of illness. Personality among fellow middle-class or upper-middle-
class people also mattered. Communities or social organizations
dominated by harsh, judgmental personalities certainly existed.
Social arrangements could be rigid, as leaders worked to enforce

moral codes or social practices. Brookings, like other aspiring towns, had individuals and families who sought prosperity and respectability, both markers of middle-class status. In the rural West, however, the latter was often more important.[47]

The 1898 suffrage campaign failed, with 19,698 votes for suffrage and 22,983 against. Historian Dorinda Riessen Reed blamed the loss on Marietta Bones's public switch from pro- to anti-suffrage. Elizabeth Crannell's campaign also played an important role. A South Dakota correspondent to a Minneapolis paper believed Crannell to be "more effective in defeating the proposition than would have been the combined efforts of a dozen male orators."[48] If the Brookings anti-suffrage group is any indication, anti-suffrage literature from the East, as well as Crannell's printed speeches from her appearances at Republican and Democratic national conventions in 1896, provided local Anti chapters with an intellectual rationale that may have given individuals ways to organize otherwise inchoate thoughts into informed opposition. While the loss was painful for suffrage organizers, it demonstrated gains for the cause. Forty-six percent of male voters said yes to votes for women, the highest total in the three election campaigns. Antis from the East and locally would have to expand their efforts to maintain their majorities.[49]

South Dakota did not hold another vote on suffrage until 1910, although suffragists remained organized and active for the ensuing twelve years. The WCTU and suffrage workers continued to collaborate, perhaps confusing their message. Support from the national organization was limited. In 1899, Carrie Chapman Catt wrote South Dakota suffrage president Anna Simmons that she "did not urge people to give to South Dakota, because I have no faith in its prospects."[50] The 1910 referendum failed by a wide margin; only 38 percent voted for suffrage, a decrease of 8 percent from the 1898 referendum. The Antis' work in the state played a role in its defeat.[51] Eastern organizations continued to ship in literature. George Clarke, a "married man from Chicago," traveled the state late in 1909 on behalf of Anti groups in New York and Illinois to ascertain whether South Dakota was ready for its own anti-suffrage organization, though "none was founded."[52]

By the next referendum in 1914, much had changed. The WCTU

Defending Separate Spheres

had removed itself from direct involvement. Alice Pickler and Anna Simmons, both giants of the South Dakota suffrage movement, moved the state WCTU's headquarters to Faulk County, where they concentrated on temperance issues. Mary ("Mamie") Shields Pyle became head of the suffrage organization, newly renamed the South Dakota Universal Franchise League (SDUFL), and headquartered it in Huron. The changes refocused the South Dakota campaign and organized it around suffrage only, as NAWSA had long urged. Pyle emphasized better organization, systematic outreach, and firm leadership.[53]

The drive to organize and systemize that characterized Progressive Era social movements informed the structures and tactics of the Antis' work as well. In 1911, the various anti-suffrage state and local groups agreed to combine as the National Association Opposed to Woman Suffrage (NAOWS). The next year, a national Man Suffrage Association pulled the various male auxiliaries of the anti-suffrage organizations into a new national organization to assist their cause. Anti-suffrage groups put more speakers and organizers on the campaign trail to spread the Anti message far and wide. The state chapters organized under the auspices of the Massachusetts association in earlier years continued under the NAOWS. There were "permanent chapters" of Antis in New Hampshire, Vermont, Maine, Rhode Island, Washington, D.C., and Maryland by 1910. Antis organized the New England Anti-Suffrage League in 1914 to oversee that region. No official membership tallies exist, just "branches," "committees," or "auxiliaries."[54]

South Dakota was an "auxiliary state." Ethel C. Jacobsen of Pierre, the wife of an employee of the state school lands office and a mother of five children, was the secretary of the South Dakota auxiliary to NAOWS and served as the public face of the state Antis, who organized in 1916. Jacobsen traveled extensively, gave occasional speeches, and wrote letters to local papers. Based in Pierre, the group's chapter officers came from towns around the state. According to historian Jane Jerome Camhi, "the resistance was centered in one or two major cities [in South Dakota] and operated only sporadically" when claims made by a suffrage speaker or a letter to the editor needed to be challenged.[55]

Anti-suffrage literature continued to spread throughout the state and nation. The Albany group published *The Anti-Suffragist* quarterly, edited by Crannell, from 1908 to 1912. After NAOWS organized in 1911, it began publishing *The Woman's Protest*. Anti-suffrage books proliferated as well.[56] For example, Almroth Wright, a British biologist, authored a book titled *The Unexpurgated Case against Woman Suffrage* (1913). A highly respected biologist and medical doctor, he found deep-seated differences in male and female intellects and psychologies. Men, he argued, had "stable and relatively unresponsive nervous systems," which provided a foundation "for intellectual work." Women, in contrast, had responsive and excitable nervous systems, making them unsuitable for intellectual work. Men had "independence of thought, a faculty of felicitous generalization [and] relative immunity to fallacy," among several other traits that led "ordinary men" to be better intellectually than "intelligent women." Women, on the other hand, "appraised a statement with mental images only . . . and were over influenced by individual instances." Women considered themselves as efficient and hardworking as men but could not perform physical or mental work. Wright argued that these sex differences had been known since ancient times, and observation over the centuries had confirmed them. "The Woman's Suffrage Movement has no real intellectual or moral sanction," according to Wright.[57]

NAOWS lecturer Grace Duffield Goodwin produced several titles on anti-suffrage subjects, including *Anti-Suffrage: Ten Good Reasons* (1913). The reasons encompassed governmental, political, and biological themes. For example, Goodwin argued that voting was not a right, but a privilege, according to the United States Supreme Court. She also explained the issue of government as compulsion that frequently appeared in Anti literature. Women could not enforce their vote through physical strength or military service, whereas men could. Goodwin reminded readers of women's biological differences and disabilities, noting that each pregnancy resulted in nearly a year of special care and protection. Women's "affectability" or "life of feeling" meant different approaches to life compared to men. Women were as intelligent but possessed overactive nervous systems. The campaign for the vote, she feared, created sex antagonism, with men labeled as oppressors. If women voted, she warned, sex antagonism could infect marriage and the home. Like many Antis, Goodwin claimed that suffragists' belief that "wifehood and motherhood are incidental relations" challenged the basic foundations of society.[58]

Molly Elliot Seawell's anti-suffrage book, *The Ladies Battle* (1911), also described problems that the drive for woman suffrage created. Seawell was a well-known historian and novelist from Virginia who had supported herself through her writing for decades. Seawell addressed the need for voters to defend their votes and their government. She argued, too, that women, most of whom depended on their husbands financially and legally, could not vote without sacrificing their right to support. No voter could depend on the maintenance of another. Seawell examined the records of suffrage states to see if women's votes had purified those places as suffragists believed they would. In Utah, women had voted to sustain polygamy, and in six cases, husbands had sued their wives for financial support. Colorado had higher divorce rates, increasing juvenile delinquency, and liquor laws that increased rather than limited consumption. Women had even participated in a voter fraud scheme in the First Congressional District. Both Seawell and Goodwin noted the problem of voting by unassimilated immigrants and uneducated African Americans, whose wives would be able to vote if suffrage passed. They argued that immigrant and black women were less able than their husbands to understand their voting privilege.[59] Many suffragists also feared the impact of immigrants and uneducated voters, believing that the votes of white, middle-class women could counter those of the "less desirable." Seawall and Goodwin feared that undesirables could outvote the "better class" of women, especially, according to Goodwin, when considering the votes of "vicious women," meaning prostitutes, criminals, or the drug or liquor addled, and of the "intelligent, conscienceless" women, partners to big city bosses and others who used government positions for personal gain.[60]

The organized and energized anti-suffrage movement met the optimistic and focused South Dakota suffrage movement in three

In the 1910s, suffragists marched in a parade in Armour, South Dakota.
South Dakota State Historical Society

more referenda. Suffragists became increasingly visible in the 1910s. They flew yellow "Votes for Women" pennants, marched in local parades, spoke from automobiles and soap boxes in parks and on streets, and campaigned at the state fair, where they decorated the interiors of exhibit buildings with suffrage colors. The suffragists enjoyed the endorsement of one faction within the Republican Party, of the South Dakota Methodist church, and of the General Federation of Women's Clubs, which had voted in 1914 to support woman suffrage. Both political parties endorsed suffrage in 1918. The legislature easily passed suffrage amendments to place on the ballot in both 1916 and 1918, after the 1914 referendum failed.[61]

Suffragists' adoption of modern political techniques placed the Antis at a disadvantage. They, too, had a recognizable symbol, the Mrs. Arthur Murray (Josephine) Dodge pink rose, named for the first president of NAOWS and an editor of *The Woman's Protest*. Antis wore the Dodge rose pinned to their dresses on special occasions and decorated their booths and halls in rose and black, the official anti-suffrage colors. They did not, however, march in parades, speak on the streets, carry banners or signs, or invade suffrage lectures or debates. Antis emphasized ladylike behavior, which allowed public speaking and planned debates but not spectacles. To them, soapbox harangues, public parading, buttonholing people at rallies, heckling, or other loud, aggressive behavior violated the values they sought to preserve.[62]

The Antis did have a roster of active speakers who knew how to argue effectively and reach an audience. The best-known anti-suffrage speakers in South Dakota were Minnie Bronson and Lucy Price. Bronson, who also traveled Montana and North Dakota for the cause, visited most frequently from 1910 to 1918. Lucy Price campaigned in the state during the last three campaigns. Neither were the well-fed, well-connected rich women with fancy clothes, plumed hats, and nothing else to do that suffragists' proclaimed all anti-suffragists to be.

Minnie Bronson, the older of the two women, turned fifty in 1914. She was born on a farm in Fayette County, Iowa, and supported herself from age twenty. She earned B.A. and M.A. degrees at Upper Iowa University and taught high-school math in Saint Paul, Minnesota, for ten years. In 1900, she began a series of appointments with the Office of Education for various commissions created to represent the United States at international expositions, including the Saint Louis World's Fair in 1904. She also served as special agent of the Bureau of Labor from 1907 to 1909 to investigate working conditions for women and children and again in 1910 to monitor the Shirt Waist Makers strike. Bronson served as NAOWS's general secretary and published pamphlets on women, work, and wages. The Massachusetts Association Opposed to Further State Expansion of Suffrage to Women published and distributed Bronson's booklet, *Wage-Earning Women and the State* (1912). This document suggested that states without votes for women had labor laws as good or even better than the suffrage states. Protective legislation, including laws limiting women's working hours and mandating employees provide them with chairs, was vital, Bronson believed, to save women's strength and vitality and to preserve their childbearing capabilities. As Antis frequently argued, Bronson also suggested that voters do not receive special protective laws. Bronson traveled and spoke extensively on behalf of anti-suffrage, edited the anti-suffrage journal *Woman's Protest*, and served in key offices within anti-suffrage organizations.[63]

Lucy Price, thirty-one years old in 1914, came to Sargent County, Dakota Territory, with her parents as a baby. Her father was register of deeds for the county, raised cattle, and later became a United States marshal stationed in Fargo. Price received a B.A. from Vassar in 1905. She taught school and worked as a journalist in Fremont, Ohio, the family's hometown, then moved to Cleveland, where she served as women's editor, assistant editor, and city editor of the *Cleveland Leader*. After first supporting votes for women, she affiliated with the anti-suffrage movement and traveled extensively on behalf of their cause. Price was an excellent debater. She and Fola LaFollette, the suffragist daughter of Senator Robert LaFollette of Wisconsin, frequently debated the issue in front of large audiences.[64]

Minnie Bronson bore the brunt of suffragist ire in South Dakota. While pro- and anti-suffrage organizers had always fought with vigor and bite, the last three campaigns saw sharper, more personal conflict. Suffragists were convinced that liquor interests funded the anti-suffragist groups. Dr. Anna Howard Shaw, the famous suffragist, linked the Antis to liquor-industry money on mere supposition in her South Dakota speeches. Ruth Hipple, editor of the *South Dakota Messenger*, a suffrage paper published in Pierre from 1912 to 1914, printed Shaw's allegations and created an enduring canard. Dorinda Riessen Reed, author of the only historical overview of the entire South Dakota woman suffrage movement, accepted the *Messenger*'s charges as truth. Historian Patricia O'Keefe Easton argued that Henry Schlicting of Black Hills Brewing and Edward Dietrich of the Sioux Falls Brewing and Malting Company played a major role in suffrage defeats during the 1911–1920 period. Both men served as liaisons between their businesses and the United States Brewing Association, which a United States Senate committee investigated for pro-German activities during World War I. The investigation revealed that the brewers donated millions of dollars to groups that feared woman suffrage, such as the German-American Alliance, leading Easton to suggest that while women's anti-suffrage groups "appeared to be a public protest against equal suffrage, it was, in fact, most likely controlled by brewers' money."[65] Eastern Antis, however, had no ties to the German-American Alliance, a group dedicated to aiding German immigrants, maintaining culture, and teaching them American systems and structures. South Dakota suffragists nonetheless believed their common opposition to woman suffrage meant cooperation.[66]

Ruth Hipple certainly did. She told readers that the Anti newspaper columns published locally "were tools of organized vice." In another editorial, Hipple inferred that Edward Dietrich, Minnie Bronson, and Ethel Jacobsen were linked, then indicated her suspicions that Antis "were getting money from the 'jackpot,'" or liquor interests.[67] Shaw also continued to insist that liquor interests supported the Antis. Dietrich had offered Shaw a quid pro quo, she said: no liquor opposition to suffrage if suffragists would leave the liquor industry alone. As a result, Shaw assumed he must be making deals with the other side. Further, she claimed that the Antis had thirty thousand sample ballots printed and sent out three circulars in one week. Who paid these bills? Suffragists also pointed out that Dietrich and an array of "gamblers and toughs" had attended Bronson's talk in Sioux Falls. Surely this attendance meant that Antis received money from the liquor industry.[68]

Instead, close examinations of anti-suffrage groups' financial records indicate that they were shoestring operations that frequently requested donations from members. Many members of Anti groups were also prohibitionists, including the male editor of the *Remonstrance*, who led the No License Committee of Cambridge. Alice Paul, famous for her radical suffrage tactics, founder of the National Woman's Party, and no friend of Antis, stated publicly that the Antis were not linked to liquor money.[69] Carrie Chapman Catt, in her 1924 book *Women and Politics*, "absolved the anti-suffrage women with involvement with liquor interests and brewers," although they were on the same side of the suffrage question.[70] Perhaps it was easier to blame secretive deals with unsavory characters for suffrage losses than to recognize that many women simply opposed or were indifferent to the suffrage movement.

Other conflicts shaped the suffrage struggle in South Dakota. In 1914, Jacobsen began writing letters to newspapers to refute what she deemed misrepresentations or falsehoods. In one letter, she castigated Jean Wilkinson, a young woman from Faulkton, who had ridiculed the Antis' efforts in a letter to the Watertown paper. South Dakota voters, Wilkinson wrote, should "have [Antis] canned because the species to which they belong is so nearly extinct." Jacobsen refused to debate the other side, citing family cares and obligations and suggesting that many suffragists could do a better job of caring for their families.[71] Suffragists, in turn, ridiculed her for working outside of the home as locals editor for the *Pierre Dakotan*. While Jacobsen did not reply, census records indicate that her youngest child was fourteen in 1914.[72]

In 1916, the flamboyant suffragist speaker Elsie Benedict came to South Dakota from Denver to rally voters. Benedict employed new methods to challenge the opposition. When Antis had lectures scheduled, Benedict held rallies on the streets near their speaking venues. During the Anti lectures, she and several followers would march in, often carrying Votes for Women pennants. Benedict's methods caused conflict when Bronson, accompanied by Jacobsen, spoke at the Brookings Opera House in October. E. H. Carlisle, a suffrage supporter and manager of the venue, believed that the Antis, having paid for use of the hall, deserved their reserved time. He asked attendees to leave pennants and banners in the box office. Benedict arrived late, as was her wont, with a retinue of fifteen or twenty suffragists and refused to give up her pennants. At the entrance to the auditorium, she argued with Carlisle, who pushed her back outside. In return, she hit him in the face and on the head with her fists. Benedict claimed later, in an interview with a Watertown paper, that Carlisle had hit her, pushed her, and kicked her. She and her party gave up their banners, but Benedict concealed a Votes for Women pennant under her cloak as she rushed down to the front row to take a seat. She continued to disrupt the speech by shouting out questions that Bronson deferred to the end. After the speech, Benedict returned to the street to speak on anti-suffragists' ties to liquor and vice. Carlisle told his side of the story in an advertisement that the Antis purchased. Embarrassed by what he saw as an attack on his character, Carlisle had the police chief and his assistant verify his story. R. F. Kerr, a professor at South Dakota State College and a suffrage supporter, wrote to Mary Pyle, Universal Franchise League president, to defend Carlisle's version of events and to inform her that Benedict's tactics were hurting the cause.[73]

Benedict used the same tactics in Yankton, Mitchell, and Watertown. Antis, in turn, used Benedict and the Brookings affair to campaign against suffrage. Voters should decide, they wrote, "whether the thrusting of women into politics is desirable from the standpoint of decorum in public life, or her own delicacy, gentleness, and refinement."[74] The *Argus-Leader* published coverage of the Benedict onslaught there. She drew crowds in the street, where she "proceeded to lay her rival sisters out by clever argument." The men in the crowd were amused and concluded "that if women got the franchise, elections would be real interesting in the future."[75]

Benedict's visit to South Dakota coincided with a potentially serious misstep by Ruth Hipple. In her eagerness to tie the visiting Antis to liquor money and influence, Hipple wrote an inflammatory article for the 21 October 1916 issue of *Woman's Journal*. Charles McLean, an anti-suffragist from Dubuque, Iowa, had traveled to South Dakota with the Anti speakers that fall, and while the group visited Deadwood, Hipple wrote, "he divided his time, we are told," between the bank owned "by the ultra-wet" mayor and "the Mansion, [Deadwood's] most notorious resort," a reference to a house of prostitution. Hipple also declared Dubuque "the wettest city in Iowa."[76]

On 26 October, a Redfield, South Dakota, newspaper reprinted the story. McLean then wrote a strong "warning letter" to Hipple that stated he was a life-long abstainer, did not know the mayor of Deadwood, and had never heard of the Mansion. Iowa had voted in prohibition in 1916, he informed them, so there were no longer any wet cities or liquor interests. McLean then heard Elsie Benedict, speaking in the street in Pierre, making similar charges and ridiculing his denial. Dubuque, she said, was one of the "worst

EQUALITY AT THE BALLOT BOX

rum-soaked holes in the country."[77] When McLean tried to re-spond, Benedict demanded to know why he had not sued for libel. At this point, John Hipple, Ruth Hipple's husband and publisher of the *Pierre Capitol Journal*, stepped out of the crowd and told Benedict to allow McLean to speak. McLean defended himself to the gathering and refuted the charges. Ruth Hipple retracted her statement in McLean's attorney's office in Pierre three days later. McLean had it published, along with a printed card stating his defense.[78]

Suffrage lost again in 1916 but garnered 48 percent of the vote. Two years later, it passed with the help of legislative innovation. The South Dakota legislature, at the urging of Governor Peter Norbeck, asked voters to base the right to vote on citizenship not sex. Amendment E removed the word "male" from article seven of the state's constitution so that any otherwise eligible "citizen" had the right to vote. The amendment also inserted evidence requirements for immigrants, who would have to provide proof of citizenship before voting. This requirement would eliminate from the voting rolls those immigrants who had only filed their intent to become citizens, a process they had to complete within seven years to maintain voter eligibility. Suffrage workers moni-tored the polls in German areas to make sure that immigrants voting on first papers were within the seven-year limit. The in-tense emotions surrounding World War I permeated the election. Concern about German perfidy ensured that men who might not approve of votes for women would vote for suffrage if it kept Ger-man immigrants in line. After years of painstaking labor, suf-frage seemed likely to pass, thanks in part to the emphasis on American democracy and fairness in contrast to Germany and, perhaps, the urge among some South Dakotans to quiet suffrag-ists' demands. Even the *Argus-Leader*'s editor, a longtime Anti, changed his mind. In an editorial published 25 October 1918, he announced he would vote for woman suffrage.[79]

Ethel Jacobsen responded quickly, amazed at his reversal. The editor "endorsed the 'patriotic amendment' [i.e., woman suffrage and alien restriction] and the defeat of the socialist (!) amend-ments [also on the ballot]. Where have you been all this time not to know that woman suffrage is one of the foremost socialist doctrines?" she asked.[80] Alice Wadsworth, national president of NAOWS, had begun conflating the Anti cause with wartime movements against Germans, Bolsheviks, communists, and socialists. Mary Hildreth, her successor, continued down that path. Historian Thomas Jablonsky argues that the anti-suffrage movement at this point became "a clearing house for anti-radical rhetoric" and lost its suffrage focus.[81] Jacobsen clearly had read this new literature. She claimed, for instance, that socialists carried suffrage banners in their parades, that the *New York Call*, a socialist paper, was "one of the strongest supporters the militant suffragists have," that New York suffrage leaders asked Max Eastman, a former college professor who was fired for his radical views, and the socialist paper he edited, *The Masses*, to assist them, and so on. Her conclusion reflected the prevailing Anti sentiment: "Amendment E is truly a socialist amendment. Since suffrage has been defeated six times in South Dakota and would be again on its merits, therefore it is this year camouflaged with an alien vote clause."[82] Antis had long alleged that suffragists' calls for independent incomes for all women and state-provided daycare for children were socialist. They made the same case much more strongly as the emotions spawned by World War I swept the country.

On 6 November 1918, the men of South Dakota voted 49,318 to 28,934 to grant women the full franchise. After twenty-eight years of statehood, South Dakota women finally won the vote. The charged atmosphere of wartime aided the measure. By 1918, thousands of German immigrants in South Dakota, were subjects of suspicion and fear. Although Antis believed the double amendment was illegal and threatened to sue, South Dakota forged ahead.[83] Suffrage advocates had used themes of patriotism and German inhumanity to win votes. Edith Medberry Fitch of Yankton, a former state suffrage association officer, linked opposition to woman suffrage to pro-German sentiment: "If you are not a pro-German, we expect your vote this fall."[84] Suffrage advertisements repeated the theme. A full page of pro-Amendment E columns that appeared in the Lead newspaper the day before the election featured a map of South Dakota divided into counties. Those in white were counties that voted for suffrage in 1916.

Those shaded black were "German" counties, which had voted against suffrage. A column touting the leading South Dakota men who supported suffrage labeled the upcoming vote "A Test of Americanism."[85] After six failed tries, the dramatic circumstances of 1918 helped secure woman suffrage.

When South Dakota, and soon, the entire nation adopted woman suffrage, Antis did their duty and voted. They proclaimed their commitment to the new obligation, because the vote, they believed, was "so big, so sacred, so binding" that women should vote if their state enacted woman suffrage.[86] In Missouri, Laura Ingalls Wilder, a locally known writer for the *Missouri Ruralist* and former South Dakotan, followed this path. A strong proponent of separate spheres and small farms, Wilder told her readers that they had the duty to vote when suffrage came. She even ran, unsuccessfully, for a local tax-collection office in 1924. Former Antis wanted to counter the votes of suffragists, as well as the women they claimed were lost in prostitution, alcohol, and other vices, and their male compatriots. Although Antis participated in politics with surprising comfort, women did not vote in numbers similar to men until much later.[87] In South Dakota, the once-prominent anti-suffragist Ethel Jacobsen became a librarian at the Pierre library, then the president of the South Dakota State Library Association. She later wrote a column on Pierre social news for the Huron newspaper and contributed letters to the editor about local issues, especially about local history. The gravestone for her and her husband, Elias, calls them Hughes County pioneers, but there is no way to know if she ever voted.[88]

Antis faced harsh criticism, even ridicule, from more belligerent women who wanted immediate suffrage and had no patience for separate spheres. A member of the new National Woman's Party, the creation of Alice Paul and the more militant wing of the suffrage movement, demanded that Antis: "Cease from being over-fed, over-dressed parasitical barnacles on the ship of progress! Join the ranks of those women who at least are not a disgrace to the Mothers who bore them, a menace to the State in which they reside, and a cancer upon the bosom of their native land."[89] Of course, anti-suffragists were none of those things. They tended to be well-off conservative Protestants of Anglo-Saxon heritage with more education than average and married. Suffragists followed the same ethnic, religious, and marital pattern. Two major differences, however, stand out. Suffragists graduated from college at five times the rate of Antis, and sixty-two percent of suffragists made their own living at some point. Minnie Bronson was the only Anti leader with an advanced degree.[90]

Antis in general were economically secure and did not have to pursue greater education or employment. They believed they could do public-service work and improve society without the vote or immersion in partisan politics. Lucy Price explained the Anti vision: "It is not more laws, but better customs that we need and women, as a non-political factor, have the making of the customs in their own hands."[91] Ethel Jacobsen believed the anti-suffrage position could be compared to the prohibition question. No one forced prohibitionists to visit saloons, but "they believe the influence of the thing they oppose must be evil" and therefore had to be outlawed. Jacobsen also made a vital distinction: "Suffragists mention at all times that anyone opposed to suffrage is necessarily opposed to temperance, uplift movements, and other social good, and that suffrage and 'reform for the better' are almost synonymous terms. This the anti-suffragists resent." Those who oppose suffrage, she wrote, do so as a political question, "not a moral issue. . . . The right to vote, of itself, is not a moral question."[92] Many Antis agreed with the leading social reform causes of the day but believed women should influence public opinion rather than engage in partisan politics. Separate spheres built a successful society, one that best suited the needs of women, children, and family, they argued. Long after gaining the vote, untold numbers of women would continue to insist that their true power stemmed from their influence over home and community.[93]

NOTES

1. *Remonstrance*, Special South Dakota Edition, p. 1, copy in folder 48, box 6674, Pickler Family Papers, 1865–1976, State Archives Collection, South Dakota State Historical Society (SDSHS), Pierre.

2. *Yankton Press and Dakotan*, 15 Aug. 1890.

3. *Remonstrance*, p. 1.

4. Ibid., p. 2.

EQUALITY AT THE BALLOT BOX

5. Ibid., pp. 3-4.

6. Goodspeed to *Dakota Ruralist*, 11 Aug. 1890, copy in folder 2, box 6674, Pickler Family Papers.

7. Dorinda Riessen Reed, *The Woman Suffrage Movement in South Dakota*, 2d ed. (Pierre: South Dakota Commission on the Status of Women, 1975). Reed details the suffrage battle from territorial days to victory and after. *See also* Cecelia Wittmayer, "The 1889–1890 Woman Suffrage Campaign: A Need to Organize," *South Dakota History* 11 (Summer 1981): 199–225; Patricia O'Keefe Easton, "Woman Suffrage in South Dakota: The Final Decade, 1911–1920," *South Dakota History* 13 (Fall 1983): 206–26.

8. Easton, "Woman Suffrage in South Dakota," p. 226.

9. Wittmayer, "1889–1890 Woman Suffrage Campaign," pp. 199–225.

10. Ibid., p. 224.

11. Adams to My Dear Friend, 26 Nov. 1890, folder 1, box 6674, Pickler Family Papers.

12. Jane Jerome Camhi, *Women against Women: American Anti-Suffragism, 1880–1920* (Brooklyn: Carlson Publishing, 1994); Susan Goodier, *No Votes for Women: The New York Anti-Suffrage Movement* (Urbana: University of Illinois Press, 2013); Thomas J. Jablonsky, *The Home, Heaven, and Mother Party: Female Anti-Suffragists in the United States, 1868–1920* (Brooklyn: Carlson Publishing, 1994); Susan E. Marshall, *Splintered Sisterhood: Gender and Class in the Campaign against Woman Suffrage* (Madison: University of Wisconsin Press, 1997).

13. For examples of women's place in the civil community, *see* Paula M. Nelson, "'Do Everything:' Women in Small Prairie Towns, 1870–1920" *Journal of the West* 36 (Oct. 1997): 52–60.

14. Nancy Woloch, *Women and the American Experience: A Concise History* (New York: Alfred A. Knopf, 1984), offers an excellent synthesis of the roles and place of women in the United States from the earliest European arrivals to 1984. *See* Barbara Welter, "The Cult of True Womanhood, 1820–1860," *American Quarterly* 18 (Summer 1966): 151–74, for a discussion of the ideology of "separate spheres." Linda K. Kerber, "Separate Spheres, Female World, Woman's Place: The Rhetoric of Women's History," *Journal of American History* 75 (June 1988): 9–39, provides a historiography of the term and rejects it because of the dualism it presents, although, she notes, "historians of women who did not consider themselves Marxists, employed the sphere language because it offered opportunities for social, cultural, political, and material analysis" (p. 14). I employ it here because many of the women I study understood and explained their world in this way. Linda K. Kerber, *Women of the Republic: Intellect and Ideology in Revolutionary America* (Chapel Hill: University of North Carolina Press, 1989), pp. 7, 120, 139–55, 189–221,

269–88, explains how the Revolution expanded women's place, laying the foundation for separate spheres. On issues of ideology versus the reality of lives of women in the West, *see* Elizabeth Jameson, "Women as Workers, Women as Civilizers," in *The Women's West*, ed. Susan Armitage and Jameson, (Norman: University of Oklahoma Press, 1987), pp. 145–64; Robert Griswold, "Anglo Women and Domestic Ideology in the American West in the Nineteenth and Early Twentieth Centuries," in *Western Women: Their Land, Their Lives*, ed. Lillian Schlissel, Vicki L. Ruiz, and Janice Monk (Albuquerque: University of New Mexico Press, 1988), pp. 15–33. On the anti-suffrage movement, *see* Goodier, *No Votes for Women*, p. 2.

The term "separate spheres" may not describe the lives of immigrants who came to the United States to farm or to labor in towns and cities. The United States also had native-born families who did not practice separate spheres ideology. Men and women within most groups, however, had duties and obligations linked to their sex, but perhaps without the sentimentality or the rarefication of motherhood. For divisions of labor in the Great Plains and Midwest, *see* Shirley Fischer Arends, *The Central Dakota Germans: Their History, Language, and Culture* (Washington, D.C.: Georgetown University Press, 1989); Betty A. Bergland and Lori Ann Lahlum, *Norwegian-American Women: Migration, Communities, and Identities* (Saint Paul: Minnesota Historical Society Press, 2011); Linda Schelbitzki Pickle, *Contented among Strangers: Rural German-Speaking Women and Their Families in the Nineteenth-Century Midwest* (Urbana: University of Illinois Press, 1996).

15. Aileen S. Kraditor, *The Ideas of the Woman Suffrage Movement, 1890–1920* (Garden City, N.Y.: Doubleday Anchor Books, 1971), pp. 39, 43–57. On the Progressive Era, *see* Robert A. Wiebe, *The Search for Order, 1877–1920* (New York: Hill & Wang, 1966); John Whiteclay Chambers, *The Tyranny of Change: America in the Progressive Era* (New York: St. Martin's Press, 1992).

16. *Bismarck Tribune*, 8 Dec. 1915, 11 Sept. 1918; U.S., Bureau of the Census, *Census of the United States*, 1880, 1900, 1910, 1920, 1930; Find-a-Grave. com; Paul A. Hefti, "The Pull of Tradition: The North Dakota Association Opposed to Woman Suffrage," in *Day In, Day Out: Women's Lives in North Dakota*, ed. Bjorn Benson, Elizabeth Hampsten, and Kathryn Sweney (Grand Forks: University of North Dakota, 1988), pp. 197–204; Grace Duffield Goodwin, *Anti-Suffrage: Ten Good Reasons* (New York: Duffield & Co., 1913), p. 86.

17. For example, M. Lyons wrote, "Man, if you believe in anti-suffrage, give woman back her knitting needles, place her chair at the window where she can have a good view of the neighbors, don't forget that part . . . and go back to the dark ages" (*Bismarck Tribune*, 22 Apr. 1914).

18. Dennis A. Norlin, "The Suffrage Movement and South Dakota Churches: Radicals and the Status Quo, 1890" *South Dakota History* 14 (Winter 1984): 309–10.

19. Ibid., pp. 309–20.

20. Mrs. W. A. Woolege to the editor, *Sioux Falls Argus-Leader*, 27 May 1918. The United States census shows no W. A. Woolege, but William A. Wooledge had a homestead in Elvira Township, Buffalo County, not far from White Lake. He served a term as Buffalo County sheriff and sold insurance after 1910. "Mrs. W. A. Woolege" may be "Luna Wooledge," whom William A. Wooledge married as Luna Yakey in Groton, South Dakota, in 1891. They had eight children.

21. Jablonsky, *Home, Heaven, and Mother Party*, pp. 32–34, 50.

22. Eleanor Flexner, *Century of Struggle: The Woman's Rights Movement in the United States* (Cambridge: Harvard University Press, 1959), pp. 295–305; Ann Douglas, *The Feminization of American Culture* (New York: Alfred Knopf, 1977), pp. 17–120. Douglas suggests that ministers in Congregationalist and other prominent northeast denominations who were losing status in the industrializing nineteenth-century culture allied with women in their congregations to create a feminized culture.

23. *Sioux Falls Argus-Leader*, 10 Apr. 1894.

24. Reed, *Woman Suffrage Movement in South Dakota*, p. 49. One of the 1894 amendments proposed to lift the two-term limit for superintendents, and the other allowed women to vote for any school office, including county and state superintendents of public instruction. *See* Ruth Page Jones, "The Women Voted," herein.

25. Reed, *Woman Suffrage Movement in South Dakota*, p. 52; Jablonsky, *Home, Heaven, and Mother Party*, pp. 6–11, 20–24; Marshall, *Splintered Sisterhood*, pp. 25–27.

26. Goodier, *No Votes for Women*, p. 47; *United States Census*, 1850, 1860, 1870, 1900, AncestryLibrary.com; Women's Anti-Suffrage Association, *Pamphlets Printed and Distributed by the Women's Anti-Suffrage Association of the Third Judicial District of New York* (Albany: By the Association, 1905). Elizabeth Crannell also edited a periodical, *The Anti-Suffragist*, from 1908 to 1912. *See* Kathleen L. Endres and Theresa L. Lueck, *Women's Periodicals in the United States: Social and Political Issues* (Santa Barbara, Calif.: Greenwood Publishing Group, 1996), pp. 20–27.

27. "Address of Mrs. W. Winslow Crannell," in *Pamphlets Printed and Distributed*, pp. 1–8.

28. Goodier, *No Votes for Women*, pp. 45–47.

29. Howe, quoted in Nancy Tystad Koupal, "Marietta Bones, Personality

and Politics in the South Dakota Suffrage Movement," in *Feminist Frontiers: Women Who Shaped the Midwest*, ed. Yvonne J. Johnson (Kirksville, Mo.: Truman University Press, 2010), p. 70.

30. Ibid., pp. 73–81.

31. *Huron Daily Plainsman*, 18 June 1891.

32. Bones, quoted in *Sioux Falls Argus-Leader*, 9 Dec. 1898, under a headline with an unfortunate typographical error, "Mrs. M. E. Boner Rejoices."

33. Ibid., 27, 28, 29 Sept., 17 Oct. 1898; Linda Perry to Clare Williams, 15 Oct. 1898, folder 15, box 6676, Pickler Family Papers. Crannell also traveled to Washington state to promote anti-suffrage.

34. Gregg to Williams, 5 Oct. 1898, folder 17, box 6676, Pickler Family Papers.

35. Frances Brookman to Williams, 13 Oct. 1898, folder 15, ibid.

36. Morrow to Williams, n.d., folder 19, ibid.

37. Linda Perry to Williams, 15 Oct. 1898, folder 15, ibid.

38. McCulloch to Williams, 6 Oct. 1898, folder 21, ibid. German Russians, known colloquially as Russians, descended from German-speaking families who accepted Catherine the Great's 1763 invitation to migrate to Russian lands to farm. Among several other privileges, Catherine promised that they would not be subject to the military draft, as they had been in their home provinces. When Czar Alexander II instituted universal conscription in 1874, he voided that promise. Notably anti-German, Alexander began intensive "Russification" of German colonists in 1881, which effectively nullified any remaining privileges. In response, many German Russians migrated to Dakota Territory, Kansas, and other Plains states. "A Brief History of the Germans from Russia," Germans from Russia Heritage Collection, library.ndsu. edu.

39. Breeden to Williams, 25 Oct. 1898, folder 4, box 6676, Pickler Family Papers.

40. Gregg to Williams, 1 Nov. 1898, folder 19, ibid.

41. Hyde to NAWSA, 15 Dec. 1897, folder 24, ibid.

42. *Brookings Press*, 3 Nov. 1898.

43. Williams to *Brookings Press*, 6 Oct. 1898.

44. *Brookings Press*, 20 Oct. 1898. The owner and editor, C. F. Allen, and his wife moved to Washington State before 1900.

45. *United States Census*, 1850–1930. *See also* Find-a-Grave and other documents on AncestryLibrary.com for background information on anti-suffrage women listed in the *Brookings Press*. Interestingly, Clare Williams, ESA secretary, had also moved from Brookings by 1900. She and her husband moved to Watertown, South Dakota, where he worked for International Harvester and she became assistant librarian at the city library (*Watertown*

City Directory). The Brookings membership list seems to be the only record of anti-suffrage club members in South Dakota. During the 1890 suffrage campaign, newspapers mentioned the organization of anti-suffrage groups in Huron, Woonsocket, and Artesian. No other information appeared, but the *Sioux Falls Argus-Leader* editor wrote that anti-suffrage clubs were "not uncommon" (17 Apr. 1890). *See also Hot Springs Star*, 14 Mar. 1890; *Huron Daily Plainsman*, 19 June 1890.

46. Marshall, *Splintered Sisterhood*, pp. xi–5, 20–57.

47. This discussion of class and behavior in rural communities and small towns on the Great Plains and in the Midwest comes from my close reading of thirty years of the *Sioux Valley News* (Canton, S.Dak.), 1875–1905, and from four decades of research and writing about rural life and culture, families, neighborhoods, and towns in those regions. One theme that stands out is the importance of individuals in these places; by personality and leadership, people changed the atmosphere and direction of their home places in ways both positive and negative.

48. Quoted in Reed, *Woman Suffrage Movement in South Dakota*, p. 5.

49. Ibid., pp. 62, 117.

50. Quoted in Paula M. Nelson, "Home and Family First: Women and Political Culture," in *The Plains Political Tradition: Essays on South Dakota Political Culture*, ed. Jon K. Lauck, John E. Miller, and Donald C. Simmons, Jr. (Pierre: South Dakota Historical Society Press, 2011), p. 142. *See also* pp. 136–43 for a discussion of the suffrage campaigns prior to 1914.

51. Reed, *Woman Suffrage Movement in South Dakota*, pp. 55–58, 117.

52. *Sioux Falls Argus-Leader*, 29 Nov. 1909.

53. Reed, *Woman Suffrage Movement in South Dakota*, pp. 58–92; Easton, "Women Suffrage in South Dakota," pp. 208–16.

54. Camhi, *Women against Women*, pp. 81–88.

55. Ibid., p. 82; *Sioux Falls Argus-Leader*, 28 Sept. 1916. Officers listed were president, Mrs. Ernest Jackson of Dallas, whose husband dealt in real estate and ranched; vice-presidents, Mrs. George Mansfield of Rapid City, whose husband was superintendent of the electric plant in town, Mrs. Roy McMillan Wheeler of Hot Springs, who was married to a physician, Mrs. C. M. Barnes of Aberdeen, whose husband was a businessman selling lighting supplies, Mrs. H. R. Hinckley of Hoven, who farmed with her husband; secretary, Ethel Jacobsen, Pierre. Local officers in Pierre, who oversaw the headquarters office, were president, Mrs. C. M. Hollister, who was married to a physician, vice-president, Mrs. J. L. Lockhart, who was married to a real estate magnate with several businesses; treasurer, Mrs. S. S Ruble, who was married to an undertaker and furniture-store owner.

56. Camhi, *Women against Women*, pp. 88–91. *See Minneapolis Morning*

Tribune, 15 Apr. 1915, for a list of book titles. The Minneapolis anti-suffrage group maintained a three-room office suite. One room contained a library, with comfortable chairs for working women to spend their lunch time relaxing or reading. Visitors could check out books as well.

57. Wright, *The Unexpurgated Case against Woman Suffrage* (London: Constable & Co., 1913), pp. 1, 21, 31–37.

58. Goodwin, *Anti-Suffrage,* pp. 92, 103. *See also* pp. 15–24, 43–87, 85–104.

59. Seawell, *The Ladies' Battle* (New York: Macmillan Co., 1911), pp. 7–14, 20–61, 91–101.

60. Goodwin, *Anti-Suffrage,* pp. 43–48. *See also* Seawell, *Ladies' Battle,* pp. 18–20. Seawell was most concerned about former slaves, whom she deemed but "a few generations removed from cannibalism" (p. 20).

61. Reed, *Woman Suffrage Movement in South Dakota,* pp. 67–69, 104.

62. Jablonsky, *Home, Heaven, and Mother Party,* p. 85.

63. *United States Census,* 1870–1910, and travel documents, AncestryLibrary .com. For a brief biography, *see* Bronson, *Wage-Earning Woman and the State* (Boston: Massachusetts Association Opposed to Further Extension of Suffrage to Women, 1912), p. 2.; Camhi, *Women against Women,* p. 238.

64. *United States Census,* 1900, 1910, AncestryLibrary.com; John William Leonard, *Women's Who's Who of America, 1914–1915* (New York: American Commonwealth Co., 1915), p. 662; *Sioux Falls Argus-Leader,* 19, 23 Oct. 1916; *Deadwood Weekly Pioneer Times,* 2 Nov. 1916.

65. Easton, "Woman Suffrage in South Dakota," pp. 207–10. *See also* Reed, *Woman Suffrage Movement in South Dakota,* pp. 84–86, 88–89; Carrie Chapman Catt and Nettie Rogers Shaw, *Woman Suffrage and Politics: The Inner Story of the Suffrage Movement* (Buffalo: William S. Hein, 1926), pp. 147, 272–78.

66. Reed, *Woman Suffrage Movement in South Dakota,* p. 85.

67. Quoted ibid., p. 85. *See also* pp. 88–89.

68. Ibid., p. 93.

69. Camhi, *Women against Women,* p. 89; Jablonsky, *Home, Heaven, and Mother Party,* p. 75.

70. Quoted in Goodier, *No Votes for Women,* p. 178n41.

71. Jacobsen to editor, *Deadwood Daily Pioneer Times,* 12 Oct. 1914. The first letters under the signature of Ethel C. Jacobsen, secretary of the auxiliary, appeared in the summer of 1914. *Daily Deadwood Pioneer Times,* 12 Aug., 17 Oct. 1914.

72. Reed, *Woman Suffrage Movement in South Dakota,* p. 79.

73. *Sioux Falls Argus-Leader,* 24 Oct., 4 Nov. 1916.

74. Quoted ibid., 24 Oct. 1916.

75. Ibid.

       EQUALITY AT THE BALLOT BOX

76. Quoted in *Des Moines Register*, 27 Nov. 1916.

77. Quoted ibid. Mrs. Simon Casaday, chair of the Iowa Anti-Suffrage group, gave the *Des Moines Register* much of McLean's letter for publication.

78. *Sioux Falls Argus-Leader*, 4 Nov., 1916.

79. Reed, *Woman Suffrage Movement in South Dakota*, p. 6; *Sioux Falls Argus-Leader*, 25 Oct. 1918.

80. Jacobsen to the editor, *Sioux Falls Argus-Leader*, 31 Oct. 1918.

81. Jablonsky, *Home, Heaven, and Mother Party*, p. 111.

82. Jacobsen to editor, *Sioux Falls Argus-Leader*, 31 Oct. 1918.

83. Reed, *Woman Suffrage Movement in South Dakota*, pp. 95–100, 105–12.

84. Quoted in *Sioux Falls Argus-Leader*, 4 May 1918.

85. *Lead Daily Call*, 4 Nov. 1918.

86. Jablonsky, *Home, Heaven, and Mother Party*, p. 115.

87. Paula M. Nelson, "Women's Place: Family, Home, and Farm," in *Pioneer Girl Perspectives: Exploring Laura Ingalls Wilder*, ed. Nancy Tystad Koupal (Pierre: South Dakota Historical Society Press, 2017), pp. 177–208; "Gender Differences in Voter Turnout," Center for American Women and Politics, Eagleton Institute of Politics, Rutgers University, 20 July 2017, cawp.rutgers.edu.

88. *United States Census*, 1880–1940, and Find-a-Grave for Ethel C. Jacobsen. Jacobsen wrote the "Capital Society" column for the *Huronite and Daily Plainsmen*.

89. Quoted in Jablonsky, *Home, Heaven, and Mother Party*, p. xxiii.

90. Ibid., pp. 56–58.

91. Quoted in *Sioux Falls Argus-Leader*, 26 Oct. 1916.

92. Jacobsen to editor, *Pierre Weekly Free Press*, 16 Dec. 1915.

93. Manuela Thurner, "'Better Citizens without the Ballot: American Anti-suffrage Women and Their Rationale during the Progressive Era," in *One Woman, One Vote*, ed. Marjorie Spruill Wheeler (Troutdale, Oreg.: NewSage Press, 1995), pp. 203–20. Thurner argues that the opportunity to be a nonpartisan political force, not family or separate spheres issues, motivated anti-suffrage women after 1900. Nonpartisanship was important to wealthier urban women who could influence male movers and shakers. For women outside that milieu, the rarified role of motherhood and their position as the moral center of the home carried more weight.

SNAPSHOTS

A SENTIMENT OF JUSTICE
The Woman Suffrage Question and Wyoming Statehood

AMY L. MCKINNEY

When delegates from Wyoming Territory met in 1889 to draft a state constitution, most believed woman suffrage would be included, making it not only the first territory but also the first state to grant women the right to vote. The all-male delegation that met in Cheyenne formed committees to draft specific sections, including one on suffrage and elections. Few predicted any controversary surrounding the issue of women's suffrage, but a small group of dissenters emerged. For the second time since its passage, the fate of woman suffrage in Wyoming seemed uncertain.

The first repeal attempt came at the 1871 legislative session, when C. E. Castle, a Democrat from Uinta County, proposed a bill to rescind women's voting rights, which had been enshrined in the territorial constitution just two years earlier. The *Laramie Daily Sentinel* reported that in the first election to include women, in September 1870, sixty-four of Laramie's ninety-three women voters cast ballots for Republicans, which might help explain why majority Democrats carried the vote in both houses of the territorial assembly for the repeal of woman suffrage. In turn, the first territorial governor, Republican John A. Campbell, vetoed the repeal bill.[1]

After years of silence, the debate over woman suffrage began anew as soon as Republican governor Francis E. Warren called for a state constitutional convention in the summer of 1889. In contrast with the 1871 call for repeal, few now doubted the wisdom of woman suffrage. Those who raised the question admitted woman suffrage had been "something of a success in its operation here." Rather, opponents expressed concern that the inclusion of women's voting rights would jeopardize Wyoming's chance for statehood. In Wyoming, as in other Northern Great Plains states, many believed the United States Congress would reject any state constitution that included woman suffrage. They did not consider it prudent to "make unreasonable demands upon congress" and instead advocated a separate referendum.[2] The opposition remained "very small, but there are several members who believe that it should be submitted separately to the people," reported the *Laramie Boomerang*, a Republican-leaning newspaper.[3]

Those who opposed the inclusion of woman suffrage in the state's constitution pointed to congressmen who made their opposition to woman suffrage clear. Outspoken Illinois Democrat William M. Springer, the *Cheyenne Sun* reported, "opposed woman suffrage and . . . would oppose Wyoming's admission under the circumstances, on the ground that women are proverbially favorable to temperance." Barely considered in Wyoming Territory in 1869, by 1889 temperance had become a leading issue throughout the Northern Great Plains states.[4]

Those supporting a post-statehood referendum argued that, by making woman suffrage a separate vote, both the state constitution and woman suffrage would easily pass. In line with this thinking, delegate Anthony C. Campbell, a Democrat from Laramie County, "moved to amend by making [woman suffrage] a separate proposition to be submitted to a vote of the people." According to the *Cheyenne Daily Sun*, a Republican publication edited by E. A. Slack, the eldest son of suffragist Esther Morris, Campbell's proposition "took many of the members by surprise" because "sentiment in favor of incorporating the female suffrage clause into the constitution" was strong.[5] Indeed, Campbell made it clear he did not oppose woman suffrage, and the *Laramie Boomerang* explained, "If the question was submitted separately he would vote in its favor."[6] Campbell's idea of a separate referendum was not unique. Legislators in Montana and North Dakota also discussed holding post-statehood referendums during their constitutional conventions, though none materialized. South Dakota held an unsuccessful referendum in 1890.[7]

Campbell's amendment caused a stir on the delegation floor. Those supporting the inclusion of woman suffrage in the con-

UNCLE SAM   Have been waiting for you, Miss Wyoming. Welcome to my house.
MISS WYOMING   I bring with me a constitution giving equal rights to ALL.

On 28 June 1890, one day after the United States Senate approved
the Wyoming constitution, a cartoon in the Cheyenne Sun *lauded the*
new state's status as the first to grant women full voting rights.
Wyoming State Archives

stitution spoke in great numbers. Judge Melville C. Brown, who
had been a member of the second territorial legislature when the
repeal bill was introduced, sardonically suggested "submitting to
the people of Wyoming a separate and distinct proposition as to
whether a male citizen should be entitled to vote." C. W. Holden
of Uinta County, meanwhile, gave an impassioned plea, claiming, "rather than surrender the right which the women of this
territory have so long enjoyed, a privilege which they have not

only used with credit to themselves but with profit to the country, . . . we would rather remain in a territorial condition throughout the endless cycles of time." Former territorial governor John Hoyt agreed and expressed his willingness to "remain out of the union until a sentiment of justice shall prevail." Charles Burritt of Johnson County echoed this sentiment by stating that, in "believing that woman's suffrage is right, this convention has the courage, and this state has the courage, to go before congress and the world with this suffrage plank in its constitution, and if they will not let us in with [it] we will stay out forever."[8] After a heated and lively debate, the convention voted down Campbell's amendment, thirty to eight. Woman suffrage would be a part of Wyoming's proposed constitution.[9]

Concern over Congress's response still loomed as Wyoming prepared to send their newly drafted constitution to Washington, D.C., for approval. Nationally recognized suffrage supporter Henry Blackwell sent out letters to newspapers from members of Congress who reassured those concerned about possible rejection of state constitutions that granted woman suffrage. Senator Henry M. Teller, for example, told Blackwell that he was "confident that recognition of woman's suffrage in the constitutions of the proposed states will not in any way hinder, delay or endanger their admission."[10] Emboldened, supporters in the territorial legislature sent a message to Wyoming's congressional delegate instructing him to tell Congress, "We will remain out of the Union a hundred years rather than come in without woman suffrage."[11] Despite opposition at both the local and national level, Wyoming became the forty-fourth state in 1890, and the first to include woman suffrage in its constitution.

NOTES

1. T. A. Larson, "Woman Suffrage in Wyoming," *Pacific Northwest Quarterly* 56, no. 2 (1965): 62, 64; *Laramie Daily Sentinel*, 7 Sept. 1870; "Historical Correction," *Wyoming State Journal* (Lander), 14 Feb. 1919. The territorial legislature limited the rights women received in the 1869 constitution almost immediately after it was approved. Many focused on women's jury service, which opponents claimed disrupted home life and cost the courts additional money due to the need for additional bailiffs and accommodations. By 1871,

judges argued that jury service was not a guaranteed right of suffrage. No woman would serve on a jury in Wyoming again until 1950.

2. "The Suffrage Question," *Laramie Boomerang*, 19 July 1889.

3. "Woman Suffrage," ibid., 14 Sept. 1889.

4. "Statehood for Wyoming," *Cheyenne Daily Sun*, 8 Mar. 1890.

5. "The Great Debate," ibid., 18 Sept. 1889.

6. "Concerning Revenue," *Laramie Boomerang*, 26 Sept. 1889.

7. *See* Cecelia Wittmayer, "The 1889–1890 Woman Suffrage Campaign: A Need to Organize," *South Dakota History* 11 (Summer 1981): 199–226; Leslie Wheeler, "Woman Suffrage's Grey-Bearded Champion Comes to Montana," *Montana: The Magazine of Western History* 31 (Summer 1981): 2–13.

8. All quoted in Wyoming, *Journal and Debates of the Constitutional Convention of the State of Wyoming* (Cheyenne, 1893), p. 350, 353, 356–57.

9. "The Convention," *Cheyenne Daily Leader*, 18 Sept. 1889.

10. Quoted in "Woman's Suffrage," *Bill Barlow's Budget* (Douglas, Wyo.), 14 Aug. 1889.

11. Quoted in T. A. Larson, "Petticoats at the Polls: Woman suffrage in Territorial Wyoming," *Pacific Northwest Quarterly* 44, no. 2 (1953): 79. In the end, statehood won by votes of 139 to 127 in the House of Representatives and 29 to 18 in the Senate.

THE SOUTH DAKOTA SCANDINAVIAN TEMPERANCE SOCIETY AND WOMAN SUFFRAGE

LORI ANN LAHLUM

RESOLUTIONS:

1. Resolved, we proclaim that we oppose the sale of intoxicating drink regardless of whether it is carried out privately, by the state, or by the local community.
2. For our society's future and preservation, it is desirable and necessary that all power and might are used for this cause.
3. Whereas, woman has both intelligence and moral authority, as well as power and might, and like man can partake in service to the community, it is helpful that she has the right to vote on an equal basis as man.
4. Whereas, the traffic in alcohol is one of our society's greatest fiends, and women who have political rights will fight against such trafficking and for this cause that makes society better, we declare that woman is the same as man and has the right to cast her vote for the cause, and we therefore declare ourselves in favor of woman's right to vote.

—Proceedings, *The 5th Annual Meeting of the South Dakota Scandinavian Temperance Society, which met in Bradley on 21st, 22d, and 25th June 1898.*[1]

When the South Dakota Scandinavian Temperance Society met in the summer of 1898, a campaign was underway to enfranchise women, including foreign-born women who were not citizens, with an amendment eliminating the word "male" from the state's constitution. Another amendment on the ballot sought to give the state government authority over the production and sale of alcohol through a dispensary amendment to the constitution. The

Resolutioner:

1) Besluttet, at vi erklærer os afgjort imod al Trafik med berusende Drikke uanseet, enten den drives af Private eller af Stat og Kommune.

2) For vort Samfunds Fremgang og Bevarelse er det gunstigt og nødvendigt, at alle dets Evner og Kræfter tages i Brug.

3) Da Kvinden, baade hvad Intelligens og Moral angaar, har Evner og Kræfter, der ligesaavel som Mandens kan anvendes i Samfundets Tjeneste, er det gavnligt, at hun, hvad Stemmeretten angaar, bliver sat paa lige Fod med Manden.

4) Da Drikketrafiken er en af vort Samfunds største Fiender, og Kvinden som Regel vil bekjæmpe samme, vilde det særligt, hvad denne Sag betræffer, være til Samfundets Vel, om Kvinden ligesaavel som Manden fik Lov til at kaste sin Stemme mod den, og vi erklærer os derfor i Favør af Kvindens Stemmeret.

5) Besluttet, at nærværende Totalafholdsselskabs Aarsmøde udtaler sin Tak til disse Foreninger i og udenom Bradley, som har indbudt til Aarsmødet, for deres Gjestfrihed i at modtage og gjøre det saa hyggeligt og godt for Mødets Deltagere som muligt, tillige Tak til

temperance organization's resolutions, which called for the eradication of alcohol from society and the enfranchisement of women, complicate our understanding of connections between South Dakota's foreign-born population, prohibition, and woman suffrage. National leaders may have complained about the foreign-born population in South Dakota and the linkage of woman suffrage and temperance, or prohibition, measures, but among Scandinavians, and especially Norwegians, laws restricting or banning intoxicating spirits could, in fact, increase support for woman suffrage.

In 1900, Norwegians (foreign-born and of Norwegian parentage) made up 13 percent of the South Dakota population. At that time, South Dakota allowed aliens who had taken out their first papers and begun the process of naturalization to vote in elections. Just over 40 percent of male South Dakotans over age twenty-one were foreign-born in 1900. Of these, 58 percent had been naturalized, and another 17 percent had taken out first papers.[2] Thus, while a majority of the state's foreign-born male population had become citizens, slightly more than seventy-five hundred men who had not become citizens could still vote. In a state the size of South Dakota, the immigrant vote could be a deciding factor.

For the most part, the counties with the highest concentrations of Norwegians supported female suffrage and the dispensary law in 1898 at a level higher than the state average. The five counties with the highest percentages of Norwegian Americans in 1900 were Deuel (41 percent), Day (31 percent), Brookings (30 percent), Minnehaha (27 percent), and Kingsbury (24 percent). In 1898, approximately 60 percent of Kingsbury County voters cast their ballots in favor of female suffrage, far above the 46 percent statewide. In part, this outcome reflected the outsized presence of the Farmers' Alliance and the Populist/Independent Party in the county. Both Brookings County (53 percent) and Deuel County (50 percent—by two votes) supported the measure, while Minnehaha County recorded two percentage points higher, and Day County about one percentage point lower than the state average.[3] The 1898 dispensary amendment, which carried the state with 52 percent of the vote, found even higher rates of support in these five heavily Norwegian counties. Deuel County (66 percent), Day County (63 percent), and Kingsbury County (63 percent) all polled more than 60 percent of the vote, and Brookings County (57 percent) and Minnehaha County (55 percent) both outpaced the state average.[4]

Looking at how counties with large Norwegian American populations voted on woman suffrage and the dispensary measure suggests that suffragists might have been able to garner additional support in Norwegian American communities by linking their cause with prohibition. To be sure, many Norwegian Americans supported prohibition but not woman suffrage, especially those in the conservative Norwegian Synod. According to Dennis A. Norlin, not a single Lutheran minister spoke out in favor of woman suffrage in 1890. By the mid-1890s, however, some Hauge Synod churches began altering their constitutions to allow women to vote in congregational matters, a trend that continued

EQUALITY AT THE BALLOT BOX

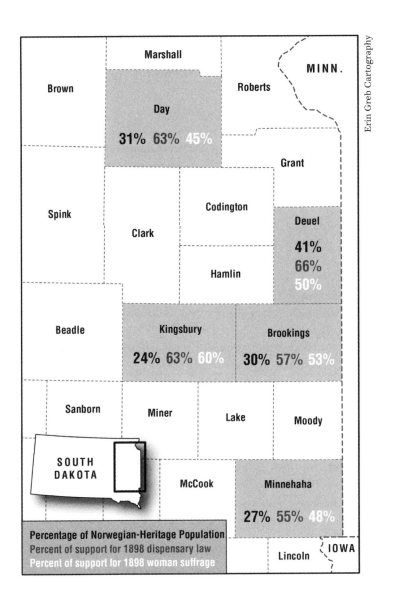

Percentage of Norwegian-Heritage Population
Percent of support for 1898 dispensary law
Percent of support for 1898 woman suffrage

into the early twentieth century. It was not unusual, however, for former Norwegian Synod churches to deny voting rights to women at congregational meetings until the 1940s and 1950s.[5] There were important ethnic differences within the Lutheran church, and more work needs to be done on the relationship between Lutheran synodical affiliation, ethnicity, and support for woman suffrage. The example of the South Dakota Scandinavian Temperance Society nonetheless helps us think about the ways in which linking woman suffrage and prohibition could garner support for both in some immigrant communities.

NOTES

I would like to thank Jeff Sauve of the Norwegian American Historical Association (NAHA) for securing the image for me and facilitating research trips to NAHA that have been at the core of my academic pursuits for twenty years.

1. Author's translation of *Beretning om Det 5te Aarsmöde af Syd Dakota Skandinaviske Afholdsselskab afholdt i Bradley, S. Dak., den 21se, 22de og 25de Juni 1898* (Eau Claire, Wisc., 1898), p. 21, Temperance Movement Papers, P0574, Norwegian American Historical Association, Northfield, Minnesota. All four of the society's officers were men, but women held two of the three directorships. *See* the report's inside cover for the officers and directors. Knute Lewis of Kingsbury County (and future Prohibition Party candidate) served as president. Although the organization used the term Scandinavian and welcomed Norwegians, Swedes, and Danes, the vast majority of Scandinavians in South Dakota were Norwegians.

2. Carleton C. Qualey, *Norwegian Settlement in the United States* (New York: Arno Press & the *New York Times*, 1970), p. 134; U.S., Senate, Immigration Commission, *Statistical Review of Immigration, 1820–1910: Distribution of Immigrants, 1850–1910* (Washington, D.C.: GPO, 1911), pp. 430–31.

3. I use the figures compiled by Qualey, *Norwegian Settlement in the United States*, pp. 238–39. These numbers are a bit low because by this time a number of third-generation Norwegians appeared on the census with no reference to their grandparents. South Dakota, *Official Vote of South Dakota by Counties: From October, 1889, to November, 1914* (Sioux Falls, 1914), p. 57. Finding township votes on the woman suffrage measure has been challenging. I have not been able to locate consistent township data beyond Day County. In Grant County, Elwin Rogers looked at the 1910 suffrage vote at the township level. He found that one of the county's "most heavily Scandinavian" townships voted to extend the franchise to women, but the county rejected the amendment (430 yes to 824 no). *See* Elwin E. Rogers, "Almost Scandinavia: Scandinavian Immigrant Experience in Grant County, 1877–1920," *South Dakota Historical Collection* 41 (1982): 367; *Statistical Review of Immigration*, p. 190.

4. *Official Vote*, p. 59. In Grant County, all of the townships Rogers classified as Scandinavian passed the 1898 prohibition measure. Rogers, "Almost

Scandinavia," p. 374. I have done analysis for some townships on the dispensary vote.

5. Dennis A. Norlin, "The Suffrage Movement and South Dakota Churches: Radicals and the Status Quo, 1890," *South Dakota History* 14 (Dec. 1984): 309, 311, 313–14; Lori Ann Lahlum, "Women, Work, and Community in Rural Norwegian America, 1840–1920, in *Norwegian American Women: Migration, Communities, and Identities*, ed. Betty A. Bergland and Lahlum (Saint Paul: Minnesota Historical Society Press, 2011), pp. 96–98.

FRAUENSTIMMRECHT IN SÜD-DAKOTA
German-Language Newspapers in South Dakota on Woman Suffrage

KELLY O'DEA

To the voters of South Dakota!

Wherever woman suffrage was introduced in this country a tax increase has followed.

On 25 October 1916, the "Pierre Capital Journal," the official publication of the woman suffragists explained: "The adoption of woman suffrage must be followed by a campaign for a law, which forces women and men to cast their votes."

German voters, do you wish higher taxes and compulsory voting?

If not, then vote 'NO' on 7 November regarding Amendment No. 6.

Amendment No. 6, on the longest, separate ballot, pertains to woman suffrage.

—Women's Anti Suffrage Ass'n of So. Dak.[1]

Throughout the late-nineteenth and early-twentieth centuries, Germans from Europe and Germans from Russia immigrated to Dakota Territory and, later, South Dakota in large numbers. The state's German-speaking population soon supported many German-language newspapers. Woman suffrage was a regular topic in at least two of these publications, the *Dakota Freie Presse* ("Dakota Free Press") and the *Deutscher Herold* ("German Herald"). In 1916, for example, the Women's Anti-Suffrage Association of South Dakota bought multiple advertisements in the *Deutscher Herold* that warned against Amendment No. 6, which would have enfranchised South Dakota women. When this measure failed, South Dakota suffragists believed that German immigrants' lack of support cost them a victory.[2] While much research on woman suffrage in South Dakota focuses on English-language

An die Stimmgeber von Süd Dakota!

Wo immer Frauenstimmrecht in diesem Lande eingeführt wurde, folgte eine Erhöhung der Steuern.

Am 25. Oktober 1916 erklärte das „Pierre Capital Journal", das Organ der Frauenstimmrechtler, editoriell:

„Der Annahme des Frauenstimmrechts muß eine Kampagne für ein Gesetz folgen, welches Frauen und Männer zwingt, ihre Stimme abzugeben."

Deutsche Stimmgeber wünscht Ihr höhere Steuern und Stimm-Zwang?

Wenn nicht,

Dann stimmt „NO" am 7. November betreffs Amendements No. 6

Amendement No. 6, auf dem längsten separaten Stimmzettel betrifft Frauenstimmrecht.

Women's Anti Suffrage Ass'n of So. Dak.

sources, German-language newspapers provide insight into the attitudes of the German-speaking populations in South Dakota and the effect they had on the failure of suffrage amendments. These newspapers also suggest why women's enfranchisement lacked support in many German communities.

German-speaking residents supported some sixty-four publications in South Dakota before becoming fully assimilated into American society. These newspapers provided an important tool for immigrants, "providing instruction in the history, ideals, and procedures of the new country." The *Dakota Freie Presse*, which politicians referred to as "the bible of the Russian-Germans," was one of the state's longest-running foreign-language newspapers. Originally based in Yankton, it relocated to Aberdeen in 1909. While some German newspapers simply translated articles from English-language newspapers, the editors of the *Dakota Freie Presse* and *Deutscher Herold* primarily published material written by German reporters and German community members. Both provided regional, national, and international news. Until the outbreak of World War I, news from Germany and Russia received particular attention. After its relocation to Aberdeen, the *Dakota Freie Presse* struck a Republican tone in a majority of its political articles, while the *Deutscher Herold* more often espoused Democratic viewpoints. Although they had essentially become rival publications, neither supported a woman suffrage amendment.[3]

In the months leading up to the vote on woman suffrage in 1914, German-language newspapers included material on the topic. The 3 September 1914 *Deutscher Herold* included a short blurb in its "Politics" section that asked rhetorically if women's influence would make a political campaign "more decent." The author answered: "Not in the least. After all, the editor of the state organ of woman suffragists in South Dakota has already insulted the Germans because of their negative attitude on this issue."[4] This article may be a response to a 27 November 1913 editorial in the *South Dakota Messenger*, the Universal Franchise League's official paper, in which Ruth B. Hipple wrote critically about German and German Russian men, who "could not be expected to be in favor of equal suffrage when they allowed their own women to take week-old babies out into the fields while they worked."[5]

In a *Deutscher Herold* letter to the editor from 22 January 1914, Fred Barth from Olivet, South Dakota, claimed he had "respect and honor" for women, but he did not support woman suffrage because he doubted "one of one-hundred women would make use of it." He claimed he had "already spoken to many women" about suffrage, who told him they already had enough to do at home. "They want to nurture their children in the position that

God has instructed them," he concluded. The opening of Barth's letter also referenced the inconvenience that prohibition would pose for traveling farmers who visited pubs and saloons on their way home. Barth argued, "the community has previously had little criminal activity." Presumably, he meant that the amendment on prohibition was unnecessary.[6]

As the 1914 election drew closer, the political section continued to argue against woman suffrage. A 10 September article quoted a pro-suffrage claim, "No political corruption will exist anymore under universal suffrage for women and men," before asking: "Since when is the female sex naturally immune to contestation and influence? If 'Frau' policeman Murphy turns out to be just as weak with bribes as Herr policemen Murphy, where is the 'reform'?"[7] The *Deutscher Herold* also published a translated article from the *Deadwood Pioneer Times* that offered, "The answers of a woman from Deadwood, on the arguments of woman suffragists." The 22 October 1914 article listed ten claims from pro-suffrage advocates to which a woman identified as "D. H." responded. The first read, "Advocates of woman suffrage claim 'the right to vote is inherent or innate.'" D. H. answered: "In truth, it is a duty, not a privilege. The compulsion or the duty to exercise the right to vote is often a burden that most women would shrink from." The numbered list concluded with a claim about the educational value of the right to vote. In opposition, D. H. responded: "For some women who have no plans for anything else, it may seem like a duty to mix themselves in politics. . . . But for the God-fearing, faithful, and natural mother . . . politics has no appeal. With more such 'old-fashioned' German mothers, the world will become ever purer and better."[8]

Although many state and national suffragists had attempted to divorce themselves from the temperance movement, content on woman suffrage and prohibition often appeared side-by-side in the German-language newspapers. The *Deutscher Herold* placed the 1916 advertisement denouncing Amendment 6 directly next to a page-length advertisment about voting "NO" on Amendment 7, the prohibition amendment. The anti-prohibition advertisement did not reference suffragists, and the only reference to women was part of a pro-prohibition argument that it aimed to discredit. On 24 October 1916, the *Dakota Freie Presse* published an almost identical anti-prohibition advertisement.[9]

The news coverage prior to the 1916 election not only contained articles referencing anti-prohibition and anti-suffrage separately, it occasionally connected the issues. The 19 October 1916 issue of the *Deutscher Herold* included an advertisement promoting an anti-prohibition lecture from Clarence Darrow, "the famous defense lawyer of the Workers' Rights and Chicago Advocate," planned for 23 October. An article titled "Personal Freedom against Prohibition" followed, asking if "the opponents of woman suffrage [would] speak up." The article also invited "all Germans of the city" to attend Darrow's speech about the "dangers of prohibition." It then listed dates for evening lectures by the Women's Anti-Suffrage Association of South Dakota and officials from the state and national associations of Women Against General Women's Voting, suggesting, "No German voter and no woman should be missing [from the events]."[10]

As the election approached, the *Dakota Freie Presse* and the *Deutscher Herold* also included explanatory articles on the ballot measures. In the *Dakota Freie Presse* for Amendment 6, on woman suffrage, editor John Schroeder declared: "No. 6 is . . . a measure of the prohibitionists who hope to suppress the personal freedom with the help of the women. Make a thick cross before the word 'No.'"[11] Schroeder used the German word *Weiber,* meaning "female," instead of *Frauen,* meaning "women." The subtly derogatory phrasing suggested real German women and men did not support suffrage. In the *Deutscher Herold,* however, the proposed sample ballot simply suggested that voters choose "No" on Amendments 6 and 7 without additional reasoning. The "Staatsverband" (State Association) article directly after the sample ballot suggested, "Furthermore, vote like a man against Amendment No. 7 (Prohibition) and No. 6 (Woman Suffrage)."[12]

After the November election, news coverage focused on election returns. The *Deutscher Herold* published results on both amendments for Sioux Falls in a table of ward results (with the exception of ward six). In wards three, five, seven, eight, ten, and eleven, the majority had voted "Yes" on the amendment for woman suffrage. At the end of the month, in a 30 November 1916 article, the same newspaper published the official voting results for the state, showing a majority of South Dakotans had voted against the woman suffrage amendment by a margin of less than five thousand votes. The *Dakota Freie Presse* included the national results of the presidential election but said nothing else about Amendments 6 and 7.[13]

In 1918, both newspapers were curiously silent on woman suffrage. When the *Dakota Freie Presse* published its weekly edition on 5 November 1918, election day, nothing about the issue appeared. Throughout 1918, the *Dakota Freie Presse* made only a couple of references to the topic, both as side notes in articles about President Woodrow Wilson's appeal for a federal amendment in favor of woman suffrage. The articles claimed that Wilson believed suffrage rights should be extended because of the "value of women."[14] The *Deutscher Herold* included only one odd and incorrect reference to Hawaii being "blessed with suffrage for women." The two sentences concluded a page in the newspaper dedicated to regional and national news, which provided no further context concerning Hawaii.[15]

While most German arguments against woman suffrage revolved around the preservation of the mother and her duties to the family, the association between anti-prohibition and anti-suffrage sentiments also drove opposition. After passage of the state's prohibition amendment in 1916, news coverage on woman suffrage dropped dramatically. The outbreak of World War I proved even more consequential for South Dakota's Germans. Amid rising anti-German sentiment, the *Dakota Freie Presse* almost exclusively dedicated its front page to news of the war. It moved to New Ulm, Minnesota, in 1918. The *Deutscher Herold*, meanwhile, closed that same year.[16]

NOTES

Many thanks to Carol Leibiger of the University of South Dakota for constructive suggestions and reviewing my translations. And a special thanks to Molly Rozum for this wonderful opportunity and her support throughout the research and writing processes.

1. Author's translation of advertisement, *Deutscher Herold*, 19 Oct., 2 Nov. 1916.

2. Patricia O'Keefe Easton, "Woman Suffrage in South Dakota: The Final Decade, 1911–1920," *South Dakota History* 13 (Fall 1983): 208, 224.

3. Anton H. Richter, "'Gebt ihr den Vorzug': The German-Language Press of North and South Dakota," *South Dakota History* 10 (Summer 1980): 189–94, 196–98.

4. *Deutscher Herold*, 3 Sept. 1914. Original text: "Wird der Einfluss der Frau eine politische Kampagne anständiger machen?—Nach den Proben, die wir bis jetzt bereits gesehen, nicht im geringsten. Hat doch die Redakteurin des Staatlichen Organs der Frauen-Stimmrechtlerinnen in South Dakota die Deutschen wegen ihrer ablehnenden Haltung in dieser Frage schon geradezu beschimpft."

5. Quoted in Easton, "Woman Suffrage in South Dakota," pp. 210–14.

6. *Deutscher Herold*, 22 Jan. 1914. Original text: "Wir sind auch gegan das Frauenstimmrecht. Ich glaube geiß, daß von unseren deutschen Frauen nicht eine aus hundert ist, die Gebrauch davon machen würde. Ich habe schon mit vielen Frauen darüber gesprochen, erhielt aber immer zur Antwort: 'Wir haven genug zu hause zu tun und wollen unsere Kinder gut erziehen, das ist unser Platz, welchen uns der liebe Gott angewiesen hat'. Ich hoffe, daß unsere nächste Gesetzgebung darauf bezüglicht Bills in den Papierkorb wander läßt, oder sie verbrennt, damit sie nicht wieder zu in Vorschein kommen. Zum Schluß will ich bemerken, daß ich nicht etwa ein Feind des weiblichen Geschlechts bin, sondern dasselbe hochachte und ehre!"

7. Ibid., 10 Sept. 1914. Original text: "'Keine politische Korruption wird mehr unter allgemeinem Stimmrecht für Frauen und Männer existieren [*sic*].' . . . Seit wann ist das weibliche Geschlecht von Natur gefeit gegen Anfechtung und Beeinflussung? . . . Und wenn 'Frau' Polizist Murphy sich Bestechungskünsten gegenüber als eben so schwach erweist, wie Herr Polizist Murphy, wo bleibt dann die 'Reform'?"

8. Ibid., 22 Oct. 1914. Original text: "Befürworter des Frauenstimmrechts behaupten, 'das Stimmrecht sei ein angestammtes oder angeborenes Recht.'" "Antwort: In Wahrheit ist es eine Pflicht, und nicht ein Privilegium. Der Zwang oder die Pflicht, das Stimmrecht auszuüben, ist oft eine Bürde, vor welcher die meisten Frauen zurückschrecken würden." "Das Stimmrecht wirkt in erzieherischer Weise, sagen die Frauenstimmrechtler, und Frauen würden durch daselbe fähiger warden und in verständigere Wege geleitet. Antwort: Manchen Frauen, welche sonst nichts anderes vorhaben, mag es als Pflicht erscheinen, sich in die Politik zu mischen und ihre Frauenwürde damit zu beschmutzen. Aber für die gottesfürchtige, treuherzige und natürliche Mutter, wenn sie dadurch auch etwas altmodisch erscheint, hat die Politik keine Anziehungskraft. Mit mehr solchen 'altmodischen' deutschen Müttern wird die Welt immer reiner und besser werden."

9. Ibid., 2 Nov. 1916; *Dakota Freie Presse* (Aberdeen, S.Dak.), 24 Oct. 1916.

10. *Deutscher Herold*, 19 Oct. 1916. Original text: "'Persönliche Freiheit gegen Prohibition' Die Gegnerinnen des Frauenstimmrechts melden sich zum Wort. Während der berühmte Verteidiger der Arbeiterrechte und Chicagoer Advocat, Clarence Darrow, heute Abend, den 19 Oktober, im hiesigen Auditorium eine gewaltige Rede gegen die Gefahren von Prohibition halt, wozu alle Deutschen der Stadt dringend eingeladen sind, wisen wir zugleich auf einen anderen Redeabend hin, unter Leitung der Womens Anti-Suffrage Association of South Dakota." "Am nächsten Montag Abend, den 23 Oktober, findet ebenfalls im Auditorium ein hochinteressanter Redeabend statt, bei dem Beamtinnen der Staatlichen und nationalen Vereinigung von Frauen, welche gegen das allgemeine Frauenstimmrecht sind, ihre besten und überzeugendsten Redekräfte ins Feld führen werden." "Kein deutscher Stimmgeber und keine Frau sollte fehlen."

11. *Dakota Freie Presse*, 31 Oct. 1916. Original text: "No. 6 ist eine Gesetzvorlage zur Einfürung des Frauenstimmrechts in Süd-Dakota. Auch eine Maßregel der Prohibitionisten, welche hoffen, mit Hilfe der Weiber die persönliche Freiheit zu unterdrücken. Macht ein dickes Kreuz vor das Wort 'No.'"

12. *Deutscher Herold*, 26 Oct. 1916. Original text: "Ferner stimmt wie ein Mann gegen Amendment No. 7 (Prohibition) und No. 6 (Frauenstimmrecht)."

13. Ibid., 9, 30 Nov. 1916; *Dakota Freie Presse*, 14 Nov. 1916.

14. *Dakota Freie Presse*, 3 Dec. 1918. Original text: "Bezugnehmend auf die Frauenfrage sprach er über das Wert der Frauen und appellierte wiederum zugunsten des Stimmrechts für Frauen auf dem Wege eines Bundes-Amendments."

15. *Deutscher Herold*, 27 June 1918. Original text: "Auch Hawaii soll jetzt mit dem Frauenstimmrecht beglükt werden. Wenn das die sel'ge Lil' noch erlebt hätte!" Hawaii Territory did not pass territorial woman suffrage before the ratification of the Nineteenth Amendment, which also applied to territorial voting, and was not admitted as a state until 1959. In June 1918, however, the United States Congress passed a bill that enabled the Hawaiian territorial legislature to enfranchise women. Congress had inserted the word "male" into the territorial constitution it created with the Hawaiian Organic Act of 1900. Allison L. Sneider, *Suffragists in an Imperial Age: U.S. Expansion and the Woman Question, 1870–1929* (New York: Oxford University Press, 2008), pp. 90–92, 114–15, 128–29; Ida Husted Harper, ed. *History of Woman Suffrage*, Vol. 6 (New York: J. J. Little & Ives Co., 1922), pp. 715–19.

16. Richter, "Gebt ihr den Vorzug," pp. 196–98. On gender relations in German-American communities, *see* Linda Schelbitzki Pickle, *Contented among Strangers: Rural German-Speaking Women and Their Families in*

the Nineteenth-Century Midwest (Urbana: University of Illinois Press, 1996), pp. 23–38, 72–73, 138–40, 146–47, 185–92; Ruth Seifert, "Women's Pages in the German-American Radical Press, 1910–1914: The Debate on Socialism, Emancipation, and the Suffrage," in *The German-American Radical Press: The Shaping of a Left Political Culture, 1850–1940*, ed. Elliott Shore, Ken Fones-Wolf, and James P. Danky (Urbana: University of Illinois Press, 1992), pp. 127–28.

PART 2

"THE WOMEN VOTED"

School Suffrage in Dakota Territory and South Dakota

RUTH PAGE JONES

An 1890 report of a school election in Hurley, South Dakota, captured both the excitement and strangeness women experienced when casting their first votes in public elections: "Some of the women approached the ballot box, with fear and trembling, and at first refused to pass their ballots over to the judge to be deposited. They soon gained courage, however, and when they again take part in an election they will be ready to corner an opponent, male or female, and talk for their favorite candidate."[1] Two months before the Hurley election, a women's convention in Rapid City had drawn a number of women to select a slate of female contenders to run for the school board there. On 10 April, in a filled meeting hall, the attendees chose Lizzie Kercheval, Helen Lewis, Lydia A. Knull, and Anna S. Cooper as their candidates. Soon after, the Republican Party endorsed the same nominees for four of eight open seats, while Democrats fielded eight men and no women.[2] The *Rapid City Republican* announced, "Tomorrow a selection will be made at the polls and the sisters, wives and mothers stand equal before the law." Calling out Democrats for not endorsing the women's slate, the newspaper predicted, "The female quartette will, by the votes of their friends, pulverize these mossbacks at the polls tomorrow."[3] Whether they voted tentatively, as the women in Hurley had, or with confidence, about one-fourth of the city's eligible women turned out, with results showing wins for three of the female candidates: Kercheval, Lewis, and Knull.[4] These women and countless others participated in public elections decades before the United States granted all women equal voting rights in 1920. Often limited to voting on school matters only, many women nonetheless seized this opportunity to enter electoral politics and helped change perceptions about woman suffrage in the process.

The territories of the Northern Great Plains—Wyoming, Dakota, and Montana—granted varying degrees of woman suffrage earlier than most other areas of the country. Wyoming Territory gave women full suffrage in 1869, while the territories of Montana and Dakota limited women to voting only on school matters, establishing that right from 1879 in Dakota and 1883 in Montana. When the territories achieved statehood, the Dakotas and Montana in 1889 and Wyoming in 1890, women retained their prior territorial suffrage rights. Montana later amended its constitution to give women full suffrage in 1914. North Dakota women gained presidential suffrage in 1917, and South Dakota women gained full suffrage rights in 1918, two years before woman suffrage became legal nationwide.[5]

Meanwhile, women exercised their school suffrage rights. Casting votes, campaigning for political positions, and serving as elected officials helped them gain experience and respect, thereby normalizing the concept of women voting and holding office. While most scholarly treatments of the woman suffrage movement have focused primarily on the efforts of state and national leaders and organizations to achieve full voting rights, few have studied the role partial suffrage, especially school suffrage, played in that movement.[6] Women's use of limited suffrage in South Dakota changed the social reality and increased support for women's right to participate fully in the franchise. The progression of school suffrage legislation in South Dakota between 1879 and 1920 and the ways that women took advantage of those laws, both as voters and as elected officials, reveals that school suffrage contributed significantly to efforts to secure full voting rights for women.

Many American women had access to the ballot box on a limited basis before achieving full voting rights through the Nineteenth Amendment to the United States Constitution. Starting with Kentucky, as early as 1838, and then Kansas in 1861, several states granted some type of limited voting rights: in school or municipal elections, in presidential primaries, or on tax and bond issues. Seven states or territories gave women some level of school suffrage before Dakota Territory lawmakers included women as voters in official school meetings in 1879. Upon statehood in 1876, Colorado granted school suffrage rights. In 1893, the state's newly elected Populist governor, Davis Waite, lauded women's participation in school elections, noting, "The heavens have not fallen and the efficacy of the public schools have been greatly improved."[7] That same year, Colorado voters approved a constitutional amendment granting women full voting rights. By 1900, Wyoming, Colorado, Utah, and Idaho had provided full woman suffrage and twenty-five states and territories, including Montana, North Dakota, and South Dakota, had granted school suffrage to women. By the time the Nineteenth Amendment became law, women could exercise full suffrage in fifteen states plus Alaska Territory. In another sixteen states, they held school suffrage rights. With additional states allowing municipal or other limited voting rights, only eight states had failed to grant women any type of access to the ballot before 1920.[8]

Most partial-suffrage successes stemmed from grassroots campaigns organized by local activists rather than through any coordinated national efforts. Concentrating their work on achieving full suffrage through a constitutional amendment, suffrage leaders Susan B. Anthony and Elizabeth Cady Stanton of the National Woman's Suffrage Association (NWSA) did not pursue partial suffrage as a significant strategy. They believed the tactic to be counterproductive, as low-turnout elections would feed into the anti-suffrage argument that women did not want the vote. While Lucy Stone and Henry Blackwell of the American Woman Suffrage Association (AWSA) focused on achieving full suffrage state by state, they sometimes encouraged local activists to work with legislators to achieve any kind of progress, arguing in their weekly newsletter, *The Woman's Column*, "the right of women to vote for anything concedes the principal," and "nothing educates the public mind like seeing women legally empowered to vote," as "every step promotes a further step."[9]

At the local level, school suffrage advocates believed they could overcome societal objections to women's engagement in politics by arguing that voting on school issues properly fit woman's role

After gaining school suffrage, some South Dakota women used their roles as teachers in rural schoolhouses, such as this one near Philip, as an entry point into local politics. South Dakota State Historical Society

as mother. Clarina Howard Nichols, one of the first women to promote school suffrage publicly, unsuccessfully lobbied the 1852 Vermont legislature before securing that right in the 1861 Kansas constitution, thereby creating an opening for similar successes in other states. Rather than promoting equal rights for women, Nichols maintained that voting on school matters simply extended women's role in childhood education and did not compromise their femininity. In so doing, she promoted school suffrage as an opening for women to engage in politics in a nonthreatening manner and a chance to prove their value as voting citizens.[10]

An early supporter of school suffrage, Dakota Territory gave women limited rights to vote in school elections and hold elective office, but a lack of consistency and clarity in education and election laws, even after statehood, created barriers to the ballot box. As territorial legislators and, later, South Dakota lawmakers modified education statutes, they wrote separate laws for three distinct school systems, producing different and changing rules regarding types of elective positions, dates of school elections, and qualifications for those running for office, as well as for voting. Prior to 1883, the "district plan" permitted any number of school districts per county, usually with one school per district. That law allowed voters to make most decisions at district meetings, such as voting on taxes and deciding on school sites. They could also "choose persons" for the offices of director, clerk, and treasurer. No private ballot was required.[11] In addition, between 1875 and 1881, a second set of laws authorized incorporated cities, towns, and villages with at least 175 school-aged children to establish independent school districts. Initially, mayors and city councils or presidents and boards of trustees elected members to those boards of education, selecting two members from each voting ward to serve two year terms.[12]

As the number of school districts grew to 1,644 in forty-four counties in 1883, lawmakers revised the district system to reduce the number of school boards, provide for more uniform decisions, and transfer more authority to governing boards. The new law established the third system, the "township plan," which aligned school districts with civil townships and established one school board per township with authority over all township schools. While the township law applied to all new counties, fifteen older counties could choose to maintain their schools under the old district system, and independent school districts operated under their own set of statutes.[13] Within each of these three separate education systems, women obtained distinct voting rights.

Each time legislators rewrote education statutes, they modified voting rules, sometimes expanding and sometimes limiting the female franchise in school matters. The 1879 education law included women for the first time by modifying the definition of voters at district school meetings and shifting voting rights from "free white males" to "all persons over the age of twenty-one." The law continued to require all voters to meet certain citizenship and residency rules. According to the law for school districts,

"The Women Voted"

women could vote at school meetings on school officers, tax issues, teachers' wages, schoolhouse locations, and other items.[14] The 1879 law did not apply to independent school districts that had their own specific statues.

In 1883, the new township plan effectively barred women from participating as candidates and from voting for school officers because the law required school township boards to be made up of "qualified electors of the county." Only men could vote in county elections. Some women "belonging to and forming a particular school, who are parents, guardians or other persons having in charge children of school age," however, could vote at school meetings.[15] The law acknowledged that mothers had some rights to participate in decision-making regarding schools, but those rights were limited. For example, only male voters could cast ballots to elect township school boards because those ballots included races for additional township offices, for which women could not vote. While each township board managed all schools within its boundaries, each school could hold its own meeting where both men and women with school-aged children, living in the attendance area for that school, could vote. The law did not require paper ballots for school meetings at individual schools. Without the right to elect officers or make taxing and bonding decisions, voting at school meetings gave women limited authority.

Territorial legislators modified school statutes again in 1887. This time, they expanded women's authority by calling for school elections to be held the same day as the annual school meeting rather than during township or county elections. Women could now vote for elected school officials, including county superintendent. In addition, the law extended voting rights to "all resident taxpayers," male or female, including those without school-aged children. The law also called for the public, rather than city councils, to elect school officers in independent school districts. Those living in counties operating under the 1879 school district law, rather than township law, could still vote by those earlier rules, giving some women more rights than others depending on where they lived.[16]

When South Dakota became a state in 1889, the state constitution codified women's school suffrage rights, identifying who could vote, when they could vote, and which offices they could hold. According to the constitution, "Any woman having the qualifications enumerated in Section 1, of this article, as to age, residence and citizenship, and including those now qualified by the laws of the territory, may vote at any election held solely for school purposes, and may hold any office in this State except as otherwise provided in this constitution."[17] Regarding who could vote, the phrase "including those now qualified by the laws of the territory" received clarification on 21 April 1890, when state attorney general Robert Dolard appeared to expand women's voting rights by including "those in addition thereto, if any, who under the school law had a right to vote by reason of having school children in charge."[18] Whether that ruling addressed residency rules or added voting rights, for example, to noncitizen women, remains unclear. Some women tested that theory in 1890, when the votes of two Scandinavian women in Slaughter were challenged because they had not taken out naturalization papers.[19]

Although the constitution specified women could vote "at any election held solely for school purposes," different interpretations of that phrase meant women could vote on school questions in some cities but not others. While township voters elected school trustees at their annual school elections in June, cities with independent districts selected school trustees during municipal elections. Some locales hostile to the idea of women voting simply failed to provide women with separate school ballots. For example, judges of elections in Madison refused to accept women's votes, even though several tried to vote. Expressing disdain for women's rights, and possibly reflecting community sentiment, a local newspaper ridiculed their attempt, as noted by the pro-suffrage *Madison Sentinel*.[20] In Rapid City, women met with greater success when the mayor and city council ordered two sets of ballot boxes for each ward, separating ballots for school board members and school treasurer from those for mayor and other city offices.[21] The third clause, specifying that women "may hold any office in this State except as otherwise provided in this constitution," essentially restricted women from running for any office other than those related to education. In addition to local school offices, women could run for county and state superintendent of public instruction. School suffrage, though, did not include the right to vote for those positions, as they appeared on general election ballots in November, an election not held "solely for school purposes."[22]

New legislation in 1893 reinforced women's right to vote for school trustees by requiring two ballot boxes at each polling place, one for city ballots and one for school ballots. The *Hot Springs Weekly Star* reported that those boxes should be "so arranged as to be accessible to all persons entitled to vote at school elections. As women are entitled to vote at all school elections in South Dakota it is expected a large number will be at the polls."[23] After 1893, only social custom and lack of interest kept women from voting in school elections.

In the state's last attempt to expand school suffrage laws, legislators in 1893 agreed to submit two constitutional amendments to the voters the following year. The South Dakota Educational Association formally requested this legislation after the organization's annual meeting in 1892. The first amendment removed the restriction preventing people from holding the county office for more than two terms. The second amendment allowed women to vote for any school office, expanding that right to include county and state superintendents of public instruction. Voters in 1894 rejected both amendments, with only 28 percent voicing approval for the first one and a minority of 43 percent supporting the second one. The attempt to expand voting rights failed by 5,672 votes in that low-turnout election. Exhibiting little interest in either measure, only about one-half of those voting in the governor's race voted on the two amendments.[24]

In part, these amendments failed because no one, including suffrage leaders, organized a campaign to advance compelling reasons for voting "yes." Several factors contributed to suffragists' lack of zeal in promoting the amendments. That same year, suffrage proponents had successfully petitioned the state senate to extend women's voting rights to include city and town elections but failed to gain approval in the house. That disappointing loss may have discouraged them from promoting amendments that seemed to yield such small gains.[25] Proponents of the amendments also assumed that the measures would pass on their own merits, and therefore, voters needed little persuasion. State Woman's Christian Temperance Union (WCTU) officials expressed such assurance in the *Union Signal*, the national WCTU weekly newspaper, claiming, "The outlook for the passage for this proposed amendment to the constitution is most flattering." They expressed similar confidence a few months later: "It is hoped that the 'men people' will feel that we have rights as well as they and cast their votes accordingly."[26] In her 1902 history of the state suffrage movement, proponent Alice M. A. Pickler confirmed their misplaced confidence, explaining, "As there seemed to be no objection to women's voting for school trustees it was not supposed there would be any to extending the privilege for the other school officers."[27] Some state newspapers also shared this assumption. The *Turner County Herald* confidently stated, "to the first two propositions there can be no serious objection."[28] Local voters voiced a contrary opinion, with 71 percent voting to defeat term extension and 69 percent voting to defeat expansion of school suffrage.[29]

State suffrage leaders also prioritized temperance over suffrage. In this era, the most ardent suffragists were also ardent prohibitionists. Leading both movements, Anna R. Simmons and Emma A. Cranmer, officers of the South Dakota Equal Rights Association, endorsed legislation for the amendments in 1893 while also lobbying on temperance matters as officers of the state Woman's Christian Temperance Union. The state's prohibition law, approved by voters in 1889, barely survived a legislative vote in 1893 to resubmit the issue to voters. If temperance-friendly lawmakers failed to win the legislature the following year, the issue might go to voters again. Their fervent desire to save prohibition dominated women's activism in that election. As a result, the WCTU did not place much emphasis on the amendments. Kate B. Haines, legislative superintendent of the state WCTU, for example, described efforts to fight resubmission but made no mention of the upcoming amendments in her report to the 1893 national meeting.[30] In the following year's minutes, corresponding secretary Emma P. Myers wrote about the importance of the fall election, with women pledging their "earnest and unwearied efforts" to secure wins for their candidates. Again, she said nothing about the amendments.[31] Just after the election, the *Union*

Signal report for South Dakota once more asserted that all of the organization's efforts had focused on securing "the election of legislative candidates pledged against resubmission and the defeat of those favoring the same."[32] Their drive to preserve the prohibition law superseded their desire to obtain incremental advantages in school suffrage. Lack of an active campaign undoubtedly contributed to the defeat of the amendments. Whatever the reason—lack of enthusiasm, naive assumption of success, or pursuit of a different cause—by failing to educate voters on the merits of the two amendments, those supporting full suffrage lost an opportunity to advocate for the expansion of women's voting rights.

Dating back to the first Dakota school suffrage law passed in 1879, local newspapers reported on those voting rights and women voters, sometimes positively and other times negatively. In 1879, for example, the *Canton Advocate* announced, "Our Dakota Legislature has conferred the right of suffrage upon women to the extent that they can vote at school district meetings."[33] Several territorial newspapers highlighted women's modified suffrage rights in 1887, with more than one paper, including the *Turner County Herald*, announcing that women over age twenty-one with school-aged children could vote in school elections. These notices revealed a dismissive attitude towards women voting, however, concluding: "That [law] will evidently admit all ladies of the required age who live where there are school children. The restriction is evidently intended as an encouragement to the production of juvenile population."[34] That same year, rather than ridicule the female vote, the *Wessington Springs Herald* encouraged women: "Remember the school elections next Tuesday. Wife, take the children, go with your husband and vote. You are as much interested as to who shall control the schools and teach your children as is your husband." Three years later, the newspaper again encouraged women to vote at the school election, "I trust that every woman will feel it her duty to accompany her husband to the voting place and, perhaps for the first time, exercise the right of suffrage."[35] While some newspapers encouraged women to vote and others ridiculed the concept, those reports nevertheless raised awareness regarding women's right to vote.

Interest in voting increased in 1890, the year after the state constitution codified school suffrage for women. With a vote scheduled for that November to amend the constitution and obtain full suffrage, motivated women may have been eager to prove a point.[36] As the *Aberdeen News* suggested, "There will be an opportunity for the friends of woman suffrage to demonstrate the sincerity of their sex in desiring to exercise the elective franchise."[37] Although some women, depending upon their type of school system, had previously voted, that year would be the first opportunity for many. In addition to the large female turnout in Rapid City, where three women won school board seats in April, women took to the polls throughout the state. In a hotly contested school election in nearby Banner Township, the *Hot Springs Star* noted that among sixty-one people casting votes, "about twenty ladies voted, being the first time any woman ever voted in Oelrichs."[38] After the 1890 September school election in Huron, the *Wessington Springs Herald* reported that 240 women out of 714 voters turned in ballots. Although numbers for total female participation in South Dakota during this era are unavailable, a report to the WCTU indicated that 60 percent of women in North Dakota voted in school elections just seven years later.[39]

Once women started voting, turnout rates became the target of suffrage opponents, even though low voter counts characterized school elections long before women could vote. For example, after noting that only 36 women out of 125 possible voted in the 1890 school election in Woonsocket, the *Kimball Graphic*, without reporting the male vote, opined, "The fact of the matter is the great body of women do not want the ballot."[40] That argument failed to acknowledge a more likely cause of low voter counts: lack of competition and controversy in such elections. In one such case, in 1896, an uncontested school board seat in Parker brought only one woman and twenty-one men to the polls. Yet, in a "spirited" 1918 school election in Scotland, South Dakota, women represented 43 percent of votes cast to select two school-board members from a field of four male candidates.[41] Rather than reflecting women's desire to vote, turnout depended upon the circumstances of each election.

As women gained confidence as voters, they used their voting rights to support school decisions and candidates that aligned

with their political, educational, and moral goals. When suffragists in Beadle County organized an Equal Suffrage Association in
Huron in 1890 to advocate for the state equal rights amendment
that fall, they resolved, "That no man is worthy of support for office except he be a pronounced equal suffragist" and "that it is the
duty of every married woman in this county to vote at the school
election in June next."[42] Two years later, the *Hot Springs Weekly
Star* urged women to vote on a bonding issue to build and furnish
a new school.[43] In 1896, two years after Populists had endorsed
equal suffrage at their convention in Mitchell, a story in the *Black
Hills Union* of Rapid City admonished women to rally support for
the Populist members of the school board, arguing: "If you do not
use what privileges you have, how can you expect greater ones?
Your rights 'will grow green-moldy for want of use.'"[44]

Despite their seeming indifference in the election of 1894, the
crusading women of the WCTU viewed school suffrage as a useful
tool to further their cause. In several annual reports, local WCTU
chapters reported on women voting in school elections, sometimes providing vote counts. In 1902, the franchise report noted
that women cast forty-two out of ninety-six school votes in Highmore, a town with a population of about four hundred.[45] WCTU
women in White Lake organized their votes in accordance with
their views on temperance and then reported successful results
to state leaders in 1906, explaining: "Our specific work has been
an effort to remove the saloon by creating public sentiment. All
women use right of school suffrage and by their efforts secured a
clean man on the school board."[46] Whether advancing local school
issues, endorsing partisan candidates, or promoting moral causes
such as full suffrage or temperance, women employed school suffrage as a means of exerting influence on their communities.

School suffrage laws not only gave women access to the ballot,
they also gave them the opportunity to run for office. The 1879
law allowed women to be chosen for the school offices of director,
clerk, and treasurer. Two years later, the legislature made women
eligible to run for county superintendent of public instruction.
While the 1883 township law prevented women from qualify-
ing as school board members, it did allow women to be elected
moderators for their specific schools.[47] Rewriting the rules again

in 1887, legislators enacted new laws making "all persons, either male or female," who met general voter qualification, "eligible to the office of school director, judge or clerk of elections, township clerk, or county superintendent of public schools."[48] Although women could vote for township treasurer, they could not run for that office. When South Dakota became a state in 1889, the constitution provided that women could hold any school office but restricted women to voting solely in school elections. Therefore, women could run for, but not vote for, state and county superintendents in November elections.[49]

Throughout the state, female leaders won and lost elections for school board seats, although their numbers remained small. Dr. Nettie C. Hall, elected school trustee of Wessington Springs Township, Jerauld County, in 1887, presented uncommon leadership qualities in the public sphere. Three years earlier, Hall, a practicing physician, pharmacist, and dedicated temperance advocate, had shown an interest in public education. She circulated a local petition to adopt temperance textbooks for public classrooms so that "children are taught the effects of alcohol on the human system."[50] A prolific speaker and writer, Hall traveled throughout the state promoting better hygiene in homes as WCTU's state superintendent of hygiene, and she later became an organizer and statewide lecturer in the suffragists' unsuccessful 1890 campaign to pass the equal suffrage amendment in South Dakota. She joined the Farmers' Alliance in 1891, an organization formed to advocate for farmers that was sympathetic to woman suffrage and closely aligned with the Populist movement. Elected as vice president of the South Dakota Pharmaceutical Association in 1894, Hall also demonstrated leadership in her profession.[51]

Writing in the *Wessington Springs Herald* a year after winning her election, Hall detailed her role as school trustee. Reporting an income of one dollar, she then itemized her personal expenses at seventy-nine cents to cover the costs of stabling her horse team during meetings, postage, and stationary. She also "furnished extra kindling to the amount of 25cts besides the strategic movements I made to get the male portion of my household to prepare the kindling." Once, she even drove her own team to collect and deliver coal to the school. Hall then listed all purchases and improvements made to the school. She complained about male board members being late or completely missing meetings. Announcing she would not be a candidate that year, Hall noted, "I did not aspire to the office, in fact knew nothing of it until after the election and refused to serve until I had consulted an attorney who told me I must either serve or pay $10.00 fine." She added, "If serving in this capacity has been a step towards lifting women to the plane justly due her, I am gratified."[52] Despite her announcement, voters re-elected Hall as school director in 1888. Signifying her stature among local citizens, the *Wessington Springs Herald* reported that she was also elected judge of that election, possibly "the first woman so acting in Dakota."[53]

Hall was not the only woman to win elections. In 1890, when Rapid City women won three school board seats, forty-seven women in Hurley "polled their maiden vote" and, along with sixty-three men, elected two female and two male directors among a field of three women and three men.[54] That same year, three women in De Smet won school board seats. The following year, voters in three of twenty townships in Aurora County elected a total of four female school board members. By 1896, sixteen women had won seats on local school boards in South Dakota. In contrast, 125 women had won such elections in North Dakota. Once elected, some women served for several years, giving them greater influence in local policies. In 1913, women in Plankinton organized a meeting and selected two women for membership on the school board. Although unsuccessful in that election, one of those women, Agnes Sullivan, and another local woman, Martha Cawley Bakewell, won their seats five years later. Sullivan served for eight years and Bakewell, Plankinton's first school principal in 1882, served ten years, including seven as chairman of the board.[55]

In addition to winning seats on school boards, women enjoyed numerous electoral successes as school superintendents, taking advantage of school suffrage laws to pursue new leadership opportunities in the public arena. While laws changed regarding the duties of the position, county superintendents, in general, administrated all public schools in their county, except for those in towns with independent school districts. Superintendents reported school statistics to the state office of public instruction, held public examinations, issued teaching certificates, visited schools, provided guidance to teachers, and worked with school trustees to ensure they followed school laws. Four years before the 1881 law explicitly made women eligible for the office of county superintendent, Linda Warfel Slaughter occupied that seat in Bismarck, Burleigh County. Slaughter later led the unsuccessful effort to include full woman suffrage rights in the North Dakota constitution of 1889. In the first election after becoming eligible, territorial women won superintendent seats in three southern counties, Custer, Faulk, and Lawrence, and two northern counties, Ransom and Sargent.[56]

Sometimes, female candidates proved much more popular than the male candidates. In 1886, Alice Sanborn won office in Brule County with a sizeable 402-vote majority over her male Republican opponent. Women throughout the Northern Great Plains also won elections for superintendent. In 1888, Montana voters elected twelve women in the territory's sixteen counties, and Wyoming voters elected six women in its ten counties. Also that year, in the first and only election held when women could vote for county superintendent before achieving full suffrage, Dakota Territory reported twelve women winning in eighty-six counties, eight of them from present-day North Dakota. One of those elected, Laura J. Eisenhuth, successfully ran for state superintendent of public instruction in North Dakota in 1892, becoming the first woman in the United States to hold statewide public office.[57] Voters appeared to have agreed with a sentiment that state superintendent of schools Gilbert L. Pinkham expressed in the *Rapid City Republican* in 1890: "Women superintendents of schools exert a better influence than do men, they visit the schools oftener and have more pride in their mission."[58]

As women proved themselves capable leaders in that position, the public took notice. Some counties favored women over men in a majority of elections. Starting in 1882, Lawrence County elected women in seventeen out of nineteen biennial elections held before women gained full suffrage in 1918. Fourteen other counties each elected women ten or more times in those years. During that same period, only four counties failed to elect a female superintendent, those being Campbell, Dewey, Walworth, and Yankton counties. Voters' growing confidence in female superintendents led them to place women in that position in fifty-two out of sixty-six counties in South Dakota in the same election year that woman achieved equal voting rights.[59] By providing women with access to elective office covering an entire county, school suffrage laws gave women the ability to display leadership skills beyond local school districts. They proved themselves capable of succeeding in the public realm and helped build support for women's full rights of citizenship, including suffrage.

Increased opportunities in the western United States, such as the ability to homestead, teach, and run for elective office, provided key avenues for women's empowerment. Grace Reed Porter and Kate Taubman, for instance, employed all three strategies to become leaders in the public arena. Highly educated, both women came to South Dakota to homestead, obtained teaching positions, and then won elections for county superintendent. They held positions as high school principals, provided leadership in state organizations, and participated in national organizations. In addition, Taubman ran for the statewide position of superintendent of public instruction, coming within 270 votes of winning.[60]

Grace Reed Porter's memoirs offer a glimpse into the politics of campaigning for county superintendent and provide a sense of the work the position required. Porter, born in 1869, called Spring Green, Wisconsin, her home until finishing high school. She then attended Muskingam College, a private co-educational institution in New Concord, Ohio, before studying at a home economics school in Chicago. She also completed a hotel training course. Porter worked as a teacher at several levels, including rural school, grade school, high school, normal school, and university. Lured by the promise of free land in 1906, she resigned as head of the Latin department in a high school in Boone, Iowa, to homestead and teach in a one-room school near family members northwest of Fort Pierre. Two years later, the county school superintendent, Mrs. M. I. Weed, recruited Porter, then known as Grace Reed, to serve as her deputy in an office in Stanley County's courthouse. Accepting the job, Porter continued to hold down her claim by riding horseback to her homestead every week, twenty

Your Vote Will Be Appreciated

GRACE AIMEE REED

Republican Candidate For
County Superintendent of Schools

Grace Reed Porter taught in a one-room school near Fort Pierre
before running for superintendent of schools in Stanley County.
South Dakota State Historical Society

miles in each direction.[61] That fall, Porter ran for Stanley County
superintendent on the progressive ticket of the Republican Party.
After winning a "lively" primary against several opponents, she
entered the general election, running against the Democratic
candidate, Mrs. Culp. Porter made trips throughout the large
county to meet people and speak at meetings. Weed aided her

campaign by introducing Porter to many influential people. On election night, rumors about her opponent's high level of confidence caused Porter significant anxiety. She need not have worried. Porter won the largest vote of anyone in the county and carried every precinct but one.[62]

Once elected, Porter oversaw 120 rural schools, wrote bonds for new schoolhouses, audited records, and supervised the building of new schools, among other tasks. She wrote about the challenge of traveling close to three thousand miles each year: "The railroads only reached the town schools, the others had to be reached by the use of horses. My first year I traveled by horseback. School houses were in pastures, roads were closed by wire gates and there were creeks to cross, so horseback was the best way to travel." She later organized a teacher institute, providing two weeks of training to 150 teachers.[63] Porter, who married between her first and second elections, served as county superintendent for four years, the maximum allowed by law. Her capability and leadership skills led to other opportunities, including four years as principal of Fort Pierre High School, five years on the state board of education, and appointments to other roles in state and national organizations. In addition, she served as the dean of women at Dakota Wesleyan University in Mitchell from 1926 to 1932.[64] Laws that allowed women to win elective offices, such as county superintendent, gave Porter and others an opening to develop skills, build reputations, and prove their suitability as leaders for other public roles.

Like Porter, Kate Taubman used elective office to demonstrate leadership in the public sphere. Born in 1862 in Iowa, she earned her degree from Iowa State Normal School and taught in Iowa before moving to Dakota Territory at the age of twenty. In her first years in the territory, Taubman took advantage of homesteading laws to become a landowner. By 1884, she had obtained patents to two quarter-sections of land, one in Aurora County and one in Jerauld County. Hired as a teacher for Plankinton and then as principal, Taubman later won the 1890 and 1892 elections for school superintendent in Aurora County. Expanding her influence beyond the county, Taubman accepted the role of recording secretary of the South Dakota Education Association during her

OFFICERS OF THE GENERAL ASSOCIATION.

CLARK M. YOUNG,
PRES., Vermillion, S. D.

KATE TAUBMAN,
Rec. Sec'y,
Plankinton, S. D.

WEDNESDAY, DEC. 27.

EVENING SESSION, 7:30 O'CLOCK.

Address of Welcome - - - MAYOR F.C. DANFORTH
Response and Annual Address PRES. C. M. YOUNG, Vermillion
Sociable and Acquaintance Meeting.

THURSDAY, DEC. 28.

FORENOON SESSION, 8:30 O'CLOCK.

The End of Common School Training, SUPT. W.W. GIRTON, Howard
Discussion—Opened by - PRES. W. H. H. BEADLE, Madison
The Relation of Teacher and Supt., SUPT. A. M. ROWE, Sioux Falls
Discussion—Opened by - - - - - -
 - SUPT. N. M. HILLS, Yankton, SUPT. M. A. LANGE, Salem
Methods versus Results - MISS J. M. J. PRYNE, Madison
Discussion—Opened by - - SUPT. I. F. NICKELL, Huron

AFTERNOON SESSION 1:30 O'CLOCK.

Political Methods in School Management - • •
 - - - - PROF. R. B. McCLENNON, Madison
Discussion—Opened by - PROF. M. D. MILLER, Canton
American Literature in Our Public Schools - • •
 - - - - MRS. E. M. LOVEJOY, Aberdeen
Discussion—Opened by - PROF. J. O. DUGUID, Scotland
Moral Education Necessary - PROF. H. C. FRYE, Elk Point
Discussion—Opened by - - PROF. L. A. STOUT, Mitchell
Report from Educational Council.

Kate Taubman, depicted here in a program from a meeting of the South Dakota Education Association, became a major figure in state educational politics. South Dakota State Historical Society

second term. After serving for three years, she became the first woman elected as president of the state association.[65]

By 1896, when Taubman ran for state superintendent of public instruction, she held the position of high school principal in Aberdeen and had joined the National Education Association. Her prospects for electoral victory seemed promising, as three women in the Northern Great Plains states had recently won their elections for state superintendent. In North Dakota, two years earlier, Emma F. Bates had replaced Laura J. Eisenhuth, the first women to achieve statewide elective office in the country. Estelle Reel had won in Wyoming in 1894. Running on the People's Party (Populist) ticket, Taubman narrowly lost, having received 49.6 percent of the state vote and 59.4 percent of Aurora County's vote. Needing only another 270 votes to win, Taubman came close to becoming the first woman elected to statewide office in South Dakota. Other members of her party had achieved remarkable success, with Populists winning two seats in Congress, the governorship, and several state legislative seats. Even the Populist candidate for president, William Jennings Bryan, who ran as a Democrat, carried the state.[66] After the election, Taubman continued her role as president of the South Dakota Education Association and later moved to Deadwood to serve as assistant principal of the local high school. Through her leadership in education and her electoral victories and campaigns, Taubman achieved a remarkable level of prominence for a woman of her era. Sadly, her sudden death in 1902 cut short her legacy.

Often ignored or downplayed by historians, school suffrage served an important role in the fight for full suffrage. Living in a gendered society that accepted childhood education as a proper aspect of motherhood, women successfully fought to extend their educational role through limited suffrage and elective office. In South Dakota, newspaper accounts and state reports show that women used school suffrage laws, decades before achieving full voting rights, to vote, to organize others to vote, to advocate for issues important to them, and to seek public office. Although an 1894 constitutional amendment to allow women to vote for school superintendents failed, South Dakota women who ran for county school superintendent made impressive gains, winning their first seats in 1882 and achieving that position in 80 percent of the state's counties by 1918.[67] Long before they obtained full voting rights, school suffrage served as a pathway to public leadership for Taubman, Porter, and many other ambitious and talented women.

By the time South Dakota passed its full-suffrage amendment in 1918, women had been voting on school matters and holding elective offices for close to forty years. Their engagement in elections and school governance, which took place throughout the Northern Great Plains and beyond, helped change the social reality, fostering greater support for female participation in the public arena. Countless Americans learned to envision women at the polls and to value their public contributions. As a result, many acknowledged the changing social order and endorsed the rights of women to engage as equals in the electoral process.

NOTES

Special thanks go to Molly Rozum and Lori Lahlum for inviting me to explore this subject and discover the untold story of school suffrage. In addition, their insightful feedback and excellent suggestions helped me deliver a more organized and appealing essay.

1. "The School Election," *Turner County Herald* (Hurley, S.Dak.), 19 June 1890.

2. "The Women Voted," *Mitchell Capital*, 18 Apr. 1890; "Candidates," *Rapid City Daily Republican*, 11 Apr. 1890; Editorial, *Rapid City Republican*, 15 Apr. 1890.

3. Editorial, *Rapid City Republican*, 15 Apr. 1890.

4. "The Women Voted"; "The Election," *Rapid City Republican*, 17 Apr. 1890; "City Council Proceedings," *Black Hills Union*, 25 Apr. 1890; "Annual Meeting," ibid., 25 July 1890. First reports indicated that only two women had won, but later reports confirmed that three female school board members had been elected. Not all women supported the female candidates. Hinting at houses of prostitution in the fourth ward, the *Rapid City Daily Republican* blamed Cooper's loss on disreputable women, "who have the same legal right to vote" and voted in accordance with the men "without whose financial aid they could not exist" ("The Election"). The women elected also won leadership positions in the Woman's Christian Temperance Union annual meeting in July.

5. Alexander Keyssar, *The Right to Vote: The Contested History of Democracy in the United States*, rev. ed. (New York: Basic Books, 2009), pp. 365–68; Doris Buck Ward, "The Winning of Woman Suffrage in Montana" (master's thesis, Montana State University, 1974), p. 6; Dakota Territory, *Fifteenth Annual Report of the Superintendent of Public Instruction* (Yankton, 1884), p. 30; Sally Roesch Wagner, ed., *Fighting for the Vote in South Dakota* (Aberdeen, S.Dak.: Sky Carrier Press, 1995), pp. 90–98. Keyssar mistakenly lists Montana as a full-suffrage territory.

6. Gaylynn Welch, "Local and National Forces Shaping the American Woman Suffrage Movement, 1870–1890" (Ph.D. diss., Binghamton University, 2009), pp. 68–112; Marilyn Schultz Blackwell, "The Politics of Motherhood: Clarina Howard Nichols and School Suffrage," *New England Quarterly* 78, no. 4 (2005): 570–98; Edmund B. Thomas, Jr., "School Suffrage and the Campaign for Women's Suffrage in Massachusetts, 1879–1920," *Historical Journal of Massachusetts* 25, no. 1 (1997): 1–17; Frances Maule Björkman, ed., *Woman Suffrage: History, Arguments, and Results* (New York: National American Woman Suffrage Assoc., 1913), pp. 65–66; Keyssar, *The Right to Vote*, p. 365; Elizabeth Cady Stanton, Susan B. Anthony, and Matilda Joslyn Gage, eds., *History of Woman Suffrage*, Vol. 3 (Rochester, N.Y.: Susan B. Anthony, 1886), pp. 662–63; Dorinda Riessen Reed, *The Woman Suffrage Movement in South Dakota*, Governmental Research Bureau, Report no. 41 (Vermillion: State University of South Dakota, 1958), pp. 5–6, 49. Welch devotes one chapter to school suffrage in her 2009 dissertation, noting that the subject needs more academic analysis. In her 2005 article about the school-suffrage movement in Vermont and Kansas, Blackwell lists only a few articles and books that focus on school or partial suffrage, all published before 1999. Most historians who discuss school suffrage, even briefly, inaccurately portray dates and details regarding such laws in Dakota Territory and South Dakota. Both Björkman and Keyssar fail to recognize the 1879 date as the origin of school suffrage in Dakota Territory. Keyssar, for example, cites 1883 as the first date of school suffrage in Dakota Territory and 1890 as the first date for North Dakota, providing no date for South Dakota. Björkman mistakenly lists 1887 as the first date for the two Dakotas. Suffragist Marietta Bones, who wrote the first history of the territory's fight for woman suffrage, published in the *History of Woman Suffrage*, Vol. 3, accurately portrays the 1879 law, but Reed, in her 1958 history, confuses and combines the details of the 1879 and 1883 laws. Reed also mistakenly states that voters rejected an amendment for full suffrage in 1894. The failed amendment only attempted to extend school suffrage.

7. Colorado, *Message of Governor John L. Routt to the Ninth General Assembly of the State of Colorado* (Denver, 1893), p. 48.

8. Keyssar, *Right to Vote*, pp. 365–68. Keyssar's tables A.17 and A.20 list all states that allowed full and partial suffrage before 1920. Since those tables show inaccurate dates for South Dakota, other information could contain similar inaccuracies. States with no prior type of woman suffrage include Alabama, Georgia, Maryland, North Carolina, Pennsylvania, South Carolina, Virginia, and West Virginia.

9. "Twenty-Two State Legislatures," *The Woman's Column* 8 (5 Jan. 1895): 1; Blackwell, "Politics of Motherhood," p. 595; Welch, "Local and National

Forces," pp. 68–70; National American Woman's Suffrage Association, *Victory: How Women Won It: A Centennial Symposium, 1840–1940* (New York: H. W. Wilson, 1940), pp. 73–74.

10. Blackwell, "Politics of Motherhood," pp. 573–74, 585, 595.

11. Dakota Territory, *Laws Passed at the Thirteenth Session of the Legislative Assembly of the Territory of Dakota* (Yankton, 1879), chap. 14, secs. 29–30 (hereafter cited as *Session Laws*).

12. *Session Laws*, 1881, chaps. 41–47. Lawmakers wrote a special statute to establish the first independent school district in Yankton in 1875, followed by Fargo and Sioux Falls in 1879. The statute for Sioux Falls called for village electors to select board members by ballot. The 1881 law created similar districts in Bismarck and Deadwood, with the law for Bismarck also defining general rules for establishing independent districts. The 1887 education law called for public elections for all school trustees.

13. *Fifteenth Annual Report of the Superintendent of Public Instruction*, p. 17; Dakota Territory, *Annotated Revised Codes of the Territory of Dakota* (Yankton, 1883), vol. 2, chap. 40 (hereafter cited as *Revised Codes*). Legislators completely rewrote the education statute in 1883 to define the township system. In sections 128 and 148, the law exempted identified independent school districts and fifteen specified "district plan" counties from most of the new laws, but not all.

14. *Session Laws*, 1862, chap. 32, sec. 51; *Revised Codes*, 1877, chap. 40, secs. 21, 42; *Session Laws*, 1879, chap. 14, secs. 29–30. The 1877 law defined those who could vote at school district meetings as "all persons possessing the qualifications of electors as defined by the laws of the territory." Those laws, enacted in 1862, required a voter to be a "free white male" and also specified citizenship rules. The 1879 school law replaced the qualification that limited voting to males to "all persons over the age of twenty-one years who are citizens of the United States, or have declared their intention to become such, and who shall have resided in the district five days next preceding any district meeting." The citizenship rule remained in place for all elections until women received full voting rights.

15. *Revised Codes*, 1883, chap. 40, secs. 30–31, 66–68.

16. *Session Laws*, 1887, chap. 46, sec. 2; chap. 47, secs. 10, 20.

17. South Dakota, *Constitution and the Laws Passed at the First Session of the Legislature of the State of South Dakota* (Pierre, 1890), art. 7, sec. 9 (hereafter cited as *Constitution*).

18. "Present Extent of Woman Suffrage in South Dakota," *Turner County Herald*, 8 May 1890.

19. *Black Hills Union*, 18 July 1890.

20. Mary Kay Jennings, "Lake County Woman Suffrage Campaign in

1890," *South Dakota History* 5 (Fall 1975): pp. 396–97; "Women Did Vote," *Madison Sentinel*, 18 Apr. 1890.

21. "To Voters," *Rapid City Daily Republican*, 14 Apr. 1890; "Women Voted."

22. *Constitution*, art. 4, sec. 12; art. 7, sec. 9; art. 9, sec. 5.

23. "South Dakota News," *Hot Springs Weekly Star*, 31 Mar. 1893.

24. South Dakota Educational Association, *Minutes of the Annual Meeting of the South Dakota Educational Association* (Pierre, 1884), p. 61; Wagner, *Fighting for the Vote in South Dakota*, p. 93; South Dakota, *Fifth Biennial Report of the Secretary of State* (Pierre, 1900), pp. 147, 153.

25. Ida Husted Harper and Susan B. Anthony, eds., *The History of Woman Suffrage*, Vol. 4 (Rochester, N.Y.: Susan B. Anthony, 1902), p. 557; George W. Kingsbury, *History of Dakota Territory*, Vol. 3 (Chicago: S. J. Clarke, 1915), pp. 768–69, 789; Wagner, *Fighting for the Vote in South Dakota*, pp. 93, 99.

26. "South Dakota: The Outlook," *Union Signal*, 6 Sept. 1894; "South Dakota: Yearly Ingathering," ibid., 29 Nov. 1894.

27. Quoted in Harper and Anthony, eds., *History of Woman Suffrage*, p. 557. Pickler wrote the South Dakota chapter in this volume.

28. "The Proposed Amendments," *Turner County Herald*, 1 Nov. 1894.

29. "Election Results as Officially Declared by the County Board," ibid., 29 Nov. 1894.

30. "South Dakota Legislative Notes," *Union Signal*, 30 Mar. 1893; Kingsbury, *History of Dakota Territory*, p. 746; *Minutes of the National WCTU Twentieth Annual Meeting, Chicago, Illinois* (Chicago: Woman's Temperance Publishing Assoc., 1893), p. 421.

31. Quoted in *Minutes of the National Woman's Christian Temperance Union at the Twenty-first Annual Meeting, Cleveland, Ohio* (Chicago: Woman's Temperance Publishing Assoc., 1894), p. 197.

32. "Siftings from South Dakota," *Union Signal*, 29 Nov. 1894.

33. "Territorial Items," *Canton Advocate*, 6 Mar. 1879.

34. "The School Law," *Turner County Herald*, 28 Apr. 1887; "The School Law," *Cooperstown Griggs Courier*, 29 Apr. 1887; "The School Law," *Dickinson Press*, 23 Apr. 1887.

35. "Locals," 17 June 1887 and "Notice," 13 June 1890, *Wessington Springs Herald*.

36. *Constitution*, art. 7, secs. 2, 9.

37. *Aberdeen News*, reprinted in *Mitchell Capital*, 28 Mar. 1890.

38. *Hot Springs Star*, 27 June 1890.

39. *Wessington Springs Herald*, 3 Oct. 1890; *Minutes of the Twenty-fourth Annual Meeting of the National WCTU, Buffalo, New York* (Chicago: Woman's Temperance Publishing Assoc., 1897), p. 478.

40. *Kimball Graphic*, 18 Apr. 1890.

41. "Parker: From the Press," *Turner County Herald*, 23 Apr. 1896; *Scotland Citizen Republican*, 20 June 1918. Women cast 129 of 297 votes in the Scotland election.

42. Quoted in "For Female Suffrage," *Wessington Springs Herald*, 14 Mar. 1890.

43. "Vote for a School House," *Hot Springs Weekly Star*, 2 Dec. 1892.

44. "A Word to the Fair Sex," *Black Hills Union*, 10 Apr. 1896. *See also* "Equal Suffrage among South Dakota Populists," *Union Signal*, 23 Aug. 1894. For more information about the Populist movement, *see* R. Alton Lee, *Principle over Party: The Farmers' Alliance and Populism in South Dakota, 1880–1900* (Pierre: South Dakota Historical Society Press, 2011).

45. *Minutes of the Thirteenth Annual Convention of the WCTU of South Dakota* (Watertown, 1901), p. 124; *Minutes of the Fourteenth Annual Convention of the WCTU of South Dakota* (Mitchell, 1902), p. 81; U.S., Bureau of the Census, *Twelfth Census of the United States: 1900, Population*, Vol. 1 (Washington, D.C.: Government Printing Office, 1901), p. 475. The WCTU report indicated Highmore's population at 600, but the 1900 census counted only 376 residents.

46. *Minutes of the Eighteenth Annual Convention of the WCTU of South Dakota* (Parker, 1906), p. 51.

47. *Session Laws*, 1879, chap. 14, sec. 33; *Session Laws*, 1881, chap. 65, sec. 1; *Revised Codes*, 1883, chap. 40, secs. 66–67.

48. *Session Laws*, 1887, chap. 47, secs. 27–28.

49. Ibid., chap. 47, sec. 14; *Constitution*, art. 7, secs. 9; art. 4, sec. 12.

50. "Temperance, W.C.T.U.," *Wessington Springs Herald*, 26 Sept. 1884. *See also* ibid., 27 June 1884.

51. "Report of the 'One Woman' on School Board in Jerauld County," ibid., 15 June 1888; N. J. Dunham, *A History of Jerauld County, South Dakota* (Wessington Springs, S.Dak.: n.p. 1910), pp. 113, 133, 204, 244; "Press Notices of Our Worthy Townswoman and Her Noble Work," ibid., 22 Mar. 1888; "At the Court House," *Mitchell Capital*, 29 Aug. 1890; "Flattery or Policy—Which?," *Wessington Springs Herald*, 3 Apr. 1891; "South Dakota News," *Turner County Herald*, 16 Aug. 1894. These sources and other newspaper accounts indicate that Hall lectured frequently throughout the state and in Nebraska on issues of hygiene, temperance, and suffrage. Hall moved to Georgia in 1894.

52. "Report of the 'One Woman' on School Board in Jerauld County."

53. *Wessington Springs Herald*, 29 June 1888. Nettie Hall also served as the president of the Jerauld County WCTU.

54. "The School Election," *Turner County Herald*, 19 June 1890.

55. "Women Did Vote"; Aurora County Superintendent of Schools, Superintendent's Record, 1885–1891, pp. 284–88, Township Misc. Box, Aurora County Historical Society, Plankinton, S.Dak.; *Minutes of the National WCTU at the Twenty-Third Annual Meeting, St. Louis, Missouri* (Chicago: Woman's Temperance Publishing Assoc., 1896), p. 386; *South Dakota Mail* (Plankinton), 5 June 1913; Lennis J. Long, "A History of the Plankinton School, Plankinton, South Dakota: 1882–1954" (master's thesis, University of South Dakota, 1954), pp. 80–81; *Aurora County History* (Stickney, S.Dak.: Aurora County Historical Society, 1983), p. 143. "Mrs. Thomas Bray Dead," 1931, in Scrapbook of Newspaper Obituaries, 1930s–1940s, Ella Todd Wilson Papers, Adeline Van Genderen Collection, Plankinton, S.Dak. The women nominated Maud Bray and Agnes Sullivan in 1913. Although Bray's obituary indicates that she served on the local school board, her name does not appear in the Long thesis that lists all school board members starting in 1897.

56. *Revised Codes*, 1883, chap. 40, secs. 10–22, 94; Dakota Territory, *Eighth Annual Report of the Superintendent of Public Instruction*, 1877, p. 18; *Fifteenth Annual Report*, pp. 14–15; "Woman Suffrage at Statehood—Introduction," State Historical Society of North Dakota, history.nd.gov.

57. "Compliments to Miss Sanborn," *Turner County Herald*, 2 Dec. 1886; *Eleventh Census of the United States*, 1890, Brule County; Montana, *First Annual Report of the Montana Superintendent of Public Instruction* (Helena, 1890), p. 5; Virginia Cole Trenholm, ed., *Wyoming Blue Book*, Vol. 1 (Cheyenne, Wyoming State Archives & Historical Dept., 1974), p. 440; Dakota Territory, *Nineteenth Annual Report of the Superintendent of Public Instruction*, 1888, pp. 66–67; "History: ND Elected First Woman to Be Administrator of a State Office," *Bismarck Tribune*, 25 Apr. 2010; "County Superintendents," *Turner County Herald*, 3 May 1888. Because people living in cities voted for school board members during municipal elections in other months, those electors could not vote for the county superintendent during the June 1888 township elections.

58. "Candidates," *Rapid City Daily Republican*, 11 Apr. 1890.

59. Dakota Territory, *Fifteenth Annual Report of the Superintendent of Public Instruction*, pp. 14–15; *Sixteenth Annual Report*, pp. 30–31; *Seventeenth Annual Report*, pp. 63–64; *Nineteenth Annual Report*, pp. 66–67; South Dakota, *First Biennial Report of the Superintendent of Public Instruction*, 1892, p. 68; *Second Biennial Report*, p. 126; *Third Biennial Report*, pp. 24–51; *Fourth Biennial Report*, pp. xiii–xiv; *Fifth Biennial Report*, p. 19; *Sixth Biennial Report*, p. 35; *Seventh Biennial Report*, p. 197; *Eighth Biennial Report*, p. 97; *Ninth Biennial Report*, p. 26; *Tenth Biennial Report*, p. 33; *Eleventh Biennial Report*, pp. 328–29; *Twelfth Biennial Report*, pp. 276–77; *Thirteenth Biennial Report*, pp. 141–42, 207–8; *Fifteenth Biennial Report*, pp.

264–65. Based upon female first names, I tabulated the counts for female county superintendents elected from 1882 through 1918.

60. South Dakota, *Fifth Biennial Report of the Secretary of State*, p. 142.

61. Grace Reed Porter, "Grace Reed Porter Autobiography," 1957, pp. 1–7, folder 1, box 3749B, Grace Reed Porter Papers, State Archives Collection, South Dakota State Historical Society, Pierre; "Grace Aimee Porter, formerly Grace Aimee Reed," 21 Dec. 1914, Stanley County, S.Dak., Homestead Accession Number SDMTAA 450319, Bureau of Land Management (BLM) Land Patents; *Ninth Biennial Report of the Superintendent of Public Instruction*, p. 26. Porter met the requirements to obtain her land patent as a homestead in 1914, paying only a small administrative fee.

62. Porter, "Grace Reed Porter Autobiography," pp. 1–7.

63. Ibid., pp. 7, 9.

64. Ibid., pp. 20–25; *Tenth Biennial Report of the Superintendent of Public Instruction*, p. 33; *Eleventh Biennial Report*, p. 328.

65. "Proud of an Iowa Girl," *Waterloo Courier*, 26 Oct. 1896; "Kate Taubman," 20 Dec. 1884, Aurora County, S.Dak., Homestead Accession Number SDMTAA 140298, BLM Land Patents; "Kate Taubman," 4 Dec. 1884, Jerauld County, S.Dak., Homestead Accession Number SDMTAA 145218, BLM Land Patents; "High School Items," *Mitchell Daily Republican*, 13 Mar. 1886; *First Biennial Report of the Superintendent of Public Instruction*, p. 68; *Second Biennial Report*, p. 126; South Dakota, *Biennial Address of Governor Charles N. Herreid to the Ninth Legislative Session* (Pierre, 1905), p. 182. Taubman paid cash for both of her land patents in 1884, likely pre-empting one tract of land and commuting the other tract from a homestead to a cash payment.

66. National Education Association, *Journal of Proceedings and Addresses of the Forty-First Annual Meeting* (Minneapolis, 1902), p. 899; "Department of Public Instruction," State Historical Society of North Dakota, history.nd.gov; Kerry Drake, "Estelle Reel, First Woman Elected to Statewide Office in Wyoming," Wyoming Historical Society Encyclopedia, www.wyohistory.org; South Dakota, *Fifth Biennial Report of the Secretary of State*, p. 142; *Sixth Biennial Report of the Superintendent of Public Instruction*, p. 41; R. Alton Lee, *Principle over Party*, pp. 137–39. Taubman received 345 votes in Aurora County and 40,854 statewide. Frank Crane, her Republican opponent and the incumbent, received 423 county votes and 41,124 state votes. With no Democratic candidate on the ballot, the only other votes equaled less than one percent of the state total.

67. *Fifth Biennial Report of the Superintendent of Public Instruction*, p. 112.

ETHNICITY AND WOMAN SUFFRAGE
ON THE SOUTH DAKOTA PLAINS

SARA EGGE

Rain, "wind and blackness of heavens" greeted Nettie Hall, a lecturer and organizer for the South Dakota Equal Suffrage Association (SDESA), after she left yet another disappointing meeting
in Yankton County, South Dakota, in August 1890. Hall had rid-
den seven miles on horseback to Volin, a tiny hamlet of mostly
Norwegian immigrants, only to find her audience had disbanded
as the storm approached. She had even worse luck in Lesterville,
a German Catholic enclave, where locals "would or could *not
provide any place* for a meeting." She was so aggravated at their
reluctance she admitted that she "would have stood on the street
and talked if anyone would" have listened. While she was able to
organize two suffrage clubs in Yankton County, it was not without "difficulties." Despite the obstacles she faced, Hall remained
resolute, vowing to continue her canvass to "make things count."[1]
In less than three months, eligible voters would cast their ballots
on a proposed state constitutional amendment to enfranchise
women in South Dakota. Hall remained hopeful, but time was
running out.

A number of difficulties plagued the 1890 suffrage campaign
in South Dakota. Political turmoil gave rise to a third-party contender that catered to immigrants over suffragists. Most South
Dakotans associated temperance with woman suffrage, frustrat-
ing national leaders who wanted the cause treated as a single
issue. State and local advocates, however, found disassociat-
ing temperance and woman suffrage almost impossible, which
fostered internal tensions with national suffragists that hurt
the campaign. Ethnic tensions linked all these issues. Since the
1880s, foreign-born individuals had arrived in increasingly large

numbers on the Northern Great Plains, settling in isolated enclaves where they could preserve their ethnic identities. Once
they had filed a Declaration of Intention to become a citizen of
the United States, immigrant men in almost two dozen states, including South Dakota, could vote after only two years' residency.
Voting without citizenship, also known as alien suffrage, allowed
noncitizen immigrants extraordinary access to political institutions. Immigrants' access to political power, combined with their
numerical strength, produced a quagmire for national suffrage
leaders who struggled to address this diverse population.[2]

During the 1890s, South Dakota held two state referenda for
full woman suffrage, first in 1890 and then in 1898.[3] Leaders in
the National American Woman Suffrage Association (NAWSA),
participated extensively in the 1890 effort, but they backed off in
1898 out of frustration. They deemed South Dakotans incapable
of supporting the cause because so many were ethnic voters who
assumed women only wanted the vote to secure prohibition.
Moreover, NAWSA leaders had essentially turned their backs on
the SDESA due to the state association's unwillingness to separate temperance from woman suffrage. By 1898, almost all of
the SDESA's officers also held executive positions in the Woman's Christian Temperance Union (WCTU). Most South Dakota
suffragists, as with countless others across the Northern Great
Plains states, found suffrage through their work in the WCTU,
which made separating the causes difficult. Finally, national
leaders disagreed with state and local advocates about how to engage with immigrants. While some NAWSA leaders considered
these voters unmovable in their opposition to woman suffrage,
the SDESA, along with local activists, recognized the political
power that foreign-born individuals held in South Dakota. Some
state and local field workers explicitly challenged NAWSA's assumptions about immigrants, arguing that these ethnic voters
could support the cause if given the chance.[4]

For most of the 1890s, NAWSA struggled to define its approach
to the ethnic communities on the Northern Great Plains. On the
one hand, most national leaders acknowledged that the immigrants' votes mattered but expressed frustration with how difficult it was to work with them. Many newcomers did not speak

Many immigrants to South Dakota in the late-nineteenth century,
such as these Russian immigrants photographed in Brule County in 1894,
lived in tight-knit ethnic enclaves. South Dakota State Historical Society

or read English. They usually lived away from towns, which made
reaching them difficult. Cultural distinctions also produced a ka-
leidoscope of diverse opinions. While most foreigners came from
northern and western Europe, they were not a unified group. In
South Dakota, Germans were the largest ethnic community, and
of their ranks, a majority came from Russia after living along the
Black Sea for a century. Scandinavians, mostly Norwegians with
some Swedes and Danes, comprised the second largest group. Religious affiliation also complicated ethnic identities. Norwegians
and Swedes were usually Lutherans, but they often chose not to
worship together. Germans split between Catholic and Lutheran,
often forming distinct congregations in the same county. The
manner of settlement also shaped ethnic communities. Many immigrants arrived in South Dakota in colonies or with neighbors
and friends from their home country. These patterns reinforced

EQUALITY AT THE BALLOT BOX

existing cultural, religious, and political customs, producing a dizzying array of political views.[5]

At statehood in 1889, foreign-born individuals comprised 26 percent of South Dakota's population. By 1900, the percentage had fallen slightly to 22 percent. These populations varied by county. For example, Yankton County's percentage of foreign-born residents in 1890 was higher than the state average, about four thousand out of a total population of ten thousand. Almost one quarter were Germans.[6] Importantly, these figures do not include second-generation children who maintained strong ethnic identities and often voted as their parents did. Moreover, immigrants enjoyed more political power than this data suggests. By 1890, immigrants comprised a significant portion of the Knights of Labor and the Farmers' Alliance, both influential pressure groups within the two-party system After the Populist Party formed from these two groups in the summer of 1890, ethnic minorities flocked to its ranks. The Populists spearheaded successful reforms, including the Austrailian (secret) ballot, the initiative and referendum, and a measure on mine safey.[7] Democrats and Republicans ultimately maintained control of partisan politics in South Dakota, but the rise of a viable third party forced politicians to make concessions to groups dominated by immigrants. While immigrant enclaves existed elsewhere in the West and throughout the United States, the particular combination of alien suffrage and local activists' attachment to temperance led NAWSA to cast additional scrutiny on South Dakota. Leaders such as Anthony saw foreigners as linchpin voters, the ones whose "persuasion" could mean victory or defeat.[8]

By the late-1880s, many NAWSA leaders began accusing foreigners of ignorance, which implied more than just a lack of education. As historian Wanda Hendricks argues, during the last two decades of the nineteenth century, NAWSA leaders began to apply racial categories to both foreign-born and black men, arguing that their inferior status meant they should not vote. In this way, Hendricks asserts, NAWSA pursued a policy of white supremacy. In the case of the foreign born, NAWSA suggested they were outsiders unfit for democracy.[9] As Olympia Brown put it at NAWSA's 1889 annual convention, European immigrants were "reckless," "political inferiors," and "riff-raff" who refused to adopt American values. Instead, they plotted to topple American democracy through the ballot box to establish rule "with a rod of iron."[10]

As NAWSA leaders increasingly espoused nativist sentiments, they also clashed with local and state leaders over temperance. In South Dakota, many activists advocated for woman suffrage through the WCTU, which by 1889 increasingly participated in partisan politics through the Prohibition Party. South Dakota activists such as Marietta Bones argued against this partisanship, and national leaders such as Susan B. Anthony also recognized that mixing temperance and woman suffrage often drew fervent opposition from anti-prohibitionists, many of whom were also foreign-born. In fact, South Dakota voters had stirred up liquor interests in the state as early as 1889, when the majority had voted in favor of prohibition at statehood. Subsequent woman suffrage measures met hostility from brewers because they assumed women wanted the ballot to keep prohibition intact. Liquor interests in the state sought to resubmit the issue to the public to repeal prohibition. During the 1890 effort, Anthony advised pro-suffrage members of the WCTU to work only for woman suffrage, but activists whose support of the cause came from promoting temperance ignored the directive.[11]

As the election season began, South Dakota voters began considering a constitutional amendment to enfranchise the state's women, and suffragists across the country sprang into action. The NAWSA and the SDESA orchestrated a tripartite campaign that Susan B. Anthony directed. Anthony ordered lecturers into every county, where they were to organize local suffrage clubs. She and other leaders also planned to secure endorsements from Republicans and Democrats, using their connections in the Knights of Labor and Farmers' Alliance to do so. Both associations, with their large foreign-born memberships, had endorsed woman suffrage prior to the spring of 1890, and Anthony counted on their influence to help shape the major parties' platforms.[12] When these groups then formed the Independent Party in June without endorsing woman suffrage, Anthony was furious. The party had "ignored in its platform . . . woman suffrage . . . for the avowed object of *winning* the *votes* of the . . . *Foreigners* among them,"

EQUALITY AT THE BALLOT BOX

Anthony wrote to South Dakota suffragist Alice Pickler after the Independent Party convention.[13] As a third-party alternative, the Independents had lost whatever leverage they had with which to cajole Republicans and Democrats to support woman suffrage. The *Aberdeen Daily News* called the Independent Party, soon to be known as the People's, or Populist, Party, "one of the worst things to happen" to the cause as it splintered suffragists even further.[14] After a bitter state convention, the executive committee of the SDESA resigned, leaving pro-Anthony supporters to pick up the pieces.[15]

Despite their anger with the Independents, Anthony and the SDEA's new executives did not write off foreign-born individuals entirely. They reckoned that if they could not convince political leaders, they could still sway their constituents. On 16 July 1890, the SDESA, along with "our Deborah, Susan B. Anthony," issued a "Do-Everything" policy. Recalling Anthony's earlier tripartite plan, the new policy emphasized the role of "home talent," who were to host "oratorical suffrage contests," "tent meetings," "yellow tea parties," and "suffrage dinners" to "agitate the question" across the state.[16] The Do-Everything policy reflected the variety of perspectives suffragists held in 1890. It integrated rhetoric from both WCTU president Frances Willard, who previously had implemented a similar Do-Everything policy, and NAWSA, which had begun reframing its arguments around domesticity. NAWSA leaders slowly shifted away from claims that women were equal to men, highlighting instead women's differences, especially their selflessness and moral nature, as making them fit for the ballot.[17] The July 1890 campaign plan hinged on suffragists reaching as wide a population as possible, including immigrants. "We wish to send German and Scandinavian speakers and literature where needed," wrote the SDESA.[18] In this way, state and national suffragists conceived of the Do-Everything policy as inclusive and expansive.

Campaign activities in Yankton County from August to October 1890 exemplified the SDESA's Do-Everything policy. Nettie Hall was the first of four NAWSA lecturers to visit the area. She noted the ethnic backgrounds of her audiences, suggesting that suffragists explicitly reached out to foreign-born individuals.

She spent ten days crisscrossing the county on horseback, mostly speaking with Germans and Norwegians. While local advocates celebrated Hall's tour, they also requested more speakers from diverse backgrounds. Julia King, a suffragist and member of the local WCTU, admitted that the local suffrage club, comprised mostly of native-born town-dwellers, struggled to reach foreign-born farmers.[19] In response, SDESA sent three additional speakers, and their canvasses both confirmed and challenged NAWSA's assumptions about immigrants.

National leaders believed Germans more likely to oppose woman suffrage, while Scandinavians were allegedly more supportive. They also contended that Catholics generally opposed woman suffrage while Protestants more often favored it. These assertions reflected their understandings of ethnic traditions. Most Germans and Catholics consumed alcohol as part of rituals and traditions central to their identities, and their anti-suffrage stance stemmed from anti-prohibition concerns.[20] Hall's canvass seemed to verify these stereotypes. Other lecturers met immigrants who defied these trends. In September, a second speaker, Carrie Chapman Catt, in her first campaign as a national organizer, proudly noted that she had success among German Catholic farmers in northeast Yankton County. "Every place [I] have had a good many converts from that church," she wrote. That she boasted of her work suggests that German Catholics may have been more receptive to the cause than often assumed.[21]

In early October 1890, a third lecturer, Julia B. Nelson, arrived in Yankton County and set out on an ambitious tour of the area. Her letters provide the most incisive look at how suffragists navigated the complexities of ethnicity. Born in Connecticut, Nelson had moved to Iowa as a child before her family settled in Minnesota, another state with high numbers of northern European immigrants. When her marriage to Ole Nelson, a Norwegian immigrant, ended with his sudden death, she spent the next decade and a half in the South, teaching freedpeople and their children. By the 1880s, she had returned to Minnesota, becoming involved in the WCTU and the Minnesota Woman Suffrage Association. By 1888, NAWSA employed her as a lecturer and organizer. Nelson carried critical skills with her into the campaign. Her marriage to Ole Nelson gave her an edge among Norwegians, while her experience as a teacher made her an effective public speaker.[22]

Nelson arrived in Yankton County after a disastrous encounter in Hutchinson County. The sheriff of one small town, a German from Russia, "did all he could to intimidate" locals, threatening "political decapitation" to anyone who dared attend Nelson's lecture there. "To wear the yellow ribbon in Hutchinson Co. is like shaking a red rag at an enraged bovine or a turkey gobbler," she noted.[23] Her canvass of Yankton County started with similar disappointment. She rode fourteen miles in a rented buggy to Jamesville, a colony of Mennonite Germans from Russia. While she gave few details about what transpired there, she admitted that she never left the buggy, even after the long ride. She told the SDESA, "Don't try to arrange speakers at Jamesville," warning that they "would not give a hearing to either man or woman on the subject of suffrage." Nelson had better luck at Norway, a small village of Norwegian Lutherans, and made it plain what Norwegians thought of Germans, especially Germans from Russia. Norwegians "don't want to be classed with the Russians in prejudice against free speech," she remarked candidly.[24]

Despite the open hostility she faced in Hutchinson and Yankton counties, Nelson remained steadfast in her work with foreigners, including Germans. While she noted "much opposition" among foreign-born individuals living in rural areas, she explained that their lack of support was neither a permanent cultural hallmark nor an unchangeable political stance. She argued that when she could gather an audience, she made converts. In her opinion, national suffragists had poor organization and weak campaign strategies. Similar to many speakers, Nelson went into the field with an incomplete itinerary, if she had one at all. Many of her visits surprised locals because headquarters had failed to advertise her lecture. In addition, Nelson pointed out that, while more time-consuming, a canvass of rural school districts gave foreign-born farmers the best opportunity to hear suffrage speakers. Prominent state and national lecturers often visited only the largest towns located along railroads, and they missed rural residents who could not travel long distances. According to Nelson, suffrage leaders often wasted the opportunity to bring their message "where the battle" was "thickest."[25] While Nelson recognized that many foreigners opposed the cause, she also castigated suffragists for ignoring them. They could only blame themselves for not doing more to engage immigrants directly.

In late October, a fourth speaker, Emma Smith DeVoe, toured Yankton County in a last-ditch effort to win votes. DeVoe served as the state lecturer for SDESA and a superintendent of the franchise for the WCTU, which seemed to affirm the link between woman suffrage and temperance that NAWSA desperately tried to deny. DeVoe, however, was close to Anthony but lived in South Dakota and helped bridge national and state efforts. While DeVoe often repeated familiar arguments that national suffragists made—that women need to have a voice in making laws, that the constitution granted equal rights to women, and that as taxpayers women should vote—her talks occasionally included an implicit criticism of foreign-born voters. Near the end of one speech, she compared an American-born girl to a European-born boy. Educated and resourceful, the girl acquired property and paid taxes on it. The boy, "without property or knowledge of our institutions," became a naturalized citizen who could vote. DeVoe was not vehemently anti-immigrant and explained that she believed "in many instances, they make our best citizens." Still, her comparison suggested American-born women often had superior education and institutional knowledge when compared to foreigners.[26] It is unclear how often DeVoe used this anecdote or which audiences she believed would be receptive to such a claim. Because many newspapers published her speeches in full, however, the story, which could easily be construed as a criticism of immigrant voters, undoubtedly reached a broad audience.

South Dakotans delivered a crushing defeat to the amendment in November 1890, with 45,862 opposed and 22,072 in favor. Only 15.2 percent of voters in Yankton County favored woman suffrage, while a mere 9.4 percent in Hutchinson County approved of the measure.[27] After a grueling campaign, suffragists struggled to make sense of what went wrong. Despite clear organizational deficiencies, NAWSA placed the blame squarely on foreign-born voters. When the Independent Party abandoned woman suffrage to court immigrants, NAWSA lost whatever leverage it had

EQUALITY AT THE BALLOT BOX

with Republicans and Democrats, a fatal blow to the campaign. Moreover, Anthony, Catt, and other NAWSA leaders lambasted foreign-born voters. According to Catt, alien suffrage allowed "30,000 Russians, Germans and Scandinavians" who were "unable to read or write in any language or to speak English" to vote in South Dakota. Catt explained that these immigrants colluded with "saloon henchmen," who brought them to the polls and paid for their votes against the cause.[28] Henry Blackwell, editor of the *Woman's Journal*, also bluntly reported, "American settlers had been starved out and left for other parts of the country, but the degraded foreigners were used to hard times and stayed," thereby casting the deciding ballots against woman suffrage.[29] Few NAWSA leaders bothered to acknowledge that native-born Americans were the majority in South Dakota, and their votes had also sunk the measure.

Between 1890 and 1898, NAWSA increasingly thought victory in South Dakota impossible and declared anti-prohibitionists and foreigners responsible. In 1894, NAWSA did not participate when an amendment that called for partial suffrage in school affairs came before South Dakota voters. South Dakotans defeated the measure with 17,010 votes for and 22,682 against. Two years later, a political tempest again ensued when South Dakotans voted to repeal prohibition. When the legislature reestablished the local option law, which allowed communities to make their own decisions about alcohol regulations, many SDESA leaders also became vocal in the WCTU's efforts to reestablish prohibition. Both local option laws and the suffragists' agitation against them thrilled anti-prohibitionists, as they could explicitly point out that women only wanted the vote to restore prohibition. Partisan politics remained contentious as well. A number of Democrats and some "silver Republicans" joined the Populists, and the party did well in the 1896 election, winning two Congressional seats, the governorship, and control of the state legislature. Republicans scrambled to reassert their dominance, and amid this tumultuous political climate, even Populists who had endorsed woman suffrage became focused on other issues. Partisan jockeying and temperance entanglements increased the tensions among South Dakota suffragists and their national counterparts.[30]

The repeal of prohibition posed a new challenge to SDESA leaders. In 1897, when the legislature passed a measure to submit another woman suffrage amendment to eligible voters the following year, NAWSA leaders were dismayed. Dr. Anna Howard Shaw explained that since the SDESA refused to divorce the cause "from every other issue" and run it "along purely Suffrage lines," defeat was certain. She also saw no hope of carrying the amendment because of "apathy" and "indifference," predicting defeat because of the SDESA's ties to the WCTU.[31] Catt, now prominent in the organization, refused NAWSA support for the campaign, creating a void in leadership and financial resources. As the 1898 campaign drew near, the SDESA officer corps looked virtually identical to the executives of the state WCTU.[32]

While the 1898 campaign retained elements from the 1890 effort, it had several unique dimensons. Many suffragists in South Dakota knew that anti-prohibitionists had a point; if enfranchised, most women probably would vote to reinstate prohibition. The SDESA recycled the Do-Everything policy from 1890 but put greater emphasis on the grassroots effort. They spent most of their energy on a comprehensive canvass at the precinct level, with county leaders using detailed electoral returns to identify and persuade eligible voters. The SDESA pursued this overly ambitious plan knowing that without NAWSA's experienced field organizers they had to rely on local activists. In turn, local workers counted on family, friends, and other social networks, especially when arranging speaking tours. They also readily included foreign-born individuals in the campaign, in part because of alien suffrage and in part because settlement on the Northern Great Plains had required collaboration between foreign-born and native-born residents. Both groups often worked cooperatively on civic initiatives, founding public institutions such as libraries and schools and promoting economic development, reducing ethnic tension in the process.[33]

In Yankton County, a mother-in-law and daughter-in-law duo, Matilda Vanderhule and Adena Vanderhule, coordinated the 1898 South Dakota campaign. Born in Vermont, Matilda Vanderhule and her husband George, a pharmacist, had arrived in South Dakota before 1880. Adena Vanderhule joined the family when she married Clarence, Matilda Vanderhule's oldest son. The Vanderhules were well-known in the community, with Matilda Vanderhule in the WCTU and in the Order of the Eastern Star, the women's auxiliary to the Masons.[34] The Vanderhules spent most of their time arranging speaker schedules, soliciting precinct surveys, requesting literature from SDESA, and renegotiating itineraries. They primarily communicated through letters, which produced an intricate web of correspondence among neighbors, friends, and state officers. The duo selected a chair for each precinct, usually someone they knew. Near Marindahl, a small hamlet in northeast Yankton County, the precinct chair was most likely Ross Vanderhule, Matilda Vanderhule's brother-in-law. At Mayfield, in northern Yankton County, friend and farmer Fred Richter surveyed his precinct and declared the "chances of victory" to be "very good."[35]

The Vanderhules focused most on convincing foreigners to support the cause. In multiple letters, Adena Vanderhule and Matilda Vanderhule called for lecturers who spoke German and Norwegian. While the SDESA claimed to have no German-speaking activists to send, leaders assured the Vanderhules that a Norwegian lecturer or two would arrive once they became available. In the meantime, the SDESA informed Matilda Vanderhule that Emma Cranmer, a suffragist and WCTU member from Aberdeen who spoke only English, was on her way to Yankton County. Vanderhule eagerly arranged a schoolhouse campaign that included an intense schedule of thirteen engagements in fifteen days. Cranmer's tour of local school districts reflected Julia B. Nelson's observation that, if suffragists wanted to convince rural foreigners to support the cause, they had to reach them where they lived.[36]

When Cranmer embarked on her schoolhouse campaign, she had low expectations. Most counties did not have home talent willing to devote substantial time and effort to the cause. In the few counties that did have local organizers, they were often inexperienced, and the sheer amount of work it took to mount a successful campaign overwhelmed them. Most meetings went unadvertised, which made collections meager and audiences small. That the Vanderhules had a schedule at all was a welcome

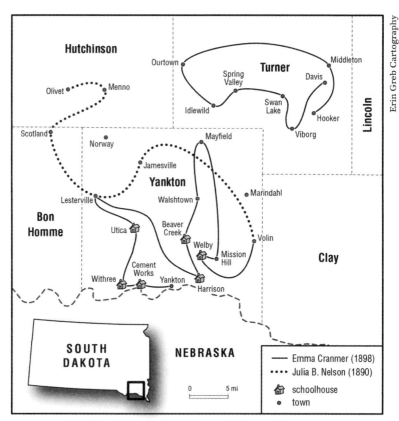

Erin Greb Cartography

*Suffragists Julia B. Nelson and Emma Cranmer
undertook lengthy tours of southeastern South Dakota in
attempting to win supporters.*

change, and on 30 August 1898, Cranmer applauded Matilda
Vanderhule for making "things come to pass." At Mission Hill,
Cranmer enjoyed a "splendid church full, more than half voters,"
although she did not indicate to what denomination the audience
members belonged. Germans at Walshtown were friendly, but
Cranmer noted they did not provide lodging or entertainment.
Although she had a "fine meeting," she noted that they "talked,
cooked & slept—*German*." She related that as she finished her
address, she joked, "*Now* gentlemen if you can't vote yes don't
you dare to vote on the measure." While Cranmer celebrated the
"schoolhouse tour" for "doing more good than all else" by en-

gaging people in face-to-face conversations, she suggested that in many German communities, the best she anticipated was abstention.[37]

When Cranmer departed Yankton County to canvass Turner County, she again encountered scheduling problems. She reported that local advocates had "done virtually nothing" to advertise her visit. When the SDESA sent press notices ahead of her meeting at Davis, someone merely scattered them "about the street with no date no place" listed. "This is hard work," she complained, noting she planned to speak at a small church that required a twenty-five-mile-round-trip voyage. Despite these trials, Cranmer remained defiant. "Work must be done," she quipped. The absence of an itinerary allowed Cranmer to reach out to prominent leaders of ethnic enclaves in order to save what seemed a wasted effort. Cranmer made inroads among Scandinavians in Turner County, when ethnic leaders agreed to take her message to their communities. To her surprise, a Norwegian newspaper editor promised to publish whatever pro-suffrage literature she could send him. A Danish storekeeper—a "radical suffragist" and a *"fine man"*—requested as much propaganda as possible to distribute among his customers. Rejuvenated by this community support, Cranmer echoed Julia B. Nelson when she noted that working among immigrants who traditionally opposed woman suffrage held more significance than canvassing those already in favor.[38]

While Cranmer's tour of southeastern South Dakota raised interest in woman suffrage, many suffragists recognized that her tour ended too soon. The SDESA desperately needed momentum yet lacked resources, especially lecturers. In their letters, the Vanderhules continued to beg SDESA officials to send German or Norwegian lecturers to Yankton County. Cranmer echoed their pleas, noting that Scandinavians in Turner County requested a speaker in their native tongue. While the Vanderhules eventually secured two Norwegian-speaking activists, the lecturers left before finishing a complete canvass of the county. Adena Vanderhule regretted their departure but promised to supplement their tour with literature where possible. The SDESA, however, produced almost all its propaganda in English, leaving the translation to locals with few resources to print it. Moreover, suffragists lacked knowledge of literacy levels in immigrant communities.[39]

South Dakotans voted down the 1898 amendment. Although the outcome was close—19,698 in support and 22,983 against—it was a blow to state and local suffragists. Yankton County showed only 29.8 percent support for woman suffrage, and Turner County 33.2 percent.[40] Home talent struggled with organization and execution without NAWSA's help. Speakers lacked itineraries until the last minute. Locals failed to advertise upcoming meetings. Slow mail service made planning almost impossible. Immigrants and ethnic communities showed interest in the cause, but they had infrequent contact with lecturers and literature in their native languages. The campaign's deficiencies made the efforts of advocates like the Vanderhules all the more impressive.

Following the loss, Carrie Chapman Catt, then chair of NAWSA's Committee on Organization, made two decisions that profoundly shaped future campaigns in the Northern Great Plains states. First, she studied electoral returns, paying particular notice to party affiliation and foreign-born voters. While she said nothing about adjusting the group's strategy based on the results, she noted, "It will be useful to know whether it paid best to let the foreigner alone or to work with him."[41] The returns confirmed for Catt that volatile partisan politics, created by third-parties comprised mainly of foreigners and anti-prohibition foreigners, made the Northern Great Plains an unattractive region in which to campaign for the cause. Her interpretation of the returns led to her second decision, to sever all ties with the SDESA. Catt refused NAWSA support of SDESA until its officers renounced their affiliation with the WCTU. In Catt's eyes, woman suffrage had to be a single issue, or ignorant foreigners would continue to collude with liquor interests to sink the cause. Members of the SDESA and WCTU also recognized this trend, but they could not extricate themselves from the strategy when so many supporters saw woman suffrage as an extension of temperance. In December 1898, Catt wrote directly to local suffrage clubs in South Dakota, asking them to bypass the SDESA and "to work with the National Association in the interest of Equal Suffrage in

South Dakota."[42] When Matilda Vanderhule received Catt's letter, she replied with her plans to send a list of suffrage supporters in Yankton County and work directly with NAWSA as a press superintendent to promote the cause in local newspapers.[43]

The 1890 and 1898 campaigns reveal how ethnicity shaped debates over woman suffrage in South Dakota. Foreign-born individuals were not a majority in the state, but they wielded political clout as part of pressure groups. Attempts to include immigrants in suffrage activism proved divisive. The NAWSA believed the SDESA's overlap with the WCTU would alienate ethnic voters, but SDESA leaders refused to give up their positions in the WCTU. How could suffragists expect foreigners to separate their attitudes toward prohibition from woman suffrage when they could not do so themselves? Immigrants, however, often defied expectations. Carrie Chapman Catt, Julia B. Nelson, and Emma Cranmer each reported receptive ethnic audiences, suggesting that such communities were open to conversion when suffragists could spend the time and effort. Unfortunately, NAWSA lacked the will and SDSEA the resources to mount a grassroots campaign to engage foreign-born people and their communities.

Twenty years after the 1898 campaign and after additional unsuccessful woman suffrage campaigns in 1910, 1914, and 1916, South Dakotans voted in favor of an amendment to enfranchise the state's eligible female voters. The results of the 1918 campaign reflect how suffragists had successfully addressed many of their late-nineteenth-century dilemmas. The SDESA had disbanded in 1910, replaced by the South Dakota Universal Franchise League, which did not share an executive corps with the WCTU. In addition, a majority of South Dakotans had voted to reestablish prohibition in 1916, even as the populace voted down woman suffrage for the fifth time. Unlike the 1890 campaign, rising nativism during World War I dampened brewers' hostility to woman suffrage. Wartime fervor marked anti-prohibitionists as pro-immigrant, a tenuous stance to take as anti-German hysteria gripped the Northern Great Plains. Suffrage leaders appealed to this heightened anti-immigrant sentiment. Claims that immigrants living on the Northern Great Plains were out to sabotage democracy only grew after the 1890s, and state leaders joined NAWSA officials in openly questioning foreign-born individuals' electoral participation.[44]

Ethnic prejudice helped to secure women the ballot. During an emergency wartime legislative session in March 1917, South Dakota's governor added a clause to the pending woman suffrage amendment that would come before voters in November 1918. The additional language extended the residency requirement for naturalization but confirmed that only naturalized citizens could vote, thereby eliminating alien suffrage in South Dakota. The measure likely resonated with suffrage campaign veterans from decades past who had struggled to win over foreigners and often cast them as the reason for their defeats. In 1918, however, suffragists leveraged anti-German sentiment as a campaign strategy, arguing voting rights for native-born women would preserve democracy from foreign influence, especially during wartime. This time, Yankton County showed 52.8 percent support for woman suffrage. Turner County supported votes for women at 53.8 percent, but the measure failed in Hutchinson County with only 28.4 percent of voters supporting the referendum.[45] While woman suffrage prevailed, ethnic tensions had profoundly shaped the debate.

NOTES

1. Nettie C. Hall to Elizabeth Wardall, 20 Aug. 1890, folder 8, box 6674, Pickler Family Papers, State Archives Collection, South Dakota State Historical Society (SDSHS), Pierre (emphasis in original).

2. Cecelia M. Wittmayer, "The 1889–1890 Woman Suffrage Campaign: A Need to Organize," *South Dakota History* 11 (Summer 1981): 199–225; Nancy Tystad Koupal, "Marietta Bones: Personality and Politics in the South Dakota Suffrage Movement," in *Feminist Frontiers: Women Who Shaped the Midwest*, ed. Yvonne J. Johnson (Kirksville, Mo.: Truman State University Press, 2010), pp. 69–82; Frederick C. Luebke, Introduction to *Ethnicity on the Great Plains*, ed. Luebke (Lincoln: University of Nebraska Press, 1980), pp. xi–xxxiii; Jamin Raskin, "Legal Aliens, Local Citizens: The Historical, Constitutional and Theoretical Meanings of Alien Suffrage," *University of Pennsylvania Law Review* 141 (Apr. 1993): 1391–1470.

3. In 1894, a third campaign attempted to enfranchise women on school matters only. The measure failed. *See* Ruth Page Jones, "'The Women Voted': School Suffrage in Dakota Territory and South Dakota," herein.

EQUALITY AT THE BALLOT BOX

4. Wittmayer, "1889–1890 Woman Suffrage Campaign," pp. 208–11; Koupal, "Marietta Bones," pp. 73–74, 78. For a sampling of comments about and thoughts on immigrants and race in the woman suffrage movement, *see* Susan B. Anthony and Ida Husted Harper, eds., *The History of Woman Suffrage*, Vol. 4 (Rochester, N.Y.: Susan B. Anthony, 1902), pp. 176–77, 555–56; Carrie Chapman Catt and Nettie Rogers Shuler, *Woman Suffrage and Politics: The Inner Story of the Suffrage Movement* (New York: Charles Scribner's Sons, 1926), pp. 160–69; Eleanor Flexner, *Century of Struggle: The Woman's Rights Movement in the United States* (New York: Athenaeum, 1972), pp. 211, 297; Beverly Beeton, *Women Vote in the West: The Woman Suffrage Movement, 1869–1896* (New York: Garland Publishing, 1986), pp. 110–13, 119, 123, 125, 129, 133; Rebecca Mead, *How the Vote Was Won: Woman Suffrage in the Western United States, 1868–1914* (New York: New York University Press, 2006), pp. 4–13; Holly McCammon, "Stirring Up Suffrage Sentiment: The Formation of the State Woman Suffrage Organizations, 1866–1914," *Social Forces* 80 (Dec. 2001): 449–80, esp. 457–58, 467, 472.

5. Rex C. Myers, "An Immigrant Heritage: South Dakota's Foreign-Born in the Era of Assimilation," *South Dakota History* 19 (Summer 1989): 137–39; Robert Karolevitz, *Yankton—The Way It Was!: Being a Collection of Historical Columns* (Yankton, S.Dak.: Yankton Daily Press & Dakotan, 1998), p. 84; Frederick Luebke, "Ethnic Group Settlement on the Great Plains," *Western Historical Quarterly* 8 (Oct. 1977): 412. Ethnic Germans first settled in the Crimea and Black Sea regions in Russia under the protection of Catherine the Great in 1763. They lived in Russia for almost a century, until Catherine's great-grandson, Alexander II, revoked their privileges and sought to "Russianize" them. Dissatisfied with Alexander II's new rules, Germans in Russia looked for a new place to settle. Their search coincided with the Great Dakota Boom, and many moved to Dakota Territory in the late nineteenth century.

6. Myers, "Immigrant Heritage," pp. 137–39; Sara Egge, *Woman Suffrage and Citizenship in the Midwest, 1870–1920* (Iowa City: University of Iowa Press, 2018), pp. 31–35, 66.

7. Herbert Schell, *History of South Dakota* (Pierre: South Dakota State Historical Society, 2004), pp. 223–30; Terrence J. Lindell, "South Dakota Populism" (master's thesis: University of Nebraska, 1982), pp. 11, 125–30, 135–37; Myers, "Immigrant Heritage," pp. 134–43; Erling Sannes, "Knowledge Is Power: The Knights of Labor in South Dakota," *South Dakota History* 22 (Winter 1992): 420–30. *See also* John Dibbern, "Who Were the Populists? A Study of Grass-Roots Alliancemen in Dakota," *Agricultural History* 56 (Oct. 1982): 678–82. Dibbern studied the "prepolitical Alliance phase of the populist movment," from 1885–1890, using Marshall County, S.Dak. as a case

study (p. 678). For the development of the Populist Party, the "ethnic farm vote," and "ethnic voting blocs," *see also* R. Alton Lee, *Principle over Party: The Farmers' Alliance and Populism in South Dakota, 1880–1900* (Pierre: South Dakota Historical Society Press, 2011), pp. 68–70, 73–74, 77, 131–32, 188. Before the Populists emerged, Lee notes, ethnic groups had formed "a major bloc" within the Republican Party (p. 109).

8. Susan B. Anthony to Frances E. Willard, 21 Mar. 1890, in *The Selected Papers of Elizabeth Cady Stanton and Susan B. Anthony: Their Place inside the Body-Politic, 1887–1895*, Vol. 5, ed. Ann D. Gordon (New Brunswick: Rutgers University Press, 2009), pp. 274–76.

9. Wanda Hendricks, *Gender, Race, and Politics in the Midwest: Black Club Women in Illinois* (Bloomington: Indiana University Press, 1998), pp. 76–78; Allison Sneider, *Suffragists in an Imperial Age: U.S. Expansion and the Woman Question, 1870–1929* (New York: Oxford University Press, 2008), pp. 5–6, 15–17, 31.

10. Quoted in Olympia Brown, "Foreign Rule," in *History of Woman Suffrage*, ed. Anthony and Harper, pp. 147–49.

11. Hendricks, *Gender, Race, and Politics in the Midwest*, pp. 76–78; Carrie Chapman Catt, "Danger to Our Government," in *Up from the Pedestal: Selected Writings in the History of American Feminism*, ed. Aileen S. Kraditor (Chicago: Quadrangle Books, 1968), pp. 261–62; Anthony to Willard, 21 Mar. 1890, in *Selected Papers of Elizabeth Cady Stanton and Susan B. Anthony*, ed. Gordon, p. 276; Koupal, "Marietta Bones," pp. 74–78; Wittmayer, "1889–1890 Woman Suffrage Campaign," pp. 202, 206.

12. Wittmayer, "1889–1890 Woman Suffrage Campaign," pp. 217–22; Lee, *Principle over Party*, pp. 68–70.

13. Anthony to Pickler, 14 June 1890, folder 27, box 6674, Pickler Family Papers (emphasis in original).

14. Quoted in Wittmayer, "1889–1890 Woman Suffrage Campaign," p. 219.

15. Ibid., pp. 217–18.

16. "Headquarters Equal Suffrage Association of South Dakota" to "Friends of Equal Suffrage," 16 July 1890, folder 42, box 6674, Pickler Family Papers.

17. Paula Baker, "The Domestification of Politics: Women and American Political Society, 1780–1920," *American Historical Review* 89 (June 1985): 620–22, 638–45; Sara Hunter Graham, *Woman Suffrage and the New Democracy* (New Haven: Yale University Press, 1996), pp. 25–29.

18. "Headquarters Equal Suffrage Association of South Dakota" to "Friends of Equal Suffrage." *See also* Jennifer Ross-Nazzal, *Winning the West for Women: The Life of Suffragist Emma Smith DeVoe* (Seattle: University of Washington Press, 2011), pp. 37–38.

19. Julia King to William Bailey, 19 Aug. 1890, folder 8, box 6674, Pickler Family Papers.

20. Eileen L. McDonagh and H. Douglas Price, "Woman Suffrage in the Progressive Era: Patterns of Opposition and Support in Referenda Voting, 1910–1918," *American Political Science Review* 79 (June 1985): 418–21.

21. Catt to "State Office," 17 Sept. 1890, folder 13, box 6674, Pickler Family Papers.

22. Julia Wiech Lief, "A Woman of Purpose: Julia B. Nelson," *Minnesota History* 47 (Winter 1981): 302–10.

23. Nelson to William Bailey, 1 Oct. 1890, folder 4, box 6674, Pickler Family Papers.

24. Ibid., 3 Oct. 1890.

25. Nelson to Elizabeth Wardall, 18 Oct. 1890, ibid.

26. Quoted in "Equal Suffrage," *Hecla Citizen*, 27 June 1890, and "South Dakota," *Union Signal*, 19 Dec. 1889, both in Scrapbook, 1880 to 1890, box 10, Emma Smith DeVoe Papers, Washington Historical Society, Tacoma.

27. Anthony and Harper, eds., *History of Woman Suffrage*, pp. 557–58; Patricia O'Keefe Easton, "Opposition to Woman Suffrage in South Dakota" (master's thesis, University of South Dakota, 1982), pp. 134–35.

28. Catt and Shuler, *Woman Suffrage and Politics*, p. 116. *See also* Elizabeth Cady Stanton, "Significance and History of the Ballot," in *History of Woman Suffrage*, ed. Anthony and Harper, pp. 316–18.

29. Blackwell, "Suffrage in the West," *Washington* Post, 1 Mar. 1891, Scrapbook, 1880 to 1890, box 10, DeVoe Papers.

30. Dorinda Riessen Reed, *The Woman Suffrage Movement in South Dakota*, 2d ed. (Pierre: South Dakota Comission on the Status of Women, 1975), pp. 49, 117; Lee, *Principle over Party*, pp. 122–23, 131–32, 138–43; Schell, *History of South Dakota*, pp. 229–41. *See also* Jones, "'Women Voted,'" herein.

31. Shaw to Clara Williams, 17 Oct. 1898, folder 22, box 6676, Pickler Family Papers.

32. Anthony and Harper, eds., *History of Woman Suffrage*, pp. 555–61; Emma Cranmer to Clare Williams, 30 Aug. 1898, and Catt to Williams, 24 Oct. 1898, both in folder 20, box 6676, Pickler Family Papers; Catt to Jane Rooker Breeden, 12 Jan. 1898, folder 1, box 1, Jane Rooker Breeden Papers, State Archies Collection, SDSHS; Reed, *Woman Suffrage Movement in South Dakota*, pp. 48–53. Eventually, NAWSA gave a paltry one-hundred-dollars worth of literature to the campaign. State suffragists raised a total of fifteen-hundred dollars. NAWSA leaders did pay to send Laura Gregg to the state on a month-long lecture tour. SDESA officials admitted, however, that poor local organization limited her effectiveness, for she sometimes went

days without a speaking engagement. *See* Anthony and Harper, eds., *History of Woman Suffrage*, p. 557; Paula M. Nelson, "Home and Family First: Women and Political Culture," in *The Plains Political Tradition: Essays on South Dakota Political Culture*, ed. Jon K. Lauck, John E. Miller, and Donald C. Simmons, Jr. (Pierre: South Dakota Historical Society Press, 2011), p. 142.

33. Andrew Cayton and Peter Onuf, *The Midwest and the Nation: Rethinking the History of an American Region* (Bloomington: Indiana University Press, 1990), pp. 68–75; Andrew Cayton and Susan E. Gray, "The Story of the Midwest: An Introduction," in *The Identity of the American Midwest: Essays on Regional History*, ed. Cayton and Gray (Bloomington: Indiana University Press, 2001), pp. 3–4.

34. Doane Robinson, *History of South Dakota*, Vol. 1 (Indianapolis: B.F. Bowen & Co., 1904), pp. 910–13; U.S., Department of Commerce, Bureau of the Census, *Twelfth Census of the United States*, 1900, and *Thirteenth Census of the United States*, 1910, Record Group 29, Records of the Bureau of the Census, Washington, D.C., NARA microfilm publication; Matilda Vanderhule to Clare Williams, 11 Aug. 1898, folder 9, box 6676, Pickler Family Papers.

35. Richter to Clare Williams, 10 Sept. 1898, folder 10, ibid.

36. Matilda Vanderhule to Williams, 10 Sept. 1898, folder 10, 4 Oct. 1898, folder 17, Cranmer to Williams, 30 Aug. 1898, folder 20, Matilda Vanderhule to Williams, 22 Aug. 1898, folder 6, 5 Aug. 1898, folder 8, 9, 11 Aug. 1898, folder 9, "Cranmer Ends Clay Co. Tues. Aug. 16," folder 8, all ibid.; "Around Home," *Yankton Press and Dakotan*, 28 Aug. 1898.

37. Cranmer to Williams, 30 Aug. 1898 (emphasis in original).

38. Ibid., 6 Sept. 1898, folder 20, box 6676, Pickler Family Papers.

39. Adena Vanderhule to Williams, 22 Aug. 1898, folder 6, Catt to Williams, 26 July 1898, folder 22, Adena Vanderhule to Williams, 4 Oct. 1898, folder 17, Cranmer to Williams, 6 Sept. 1898, folder 20, all ibid.

40. Reed, *Woman Suffrage in South Dakota*, pp. 52, 117; Easton, "Opposition to Woman Suffrage in South Dakota," p. 135.

41. Catt to Williams, 7 Nov. 1898, folder 20, box 6676, Pickler Family Papers.

42. Quoted in Matilda Vanderhule to Catt, 30 Dec. 1898, folder 24, ibid.

43. Ibid.; Catt to Williams, 7 Nov. 1898; Philena Everett Johnson to Alice Pickler, 22 July 1909, folder 19, box 6677, Pickler Family Papers.

44. Robert P. Saldin, *War, the American State, and Politics since 1898* (New York: Cambridge University Press, 2011), pp. 80–83; Erik Kirschbaum, *Burning Beethoven: The Eradication of German Culture in the United States* (New York: Berlinica Publishing, 2015), pp. 39–45, 77–82, 92–93, 149–50;

Frederic Luebke, *Bonds of Loyalty: German-Americans and World War I* (DeKalb: Northern Illinois University Press, 1974), pp. 61, 68, 98, 217–18, 255–56, 269–74.

45. Reed, *Woman Suffrage Movement in South Dakota*, pp. 96–113; Easton, "Opposition to Woman Suffrage in South Dakota," pp. 97–108, 134–35; Patricia O'Keefe Easton, "Woman Suffrage in South Dakota: The Final Decade, 1911–1920," *South Dakota History* 13 (Fall 1983): 206–26.

CITIZENSHIP, CIVILIZATION, AND PROPERTY

The 1890 South Dakota Vote on Woman Suffrage and Indian Suffrage

MOLLY P. ROZUM

"Woman Suffrage Snowed Under" headlined the *Hot Springs Star*.[1] On 4 November 1890, South Dakota's voting population soundly defeated its first post-statehood referendum on woman suffrage. Supporters had worked hard during the state's three constitutional conventions in the 1880s to ensure South Dakota entered the United States as the first woman suffrage state. They achieved only a constitutional requirement to submit woman suffrage to the electorate at the first post-statehood general election. Only 33 percent of voters supported the amendment to strike the word "male" from the year-old constitution. South Dakota voters also defeated an attempt by the state legislature to restrict American Indian voting, with 43 percent voting in favor. Amid severe drought, South Dakota entered the Union optimistic that a new wave of settlers would soon claim land on much of the former Great Sioux Reservation. Some state officials also felt apprehension about the end of Sioux jurisdiction on lands within the state; the goal of the defeated "Indian suffrage" amendment had been to restrict Lakota and Dakota men's voting rights.[2]

Woman suffrage supporters regarded the divergent results as a slight. "Woman's suffrage has been defeated . . . while the Indian has been extended the franchise. It is an insult to the intelligent womanhood of South Dakota," opined the *Woonsocket Times*.[3] The *Aberdeen Pioneer* argued, "The defeat of Equal Suffrage will stand as a lasting reproach to the state of South Dakota," while the same results "will probably give the red man the right to vote

Map: Organized South Dakota Counties in 1890

States labeled: MINN., NORTH DAKOTA, MONTANA, WYOMING, NEBRASKA

County data (bold = Percentage for restricting Indian Suffrage; regular = Percentage for Woman Suffrage):

- Grant **58%** 29%
- Deuel **25%** 26%
- Moody **44%** 38%
- Minnehaha **51%** 30%
- Lincoln **55%** 34%
- Union **28%** 21%
- Roberts **57%** 32%
- Codington **48%** 30%
- Hamlin **46%** 42%
- Brookings **32%** 33%
- Lake **55%** 35%
- Turner **44%** 24%
- Clay **35%** 31%
- Marshall **16%** 34%
- Day **40%** 32%
- Clark **35%** 42%
- Kingsbury **63%** 43%
- Miner **39%** 37%
- McCook **30%** 23%
- Hutchinson **59%** 9%
- Yankton **34%** 15%
- Brown **42%** 41%
- Spink **47%** 43%
- Beadle **47%** 43%
- Sanborn **38%** 44%
- Hanson **34%** 36%
- Davison **51%** 38%
- Bon Homme **38%** 19%
- McPherson **8%** 18%
- Edmunds **82%** 44%
- Faulk **40%** 34%
- Hand **35%** 48%
- Jerauld **35%** 45%
- Aurora **42%** 37%
- Douglas **34%** 21%
- Charles Mix **70%** 23%
- Campbell **29%** 25%
- Walworth **16%** 43%
- Potter **30%** 39%
- Sully **42%** 55%
- Hyde **30%** 47%
- Hughes **40%** 42%
- Buffalo **80%** 27%
- Brule **49%** 29%
- Stanley **45%** 38%
- Harding **24%** 41%
- Butte **24%** 38%
- Meade **42%** 27%
- Lawrence **45%** 34%
- Pennington **44%** 44%
- Custer **61%** 48%
- Fall River **35%** 50%

Unorganized Counties (no data): Boreman, Dewey, Pyatt, Pratt, Presho, Tripp, Lyman, Lyman, Gregory, Todd, Meyer, Schnasse, Wagner, Rinehart, Sterling, Nowlin, Jackson, Washabaugh, Lugenbeel, Martin, Choteau, Delano, Scobey, Ziebach, Washington, Shannon, Ewing

Legend:
- Western Sioux Reservations after 1889
  - Standing Rock
  - Cheyenne River
  - Pine Ridge
  - Lower Brule
  - Crow Creek
  - Rosebud
- Organized South Dakota Counties in 1890
- Unorganized Counties
- **Percentage for restricting Indian Suffrage**
- Percentage for Woman Suffrage

in our state hereafter!"[4] Many settlers linked the woman and Indian franchise amendments intellectually. In particular, national woman suffrage advocates reacted with an incredulity that reflected their racist assumptions.

The 1890 election reveals the complicated racialized and gendered ways in which settlers and suffragists thought about citizenship, civilization, property, and politics. On the Northern Great Plains, the primacy of land ownership in settler culture provided a new lens with which to view both women's and American Indians' voting rights positively. But the results of the twinned suffrage referenda revealed the cultural strength of universal manhood suffrage to be greater than the drive for universal suffrage. Powerful sex and gender norms kept what many suffragists called the "intelligent womanhood of South Dakota" from equality at the ballot box. Rigid racial concepts embedded in nineteenth-century United States culture eliminated unacculturated American Indian women from this intelligent womanhood and, in the end, kept American Indian men away from the polls, as well. Consideration of "the Indian vote" as important to future South Dakota "political computations," as the editor of the *Kimball Graphic* put it, turned out to be only a fleeting opportunity for a unique multiracial politics, albeit one gendered male.[5]

The results of the two referenda suggested to suffragists that South Dakotans favored the creation of a racially-inclusive, all-male electorate. In contrast, some woman suffrage advocates suggested a standard they called "educated suffrage," which they promoted to bring attention to the presumed cultural and intellectual advantages of white women voters. Elaborating on this idea in 1894, Elizabeth Cady Stanton postulated that "certain restrictions" on the vote, such as abilities to read and write English, could be implemented "without denying the general principle" of universal suffrage. Yet, this concept often reflected race-based cultural assumptions about civilization. Contemporary theories of racial hierarchy, in which white races axiomatically headed "civilized" society while the "lower orders" followed, influenced this thinking. While boundaries to voting based on education appeared permeable, allowing races or individuals to rise above "ignorance," the idea left room for exclusion from the vote based on culturally defined measures for intelligence.[6] Suffragists compared their social standing in South Dakota to both foreign-born men, who could vote without citizenship, and now, after the 1890 election returns, to unassimilated American Indian men. Many who ostensibly supported universal suffrage believed educated suffrage worked to middle-class white women's political advantage when arguing for voting rights.

After the mid-1870s, many suffragists shifted from using legal arguments based on the Fourteenth Amendment, which implied that all citizens had the right to vote, to a strategy based on the notion that suffrage would expand women's duties and work in the public sphere. The focus on the "organic" family, especially common to members of the Woman's Christian Temperance Union (WCTU), according to historian Allison L. Sneider, helped "make qualities such as ethnicity and heredity important tenets of national identity" and led to emphasizing "essential qualities and abstract capacity of individuals, rather than their universal rights as citizens."[7] Assimilation policy had presumed that American Indians possessed the ability to rise to the same levels of civilization as Europeans. By the late nineteenth century, however, "increasingly systematized theories of racial classification and hierarchy" linked inferiority to American Indians' ideas and cultural practices. As historian Jeffrey Ostler explains, "Most European Americans took for granted that the world's peoples could be divided into 'races,' with the 'white race' above all others, although the implications of this belief varied considerably in practice."[8]

The subject of Indian voting, as much as woman suffrage, had been on the minds of South Dakota settlers generally in the months leading up to the 1890 election. Two recent federal laws influenced settlers' thinking. The 1887 Dawes Severalty Act authorized the division of what the United States Congress and reformers held to be "uncivilized" communal reservation land into more "civilized" allotments of land, chosen by or assigned to individual American Indian heads of family, single male and female adults, and children. Allotted property came with United States citizenship, which to many settlers implied voting rights for American Indian men. The original act, as historian Francis

Paul Prucha explains, proclaimed, "Every Indian to whom an allotment was made and every Indian who separated himself from his tribe and adopted the ways of civilized life" to be "a citizen of the United States, without however, impairing the Indian's right to tribal or other property." The act allowed the president to authorize unilaterally the allotment of reservation land. Most reformers thought the individual property ownership outlined in the Dawes Act would help American Indians acculturate, civilize, and Christianize in the image of settler society. Initially, allottees became citizens of the United States and were issued a "trust patent," under which the federal government retained control of the land placed in trust for a period of twenty-five years. After the trust period passed, the allottee received full ownership of the land.[9]

The 1889 Sioux Agreement drew boundaries for six much smaller reservations tied to individual Sioux bands and eliminated the Great Sioux Reservation, which had covered much of western South Dakota. Settlers anticipated gradual absorption of both "surplus" unallotted reservation lands and this massive cession from the reservation into state borders through the use of federal land laws such as the Homestead Act. The state legislature had already overlaid the former Great Sioux Reservation with unorganized "paper" counties named almost exclusively for individuals prominent in settler society. As American Indians "civilized," state officials also expected to incorporate Indian-owned allotments. Federal and state governments envisioned disappearing reservations and, ideally, the emergence of assimilated new citizens of American Indian heritage who would eventually become resident, fully acculturated, property-owning citizens and, in the case of men, voters in what settlers thought of as "our state." Similar to national leaders, state officials "envisioned nothing less than the eventual extinguishment of all tribal claims to land." American Indians would disappear through assimilation and the allotment and sale of reservation lands.[10]

Early accounts of South Dakota's 1890 voting returns speculated that confusing ballot instructions for the woman and Indian amendments probably played a role in the failure of both. Ballot-marking required a voter to "scratch" (or "erase") the choice he opposed: one scratched out no to vote for striking the word "male" from the South Dakota constitution and also scratched out no to add language to restrict Indian voting to it. In a post-election newspaper column, South Dakota Equal Suffrage Association (SDESA) member Emma Smith DeVoe noted the "obscure" wording and surmised, "Many voted against it [woman suffrage] who desired to vote for it."[11] The editor of the *Queen City Mail* of Spearfish pointed to "the blind way" the legislature "submitted" the amendment to restrict Indian voting and claimed, "Thousands voted 'for' Indian suffrage under the impression they were voting 'against' it."[12]

An editorial in the *Black Hills Weekly Times* suggested the problem with the Indian suffrage ballot originated in the last-minute adoption of the amendment, when legislators "questioned [the bill] to such an extent" that it became "too late to provide by law for the manner of its submission." As a result, law-makers chose "the best means" available, that is, the same instructions drawn for "the question of woman suffrage." Without fully explaining, this writer saw the choice "at best, of doubtful legality" but said nothing about why legislators attached confusing instructions to the woman suffrage amendment.[13] Regardless of "misunderstanding," a *Woonsocket Times* editorial announced sarcastically, "Now the Indian can vote just the same, and your wife and daughter can have the supreme satisfaction of watching Mr. Indian, now a sovereign citizen of the United States, deposit his ballot."[14]

Soon after the 1889 Sioux land cession, the *Kimball Graphic* estimated that some five thousand American Indians would vote as a result of "the opening of the Sioux Reservation."[15] In February 1890, the month settlers could advance on the former Great Sioux Reservation, the *Sioux Falls Argus-Leader* carried a blurb estimating that twenty thousand "Indians will vote in South Dakota at the next presidential election."[16] An article in the *Milbank Herald* favored the vote for Sisseton Dakota "reservation Indians" in both Grant and Roberts counties, arguing they "vote just as intelligently as white men." The same author also noted "anxiety" among "some politicians" about "Indian votes which will be thrown upon the market when the Sioux reservation Indians are

Citizenship, Civilization, and Property   [245

made citizens by selecting their allotments of land."[17] The populations of Grant and Roberts counties, however, voted to restrict American Indian voting in 1890. A debate over whether reservation Indians could vote also heated up when advocates for Huron as the state's permanent capital—also to be decided at the 1890 election—charged Pierre, the other primary contender, with enfranchising Indian voters unlawfully.[18] Such discussions point to the origin of the South Dakota legislature's amendment to restrict Indian voting.

The failure of lawmakers' effort to thwart the Indian vote raised questions about what they had hoped to achieve. South Dakota's legislators almost certainly attempted to redress the omission from the state's constitution of a process by which American Indians would be qualified to vote as residents of the state. North Dakota's 1889 constitution limited American Indian voting to "civilized persons of Indian descent who shall have severed their tribal relations two years next preceding such election."[19] South Dakota's constitution did not address Indian voting at all. A writer in the *Black Hills Daily Times* wondered which "ignorant" legislator created such a measure that required only "the best of grammarians and scholars . . . to know how to vote intelligently and properly."[20] A person "acquainted with the circumstances connected with the origin" of the amendment wrote an editorial in reply. Apparently, state legislators "doubt[ed] the benefit of the flood of Indian votes about to set in upon the state" because they expected land allotments to end "Indian community jurisdiction." The amendment simply sought to "prevent such Indians from voting." Legislators focused on the phrase "not otherwise disqualified" in the voting qualifications section of the state's constitution. Among classes of persons disqualified from voting, lawmakers rationalized the amendment by placing American Indians "in the same position as persons under guardianship."[21]

An editorial in the *Kimball Graphic* expressed trepidation at the thought the state could end up with "a problem comparable to negro supremacy in the South." What if voting American Indians "happen to outnumber whites?" This writer advocated duty to law but considered it "pretty tough when it is brought right home to you." The "average Dakota Indian" ranked far above "the average Southern negro," but, the author concluded, "neither of them has intelligence enough to run a country fit for a white man to live in." In any case, the writer speculated, "In the future in making political computations the Indian vote will play an important part." To alleviate the political anxiety, the article suggested tying voting rights to "a certain standard of intelligence on the part of every voter—be he white, red, black, yellow, foreign or native born."[22] The comment suggests the broadly shared post-Reconstruction culture in which state governments used educated suffrage to create special voting spaces for old-stock, white, United States-born citizens. Some South Dakotans, echoing fears that southerners had expressed about freedpeople, worried that American Indians would "vote in sufficient numbers to change the power structure and overwhelm their white neighbors."[23]

The pro-woman suffrage South Dakota politician John Pickler argued, "The near prospect of the enfranchisement of fifteen thousand Indians makes it imperative that woman suffrage [*sic*] be adopted now, before this new element shall be admitted to participation in the state government."[24] As suffragist Elizabeth Cady Stanton phrased it, woman was "the greatest factor in civilization."[25] The success of settler colonialism throughout the country had relied on women's efforts to "civilize" space by establishing homes, schools, and churches.[26] Settler women, some suffragists suggested, could use the vote as a tool for organizing a racially and ethnically diverse society.

Settlers associated the settlement process, and particularly property ownership, with citizenship and civilization. The Dawes Severalty Act operated on this principle. The federal government expected "individualization of the Indian through private property."[27] Pickler, married to suffragist Alice Alt Pickler, reportedly believed "the chances of carrying" woman suffrage in the state excellent precisely because he figured women owned about one-fifth of the state's land. He argued that the injustice imposed on "unmarried women in the state," who "are paying taxes without any representation, and without any voice in the levying taxes on their land," gave weight to women's pleas for the vote. Although at least one Dakota Sioux descendant, Jane Van Meter Waldron, took an allotment and then served as the state corresponding

Jane Van Meter Waldron, c. 1890.
South Dakota State Historical Society

secretary of the SDESA, no evidence suggests that Pickler was speaking on behalf of any American Indian women allottees.[28] Writing in the *Wessington Springs Herald*, LoElla H. Blank also noted that farm-owning women were "an ever-present argument for their enfranchisement" because they "know by sad experience that taxation without representation is tyranny, in the case of a woman as well as a man."[29]

Many suffragists saw women's taxable real estate as justification for the right to vote. A canvas of four townships near Clifton, where Alice Pickler "did a great deal of good," revealed "nearly all of them believe that widows and property owners ought to be al[l]owed to vote."[30] National suffragist Matilda Joslyn Gage,

EQUALITY AT THE BALLOT BOX

who spent time in the state advocating for woman suffrage during South Dakota's 1883 constitutional convention, pointed to the large numbers of unmarried women and widows who took up land claims and were subsequently "taxed to help support the government." Gage also emphasized the work married women undertook to meet the homestead law requirements only to be without any right in ownership.[31]

Requirements for voting rights across the nation in the pre-Civil War years had shifted away from property as the primary qualification for voting. Yet, settlers were focused on acquiring land and believed they civilized the northern grasslands through commercial agriculture. Noncitizen immigrants could vote in South Dakota in part because of their value in settling land. Although women had long argued that voting rights should ensue from citizenship, male legislators frequently pointed out that children were citizens but nevertheless disqualified from voting. The United States Constitution did not attach voting rights to citizenship or make it a natural right. Instead, framers made the vote "a privilege conferred by government and subject to constitutional and statutory limitations" as instituted by individual states. Because the national constitution did not bind voting rights and citizenship, the states made various laws that restricted voting by race, gender, residency, age, and property; in some states, such as South Dakota, noncitizens met voting requirements that citizens could not.[32] Westward expansion elevated land in the nation's culture, and contemporary theorists conflated property ownership with heightened levels of civilization. The creation of private property also advanced the federal government's goals of territorial incorporation and domination over American Indians. In the West, land ownership reemerged in popular discussion as a basis for citizenship and political participation.[33]

The reception of American Indians and white women suffragists at the state's August 1890 Republican convention at Mitchell nevertheless showed the cultural hold that sex and gender norms had on voting rights. National suffragist Anna Howard Shaw, who was touring South Dakota as part of the state campaign, reported on the convention events. First, Republicans did not publicly support woman suffrage with a platform plank (neither did the Democrats or Populists). Then, Republicans "barely tolerated" the "eminent" suffragist Susan B. Anthony, who had crisscrossed the state twice advocating for woman suffrage before the 1890 vote, not even reserving one "good seat" for her. Party men provided the woman suffrage delegation, "the brainiest women in South Dakota," only ten seats in the back, "where we could neither see nor hear unless we stood on our chairs."[34] These same officials, however, did find three well-placed seats for Dakota Indian men from the Yankton reservation, who reportedly represented three hundred votes. Politicians expected the process of allotting the Yankton reservation to be completed by 1895.[35] Dakota Sioux men may have attended the convention to explore their status as voters. Perhaps Republican men's desire for American Indian votes to be "thrown upon the market" pushed them to gauge "how they [the Sioux] will vote" and "if their votes can easily be controlled."[36] Shaw saw only "big, dirty Indians in blankets and moccasins" cutting into the voting line in front of clean educated women.[37] Clearly exasperated, Anthony wrote a colleague, "*Good Heavens*—The Indian Bucks ahead of Civilized Women!!"[38] The remarks by both women show how suffragists felt the need to assert their superiority by denigrating American Indians.

To one observer, the situation of suffragists shunted to the back of the hall at the South Dakota Republican convention conjured up the punishment of former Confederate president Jefferson Davis for treason. After the Civil War, the federal government "put him down to the level of a woman, and disfranchised him." The local commentator, writing in the *Dakota Farmers' Leader*, speculated how suffragists had felt the power of masculinity in their rejection, saying, "She n[e]ver knew the importance of being a man forcibly, until she attended the republican state convention at Mitchell." Because they were men, three hundred potentially enfranchised Yanktons counted more than seventy thousand voteless "mothers and daughters of South Dakota." Maleness "was the reason the republicans loved their Indians more than their women."[39] In reality, the Dawes Act had created male and female United States citizens and landowners but only male voters. The same year the Dawes Act passed, 1887, Congress debated and defeated a woman suffrage amendment.[40]

SOUTH DAKOTA

EQUAL SUFFRAGE

MASS CONVENTION,

OPERA HOUSE

MITCHELL, AUGUST 25-26, 1890

"UNDER GOD THE PEOPLE RULE"---WOMEN ARE PEOPLE.

Officers of the Association:

PHILENA EVERETT JOHNSON,	PRESIDENT.
IRENE G. ADAMS,	VICE-PRESIDENT.
WILL F. BAILEY,	SECRETARY.
SARAH A. RICHARDS,	TREASURER.
ALICE M. A. PICKLER,	
HON. D. C. THOMAS,	MEMBERS EX. COM.
SUSAN B. ANTHONY.	
EMMA SMITH DeVOE,	STATE LECTURER.
ELIZABETH M. HAMMER,	SUP'T. ORATORICAL CONTEST.
ELIZABETH MURRAY WARDALL,	SUP'T. PRESS WORK.

Headquarters Room 9 Hills' Block, Huron, South Dakota.

South Dakota suffragists met in Mitchell just prior to the Republican convention in 1890. South Dakota State Historical Society

Democracy, it seemed, allowed room for men to gain the vote through land ownership, civilization, and naturalization, regardless of race. Many women, settler *and* American Indian, had achieved the same markers of political maturity, landownership and establishment of homes and communities, but in 1890 South Dakota, sex and gender proscriptions kept all women from transcending a culturally embedded level beneath men. Indeed, patriarchal family norms meant that American Indian women who were the spouses of American men received no individual allotment under the original Dawes Act, just as married women were excluded from the Homestead Act.[41] The slight at the Republican convention, where sex and gender seemed to outweigh race, helped frame the way suffragists received their loss at the polls.

After the defeat of South Dakota's 1890 woman suffrage referendum, Shaw concluded, "Of the two classes of voters it seemed the men preferred the Indians." She spoke at the 1891 National American Woman Suffrage Association convention in Washington, D.C., under the heading "Women v. Indians."[42] To woman suffrage supporters, the choices of South Dakota's male voters must have seemed all too similar to the post-Civil War moment in 1869 when the United States Congress refused to prohibit states from denying voting rights by sex in addition to race in the Fifteenth Amendment. Conceived of as "'Negro suffrage' versus woman suffrage," the disagreement split the American Equal Rights Association into the American Woman Suffrage Association, which supported the Fifteenth Amendment, and the National Woman Suffrage Association, to which Anthony and Stanton belonged, which did not.[43] The two organizations had only just reunited in 1890 in the middle of the South Dakota campaign.

Twenty years after the United States Congress passed the last of the post-Civil War Reconstruction amendments, South Dakota lawmakers struggled with whether their amendment to restrict American Indian voting violated the Fourteenth and Fifteenth Amendments. The Fourteenth Amendment, passed in 1868, defined national citizenship and its "privileges," including the right to "life, liberty, or property" and "equal protection of the laws." The Fifteenth Amendment, passed in 1870, prohibited states from denying or abridging the right to vote "on account of race, color,

EQUALITY AT THE BALLOT BOX

or previous condition of servitude." Although passed as part of an effort to protect the civil rights of freedpeople, the United States Congress had also debated how the Fourteenth Amendment applied to Indians. The 1866 Civil Rights Act originally included the phrase "excluding Indians not taxed," but a Senate vote deleted the phrase from the citizenship section of the Fourteenth Amendment. Some United States senators, however, argued that American Indians already lacked citizenship because they held allegiances to their tribes. By 1870, the Senate Judiciary Committee expressed a widely shared viewpoint that citizenship, as defined by the Fourteenth Amendment, did not apply to American Indians. Section two of the Fourteenth Amendment, which pertained to the apportionment of national representatives, however, specifically included "Indians not taxed," a phrase many states later used to deny American Indians the vote.[44]

Two decades later, some South Dakota legislators questioned whether the Fourteenth Amendment automatically made Indians citizens after "the disappearance of Indian community Jurisdiction," which they expected to occur through the Dawes allotment process. Others doubted their power to restrict Indian voting under the Fifteenth Amendment's prohibitions against denying the vote because of race.[45] The long debate delayed the Indian suffrage amendment, by which legislators sought to place American Indians under guardianship, to the last day of the legislative session. This delay reportedly caused the awkwardly worded ballot that many voters decried. The debate in the South Dakota legislature reveals how post-Civil War racial politics remained contested over a quarter century later on the Northern Great Plains.

White middle-class women and black men had been allies in the fight for equal human rights since the pre-Civil War abolitionist movement to end slavery.[46] In 1869, however, Elizabeth Cady Stanton saw no reason for women to "stand aside and see 'Sambo' walk into the kingdom first" before "the educated women of the country."[47] In failing to restrict American Indian men from voting in 1890, South Dakota's male voters placed another class of men above "educated" settler women. The state already allowed Norwegian, German, German Russian, Irish, and Bohemian

men, among others, to vote without full citizenship. Woman suffragists believed this large foreign-born immigrant population of
voters had cost them the victory.[48] Stanton understood South Dakota men to be "practically saying that they preferred Indians to
women as co-rulers within their borders."[49] Suffragists predicted
male American Indian voters might also oppose woman suffrage,
making victory in the state even more difficult.[50]

In the fall of 1890, Anna Howard Shaw remarked on the contrast between "white women . . . pleading for the rights of citizens" in South Dakota and "Indians . . . engaged in their ghost
dances."[51] Some Lakotas within the state resisted colonialism
by practicing a new spiritual ritual called the Ghost Dance, de-
rived from the teachings of the Northern Paiute prophet Wovoka.
The dance nurtured spiritual power and predicted the revival
of American Indian dominance. Wovoka foresaw that a calami-
tous natural event would eliminate non-Indians and bring back
deceased family members and ancestors. The natural calamity
prophesized took several forms: flames, cyclones, or a crushing
layer of soil. Bison would repopulate the grasslands. Participants
danced and sang for hours in a circle to access the spiritual power
thought necessary to bring on the change. The rigor of the dance
brought visons to participants rendered unconscious.[52]

Soon after the November 1890 election, the arrival of the
United States military underscored a threatening element in the
culturally affirming dance. Before official intervention, mission-
aries and agency officials primarily feared Indians' regression
from "civilization." Settlers had watched uncertainly. The increased military presence frightened them. The dance did communicate the Lakotas' desire "to see the present world destroyed
and new one come into being," though not by the use of arms.[53]
Shaw, however, shared the opinion of observers across the nation
who viewed the dance as "the delusion of superstitious savages."[54]
A humiliated Elizabeth Cady Stanton wondered if "the Indians
may have understood the insult conveyed by the returns of the
late election." She thought the "contempt" the vote expressed
may have encouraged "the present uprising of the Indians." By
their votes, Stanton argued, South Dakota men "told the ignorant
foreigners and Indians that there was nothing sacred in woman-

hood."[55] The *Huron Daily Plainsman* reported that the "Indian scare" caused "a change of heart" among some voters, "Those who voted against women suffrage and in favor of allowing the Indians to vote, are now looking for able bodied kickers to kick them."[56] Rivalry between the United States Department of Interior and the Department of War, as well the political appointment of unqualified and inexperienced onsite reservation agents, contributed to the deterioration of the situation. The United States military presence led to a confrontation with and the massacre of Minneconjou leader Big Foot and his band on Wounded Knee Creek in December 1890.

Soon after and for years to come, woman suffragists channeled their humiliation through the furrow of educated suffrage. Shaw told the story of how, while in South Dakota, she quizzed an unnamed Indian man on whether he had "a thorough instruction in the underlying principles of government." Reportedly, he blew smoke at her and grunted inarticulately. Shaw contrasted this behavior with women's assumed superior preparation for political participation. From this viewpoint, South Dakota's American Indians lacked both a formal education in political economy and the acculturation that settler society required. Shaw signaled this lack by citing the Indian man's long braided hair, uncleanliness, feather adornments, blankets, and moccasins.[57] Stanton did so by calling Indian men "bucks."[58] The racism was visceral. In 1892, a South Dakota suffragist from Wessington Springs, Dr. Nettie Hall, still "smart[ed] under the lash of injustice because of sex." Hall described the "men-people" who denied the vote to "women-people" and "gave the savage all political rights."[59] These attitudes anticipated federal policy changes that would delay citizenship for American Indian allottees. Lawmakers increasingly doubted "Indians' intellectual abilities." A new so-called scientific racism increasingly permeated United States culture over the first two decades of the twentieth century.[60] Such vitriol continued, although within a month of the election, the state's newspapers informed readers, "Notwithstanding the people of South Dakota to enfranchise certain Indians, the Indians are still not entitled to vote."[61] Suffragists, nonetheless, nurtured the slight they felt over the 1890 election returns.

The flurry of post-election speculation about ill-formulated ballot amendments and confusion at the polls communicated the "surprise" that settlers exhibited over vote totals in 1890.[62] Male voters in South Dakota failed to enfranchise women and also failed to restrict the enfranchisement of American Indian men. American Indians, men and women, as well as white women, however, all remained disenfranchised. Settler women waited nearly thirty years until 1918 to vote in South Dakota. A 1903 law ensured that most American Indian men and women would wait over sixty years to acquire full voting rights in the state. The law also prohibited American Indians from holding office. Officials at the Indian Bureau assumed that the 1924 Indian Citizenship Act enfranchised Indians, but many states continued to restrict Indian voting rights. In 1938, seven states, including South Dakota, still "effectively prohibited" American Indians from voting through devices such as "denying voting rights to Indians who maintained their tribal affiliations, lived on reservations, or were considered under the 'guardianship' of government," all ideas similar to those proposed in the 1890 South Dakota referendum to restrict Indian voting. South Dakota finally repealed laws restricting American Indian voting in 1951.[63]

While settler women cited land ownership as evidence that they deserved voting rights, they apparently did not consider property, especially untaxed property, sufficient to enfranchise "uncivilized" American Indian men or women who lacked democratic education. Nor did they suggest that American Indian men had the potential to be allies in women's claim to the vote as many had assumed of enfranchised black men. Indeed, a different calculus may have assumed that American Indian women had the power to influence the votes of American Indian men.[64] With exceptions that call out for more research, racialized assumptions born in civilization theory blinded many supporters of woman suffrage to considering such collaborations. The 1890 moment when the Dawes Act caused South Dakota settlers and suffragists to consider the potential political power of male Indians proved to be *only* a moment.

I wish to thank colleagues Sara E. Lampert and Elise Boxer at the University of South Dakota, Lori Lahlum at Minnesota State University, Mankato, James Naylor at Brandon University, and Jennifer Ritterhouse at George Mason University for reading this manuscript (more than once in a couple of cases). I also thank South Dakota historic preservation specialist Liz Almlie, who shared a newspaper about John Pickler and pointed me to the story of Jane Elizabeth Van Meter Waldron. Matthew T. Reitzel, archivist at the South Dakota State Historical Society, gave crucial and quick assistance. This research benefited from the financial support of the Allene R. Chiesman Fund at the University of South Dakota and the South Dakota Humanities Council.

1. *Hot Springs Star*, 7 Nov. 1890.

2. Dorinda Riessen Reed, *The Woman Suffrage Movement in South Dakota*, 2d ed. (Pierre: South Dakota Commission on the Status of Women, 1975), pp. 6–11; South Dakota, *Journal of the Senate* (Pierre, 1890), pp. 42, 44. For a general overview of the 1890 woman suffrage campaign, *see* Cecelia M. Wittmayer, "The 1889–1890 Woman Suffrage Campaign: A Need to Organize," *South Dakota History* 11 (Summer 1981): 199–225. For official election returns, *see* Alan L. Clem, *South Dakota Political Almanac*, 2d ed. (Vermillion, S.Dak.: Dakota Press, 1969), p. 33; Official Election Returns, 1862–1986, box 2, 1890–1892, Records of the Secretary of State, State Archives Collection, South Dakota State Historical Society (SDSHS), Pierre.

3. *Woonsocket Times*, quoted in *Wessington Springs Herald*, 14 Nov. 1890.

4. *Aberdeen Pioneer*, quoted in *Turner County Herald* (Hurley), 20 Nov. 1890.

5. *Kimball Graphic*, 22 Nov. 1889.

6. Stanton, "Educated Suffrage Justified," 2 Nov. 1894, and "Educated Suffrage Again," 2 Jan. 1895, both in *The Selected Papers of Elizabeth Cady Stanton and Susan B. Anthony*, ed. Ann D. Gordon (New Brunswick: Rutgers University Press, 2009), pp. 656, 665. Stanton spoke of potential voters with "shades and degrees of intelligence and ignorance" (p. 656)

7. Allison L. Sneider, *Suffragists in an Imperial Age: U.S. Expansion and the Woman Question, 1870–1929* (New York: Oxford University Press, 2008), pp. 70–72.

8. Jeffrey Ostler, *The Plains Sioux and U.S. Colonialism from Lewis and Clark to Wounded Knee* (New York: Cambridge University Press, 2004), pp. 6, 15–17, 38. *See also* John Higham, *Strangers in the Land: Patterns of American Nativism, 1860–1925* (New Brunswick: Rutgers University Press, 1998), pp. 133–34.

9. Francis Paul Prucha, *The Great Father: The United States Government and the American Indians,* abr. ed. (Lincoln: University of Nebraska Press, 1984 & 1986), pp. 224–27, 231–32, 267, 271, 298. *See also* Frederick E. Hoxie, *A Final Promise: The Campaign to Assimilate the Indians, 1880–1920* (Lincoln: University of Nebraska Press, 1984), pp. 75, 78–79, 213, 219–21. According to Prucha, one federal official called the original 1887 Dawes Severalty Act "practically a general naturalization law for the American Indians" (p. 227). After the passage of the 1906 Burke Act, instead of receiving citizenship upon allotment, an allottee received citizenship with the issuance of the "fee patent" at the end of the trust period, the duration of which was based on the "competence" of individual allottees.

10. *Turner County Herald,* 20 Nov. 1890; Ostler, *Plains Sioux,* p. 15. Regardless of intentions of Indian policy reformers or state officials who might have expected the Sioux to become assimilated landowners, the Dawes Act resulted in the decline of Indian land ownership, from 138 million acres in 1887 to 52 million in 1934. Prucha, *Great Father,* p. 895. Hoxie argued that westerners in particular supported the expansion of American Indian rights as citizens because it "promised to reduce federal interference in their local affairs" (*Final Promise,* pp. 211–12). On the Homestead Act, *see* Sheila McManus, *The Line Which Separates: Race, Gender, and the Making of the Alberta-Montana Borderlands* (Lincoln: University of Nebraska Press, 2005), pp. 37–41.

11. Quoted in *Black Hills Union,* 4 Dec. 1890. Further, DeVoe cited what she held to be credible examples of ballot "tickets" listing only a "no" option or, worse, instructions "not in accordance with law." Reportedly, one ballot offered: "For woman suffrage, 'No'; Against woman suffrage, 'Yes.'" The problem DeVoe cites may have originated in the original House Bill No. 9 "Instructions to Voters," which read, "All persons who desire to vote against striking out the word 'male' must erase the words 'For Woman Suffrage.' All persons who desire to vote for striking out the word must erase the words 'Against Woman Suffrage.'" The senate changed the original instructions. South Dakota, *Journal of the House* (Pierre, 1890), pp. 447–48.

12. *Queen City Mail,* 17 Dec. 1890.

13. *Black Hills Weekly Times,* 29 Nov. 1890, also printed in *Black Hills Daily Times,* 23 Nov. 1890. This editorial was written in response to one published in the *Black Hills Weekly Times,* 21 Nov. 1890, that criticized the state legislature for the poor language of the "Indian Suffrage" amendment. Suggesting the haste implied by the editorial, the house introduced Joint Resolution No. 352 regarding Indian suffrage on 17 February 1890 but did not pass the measure until 5 March, two days before the end of the session. Also, suggesting some laborious debate, immediately after the house agreed on the

title to the bill, a member moved, "That the vote by which House Bill No. 352 Passed the House Be reconsidered And That the motion to reconsider be laid on the table, Which motion prevailed." The senate voted on the measure on 7 March, and the house received the bill, signed, and delivered it to the governor all on the same day. South Dakota, *Journal of the House*, pp. 785–86, 1087–88, 1186, 1194, 1212, 1215.

14. *Woonsocket Times*, quoted in *Wessington Springs Herald*, 14 Nov. 1890.

15. *Kimball Graphic*, 22 Nov. 1889.

16. *Sioux Falls Argus-Leader*, 14 Feb. 1890. *See also* Ostler, *Plains Sioux*, p. 238.

17. *Milbank Herald*, 29 Oct. 1889.

18. *Sioux Falls Argus-Leader*, 30 Sept. 1890. *See also Huron Daily Plainsman*, 29 Sept. 1890. Susan B. Anthony reportedly blamed the loss of woman suffrage in part to "the absorbing capital contest" between Huron and Pierre (quoted in *Daily Plainsman*, 18 Nov. 1890). In *History of Woman Suffrage*, she and Ida Husted Harper argued that politicians "freely used" the issue of woman suffrage "as an article of barter" with reference to the capital vote (Anthony and Harper, eds., *History of Woman Suffrage*, Vol. 4 [Rochester, N.Y.: Susan B. Anthony, 1902], p. 556).

19. North Dakota, *Official Report of the Proceedings and Debates of the First Constitutional Convention of North Dakota* (Bismarck, 1889), p. xxi.

20. *Black Hills Daily Times*, 21 Nov. 1890.

21. *Black Hills Weekly Times*, 29 Nov. 1890.

22. *Kimball Graphic*, 22 Nov. 1889.

23. Daniel McCool, Susan M. Olson, Jennifer L. Robinson, *Native Vote: American Indians, the Voting Rights Act, and the Right to Vote* (New York: Cambridge University Press, 2007), pp. 3–4. Rosalyn Terborg-Penn, *African American Women in the Struggle for the Vote, 1850–1920* (Bloomington: Indiana University Press, 1999), pp. 10, 68–69, 108–12, argued that educated suffrage became especially visible in the 1890s, after the National Woman Suffrage Association and the American Woman Suffrage Association reunited.

24. John Pickler, quoted in *Black Hills Union*, 21 Feb. 1890.

25. Stanton, "Educated Suffrage Again," p. 665. The statement was made in regard to "ignorant, impecunious, immoral, 'mankind suffrage,' while sex is made a disqualification for all women."

26. McManus, *Line Which Separates*, p. 143; Andrea G. Radke-Moss, "'Willing Challengers': Women's Experiences on the Northern Plains, 1862–1930," in *Women on the North American Plains*, ed. Renee Laegreid and Sandra J. Mathews (Lubbock: Texas Tech University Press, 2011), p. 49. McManus argues, "White women were constructed as *the* symbol of domesticated civi-

lization in the late nineteenth century" and "their mere presence in colonial contexts did represent on one level the triumph of that civilization" (p. 143, emphasis in original). The work of civilizing through organization-building also held true for immigrant women. *See* Lori Ann Lahlum, "'Everything was changed and looked strange': Norwegian Women in South Dakota," *South Dakota History* 35 (Fall 2005): 209–11, 213, 215–16.

27. Prucha, *Great Father*, p. 226.

28. John Pickler, quoted in *Black Hills Union*, 21 Feb. 1890. For more on Waldron, *see* Katie O'Mara, "Dakota Images: Jane Van Meter Waldron," *South Dakota History* 28 (Winter 1998): 298–99. In the past, woman suffrage supporters had argued for the necessity of enfranchising American Indian women along with Indian men to protect the women from brutish treatment. Sneider, *Suffragists in an Imperial Age*, p. 52. Suffragists also used American Indian culture to think about "the meaning of female independence and dependence, and ideas about self-sovereignty" (ibid., p. 65). Matilda Joslyn Gage looked to the Haudenosaunees, the Iroquois Confederacy of Mohawk, Oneida Onondaga, Cayuga, Seneca, and Tuscarora as a model for "participatory democracy" that may have influenced the government established by the United States. Angelica Shirley Carpenter, *Born Criminal: Matilda Joslyn Gage, Radical Suffragist* (Pierre: South Dakota Historical Society Press, 2018), pp. 98–99. Gage, as well as Lucritia Mott, Lydia Maria Child, Harriet Converse, and Alice Fletcher, also drew ideas about gender from American Indian cultures. Gail H. Landsman, "The 'Other' as Political Symbol: Images of Indians in the Woman Suffrage Movement" *Ethnohistory* 39 (Summer 1992): 257–71.

29. Blank, "Womans [*sic*] Realm," *Wessington Springs Herald*, 25 July 1890.

30. Geo. F. Weisehedd to South Dakota Equal Suffrage Association, n. d. [1890], folder 5, box 6674, Pickler Family Papers, 1865–1976, State Archives Collection, SDSHS.

31. Carpenter, *Born Criminal*, pp. 89, 98, 144–45.

32. Allan J. Lichtman, *The Embattled Vote: From the Founding to the Present* (Cambridge, Mass.: Harvard University Press, 2018), pp. 14, 16–17, 101, 139–41. *See also* Leon E. Aylsworth, "The Passing of Alien Suffrage," *American Political Science Review* 25 (Feb. 1931): 114–15.

33. Lorenzo Veracini, *Settler Colonialism: A Theoretical Overview* (New York: Palgrave MacMillian, 2010) pp. 33–43; Ostler, *Plains Sioux*, p. 15. In the early United States, most states required a person to own a certain amount of real, personal, and/or taxable property in order to vote. Property accumulation signaled the "independence" of individuals. According to Lichtman, "To reconcile the ideal of 'universal suffrage' with the disenfranchisement

of nonwhites, political leaders insisted that certain people, like women and children, fell outside the political community, given their inherent inability to vote wisely and independently" (Lichtman, *Embattled Vote*, pp. 62–63).

34. Shaw, quoted in Ida Husted Harper, *The Life and Work of Susan B. Anthony*, Vol. 2 (Indianapolis: Bowen-Merrill Co., 1898), pp. 687–88. *See also* Anthony and Harper, eds., *History of Woman* Suffrage, pp. 182–83.

35. Gordon, ed., *Selected Papers*, p. 320n3. The Sisseton reservation allotments would be completed by 1892. Harper claimed the three men "probably" represented some five thousand votes. Harper, *Life and Work of Susan B. Anthony*, p. 687. The *Dakota Farmers' Leader* (Canton), 12 Sept. 1890, and the *Sioux Falls Argus-Leader*, 28 Aug. 1890 both cite the number of voters represented as three hundred.

36. *Milbank Herald*, 29 Oct. 1889; *Kimball Graphic*, 22 Nov. 1889.

37. Shaw, quoted in Harper, *Life and Work of Susan B. Anthony*, p. 687.

38. Anthony to Harriet Taylor Upton, 1 Sept. 1890, quoted in *Selected Papers*, ed. Gordon, p. 319. Gordon suggests that the seating of guests at the South Dakota Republican convention "became a staple of suffragists' storytelling," with the Indian men getting "dirtier and more numerous as the years passed, while the indignation went beyond the details of their treatment by Republicans to emphasize their evident racial inferiority" (p. 320n3).

39. *Dakota Farmers' Leader*, 12 Sept. 1890.

40. Sneider, *Suffragists in an Imperial Age*, pp. 30–32, 55, 58–61, 66–68.

41. Single settler women could select land under the Homestead Act of 1862, and single American Indian women could select allotments under the Dawes Act of 1887. After 1891, lawmakers revised the Dawes Act to allot equal acreages to *all* adult American Indians, single and married. The Homestead Act only allowed some married women to claim land, although all widows could. Emily Greenwald, *Reconfiguring the Reservation: The Nez Perces, Jicarilla Apaches, and the Dawes Act* (Albuquerque: University of New Mexico Press, 2002), pp. 18–35, 31–32, 60–64.

42. Quoted in Anthony and Harper, eds. *Woman Suffrage*, p. 557. While Stanton thought of American Indians as "our barbarian ancestors," she remarked that occasionally they "seem to have had a higher sense of justice to woman than American men in the 19th century, professing to believe, as they do, in our republican principles of government" (quoted in Landsman, "The 'Other' as Political Symbol," p. 267).

43. Terborg-Penn, *African American Women*, pp. 24–31.

44. Jack N. Rakove, ed. *The Annotated U.S. Constitution and Declaration of Independence* (Cambridge: Harvard University Press, 2009), pp. 258–71.

45. *Black Hills Weekly Times*, 29 Nov. 1890. On congressional debates over Indian citizenship, *see* Prucha, *Great Father*, p. 231. Apparently, the chair-

man of the judiciary committee also did not want to set a precedent of tying voting rights to wealth through a tax requirement. As late as 2007, "the argument over the connection between Indians voting and Indians paying taxes" remained debated (McCool, Olson, and Robinson, *Native Vote*, pp. 3–5).

46. Terborg-Penn, *African American Women*, pp. 13–23.

47. Quoted in Lichtman, *Embattled Vote*, p. 104.

48. Aylsworth, "Passing of Alien Suffrage," pp. 114–15.

49. Stanton to Lucy Stone, 15 Jan. 1891, in *Selected Papers*, ed. Gordon, p. 349. Anthony argued that suffragists "carried South Dakota" with "American born men" by a vote of 3 to 2, but "foreigners' votes" gave anti-suffrage "a tremendous majority against us" (*Selected Papers*, pp. 607–8).

50. Sneider, *Suffragists in an Imperial Age*, pp. 62–64.

51. Shaw, quoted in Anthony and Harper, eds., *Woman Suffrage*, pp. 182.

52. Ostler, *Plains Sioux*, pp. 243–46, 255–63, 293–308, 353–54.

53. Ibid., pp. 293–308. Authorization for a United States military operation came on 13 November, 9 days after the 1890 election (p. 300).

54. Ostler, *Plains Sioux*, pp. 244–46. *See also* Anthony and Harper, eds., *Woman Suffrage*, p. 182.

55. Stanton to Stone, 15 Jan. 1891, in *Selected Papers*, ed. Gordon, p. 349. Stanton said she would hold South Dakota men "responsible for every act of violence or injustice inflicted on the women of that State."

56. *Huron Daily Plainsman*, 29 Nov. 1890.

57. Quoted in Jennifer M. Ross-Nazzal, *Winning the West for Women: The Life of Suffragist Emma Smith DeVoe* (Seattle: University of Washington Press, 2011), p. 66; Anthony and Harper, eds., *Woman Suffrage*, p. 182.

58. Anthony to Harriet Taylor Upton, 1 Sept. 1890, quoted in *Selected Papers*, ed. Gordon, p. 319.

59. Nettie C. Hall, untitled article, *Meyer Brothers Druggist* 13 (Oct. 1892): 368–69. Clearly affected by "wild rumors" that circulated in the aftermath of the Wounded Knee Massacre, Hall charged that "red men" scalped male settlers. Nevertheless, "womankind," she thought, "may arise in the light of her intellect and triumphantly march on to victory soaring aloft, not the scalps of our brothers, but the banner awarded for highest degree of intelligence." While hundreds of American Indians died at Wounded Knee, few if any South Dakota settlers died (Ostler, *Plains Sioux*, p. 359).

60. Soon after 1900, "judges gradually shifted their justification for guardianship from treaty guarantees to racial backwardness" (Hoxie, *Final Promise*, pp. 105–7, 215). *See also* Higham, *Strangers in the Land*, pp. 131–57.

61. Similar notices appeared across the state, all apparently citing C. H. Wynn, a "Sioux Falls lawyer," who explained that an unidentified Supreme Court case had barred Indian voting. Wynn may have been referring to the

1884 *Elk* v. *Wilkins* case in which the United States Supreme Court held that an American Indian man living in Omaha had no right to vote in Nebraska, despite his nonreservation residence and a voluntary separation from his tribe. The court made clear that Congress would have to pass legislation or another "official action" would be required "to bestow" citizenship on American Indians. Wynn's research is faulty, for the Dawes Act of 1887 constituted congressional citizenship action (Prucha, *Great Father*, p. 231). Wynn apparently gave a "clear demonstration of the fact that Indians, whether connected with a tribe, or whether they have severed their tribal relations, cannot exercise the elective franchise" (*Madison Daily Leader*, 2 Dec. 1890; *Kimball Graphic*, 5 Dec. 1890; *Black Hills Weekly Journal*, 12 Dec. 1890; *Hot Springs Star*, 12 Dec. 1890). *See also* McCool, Olson, and Robinson, *Native Vote*, pp. 5–6.

62. *Rapid City Journal*, 7 Nov. 1890.

63. Lichtman, *Embattled Vote*, pp. 142–43. *See also* McCool, Olson, and Robinson, *Native Vote*, pp. 8, 11; Hoxie, *Final Promise*, p. 332.

64. Suggesting she did not see American Indians (men or women) as ready for the vote, Shaw recommended "a commission of women with [the anthropologist] Alice Fletcher at its head" to find a "solution" to "the Indian question" (Anthony and Harper, ed. *Woman Suffrage*, p. 183). Alice Fletcher, on the other hand, had "a dual perspective on Indians." She assumed they needed assimilation to survive but also admired "the Indian wife's independence in the use of her property" (Landsman, "The 'Other' as Political Symbol," p. 270).

"WAKE UP, WYOMING"

The Push to Ratify the Susan B. Anthony Amendment in the Northern Great Plains States

AMY L. MCKINNEY

Suffrage worker Frances M. Brewer stepped off the train in Laramie, Wyoming, in early January 1919 on special assignment from Carrie Chapman Catt, president of the National American Woman Suffrage Association (NAWSA). Brewer began canvassing the town, speaking to women's clubs and organizations. She hoped to establish a ratification committee of one hundred influential women in the state who would be the key force in getting the forthcoming federal woman suffrage amendment ratified in Wyoming. In anticipation of the United States Congress's passage of the Nineteenth Amendment, also called the Susan B. Anthony Amendment, NAWSA wanted to honor Wyoming as the first territory to grant woman suffrage in 1869 and the first state to allow women to vote in 1890 by ensuring that it would be the first to ratify the woman suffrage amendment to the United States Constitution. Another Wyoming first, they reasoned, would create excitement for this last phase of the suffrage movement and build the momentum needed to motivate the required thirty-six states to ratify the measure.[1] But the organizers had not allowed for the fiscal conservatism of state officials nor anticipated the actions of other Northern Great Plains states, all of which would ratify the suffrage amendment before Wyoming. While it had been first in granting its women the vote, Wyoming would be twenty-seventh in the race to ratify the Susan B. Anthony Amendment and expand the franchise beyond its borders.

In organizing the women of Wyoming, Brewer targeted the officers of the various women's clubs and organizations, including the presidents of the College Club, Presbyterian Ladies' Aid So-

In 1921, two years after Wyoming ratified the Nineteenth Amendment,
national suffrage leader Carrie Chapman Catt (center) visited Laramie.
Wyoming suffragist Grace Raymond Hebard is standing to Catt's right.
American Heritage Center, University of Wyoming

ciety, Woman's Christian Temperance Union, Woman's Club, the
secretary of the City Federation of Women's Clubs, and the regent
of the Daughters of the American Revolution. She succeeded in
organizing the committee, which included forty women from
Cheyenne, including Julia Carey, the governor's wife; twenty
women from Laramie, including Dr. Grace Raymond Hebard, a
well-known professor at the University of Wyoming; and an as-
sortment of prominent women from around the state.[2] Brewer
planned to present the list of names of influential Wyoming
women to the state senate "as an indication of the way in which
women who have had the vote more than fifty years feel on the
subject."[3] The newly elected governor, Robert D. Carey, assured
Brewer that he would recommend the ratification of the suffrage
amendment when he addressed the legislature later that month.
True to his word, he recommended HJR 1, "Memorializing the
Senate of the United States" to submit the Susan B. Anthony
Amendment for woman suffrage.[4] The state legislature passed
the recommendation unanimously.

"Wake Up, Wyoming"

In addition to gaining support for ratification of the suffrage amendment, Brewer extended a personal invitation to the women of Wyoming to attend NAWSA's national convention in Saint Louis from 24 to 29 March 1919 to celebrate the fiftieth anniversary of both national suffrage campaigning and the passage of suffrage in Wyoming. The convention also had a broader agenda, strategizing about how to protect women in industry, increase protection of children, improve campaign and election methods, and advance general social welfare policy. Carrie Chapman Catt urged creation of a League of Women Voters to aid in the final push for ratification of a federal suffrage amendment. Catt made clear, however, that the key purpose of the convention was to celebrate the fiftieth anniversary of suffrage in Wyoming. NAWSA's strategy for winning national suffrage by ratification of the Nineteenth Amendment centered on those states where women already had the right to vote. Wyoming, as the first state, was the centerpiece of that campaign. The convention toasted a delegation of Wyoming women, including Nancy Brown, wife of Judge Melville C. Brown, of Laramie, naming her Mother of the Convention because she was the oldest woman voter in attendance.[5]

Convention delegates also celebrated Esther Morris, whom national suffrage leaders portrayed as a heroic figure in the history of woman suffrage. Just prior to the Saint Louis event, the *New York Tribune* had printed an excerpt from Dr. Anna Howard Shaw's autobiography in which she claimed, "Woman suffrage in Wyoming . . . is due to the influence of one woman, Esther Morris, a pioneer who was as good a neighbor as she was a suffragist." Shaw explained that Morris had helped a neighbor through the difficult birth of a son, and the woman's husband happened to be William H. Bright, a member of the territorial legislature, who in gratitude told her he would introduce any measure concerning women that she wanted. She immediately requested the suffrage bill. Emma Bugbee, the author of the article, predicted the baby legend would be the most talked about story at the Wyoming jubilee celebration.[6]

While Morris received the bulk of the credit in 1919, she had not always been center stage in discussions of how and why the 1869 territorial legislature passed woman suffrage. For two decades following the passage of the bill, most people gave credit to the man who introduced it, William Bright. If anyone had influenced him to introduce the bill, most observers said, it had been Secretary of the Territory Edward M. Lee, who had advocated for woman suffrage to the Connecticut legislature just two years earlier. Many also credited Lee with writing the bill because Bright did not have a formal education.[7] Either way, men were at the center of Wyoming's suffrage story at the end of the 1800s. Newspapers emphasized the unique "political program by which enfranchisement of Wyoming women was affected [and] was projected by men, not women."[8] The outsized role of men in the narrative reflected the reality that, although women had voting equality in Wyoming Territory, they were not politically or economically equal. During the twenty-year period of territorial government, only two women ran for a position in the legislature. One woman received eight votes, the other received five.[9]

When Wyoming applied for statehood, the suffrage question came up again, and many feared that woman suffrage would not be included in the new constitution. Determined to maintain their voting rights, Wyoming women sought a heroine to champion the cause. Esther Morris had the public record and social connections to front the effort. In 1870, Morris had become the first female justice of the peace in the United States, serving with distinction in South Pass City, Wyoming. Over her nine-month tenure, she oversaw twenty-six cases, none of which were overturned on appeal.[10] She was not, however, selected for a second term. The first written record that directly gives Morris credit for the suffrage bill is found in the published proceedings of Wyoming's constitutional convention. While debating the inclusion of woman suffrage in the state constitution, Judge Melville Brown, her personal friend, stated, "Mrs. Esther Morris presented a bill to Mr. Bright, asking the favorable action of the legislature upon that question."[11] Suffrage proponents prevailed, and Wyoming entered the Union as the first state to enfranchise women fully.

As the new state celebrated and state and national suffragists cheered, Morris emerged as a central figure. She became a popular speaker and held such positions of honor as being chosen to present Governor Francis E. Warren with the new United

States flag containing forty-four stars. Morris never took credit, at least not publicly, for having a role in the suffrage bill, but others frequently noted her significance. During the statehood celebrations, E. A. Slack, her oldest son, bestowed upon her the title Mother of Woman Suffrage, recognizing her as a tireless worker in the campaign to achieve the vote for women. Suffragists both in Wyoming and across the nation had found their heroine, and Bright and Lee faded to the background, even though Lee's sister and niece were not happy with his diminished role and unsuccessfully asked Wyoming newspapers to print their version of the story.[12]

The fiftieth anniversary celebrations of suffrage in Wyoming and the national debate surrounding the Susan B. Anthony Amendment in 1919 cemented Morris's legacy as the Mother of Woman Suffrage. Two Wyoming newspapers, the *Kemmerer Republican* and the *Wyoming State Journal*, highlighted the fiftieth anniversary by calling on Wyomingites to remember South Pass City, the locale that had sent William Bright to the legislature. By 1919, the town where a legislator had "first conceived the great heritage of American womanhood" sat almost deserted. Commemoration advocates hoped the site would "become the famous shrine of women's suffrage."[13] Prior to 1919, little discussion had occurred about commemorating the town, which had been virtually forgotten. With the increased emphasis on Wyoming in the national suffrage debate, renewed interest in the historic site surfaced. Even though Bright was often given credit for the initial bill, the *Laramie Republican* noted, "to be sure, the 'indirect influence' of women was behind it."[14]

After the *Kemmerer Republican* and *Wyoming State Journal* printed the South Pass story with little mention of Morris, H. G. Nickerson, who lived in South Pass City in 1869, wrote to correct the record. Nickerson credited the efforts of fellow South Pass City resident Esther Morris for passage of the woman suffrage law, affirming her place in the narrative that grew from the statehood celebrations. He also introduced the most enduring story of how and why suffrage passed in Wyoming, which centers on a tea party that Morris supposedly held in her home. Nickerson had written a history of the county a few years earlier that made

During the seventy-fifth anniversary of Wyoming statehood in 1965, Wyoming secretary of state Thyra Thomson posed beside Ethel Morris's statue in Cheyenne. American Heritage Center, University of Wyoming

no mention of such an event, and neither Morris nor Bright had ever written or spoken publicly about it. Nickerson now claimed, however, that he and Bright had attended a tea party where Morris had convinced them to support woman suffrage if they won the election. As the story goes, Bright kept his word.[15]

The tea party became legendary once Grace Hebard, a strong suffrage advocate who fought for the inclusion of more women in Wyoming's history, used Morris's tea party as the cornerstone of her retelling of the Wyoming suffrage story. Hebard's 1920 pamphlet, *How Woman Suffrage Came to Wyoming*, solidified Morris's place as the champion of suffrage. Hebard also joined forces with Nickerson to place a historic marker at Morris's South Pass City home that acknowledged her as the first justice of the peace and mother of suffrage.[16] Though some considered Morris's heroine role more myth than history, Wyoming placed a statue of Morris in the Statuary Hall of the United States Congress in Washington, D.C., nearly a century later. A replica of the statue also stands outside the state capitol building in Cheyenne.[17] Both the tea party story and the anecdote of her role in the delivery of Bright's son focused attention on Morris at a time when suffragists nationally needed a heroine during their final push for ratification of the federal suffrage amendment.

The United States House of Representatives passed the Susan B. Anthony Amendment on 21 May, and the Senate followed on 4 June 1919. Although supporters of suffrage across the nation were overjoyed with the passage of the amendment, most state legislatures had already adjourned, and many of them would not convene again until 1921. In order for women to vote in the next presidential election, NAWSA needed to get thirty-six states to ratify the amendment before 2 November 1920. To meet that timeline, they had to convince states to call special sessions, and they hoped that Wyoming would take up the banner and be the first to ratify the amendment. Brewer had set the stage for this effort with her January visit and creation of the ratification committee. The women expected newly elected Governor Robert D. Carey to call a special session to ratify the amendment. After all, during Brewer's January visit, he had instructed the Wyoming legislature to send a message to Congress communicating the state's support. Carrie Chapman Catt sent the governor a telegram asking him to act. Yet, only three days after the United States Senate passed the suffrage amendment, Carey announced that Wyoming would not convene a special session to ratify it, dashing suffragists' hopes. "The fact that the cost of a special session of the legislature would be borne by the people of this state," he said, "and that the people of Wyoming would receive no direct benefit, as the women here enjoy the rights of suffrage, I am not willing to call a special session to ratify the suffrage amendment."[18] Instead, the legislatures of Wisconsin, Illinois, and Michigan had the distinction of being the first states to ratify the amendment, which they did on June 10.[19]

Throughout the summer and fall, Governor Carey refused to

call a special session despite requests from suffragists and state legislators. State senator C. D. Oviatt of Albany County assured Carey that legislators would be "more than willing" to pay their own expenses to ratify the suffrage amendment. If not, Oviatt believed the women of his county would "be willing to take a hand in some form of persuasion" to convince the governor to call the special session. Oviatt also reassured the people of Wyoming that the governor and the state legislature would not abandon the cause of woman suffrage and that Wyoming would not "be last in the ratification of the amendment."[20] For his part, Carey made it clear that he did not oppose ratification of the suffrage amendment, but he was adamant that Wyoming's support of suffrage for other women should not cost the state any money. If it appeared ratification of the amendment was in jeopardy, Carey promised that Wyoming would "step in and save the day, but at present, when only fourteen states out of the necessary thirty-six [have] ratified, I see no reason for hurry."[21] If other issues presented themselves, Carey stated on another occasion, "two birds may be killed with one stone, and the state will not be put to the expense of holding a session for the sole purpose of allowing the women in other states to vote for the next president."[22]

As Wyoming delayed, the push for ratification heated up across the Northern Plains during the fall of 1919. The *Bismarck Daily Tribune* in North Dakota reported, "The eyes of 15,000,000 women . . . are on these men," which included Governor Peter Norbeck of South Dakota and Governor Carey of Wyoming. Further, the newspaper reported, "Fifteen 'mere' men—governors of fifteen states—are holding up ratification of the woman suffrage amendment. If twelve of the fifteen do not recede from the stands they have taken they will prevent the women in twenty-one states from participation in the presidential election of 1920."[23]

By November 1919, Wyoming had yet to ratify the Nineteenth Amendment. That month, key suffrage leaders, including Julia Lathrop, Mrs. Charles H. Brooks, Dr. Valeria H. Parker, Catherine Waugh McCulloch, and Mrs. Edward P. Costigan, embarked on a multistate speaking tour to organize support for ratification. They also planned to advocate for several other issues of concern to women, including child labor laws, protection of women in in-

Wake Up, Wyoming

dustry, improvement in election laws and methods, and divorce laws.[24] Under the slogan "learn how to help the men with the use of their vote," speakers "appeal[ed] to the women to learn to use their vote—not to fight for more 'rights' and freedom, but to help the men bring about a new order of legislature that will make just laws for the care of children, the prevention of child labor, and laws fair to the women."[25]

Laramie, home of the University of Wyoming, was a key stop on the tour, where the delegation held two days of meetings on Monday and Tuesday, 10–11 November, hoping to reach university students in addition to influential women of the state. Carrie Chapman Catt gave a rousing speech entitled, "Wake Up, Wyoming," in which she encouraged the people to call for a special session to ratify the suffrage amendment. She made it clear that the people of Wyoming had disappointed suffrage leaders across the nation. Despite Frances Brewer's organizing and NAWSA's decision to fete the state's women voters at its March convention, Wyoming's leaders had not led a national charge for ratification of the Nineteenth Amendment. By the time of her address in Laramie, nineteen states had already ratified the Susan B. Anthony Amendment, and Catt raised the question, why not Wyoming?[26]

Catt's rousing call to wake up did not go unheeded. Days after the event, a group of activists organized the Wyoming League of Women Voters with the aim of convincing Governor Carey to call a special session. They presented him with the following resolution: "be it resolved that we petition our governor, the Honorable Robert D. Carey, to call the legislature in special session on December 10, 1919, to ratify the federal suffrage amendment, also known as the Susan B. Anthony amendment." They chose the date specifically because it marked the day fifty years earlier on which Governor John A. Campbell had signed woman suffrage into law in 1869. The symbolism of ratifying the amendment on the fiftieth anniversary of suffrage in Wyoming would heighten its significance. Governor Carey declined to discuss the matter with the press.[27]

Governor Carey did not call a special session for 10 December 1919, but he did issue a proclamation declaring it Wyoming Day in commemoration of the fiftieth anniversary of woman suffrage in the state. The governor's proclamation called for 10 December to be "celebrated and observed by appropriate exercises."[28] Schools across the state planned Wyoming Day festivities, and several women's clubs and organizations held Wyoming Day celebrations. The Delta Meta Delphian club celebrated with a Wyoming-themed program, including an address by Sarah Sheddon on "Pioneer Wyoming" that highlighted early suffrage history and the first women's grand jury.[29]

Other Northern Great Plains states had been slower than Wyoming in granting woman suffrage but acted more quickly in holding special sessions to ratify the Nineteenth Amendment. In Montana, which had approved a state constitutional amendment granting women the right to vote in 1914, the *Big Timber Pioneer* reported in June 1919, "Ratification will come easily and promptly."[30] Governor S. V. Stewart called for a special session of the Montana legislature in July, primarily due to the state's pressing need for drought relief. He also cited two less urgent reasons for holding the session: new funds for roads and highways and ratification of the suffrage amendment. Whether or not Governor Stewart would have been as willing to call a special session only for the purpose of ratifying the suffrage amendment is unknown. In any case, on 30 July 1919, Montana became the thirteenth state to ratify the Susan B. Anthony Amendment.[31]

Newspapers in both North Dakota and South Dakota had also reported excitement over prospects of early ratification in their states. The *Bismarck Tribune* reported that because North Dakota had been fifth in the nation to ratify the prohibition amendment, it could also be "among the first to ratify the equal suffrage amendment."[32] As in Wyoming, Governor Lynn J. Frazier initially told eastern reporters that the North Dakota legislature would address the suffrage amendment at its next session, but, if another issue presented itself, a special session might be called. North Dakota residents supported the amendment, and the legislature had granted partial suffrage to women in 1917. Even so, officials were not willing to incur any additional expense to extend the right to vote to women outside of their own state. On the same day that Montana's legislators voted to ratify the suffrage amendment, a delegation of suffragists that included Elizabeth

O'Neil of Fargo, Marjorie Shuler of the congressional committee of NAWSA, and Mrs. John G. South, former president of the Kentucky association, met with Governor Frazier to request a special session.[33] He told them "a number of things" might make a special session necessary. Suffrage, however, would not be "the impelling reason for calling the special session, but may be brought up as a side issue."[34] Two weeks later, the *Devils Lake World and Inter-Ocean* newspaper reported, "Governor Frazier never said nothing to nobody about no special [session] of the North Dakota Assembly." When asked about a date for a such a session, Frazier allegedly "growled" that he "never said there was going to be a special session."[35]

As the fall progressed, Governor Frazier faced increasing pressure from suffragists and members of the farmer-dominated Nonpartisan League to call the legislature into session to address drought relief and ratify the suffrage amendment. The *Nonpartisan Leader* of Fargo reported that organized farmers in the state "have demonstrated their attitude toward votes for women so many times that ratification is looked upon as a foregone conclusion. The majority in both houses of the assembly is overwhelming."[36] When Frazier finally called a special session for the end of November, he gave three reasons for it. Interestingly, he listed ratification first, drought relief second, and the state's industrial program third. Frazier received a personal telegram from Carrie Chapman Catt thanking him for holding the special session.[37] When Frazier addressed the joint session of the legislature on 25 November, he highlighted how North Dakotans had fought for a "square deal for all its citizens" before imploring legislators to "ratify this national amendment as your first act of this special session and demonstrate that North Dakota welcomes the opportunity to extend suffrage to the women of our state and nation."[38] On 1 December 1919, the North Dakota legislature passed the suffrage amendment with a vote of 102 to 6 in the house and 43 to 3 in the senate, making it the twentieth state to ratify the Susan B. Anthony Amendment.[39]

South Dakota suffrage supporters had also welcomed the prospect of early ratification. According to the *Philip Pioneer*, Mary ("Mamie") Pyle, former president of the South Dakota Universal

Franchise League and now president of the South Dakota League of Women Voters, believed that her state would be one of the first to ratify. In June 1919, she proclaimed, "South Dakota women while enjoying the political freedom granted to them by the voters at the last election [November 1918], . . . are ready to join the great ratification campaign to be carried on for the purpose of enabling all women in the United States to gain the same right."[40] Governor Peter Norbeck announced that same month that he would be calling a special session to ratify the suffrage amendment but not until January 1920. He, too, expressed concern about the cost of a special session and brought up the notion of state legislators paying their own expenses. By November, a majority of state senators had pledged their willingness to "attend a special one-day session of the state legislature at their own expense for the purpose of ratifying the woman suffrage amendment."[41]

When Pyle realized that many state legislators planned to be in Pierre in early December for party conventions and to nominate candidates to run in the 1920 primaries, she suggested that Norbeck call a special session during that time. Suffragists in South Dakota proceeded to secure pledges from the legislators "to remain over one day in Pierre and meet in special session on proclamation of Gov. Norbeck for the express purpose of ratifying the suffrage amendment." The *Milbank Herald-Advance* reported that members of the legislature were "thus far heard pledging to do this without expense to the state."[42] One full month ahead of Norbeck's original date, legislators met at the capitol on the wintery evening of 3 December and introduced the resolution to ratify the Nineteenth Amendment in both houses and rushed it through the requisite readings before adjourning. The body then reassembled for a midnight session. In the early hours of 4 December 1919, the South Dakota legislature voted without dissention to ratify the Susan B. Anthony Amendment, making it the twenty-first state to do so. Many legislators caught 2:00 A.M. trains out of Pierre.[43]

As news from the Dakotas reached Governor Carey, who had resisted calling a special session in Wyoming since June due to the cost, he announced that economic conditions might necessitate a special session sometime that winter. He continued to emphasize that the primary reason would be to address financial issues, not for the ratification of the suffrage amendment.[44] Suffrage workers used his announcement as another opportunity to request an immediate special session to ratify the Susan B. Anthony Amendment. Still concerned about the cost to taxpayers of what would be the first special session of the legislature in state history, Carey telegraphed legislators to ask if they would be willing to pay their own expenses in order to ratify the amendment. State senator Oviatt had suggested the option back in August, and Carey now cited South Dakota's example of asking legislators to cover their own costs for the purpose. Wyoming's 1919 legislature had appropriated a total of "$45,000 for its own expenses," the *Laramie Republican* reported, adding, "It is estimated that a special session with mileage, would cost $20,000." Carey maintained that if legislators agreed to pay their own way, the special session would not be a major expense.[45]

The governor's proposal caused considerable controversy. Some criticized Carey, a wealthy man in his own right, suggesting that it was not fair to ask state legislators, "the most poorly paid officials of the state, . . . to pay for this present. Evidently, the governor has forgotten that the legislature fixes salaries of state officials," read one opinion expressed in the *Cheyenne State Leader*. Sheridan County legislators made clear they supported the suffrage amendment but were "almost unanimous to a man in condemning Governor Carey's proposal that the legislators go to Cheyenne to perform this public function at their own expense."[46] An editorial on the front page of the *Sheridan Enterprise* made its position clear with the headline "Our Cheap Governor." The editorial called out Governor Carey for asking legislators to pay their expenses while "not [saying] that he expects to refrain from drawing his own salary from the state while the legislature is in session." The editorial also voiced concern that legislators from Sheridan County would look "hostile to the ratification of the suffrage amendment" if they did not attend the special session.[47] State legislators who lived farther from Cheyenne expressed apprehension about whether they would be able to attend without their salary. John M. Hench, an attorney from Thermopolis, volunteered to pay the expenses of a local legislator and encouraged others to do the same. Hench called out what he saw as the "cheap" nature of the governor. He believed the state "financially able to defray the cost of the special session itself."[48]

With pressure mounting, Governor Carey announced a special session of the state legislature to be held in January 1920. Although only a month previously he had maintained that a special session would not be called primarily for the suffrage amendment, he now claimed the session would meet "for the sole purpose of ratifying the suffrage amendment." He skirted the issue of payment by announcing it would be up to the legislators to determine whether or not they would be paid.[49] Ultimately, the legislators voted to receive payment.

The special session opened on 26 January 1920. Professor Grace Hebard was recognized with a seat of honor in the house chamber for her service in promoting woman suffrage. Governor Carey addressed a joint meeting on the opening day and asked legislators to ratify the amendment "without delay." He explained that he had hoped enough other states would have voted to ratify the suffrage amendment, thus allowing Wyoming to do so at the next regular session of the state legislature. But he now thought Wyoming's vote was necessary in order for women across the nation to vote in the 1920 presidential election. He also expressed concern over opponents of suffrage in other states using Wyoming's inaction as an argument against ratification by claiming that Wyoming "had not ratified for the reason that suffrage had proved a failure in this state." Carey emphasized that Wyoming "could not allow such a charge to be unchallenged."[50] At 3:30 in the afternoon on 27 January 1920, the Wyoming legislature ratified the Susan B. Anthony Amendment with little debate and no dissenting votes, making Wyoming the twenty-seventh state to do so.[51] Of the sixteen states west of the Mississippi River that had secured woman suffrage before Congress passed the Nineteenth Amendment, Wyoming was eleventh to ratify.

In the end, Wyoming did wake up and help to secure the necessary popular and legislative support to ratify the Susan B. Anthony Amendment ahead of the 1920 general election. Seeking to spark enthusiasm, NAWSA leaders had highlighted the success of suffrage in the West and Great Plains, with special emphasis on

Wyoming's status as the first territory and state to give women the right to vote. During the year in which the Nineteenth Amendment passed both houses of the United States Congress, Wyoming commemorated its commitment to woman suffrage by placing a historic landmark at South Pass City and establishing its first annual Wyoming Day. The state was slow to act, however, in making sure that women across the nation could vote as their Wyoming counterparts had been doing for fifty years. All the governments of the Northern Great Plains states supported woman suffrage, and each governor proclaimed his state's support for ratification of the Nineteenth Amendment. In Wyoming and the two Dakotas, however, the governors' focus on economic frugality led them to question the necessity of the extra expense of a special session solely for that purpose. In response to pleas of suffrage supporters, and in order to ensure that women from every state could vote in the upcoming presidential election, each governor finally called a special session that easily ratified the Susan B. Anthony Amendment, which became law on 26 August 1920.

NOTES

I would like to thank the editors of this book, Molly Rozum and Lori Lahlum, for bringing this collection to life and for their hard work and dedication in making it a reality.

1. "National Suffrage Representatives in City Today," *Laramie Daily Boomerang*, 11 Jan. 1919; "Suffrage Worker Visiting the City," *Laramie Republican*, 11 Jan. 1919.

2. Ibid.; "Mrs. Horatio Burns Heads Committee on Woman Suffrage Here," *Sheridan Daily Enterprise*, 7 Jan. 1919.

3. "In Interest of Suffrage," *Laramie Republican*, 3 Jan. 1919.

4. *Rock Springs Miner*, 31 Jan. 1919.

5. "Representative of N.A.W.S.A. Here," *Cheyenne State Leader*, 7 Jan. 1919; "The Winning of Wyoming," *Wyoming State Tribune* (Cheyenne), 18 Mar. 1919; "Plan Outlined for Suffrage Organization," *Casper Daily Tribune*, 16 Jan. 1919; "Urges Suffrage League," *New York Times*, 25 Mar. 1919, p. 11;

"To Celebrate," *Laramie Republican*, 18 Feb. 1919; "Laramie Lady Made Mother of Convention," *Laramie Republican*, 28 Mar. 1919. NAWSA's precursor organizations, the National Woman Suffrage Association and the American Woman Suffrage Association, had formed in 1869. At the 1919 Saint Louis meeting, NAWSA thus celebrated fifty years of campaigning as well as Wyoming's fiftieth anniversary of suffrage.

6. Emma Bugbee, "A Baby Gave Woman Suffrage to This Nation," *New York Tribune*, 2 Mar. 1919, p. F12.

7. T. A. Larson, "Dolls, Vassals, and Drudges—Pioneer Women in the West," *Western Historical Quarterly* 3 (Jan. 1972): 9. *See also* T. A. Larson, "Woman Suffrage in Wyoming," *The Pacific Northwest Quarterly* 56 (Apr. 1965): 57–66; Sidney Howell Fleming, "Solving the Jigsaw Puzzle: One Suffrage Story at a Time," *Annals of Wyoming* 62 (Spring 1990): 22–65; Michael A. Massie, "Reform is Where You Find It: The Roots of Woman Suffrage in Wyoming," *Annals of Wyoming* 62 (Spring 1990): 2–22.

8. "The Winning of Wyoming," *Wyoming State Tribune*, 18 Mar. 1919.

9. Larson, "Woman Suffrage in Wyoming," p. 63.

10. For more information on Esther Morris and her place in Wyoming's suffrage history, *see* Katy Morris, "'More Reputation Than She Deserves': Remembering Suffrage in Wyoming," *Rethinking History* 21, no. 1 (2017): 48–66; Marcy Lynn Karin, "Esther Morris and Her Equality State: From Council Bill 70 to Life on the Bench," *American Journal of Legal History* 46 (July 2004): 300–43.

11. Wyoming, *Journal and Debates of the Constitutional Convention of the State of Wyoming* (Cheyenne, 1893), p. 352.

12. Massie, "Reform is Where You Find It," p. 18; T. A. Larson, *History of Wyoming* (Lincoln: University of Nebraska Press, 1978), p. 93. The *Denver Post* printed the women's story in 1923, but nothing much came of it.

13. "South Pass, Suffrage Shrine Desolate and Near-Forgotten Eve of Fiftieth Anniversary," *Kemmerer Republican*, 31 Jan. 1919. *See also Casper Daily Tribune*, 6 Feb. 1919.

14. "Social News," *Laramie Republican*, 22 Mar. 1919. *See also* "The Winning of Wyoming," *Wyoming State Tribune*, 18 Mar. 1919.

15. Nickerson, "Historical Correction," *Wyoming State Journal*, 14 Feb. 1919; Nickerson, "Early History of Fremont County," *Wyoming Historical Department Quarterly Bulletin* 2 (July 1924): 1–13.

16. Hebard, *How Woman Suffrage Came to Wyoming* (1920), copy in Woman Suffrage File, American Heritage Center, University of Wyoming, Laramie.

17. Historians have long disputed the story of Morris and her tea party. Some claim it is exaggerated or even made up. T. A. Larson, for instance, outlined his objections in numerous publications, arguing, as have others, that passage of woman suffrage was simply a necessary tactic to give Wyoming enough voters to be eligible to apply for statehood. Still others argued that territorial leaders sought publicity to attract more settlers to the area,

desiring only to be first in something of national import. In the post-Civil War era, race also played a major role in suffrage debates, and many suffragists remarked that if black men and immigrant men achieved the vote, white women deserved the same right. Another theory suggested that Democrats had introduced the bill in the Wyoming legislature as a joke to embarrass the Republican territorial governor. The reasons and theories surrounding the passage of woman suffrage in Wyoming remain disputed, but the state has nonetheless assumed a key position in suffrage history. For more information, *see* Tom Rea, "Right Choice, Wrong Reasons: Wyoming Women Win the Right to Vote," *WyoHistory.org*; Michael A. Massie, "Reform is Where You Find It," pp. 2–22; Larson, "Dolls, Vassals, and Drudges," pp. 4-16; and T. A. Larson, "Petticoats at the Polls: Woman Suffrage in Territorial Wyoming," *Pacific Northwest Quarterly* 44 (Apr. 1953): 74–79.

18. Quoted in "Carey Refuses to Convene an Extra Session," *Wyoming State Tribune*, 7 June 1919.

19. Marjorie Spruill Wheeler, *One Woman, One Vote: Rediscovering the Woman Suffrage Movement* (Troutdale, Oreg.: NewSage Press, 1995), p. 378.

20. Quoted in "Will Pass Amendment," *Laramie Republican*, 18 June 1919.

21. Quoted in "Extra Session of Solons Not to Be Called," *Laramie Boomerang*, 18 Aug. 1919.

22. Quoted in "No Extra Session at This Time Says Governor," *Sheridan Post*, 21 Aug. 1919.

23. George B. Water, "Fifteen Men Bar Women's Way to Equal Suffrage," *Bismarck Daily Tribune*, 30 Oct. 1919.

24. "Social Events," *Laramie Republican*," 4 Oct. 1919.

25. "Delegation of Women Appeal to Women to Learn to Use Their Vote to Help Men," *Laramie Boomerang*, 23 Oct. 1919.

26. "Suffragist Appeals to Wyoming People," *Wyoming State Tribune*, 14 Nov. 1919.

27. Maude A. Cook, "Social News," *Laramie Republican*, 20 Nov. 1919.

28. "Governor Proclaims Dec. 10 Wyoming Day," *Cheyenne State Leader*, 3 Dec. 1919.

29. "Delta Meta Delphian Meets Celebrates 'Wyoming' Day," *Rock Springs Rocket*, 12 Dec. 1919.

30. "No Extra Sessions," *Big Timber (Mont.) Pioneer*, 12 June 1919.

31. "Call Special Session for Drouth Relief," *Fort Benton River Press*, 23 July 1919.

32. "North Dakota May Be among the First States in Union to Ratify Suffrage Plank," *Bismarck Tribune*, 7 June 1919.

33. "Prominent Suffrage Leaders Here to Interview Governor Frazier in Interest of National Amendment," ibid., 1 July 1919.

34. "'A Number of Things,'" *Valley City Weekly Times-Record*, 7 Aug. 1919.

35. "Frazier Denies Saying Would Issue Call," *Devils Lake World and Inter-Ocean*, 13 Aug.1919.

36. "A Special Session," *Nonpartisan Leader*, 17 Nov. 1919.

37. "North Dakota's Solons to Eat Thanksgiving Bird in Capital; Special Session November 25," *Bismarck Tribune*, 30 Oct. 1919; "Suffrage Chief Thanks Frazier," ibid., 4 Nov. 1919.

38. Quoted in "Farmers' Legislature Meets at Bismarck," *Nonpartisan Leader*, 8 Dec. 1919, p. 4.

39. "Suffrage Ratified," *Bismarck Tribune*, 2 Dec. 1919.

40. Quoted in "Will Ask That This State Act Upon Suffrage," *Philip Pioneer*, 19 June 1919.

41. "Legislators Meet Without Pay," *Madison Daily Leader*, 12 Nov. 1919.

42. "News of the State," *Milbank Herald-Advance*, 14 Nov. 1919.

43. "Ratify Suffrage in South Dakota," *Madison Daily Leader*, 5 Dec. 1919; Patricia O'Keefe Easton, "Opposition to Woman Suffrage in South Dakota" (master's thesis, University of South Dakota, 1982), pp. 109–11; Dorinda Riessen Reed, *The Woman Suffrage Movement in South Dakota*, Governmental Research Bureau, Report no. 41 (Vermillion: University of South Dakota, 1958), p. 113.

44. "Governor May Call Special Session of Legislature But Not at Instance of Suffragists," *Wyoming State Tribune*, 9 Dec. 1919.

45. "Asks Legislature to Serve Without Pay," *Laramie Republican*, 24 Dec. 1919.

46. "Carey's Christmas Gift to Members of the Legislature," *Cheyenne State Leader*, 28 Dec. 1919.

47. "Our Cheap Governor," *Sheridan Enterprise*, 23 Dec. 1919.

48. "Offers to Defray Expense of Solon, Thinks Carey Cheap," ibid., 19 Dec. 1919.

49. Quoted in "Pay Question Up to Solons Themselves," *Wyoming State Tribune*, 31 Dec. 1919.

50. Quoted in "Carey Wants a Solid Vote for Suffrage," *Wyoming State Tribune*, 26 Jan. 1920.

51. "Wyoming Is in Line," *Laramie Republican*, 27 Jan. 1920; "Conclude a Session," *Laramie Republican*, 28 Jan. 1920; "Ratify Suffrage Amendment," *Saratoga Sun*, 29 Jan. 1920.

SNAPSHOTS

MARTHA SYMONS BOIES ATKINSON

First Woman Bailiff

RENÉE M. LAEGREID

Martha Symons Boies Atkinson had a studio portrait taken during her later years. Middle-class and middle-aged, her face framed by a jaunty feathered hat and fur collar, she looks past the camera lens. Intentionally or not, her serious, watchful expression aligns with her role in Wyoming Territory's suffrage story. Before her marriage to James Atkinson, Boies was the first female bailiff in Wyoming. Her appointment as bailiff reveals how opportunities opened to women as part of the territory's landmark suffrage bill.[1] On 10 December 1869, a goal first proposed in Seneca Falls, New York, in 1848 had been easily and unexpectedly realized in the nation's newest territory.[2] "An Act to Grant to the Women of Wyoming Territory the Right of Suffrage and to Hold Office" guaranteed full civic equality for women.[3]

Along with voting came other rights and responsibilities. In March 1870, state chief justice John H. Howe appointed women to both the grand and petit juries in Laramie, Wyoming, for the three-week spring-court session.[4] The judge selected well-known and respected women, anticipating that perhaps "the better element" of Laramie would trust the women jurors to convict criminals because "the usual juries, consisting of men, could not or would not."[5] The women heard cases that seem right out of a Wild West novel: cattle rustling, horse thieving, illegal branding, and a murder case that began with a disagreement during a late night poker game at the Shamrock Saloon and ended with one man "quite dead."[6]

The court also faced the new responsibility of guarding women jurors "whenever the women were called to sit." The *New York*

Martha Symons Boies Atkinson, c. 1901.
American Heritage Center, University of Wyoming

Times reported on chief justice Howe's commitment to protecting women jurors, saying they would be "treated with all the respect and courtesy due, and ever paid, by true American gentlemen to true American ladies." "The Court," Howe explained, "in all the power of the Government, will secure to them all that deference, security from insult, or anything which ought to offend the most refined woman, which is accorded to women in any of the walks of life in which the good and true women of our country have heretofore been accustomed to move."[7] To ensure this outcome, the Laramie court needed a woman bailiff, a trusted and respected member of the community. Sheriff Nathaniel Kimball

Boswell, tasked with the decision, chose Martha Symons Boies, although it is difficult to know why he selected her.

Contemporary newspapers offer scant information about Boies. Later accounts depict her and her husband as a prosperous, well-loved couple, honored among the first settlers of Laramie. Her son was a prominent lawyer in town. Boies left no diaries, letters, or reminiscences. Her obituary offered a simple outline of her life as a westward traveler and an intrepid settler in Laramie. As reconstructed from these few sources, Boies's life exemplifies the rigors of travel, relocation, and frontier life that so many migrants faced in the nineteenth century. Born in England in 1830, she immigrated to Mineral Point, Wisconsin, with her parents while still an infant. The family moved again, settling in Treadwell, Wisconsin, where she married her first husband, John Symons. The couple had two sons, but her husband died while their children were still young. Martha Symons then married Jerimiah Boies, or Boyes, while still in Treadwell. Sometime in the mid-to-late 1850s, the Boies family joined the rush of emigrants moving westward, settling in Kearney, Nebraska, and "engag[ing] in the hotel business and later a boarding house." When construction of the Union Pacific Railroad approached Kearney in 1866, they saw economic opportunity. The Boieses moved from camp to camp with the railroad as construction progressed westward, arriving in Laramie in 1868, days ahead of the crews. They liked Laramie and decided to give up their itinerant life and settle, even though they continued living in a tent, as did everyone else in town, for a while longer.[8]

Perhaps her experience living with a railroad crew in Laramie during its first, most lawless years made Martha Boies a good candidate for bailiff. Grenville Dodge, the ex-Union general overseeing construction of the Union Pacific, had founded Laramie as a camp for his workers. Dodge's crew consisted of mostly young, single Civil War veterans and Irish immigrants. They earned the nickname "Hell on Wheels" for their wild, lawless behavior as they moved their camp along the rail line. After Dodge's crew left Laramie, it remained a "border town in all that the word implies . . . varied by vigilante entertainments and shooting scrapes without number."[9] Two years later, Laramie was still a rough town. As a woman who proved her mettle in helping settle it, Boies likely appeared to Sherriff Boswell as a solid choice for the role of its first woman bailiff.

According to Boies, serving as bailiff was pleasant duty. In an 1878 newspaper article, she recounted her experiences to a Laramie reporter, who explained, "The jury was locked up at night at the hotel, the lady jurors in one room the men jurors in another." Boies told the reporter the women jurors "had splendid meals given them, and enjoyed it so much that one of them, in an unguarded moment, said she 'didn't care how long the trial lasted if they could live as well as they were living.' The Judge happened to occupy an adjoining room and overheard the remark." The *Laramie Weekly Sentinel* reporter elaborated, "The next day Mrs. Boies said they had nothing but crackers and cheese for dinner." Boies described court officials as polite and kind to herself and the woman jurors. Suggesting some unease with women's public roles, the sheriff even asked if the women wanted him to relay messages home to their families or bring household items to their hotel to make them more comfortable.[10]

Wyoming's first women jurors captured national attention, but they only served three terms of court, each with Boies as bailiff. Chief Justice Howe had reasoned that the 10 December 1869 Suffrage Act superseded a law, passed just three days earlier, stipulating that only men could serve as jurors. When Howe retired in September 1871, however, his successor disapproved of woman suffrage and prohibited selecting women to serve on juries.[11] Without women jurors, Martha Boies's services were no longer needed. Questions over the constitutionality of women serving combined with an overwhelming belief that it was "a violation of all approved social customs to ask ladies to assume any duties as grim and unpleasant as jury service" ended the practice until 1950.[12] Although Boies's role as bailiff was short, her example reveals how Wyoming's decision to grant women unrestricted suffrage opened unexpected and diverse venues for women to engage in civic life.

EQUALITY AT THE BALLOT BOX

NOTES

1. Although documents in the Martha Boies File, American Heritage Center (AHC), University of Wyoming (UW), Laramie, refer to her as the first bailiff in the world, this claim is doubtful. It is more likely she served as the first woman bailiff in the United States. She was known as Martha Boies/ Boyes until she remarried following Jerimiah Boies's death in 1901. She lived until 1917.

2. Virginia Scharff, "Broadening the Battlefield: Conflict, Contingency, and the Mystery of Woman Suffrage in Wyoming, 1869," in *Civil War Wests: Testing the Limits of the United States*, ed. Adam Arenson and Andrew Graybill (Oakland: University of California Press, 2015), pp. 202–23.

3. Library of Congress, www.loc.gov/resource/ppmsca.03000/.

4. Sarah Wallace Pease, "Women as Jurors," *Cheyenne Daily Sun-Leader*, 28 Nov. 1895.

5. "Oldest Local Settler Dies of Old Age," *Laramie Daily Boomerang*, 23 Mar. 1917.

6. "Factus quarreling," Evidence before Corners Jury in the Case of John Hocter, 3 Dec. 1869, Criminal Case File #26, *Territory of Wyoming v. Andrew W. Howie*, Albany County District Court, Wyoming State Archives (WSA), Cheyenne.

7. Quoted in "Women as Jurors in Wyoming Territory," *New York Times*, 11 Mar. 1870.

8. "Oldest Local Settler Dies of Old Age."

9. "A Night Attack: Peaceful Pioneers Surprised and Captured," *Laramie Daily Boomerang*, 14 Apr. 1886.

10. "Laramie Abroad: How Our Plains, City and People Look to a Traveler," *Laramie Weekly Sentinel*, 25 May 1878.

11. Jessie C. Thompson, "History of Jury Service for Women," (Thermopolis, Wyo.: Wyoming Business and Professional Women's Clubs, March 1953), p. 13, copy in WSA.

12. Kim Viner, "Laramie Makes World History: First Women Serving on a Jury," Albany County Historical Society, 28 Apr. 2018, www.wyoachs.com /laramies-living-history-people-page2/2018/4/28/was-it-legal-downey -questions-seating-women-on-juries-in-1870.

KATE SELBY WILDER
DRESSES THE PART

ANN W. BRAATEN

The first woman in North Dakota to hold city-wide office, Kate Selby Wilder served one four-year term on the Fargo City Commission beginning in 1919. Wilder's role as a suffragist emerged from the shadows of history when her daughter donated her clothing to the Emily Reynolds Historic Costume Collection at North Dakota State University in 1988. Her cotton batiste dress with lace panels, seen here, dates from the woman suffrage campaign of the early 1910s and reveals how activists worked to manage their appearance.[1]

The Edwardian S-shaped silhouette of the dress has slight fullness in the front bodice and skirt back. As the popularity of this silhouette waned, dressmakers deemphasized this fullness, but it remained an acceptable part of women's dress throughout the 1910s. Fashionable elements of the dress include its square neckline, fitted short sleeves, and back-buttoned closure. The blending of a tried-and-true silhouette with fashionable details projected Wilder's progressive stance while suggesting women's traditional roles as wife, mother, and homemaker.

Wilder's dress was custom made with materials purchased from stores or though catalogue retailers. Fargo dressmaker Clara Hughes cut and sewed Wilder's clothing to achieve a proper profile. The dress fit over a camisole, corset and corset cover that shaped the bust and waist, and drawers (long underpants). One or two petticoats with back fullness shaped the skirt. The multiple layers provided opacity.[2]

Thin linen fabric and lacy trim were once reserved for undergarments. Indeed, the French word for linen, *linge*, is the origin of lingerie. During the late 1700s, lingerie fabrics began to be used

Kate Selby Wilder wore this white dress while campaigning for suffrage in North Dakota in the 1910s. Emily Reynolds Historic Costume Collection, North Dakota State University

in outer garments. The French called them *chemise de la reign*, or underwear of the queen, because Marie Antoinette was among the first to wear this style. During the 1800s, the style became known as the "lingerie dress."[3] In April 1909, *Harper's Bazaar* told readers that a lingerie dress was one of the most vitally important items for summer. From the late 1800s to the mid-1910s, the silhouette changed with the whims of fashion, but the thin fabric and lace remained constant.[4] When suffrage activists began staging parades in 1908 to bring attention to the cause, organizers instructed women to look their best. They wanted women representing the suffrage movement to be seen as appealing and not as stereotypically unattractive crones or aggressive hellions.[5]

By 1912, suffragists' fashionable lingerie dresses provided uniformity and symbolized purity in their campaign. An early May parade featuring ten thousand women marching in white earned the headline "Suffrage Army on Parade" in the *New York Times*. "Most of the women, particularly the younger women," the *Times* reported, "were dressed all in white, except for the out-flashing of yellow and purple and green and red that was in the ribbons they wore, the banners they carried, and the flags they waved."[6] Wilder's lingerie dress shows that women active in the Northern Great Plains suffrage movement wore this unofficial uniform as well. The soft fabric of the dress and feminine lace assured people that women's traditional roles would not be forgotten once they achieved the right to vote.

NOTES

1. Elizabeth W. Holand, daughter of Kate Selby Wilder, and her husband, Roy A. Holand, donated Wilder's clothing in 1988, accession number 1988.18, Emily Reynolds Historic Costume Collection, North Dakota State University, Fargo.

2. Notes in the Holand donor file, ibid., list Clara Hughes as Wilder's dressmaker.

3. Mary Picken, *The Fashion Dictionary* (New York: Funk & Wagnalls, 1957), p. 214, describes the term "lingerie" as borrowed from the French by Sarah Josepha Hale, editor of *Godey's Lady's Book* from 1837 to 1877.

4. "Fashion Advice for Summer 1909," *Harper's Bazaar*, Apr. 1909, p. 426.

5. T. J. Boisseau, "Women Workers and Suffrage," Roy Rosenzweig Cen-

ter for History and New Media at George Mason University, Fairfax, Va., Teaching_History.org.

6. "Suffrage Army on Parade," *New York Times*, 5 May 1912, p. 1.

JEANNETTE RANKIN ON THE ROAD

CODY DODGE EWERT

An automobile parked in the courthouse square of Missoula, Montana, was the center of attention on 2 May 1914. A report in the *Missoulian* described the scene: "About the automobile crowned by the yellow standard of the suffrage workers, the crowd hung. . . . Not a disturbing cry was raised nor a voice in opposition. When it would have been so easy to distract, children were hushed and men and women crowded closer with the attitude of disciples rather than of doubtful judges." The event, part of a nationwide Suffrage Day celebration that aimed to drum up support for a constitutional amendment that would guarantee votes for women, culminated with a speech from Jeannette Rankin, the state's most prominent suffragist. Rankin's address heralded woman suffrage as a way of securing justice. "The women of the United States are joining in this demonstration today to show that they are ready for the next step in the evolution of democracy," she declared from atop the car festooned with suffrage banners. "While we Montana women have broader opportunities than the women of any other part of the world, we want the ballot in order to give opportunity to less fortunate women."[1]

Whether used as a stage or a means of conveyance, automobiles played a key role in spreading the woman suffrage movement in the early twentieth century, as Jeannette Rankin's example makes clear. Whether attempting to reach every corner of her massive home state of Montana or bring attention to the movement on the national level, Rankin seized on the unprecedented freedom the automobile allowed. At a time when many argued that women lacked the physical and mental capacity to drive, her presence behind the wheel challenged popular assumptions. When suffragists like Rankin sat in the driver's seat,

Jeannette Rankin holds a suffrage flag atop an automobile in 1913 or 1914.
Montana Historical Society Research Center

they rebuked the restrictive gender norms of the day and boldly proclaimed women's ability to move and think independently.[2]

The dawn of the automobile age in the United States coincided with the Progressive Era, a period spanning the late-nineteenth and early-twentieth centuries when a diverse cross section of Americans launched reform crusades aimed at ameliorating a host of social and political problems. In a stark shift from the male-dominated popular politics of the nineteenth century, women often took the lead in pushing progressive reforms such as good government, school reform, labor laws, and food and water regulations, bringing them into the public sphere. The rise of the "new woman," usually depicted as a white, educated, middle-class woman who shirked traditional gender norms while pursuing social justice, challenged the Victorian-era ideal of women as homebound, timid, and nurturing. Not surprisingly, many women asserted their right to drive around the same time. Early motor travel was hazardous, complex, and cost prohibitive. As of 1900, there were only eight thousand registered automobiles in the United States. Technological advancements, however, gradually made it possible for more Americans to own and successfully operate their own cars. Private ownership ostensibly meant that women could purchase an automobile just as easily as a man. Yet, due to their unequal social roles and depressed wages, working-class women rarely had those opportunities. As a result, affluent women were the first to embrace automobiles, albeit often with the aid of a chauffeur.[3] The right to drive, then, was one of a host of rights women had to fight to secure.

Jeannette Rankin in many ways was the archetypal new woman. Born in 1880 to a prosperous Missoula family, Rankin tried her hand at feminized professions like teaching and dressmaking after graduating from the University of Montana, but her growing concern about the plight of the urban poor—fueled by the muckraking journalism of the day—soon led her to social work. After attending the New York School of Philanthropy, she secured a position in Spokane, Washington, later moving to Seattle to study at the University of Washington. There, she became convinced that meaningful social progress could be achieved only if women gained the right to vote. She worked on Washington's successful 1910 suffrage campaign before heading back to Montana. Rankin soon became a central figure among Montana suffragists, earning a position as a field secretary for the National American Woman Suffrage Association (NAWSA) in 1913.[4]

Rankin gained renown for her work as a grassroots organizer, but she also proved adept at using spectacle to promote the cause. A 1913 automobile tour from Montana to Washington, D.C., to take part in a NAWSA parade evinces her knack for generating publicity. Alice Paul, chair of NAWSA's congressional committee, concocted the idea of having suffragists from across the country conduct a five-mile automotive parade stretching from Hyattsville, Maryland, to the nation's capital. The procession, set for 31 July 1913, would deliver the signatures of over a quarter-million suffrage supporters to Congress while scandalizing onlookers with the sight of hundreds of women drivers taking over the streets. It was hardly the first time that suffragists had used automobiles to make a point. In 1910, Illinois Equal Suffrage Association members set off on an automobile tour of the state, and organizer Catherine Waugh McCulloch went on to lead similar events in Wisconsin and California.[5] Not all suffragists embraced the automobile, however. Harriot Stanton Blatch, organizer of New York City's 1912 suffrage parade, banned participants from riding in cars, which she claimed "did not demonstrate courage."[6] A few dissenters aside, suffragists across the nation began taking the wheel with aplomb, and other progressive reform groups also embraced the tactic. For instance, the Nonpartisan League, which formed in North Dakota in 1915 and became a powerful political force on behalf of farmers and workers on the Northern Great Plains, relied heavily on automobiles to reach far-flung rural communities.[7]

Rankin's cross-country journey drew significant press coverage. In Glendive, Montana, a local judge adjourned a night court session early so that she could speak in the town's assembly hall.[8] On 15 July, a *Washington Evening Star* reporter, under the headline "Suffragist is Orating Way Across Country," marveled at her wide-ranging effort to stump for women's right to vote in distant locales like "Fargo, S.D."[9] During her weeklong tour of North Dakota, Fargo's actual home, the front page of the *Grand Forks*

Evening Times announced, "Women to Make Plea for Votes from Automobile."[10] Days later, a piece in the *Jamestown Weekly Alert* informed readers, "The woman suffrage campaign in North Dakota has been started by Jeanette [*sic*] Rankin of Montana" from the running board of "a large touring auto . . . decorated with inscriptions bearing the battle cry 'Votes for Women.'"[11] In the end, Rankin did not drive all the way to Washington, D.C., making it only as far as Chicago, though she completed the journey by train.[12] Rankin's adventure nonetheless brought attention to the cause while raising her public profile.

After returning to Montana, Rankin focused on bringing suffrage to her home state. She declined to serve another term as NAWSA field secretary, instead forming a statewide equal suffrage organization to build support for a 1914 ballot referendum that would extend voting rights to Montana women. That fall, 52 percent of the state's voters approved the measure. In a massive state with a diffuse rural population, Rankin's efforts to secure victory naturally required a considerable amount of driving. In attempting to recruit workers in every county seat, she covered around thirteen hundred miles in twenty-five days—nearly as many miles as she drove en route to the nation's capital the previous year.[13] During a car campaign in rural central Montana in July 1914, Rankin learned of the onset of war in Europe. She later wrote, "It seemed to me at that time that the end of the world had come. . . . But one of the first things we had talked about in woman suffrage [was] that it was women's job to get rid of war."[14]

Indeed, Rankin's pacifism—a cause that often dovetailed with the woman suffrage movement—would largely define her career as the first woman to serve in the United States Congress. Rankin's historic 1916 congressional campaign benefitted from her experience as a suffrage activist, as she crisscrossed the state by car, train, and even a horse-drawn buggy. She advocated for a raft of progressive causes while in Congress, but her most consequential stand came in 1917 when she voted against a resolution signaling America's entrance into the war, one of only fifty-six members of the House of Representatives to do so. After an unsuccessful run for the United States Senate in 1918, Rankin was not elected to Congress again until 1940. In December of the following year, she voted against the nation's declaration of war on Japan; this time, she was the lone dissenter in either house.[15] Rankin's path into history, much like the success of woman suffrage itself, was hardly inevitable. Rather, as the key role of the automobile in her suffrage activism suggests, it stemmed from a unique intersection of far-reaching cultural, political, and technological changes.

NOTES

1. "Whole Nation Observes Woman's Day," *Missoulian*, 3 May 1914.

2. Virginia Scharff, *Taking the Wheel: Women and the Coming of the Motor Age* (Albuquerque: University of New Mexico Press, 1992), pp. 26–27.

3. On the leading role of women in progressive causes, *see* Kathryn Kish Sklar, *Florence Kelley and the Nation's Work: The Rise of Women's Political Culture, 1830–1900* (New Haven: Yale University Press, 1995), p. xv; Maureen A. Flanagan, *America Reformed: Progressives and Progressivisms, 1890s–1920s* (New York: Oxford University Press, 2007), pp. 42–48; Robert D. Johnston, "Re-Democratizing the Progressive Era: The Politics of Progressive Era Political Historiography," *Journal of the Gilded Age and Progressive Era* 1 (Jan. 2002): 80–83. On the early years of the automotive industry and women, *see* Scharff, *Taking the Wheel*, pp. 22–33; Kathleen Franz, *Tinkering: Consumers Reinvent the Early Automobile* (Philadelphia: University of Pennsylvania Press, 2005), pp. 45–53; Margaret Walsh, "Gendering Mobility: Women, Work, and Automobility in the United States," *History* 93 (July 2008): 380–82.

4. Ronald Schaffer, "The Montana Woman Suffrage Campaign, 1911–1914," *Pacific Northwest Quarterly* 55 (Jan. 1964): 9; Kathryn Anderson, "Steps to Political Equality: Woman Suffrage and Electoral Politics in the Lives of Emily Newell Blair, Anne Henrietta Martin, and Jeannette Rankin," *Frontiers* 18, no. 1 (1997): 103–5. Rankin's conviction that woman suffrage would make major social reforms like eight-hour workday laws, healthcare for mothers and children, and industrial safety measures possible echoed the thinking of leading progressive reformers like Florence Kelley and Jane Addams. *See* Flanagan, *America Reformed*, pp. 131–33.

5. Katherine H. Adams and Michael L. Keene, *Alice Paul and the American Suffrage Campaign* (Urbana: University of Illinois Press, 2007), pp. 98–99; Scharff, *Taking the Wheel*, pp. 79–80. Prior to the automotive parade, Paul had organized a two-day suffrage pageant in Washington ahead of Woodrow Wilson's inauguration. Her tactics soon led her to split with NAWSA, forming

the Congressional Union, a rival suffrage organization. Nancy F. Cott, *The Grounding of Modern Feminism* (New Haven, Conn.: Yale University Press, 1987), pp. 53–54.

6. Quoted in Johanna Neuman, "Who Won Women's Suffrage? A Case for 'Mere Men,'" *Journal of the Gilded Age and Progressive Era* 16 (July 2017): 360.

7. Michael J. Lansing, *Insurgent Democracy: The Nonpartisan League in North American Politics* (Chicago: University of Chicago Press, 2015), pp. 71–75; William C. Pratt, "Observations from My Life with Farm Movements in the Upper Midwest," *South Dakota History* 44 (Summer 2014): 140–41. *See also* Michael McGerr, "Political Style and Women's Power, 1830–1930," *Journal of American History* 77 (Dec. 1990): 873–76.

8. "Many Obstacles Met by Women," *Washington Herald*, 3 Aug. 1913.

9. "Suffragist is Orating Way Across Country," *Washington Evening Star*, 15 July 1913.

10. "Women to Make Plea for Votes from Automobile," *Grand Forks Evening Times*, 21 July 1913.

11. "'Votes for Women' Tour," *Jamestown Weekly Herald*, 31 July 1913.

12. Norma Smith, *Jeannette Rankin: America's Conscience* (Helena: Montana Historical Society Press, 2002), pp. 70–72. Several newspaper articles mentioned Rankin's decision to go to Washington from Chicago by rail. *See*, for example, "Senators Will Speak for Woman Suffrage," *Washington Herald*, 30 July 1913; "Women to Swoop Down on Capital," ibid., 31 July 1913. The *Missoulian*, in contrast, elided this detail, noting, "Miss Rankin motored all the way from Montana to the national capital" ("From Missoula to Washington, D.C., to Aid the Cause of Equal Suffrage," *Missoulian*, 10 Aug. 1913).

13. Schaffer, "Montana Woman Suffrage Campaign," p. 13; Smith, *Jeannette Rankin*, pp. 75–89; Jennifer J. Hill, "The Marathon of Montana Suffrage," herein.

14. Quoted in John C. Board, "The Lady from Montana," *Montana: The Magazine of Western History* 17 (Summer 1967): 4.

15. Ibid., pp. 5–17. As Rankin's brother, Montana politician Wellington D. Rankin, put it, "She was one of the best single-handed campaigners I ever saw" (quoted ibid., p. 6). On suffrage and peace activism, *see* Joan Hoff Wilson, "Jeannette Rankin and American Foreign Policy: The Origins of Her Pacifism," *Montana: The Magazine of Western History* 30 (Winter 1980): 33–36.

BLACK HILLS SUFFRAGIST
MABEL REWMAN

KELLY KIRK

By the spring of 1918, the normally indefatigable Mabel Rewman, member of the Round Table Club of Deadwood, local Red Cross worker, and finance chair for the South Dakota Universal Franchise League (SDUFL), was exhausted. Her weeks on the road raising funds for the 1918 woman suffrage campaign had resulted in notable successes, including significant donations to the cause. During her travels, however, her husband's assistant at the Black Hills Telephone Exchange Company had left, and the suffragist would now have to lend a hand at the office. Her frequent absences also led some of her fellow Red Cross volunteers to complain that she gave more to suffrage than to Red Cross work. Rewman informed Mary ("Mamie") Shields Pyle, president of the SDUFL, that she needed to stay in the Black Hills for a little while. There was, after all, still much work to be done in that corner of the state.[1]

Throughout the 1910s, Mabel Fontron Rewman fought for woman suffrage in the Black Hills. Originally from Kansas, she had moved around the country throughout her young adulthood and worked with loans and insurance in Missouri and Illinois before owning her own grocery business in Oklahoma. While caring for an ill sister in Washington State, she developed an ulcer, forcing her to visit a doctor. The specialist, a woman, encouraged her patient to get involved with a worthy cause and suggested the Washington State Equal Suffrage Association. Rewman not only joined, she became an extremely active member. She also met Emma Smith DeVoe, a suffragist and former South Dakota resident who had been active during that state's tumultuous 1890 campaign. After returning to Oklahoma, Mabel Fontron mar-

Mabel Fontron Rewman, c. 1918.
Adams Museum Collection, Deadwood History, Inc.

ried Paul Rewman, who managed the Black Hills Telephone Exchange Company, and the two moved to Deadwood in 1912.[2]

The move to Deadwood would be momentous, both for Rewman and for the woman suffrage movement in the Black Hills. Rewman soon assumed leadership roles in numerous organizations in Deadwood and throughout the state. Members of the Deadwood Equal Suffrage League elected her president in 1917, and the SDUFL placed her in charge of finances for the 1918 referendum campaign. She arranged gatherings and hosted key suffrage speakers such as Jane Addams, traveled extensively to give speeches, organized suffrage schools, campaigned in front of the state legislature in Pierre, and attended the 1917 national woman suffrage convention in Washington, D.C.[3]

Correspondence between Rewman and SDUFL president Pyle throughout the spring of 1918 shows her high level of activity and helps explain the eventual success of woman suffrage in South Dakota. Rewman mentioned speaking in Lead, Deadwood, and at "the Normal," or teachers college, in Spearfish to over 350 pupils. While Rewman herself provided few details about her travels, Pyle kept suffrage supporters throughout the state apprised of Rewman's achievements. For example, Pyle reported Rewman's visit to Miller, where in only three days she raised the county's fundraising quota. She then moved on to Huron.[4] Three days later, Pyle wrote to another suffragist that, while in Huron, Rewman managed to raise fifty dollars from one man, the "largest sum that any one man gave in Huron." Ironically, the man's wife had "allowed her name to be used on the board or committee of the organization opposed to suffrage."[5] Due to her successes, women across the state wrote to Pyle requesting Rewman's presence in their community.

Rewman returned to Deadwood in June 1918 to organize suffrage schools to be held across the state. National leaders such as Mrs. Frank J. Shuler, the corresponding secretary and chairman of campaigns and committees for the National American Woman Suffrage Association (NAWSA), and Mrs. Albert McMahon, field director of NAWSA, ran the two-day suffrage schools, which trained activists in organizing strategies and public relations. Rewman judged Deadwood's suffrage school a "howling success."[6]

Noted for her business acumen and speaking ability, Rewman became a suffrage leader, and both state and national organizations recognized her work. Black Hills newspapers remarked on her speeches and discussed her presence at a multitude of events. A "Who's Who of South Dakota" article praised Rewman's vocabulary, personality, "personal magnetism[,] . . . complete self-possession[,]" and "grace in gestures." While this acclaim demonstrates Rewman's leadership, it fails to account for the sheer amount of time and energy she invested in the fight for the ballot.

Rewman's activism did not end with the victory of woman suffrage in South Dakota. She continued to work for multiple organizations, including the Red Cross. In 1918, South Dakota governor Peter Norbeck appointed her to the Woman's Board of Investigation, which examined state institutions. Norbeck also asked her to serve on the Board of Charities and Corrections in 1920, making her "the first woman to hold a position on one of the constitutional boards of the state."[7] Rewman's experiences beyond the 1918 suffrage campaign not only illustrate the networks she had developed as a leader within the state but also the extent of her influence and success.

Mabel Rewman's activism extended into the 1950s, when she helped ensure the preservation of the voices of South Dakota's suffrage movement. She secured the assistance of historian Herbert S. Schell at the University of South Dakota, who "promised" Rewman, who was by then living in Vermillion and the wife of Guy G. Frary, that "he would endeavor to find a woman in the Graduate School who would write the South Dakota woman suffrage story." Not long after, in 1958, Dorinda Riessen Reed wrote a master's thesis on the subject. Reed interviewed Rewman Frary, and the former suffragist guided Reed to photographs, papers, and personal interviews with women yet alive who remembered the woman suffrage movement in South Dakota.[8] Activist Mabel Rewman not only promoted the right for women to vote, she made sure that history recorded South Dakota's woman suffrage movement.

NOTES

The author would like to thank the staff at the Homestake Adams Research and Cultural Center, especially Carolyn Weber, Rachel Lovelace-Portal, and Rose Speirs, for sharing their expertise and enthusiasm.

1. Rewman to Pyle, 7, 29 June 1918, box 2, Mamie Shields Pyle Papers, Richardson Archives Collection, University of South Dakota (USD), Vermillion. For background on Rewman, *see* Carol Bishop, *The Round Table Club, 1887–1987: The Other Ladies of Deadwood* (Deadwood: Deadwood Historic Preservation Commission, 1994), p. 90; O. W. Coursey, "Who's Who in South Dakota, Mrs. Mabel Rewman," *Deadwood (S.Dak.) Daily Pioneer Times*, 23 Nov. 1920; Dorinda Riessen Reed, *The Woman Suffrage Movement in South Dakota*, Governmental Research Bureau, Report no. 41 (Vermillion: University of South Dakota, 1958), pp. 92–94.

2. Reed, *Woman Suffrage Movement in South Dakota*, pp. 92–94; Coursey, "Who's Who in South Dakota." For more information on Emma Smith DeVoe,

see Jennifer Ross-Nazzal, "Emma Smith DeVoe and the South Dakota Suffrage Campaigns," *South Dakota History* 33 (Fall 2003): 235–62. For information on Paul Rewman, *see* Glenn D. Stratton, "Early Day Telephone in Deadwood," in *Some History of Lawrence County* (Deadwood, S.Dak.: Lawrence County Historical Society, 1981), p. 611.

3. Public notice, *Deadwood Daily Pioneer Times*, 15 Oct. 1914; "Suffragists in Annual Meeting Elect Officials," ibid., 16 Mar. 1917; "Suffrage Convention for Butte County," ibid., 21 Mar. 1917; "Mrs. Rewman Satisfied with Suffrage Status," ibid., 26 Mar. 1918; "She will Represent State at the Capital," *Weekly Pioneer Times Mining Review*, Dec. 6, 1917; Reed, *Woman Suffrage Movement in South Dakota*, pp. 100, 102.

4. Rewman to Pyle, 18 Mar. 1918, box 1, and Pyle to Alice Daley, 13 May 1918, box 2, Pyle Papers.

5. Pyle to Mrs. Frank Shuler, 16 May 1918, box 2, ibid.

6. Rewman to Pyle, 19 June 1918, ibid.

7. Coursey, "Who's Who in South Dakota."

8. Reed, *Woman Suffrage Movement in South Dakota*, p. 3.

PART 3

CORA SMITH EATON AND NORTH DAKOTA WOMAN SUFFRAGE, 1888–1897

KRISTIN MAPEL BLOOMBERG

On 4 August 1890, two Grand Forks, North Dakota, women—Cora E. Smith and her mother, Sara Emma Barnes Smith—cast ballots in a special local election called to establish an independent school district. They were the first women to vote in Grand Forks following approval of the North Dakota constitution a year earlier. Although the new state constitution granted women limited suffrage rights in conjunction with school elections, the Smiths' votes were not without controversy. In the end, the election judges accepted their ballots over the objections of some male voters.[1] While this small act of civic participation might have remained relegated to a few lines buried on the dusty pages of old newspapers, Cora E. Smith's exercise of the franchise in this minor election merits attention because it resulted from her extensive work fighting for woman suffrage in Grand Forks and the state of North Dakota.

Compared to other plains states, North Dakota and its women's rights activities have received less attention from suffrage historians, perhaps because of the better-documented campaigns held in Kansas, Nebraska, South Dakota, and Wyoming. Although most early full-suffrage campaigns on the Northern Great Plains were not fruitful, they paved the way for successful campaigns farther West. These early campaigns provided young suffragists like Cora E. Smith with valuable leadership and organizing experience. What is more, Smith's work for woman suffrage in North Dakota caused it to be a contender for the first woman suffrage state. And just as suffrage activism on the Great Plains helped launch western suffragists such as Nebraskan Clara Bewick Colby and South Dakotan Emma Smith DeVoe into the national spotlight and leadership roles in major women's organizations in the American West, North Dakota served as a launching ground for Cora E. Smith. Smith would later serve the movement through leadership roles in Minnesota and Washington State and on the National Council of Women Voters.[2] Additionally, the story of Smith's activism in North Dakota exposes examples of male resistance to woman suffrage, including the use of gendered opposition tactics that stigmatized suffragists and other women's rights advocates.

Born in Illinois in 1867, Cora E. Smith came of age in Grand Forks following her family's migration to Dakota Territory during the Great Dakota Boom in the 1880s. In 1885, she became an instructor at the recently established coeducational University of North Dakota (UND). She took a short break from UND to earn a bachelor of elocution degree from the Philadelphia National School of Elocution and Oratory in 1886. Returning to Grand Forks, she continued at UND as both instructor and student while building a reputation as a popular speaker. Her oratorical skills and her platform as an elocutionist would prove a significant asset to her suffrage activism.[3]

As Smith finished her final year at UND, residents of Dakota Territory discussed their transition to statehood, which ultimately resulted in the division of the territory into the separate states of North Dakota and South Dakota in November 1889. The question of woman suffrage complicated this process, for the future state of North Dakota had the opportunity to enact universal suffrage and bring North Dakota into the Union as the first woman suffrage state. Progressive northern Dakotans, including active clubwomen like Smith and her mother, took an interest in these debates. Suffragists had been scattered throughout the immense territory but had not been well organized in northern Dakota. With North Dakota's constitutional convention looming, Smith and her mother led a group of seventy-five women and men who called for the organization of a woman suffrage association in the spring of 1888. Thus the Grand Forks Woman Suffrage Association (GFWSA) became the first organization of its kind in North Dakota. It quickly became an auxiliary to the

American Woman Suffrage Association (AWSA) when influential members of AWSA recognized the fledgling association and sent greetings to GFWSA's first meeting.[4]

An enthusiastic standing-room crowd packed a borrowed courtroom for GFWSA's organizational meeting on the evening of 12 April 1888. Sara E. B. Smith, in her capacity as president of the Dakota Woman's Relief Corps, offered the first speech in support of women's equal rights, followed by another woman speaker who dedicated Woman's Christian Temperance Union (WCTU) workers to the joint causes of equal suffrage and temperance.[5] But not everyone in Grand Forks supported women's rights, including men who were not in favor of prohibition and feared that women voters would limit access to liquor. One male heckler, described in the *Grand Forks Herald* as "a certain individual, who was under the influence of liquor," interrupted the speakers and tried to derail the program.[6] Other men, however, were supportive. Judge John M. Cochrane, one of several judges in attendance, quickly silenced the heckler by unleashing "a scathing rebuke to all who refused to ladies their universally conceded right to courtesy." With order restored, Horace B. Woodworth, a UND professor of mathematics, physics, and astronomy, argued that suffrage and temperance should be linked together and contended that women should "obtain the use of the strong weapon of the ballot, in their brave fight against the twin evils of the day, intemperance and immorality."[7] Woodworth's remarks and his support for the WCTU reflected other suffragists' views. Prohibition, a social reform that was often entwined with woman suffrage, was energetically debated on the Northern Great Plains at the time. Ultimately, North Dakota became the first state to enter the Union under prohibition, even without the support of women's votes.

At the close of the meeting, GFWSA members elected twenty-one-year-old Cora E. Smith secretary and her mother Sara president. Soon after, GFWSA held a series of educational public lectures in support of woman suffrage, for which Ella M. S. Marble, president of the Minnesota Woman Suffrage Association and vice president of the largest Minneapolis WCTU chapter, spoke on the topic of equal suffrage. Lillie Devereux Blake, then president of the New York State Woman Suffrage Association and an orga-

Cora Smith Eaton, c. 1889. Elwyn B. Robinson
Department of Special Collections, Chester Fritz Library,
University of North Dakota

nizer for the National Woman Suffrage Association (NWSA), also traveled to Grand Forks as Smith's guest to lecture in support of North Dakota suffrage. As North Dakota's constitutional convention approached, GFWSA held weekly meetings that often featured recitations by Smith.[8]

In the spring of 1889, Smith graduated as a member of the first class of the University of North Dakota.[9] Her commencement essay, "The Position of Woman in America," set the tone for her future. She argued, "The position accorded to woman has always been regarded as a test of the nation's progress," concluding, "the tendency, the world over, is toward equality between men and women—toward removing all barriers and letting individual tastes guide both, as they formerly guided men only, in the choice of college and profession." Following her address, UND president Homer B. Sprague, an accomplished orator in his own right, complimented Smith on the soundness of her logic and "expressed himself as unqualifiedly in favor of woman suffrage."[10] With the support of many social and civic leaders in northern Dakota, the future seemed bright for woman suffrage.

Her undergraduate degree in hand, Smith resigned her position as instructor and made plans to travel to Boston University, where she had been accepted into the school of medicine. It is unclear if she planned to take an active role in the North Dakota constitutional convention, set to begin in Bismarck on 4 July 1889, because she had recently embarked on an elocutionary tour around the region. The convention, however, is where Smith's influence on North Dakota's early suffrage history became clear. It is also where Henry B. Blackwell, the long-time woman suffrage activist and co-founder of AWSA who edited *The Woman's Journal* with his wife Lucy Stone, intersects with the region's suffrage history. North Dakota, South Dakota, Montana, and Washington all held constitutional conventions at about the same time, and Blackwell aspired to convince legislators in each of the new states to add woman suffrage to their constitutions. Traveling alone on an ambitiously tight schedule, the sixty-four-year-old activist planned to attend three conventions: North Dakota, Montana, and Washington. Stone's age and declining health precluded her participation in yet another western campaign. It also appears that Blackwell's mission was not sponsored by AWSA, which at that time was in the process of merging with NWSA.[11]

Blackwell styled himself a one-man suffrage bandwagon, and upon his arrival in Bismarck, he myopically claimed that the territory had "no organized woman suffrage sentiment—no women ready to work." He lobbied convention delegates but privately expressed his frustration with the quality of men assembled for the convention, complaining to Stone that the delegates "are mostly nobodies—all the leading men have kept out of the Convention in hopes of becoming candidates for State & Federal offices."[12] Blackwell planned to lobby for including woman suffrage in North Dakota's constitution, but should the convention balk at this demand, he would advocate that the state legislature be empowered to grant suffrage at a later date.[13] Early in the process, Blackwell encountered delegates who did not favor constitutional woman suffrage but were willing to leave it to a separate measure later. As he explained to Stone: "Every man I have seen is opposed to putting woman suffrage or prohibition into the body of the State Constitution, but willing to submit both separately to the voters. They are also of the opinion that both will be voted *down*. My suggestion to refer WS [woman suffrage] to the action of future Legislatures meets with favor."[14]

Blackwell worked with allied delegates prior to the convention's opening to safeguard the possibility of future woman-suffrage legislation.[15] On the fifth day of the session, he urged the convention to adopt either constitutional woman suffrage or the future legislative provision. At the close of his lengthy speech, he declared, "Give us Woman Suffrage in the body of the Constitution or a clause empowering the Legislature to take that step when the judgment of the public will sustain it."[16] The *Bismarck Tribune* reported favorably on Blackwell's speech. However, instead of mentioning the two proposed pathways to suffrage, the *Tribune* announced, "He does not ask that the convention submit the question to the people for a vote this year, but desires that it be left to the legislature of the state."[17]

Because Blackwell had not adequately connected with suffrage supporters in northern Dakota, only a handful of women, including two wives of men who opposed suffrage, attended Blackwell's

EQUALITY AT THE BALLOT BOX

session. The speech, he said, "did not rouse any marked enthusiasm." Perhaps embittered by what he considered a lack of respect, he noted to Stone, "nor did anyone present move to give me a vote of thanks." In low spirits, he declared, "I think it will be utterly *impossible* to get woman suffrage into the body of the Constitution here." He considered arranging a public suffrage meeting but feared that few would attend. Concluding his letter to Stone, Blackwell bemoaned: "I dont [*sic*] believe more than 15 out of the 75 delegates are squarely for woman suffrage and not more than one in five of the men of the town. So expect nothing & we shall not be disappointed. I have done my best, and we *may* save the right to have the Legislature act hereafter."[18] Blackwell soon learned, however, that Frederick B. Fancher of Jamestown, who had been elected convention president, was a member of the Farmers' Alliance and brought with him the Alliance's pro-woman suffrage stand. After speaking directly to Fancher and canvassing additional delegates, Blackwell found "an evident determination to give the Legislature the power to extend suffrage to women." In addition, Blackwell connected with supportive women in Bismarck. "The prospect brightens!" he declared to Stone.[19]

A few days later, Blackwell lectured in support of suffrage at the invitation of women gathered in Bismarck. The *Bismarck Tribune* gave the event a brief, yet favorable, review. Blackwell nonetheless declared the gathering a failure because only about two hundred people—mostly women and children—attended. Despite his cynical analysis, it appeared the legislative option for woman suffrage was enjoying good support. By the time he prepared to depart for the Montana constitutional convention, he had secured thirty of the necessary thirty-eight votes needed for the measure to carry.[20] Blackwell's travel schedule did not allow him to stay until the end of the convention and secure the remaining votes. To carry on his work, he needed a forceful, intelligent, and eloquent advocate, preferably someone who had the ear of the electorate. As he explained to Stone: "If Dakota is saved it will be *wholly* due to my coming & I think I could surely save it by remaining two or three weeks longer. But I have written urging Miss Cora E. Smith, a bright talented young No[rth] Dakota lady, a graduate of the State University at Grand Forks to come down & follow up my work here. If she comes, all will be well."[21] Blackwell likely chose Smith because of her reputation as a popular orator and her role in GFWSA. GFWSA's early affiliation with AWSA may have also helped Blackwell identify Smith as capable of continuing his work.

Smith answered the call and interrupted her elocutionary tour to lead suffrage lobbying at the convention. She secured a room near the meeting hall and staffed her headquarters with supporters ready to argue the case for woman suffrage any time a delegate passed by their open door.[22] Smith's status as a regional celebrity amplified her lobbying efforts, and local newspaper editors seemed torn between supporting a homegrown personality and employing sexist descriptions to dismiss suffragists. For example, the *Jamestown Weekly Alert* offered this sidebar to its convention coverage:

> The woman's suffrage articles seem likely to make fun for the boys and fill the gallery with listeners. . . . and a female lobbyist is now in the thickest of the fray. She arrived yesterday, armed with a list of the delegates, . . . and has been enabled to see all of them personally and commence operations individually instead of collectively, like the platform shouters. The lady is young, bright and attractive, being none other than Miss Cora E. Smith. . . . Miss Smith is the exact antithesis of Artemus Ward's suffragist—"that he-looking she-male" who had a penchant for talking through her nose and jabbing people in the ribs with a cotton umbrella. She is here on a labor of love—as it were—being interested in the movement for the movement's sake and not pecuniarily.[23]

The *Alert* deliberately positioned Smith against popular caricatures of American suffragists. Her youthful age and professionally feminine deportment crafted during her years as an expert elocutionist stood in stark contrast to Blackwell's advanced age and masculine gender performance. Editors who supported Smith positively gendered her work by elevating her conventional femininity, professionalism, and intelligence. They also stressed

EQUALITY AT THE BALLOT BOX

that she entered politics as a "labor of love" rather than soiling her cause by working for money as a man might. These qualities moderated her message and opened pathways for support that might not have been available to older, less conventionally feminine or more politically radical women who supported suffrage.

After fierce debate at the convention, Blackwell's strategy to leave open a pathway for woman suffrage was successful. Ultimately, the North Dakota Constitution read: "The Legislative Assembly shall be empowered to make further extensions of suffrage hereafter, at its discretion to all citizens of mature age and sound mind, not convicted of crime without regard to sex; but no law extending or restricting the right of suffrage shall be in force until adopted by *a majority of the electors of the state voting at a general election.*"[24] As suffragist Janette Hill Knox wryly noted in her entry on North Dakota in the *History of Woman Suffrage*, "By requiring not merely a majority of those voting on the question but of the largest number voting at the election, no amendment for any purpose ever has been carried."[25]

Nevertheless, Smith and the North Dakota suffragists had achieved a victory. The *Grand Forks Daily Herald* declared, "The Ladies Win."[26] Blackwell sent an ecstatic letter to Stone, specifically praising Smith's work: "*We have saved one of the new States to Liberty!* Thanks to Cora E. Smith, our excellent young 'lobbyist,' & our good friends in the Convention, the State Legislature has been empowered to extend Suffrage to women. . . . Thank God for North Dakota! She will be a woman State within four years."[27] The editor of the *Herald* also lauded Smith's efforts: "To the indefatigable labors of Miss Cora E. Smith of this city, the friends of female suffrage are largely indebted for the adoption by the con. con. [constitutional convention] of the article . . . empowering the legislature at its discretion hereafter to extend the right of suffrage to citizens without regard to sex." The editor concluded, "Miss Smith is an enthusiastic and successful worker and deserves hearty congratulation."[28]

Yet, Cora E. Smith and North Dakota's suffrage supporters still had work to do. In mid-August, on the forty-third day of the convention, the delegates took up the question of women's ability to vote on school matters. In spite of the fact that women in Dakota

Territory had previously been granted school suffrage, the issue provoked debate.[29] Continuing this provision would allow women voters to exercise the franchise on school matters if they met the qualifications of male electors: that they were age twenty-one and older, were citizens or declared their intention to become citizens, and had established adequate residency. Importantly, the final version of the North Dakota state constitution also extended the franchise to "civilized persons of Indian descent who shall have severed their tribal relations two years next preceding such election."[30] Mandating that American Indian voters sever their tribal relations was a voter suppression tactic that served the secondary function of requiring assimilation into white American culture. While the constitution clearly separated women from the category of "persons" who qualified as electors on other matters, school suffrage equalized women, including foreign-born women who had declared their intention to become citizens as well as American Indian women who had severed their tribal relation, with men. In so doing, the North Dakota Constitution provided a pathway for non-citizen and American Indian women to vote on school matters.

Working with constitutional convention delegate William H. Rowe of Dickey County, Smith authored an amended school-suffrage provision that not only preserved women's limited franchise but also ensured additional rights for women. Rowe thus proposed that women "may vote for all school officers and upon all questions pertaining solely to school matters *and be eligible to any school office*" in substitution for the original territorial text that simply said that women "may vote at any election held solely for school purposes."[31] Yet, some men resisted continuing school suffrage for women. For example, one delegate tried to restrict voting to single women (instead of "any" woman). This measure attempted to remove limited voting rights from married women, who were most likely to be mothers of school-aged children. In response, Rueben N. Stevens, a delegate from Ransom County, facetiously hoped that the convention would not "offer a premium on old maids."[32] This comment reflected gendered opposition tactics that stigmatized single women voters as "old maids."

The convention favored Smith and Rowe's amended clause.

Delegate Eugene Rolfe from Minnewaukan, Benson County, soon identified an important technical issue that might have been rooted in the stereotype of women as deceitful: how could election judges determine that women were voting correctly on school matters and not improperly voting for other offices? Rolfe claimed that as a result of the way the article was written, "if a woman presents herself and offers to vote for school superintendent she must exhibit her vote before she will be permitted to cast her ballot." He continued, "If our elections for State School Superintendent and county school superintendent come at general elections as in all probability will be the case, any women [*sic*] offering to vote at the election cannot have reserved to her the privilege of a secret ballot, such as is guaranteed to men."[33] Smith and the suffrage supporters appear to not have anticipated this issue. Rowe, however, quickly offered a solution: separate ballot boxes for women voters. After delegates agreed that the section allowed women to vote for both local and state superintendents, the amended article was adopted, leaving the question of how women would vote in separate ballot boxes to a future legislature. Women's right to school suffrage had been preserved, but as a result of men's indifference to the practical problems of women voters, some issues remained. Still, in October 1889, North Dakota voters approved the new constitution that included Smith's school suffrage article by a vote of 27,441 to 8,107.[34]

So it was the following summer, on 4 August 1890, that Cora E. Smith and her mother Sara came to vote in Grand Forks. The two were not the first women in North Dakota to vote in a school election under the new constitution. The *Bismarck Tribune* reported that a long list of women voted in school elections that June. Women outside of Bismarck in rural Ecklund Township, however, experienced difficulties casting their votes, and when the Smiths tried to submit their ballots, some men also objected to their votes. Although the constitution granted women limited school-suffrage rights, the way they cast their ballots came under scrutiny because the constitution did not mandate separate ballot boxes for women. It is likely the objections made that day were a result of Grand Forks's failure to secure separate ballot boxes for them, even though the school measure was the only item on the ticket. It appeared that Grand Forks, like many municipalities in North Dakota, saw no need to provide separate boxes. For voters like Smith and her mother, however, the matter was urgent, given the fact that the selection of state superintendent of public instruction was scheduled for the upcoming general election in November.[35]

Again, Cora E. Smith and her mother took the lead. By the end of August, Sara E. B. Smith submitted a petition to the Grand Forks county commissioners requesting they furnish separate ballot boxes for women's use at the November election. It is probable that she served as the primary petitioner in her capacity as president of GFWSA. The county commission, however, declined to act and instead referred the request to the state's attorney for Grand Forks County, none other than John M. Cochrane, a member of GFWSA and the same Judge Cochrane who had spoken in favor of woman suffrage at the association's organizational meeting.[36]

As they waited for Cochrane's ruling, Cora E. Smith described the ballot-box problem to *Woman's Journal*. She offered a positive assessment of North Dakota women's constitutional right to vote for school matters, noting, "Many women have voted in the past year under this clause." She also expressed hope that the ballot-box issues would soon be solved, claiming, "The attorney-general is receiving requests to recommend that two ballot-boxes be provided at each polling-place, and if this is done, the obstacle to the ladies' voting will be removed."[37] But when Cochrane's decision was announced, suffragists were shocked. While his ruling conceded the necessity of separate ballot boxes, it prohibited their immediate establishment because article 128 of the constitution did not establish a provision for collecting women's votes. To do so required an act of the state legislature.[38]

Cochran's decision renewed the debate over limited voting rights for women, and many entered into the chaos that ensued. The state Democratic committee, which had nominated Laura J. Eisenhuth for superintendent of public instruction against the Republican John Ogden, argued that women should be allowed the use of separate ballot boxes. Others petitioned their county commissioners for separate ballot boxes as Sara E. B. Smith had

*Eventually, North Dakota provided separate ballot boxes
for women, such as this one with "women" crudely scratched on its side.*
Photograph by Jessica Rockeman

done—some succeeded, some failed.[39] Further complicating matters, the North Dakota attorney general decided that municipalities had "no legal obligation" to provide separate ballot boxes. Additionally, he declared, "The State Superintendent of Public Instruction is not a school officer within the meaning of the provisions of Section 128, of the Constitution." In both cases, the attorney general's decision restricted women's votes. By interpreting the statewide office of superintendent of public instruction as outside the scope of school matters on which women could vote, he had called Eisenhuth's qualifications for candidacy into question, adding to the confusion.[40]

In spite of this opposition, the Smiths remained undeterred. At its September meeting, GFWSA decided to launch a statewide campaign urging women voters to exercise their constitutionally granted voting rights on school matters.[41] Following that meeting, an announcement signed by GFWSA president Sara Smith called North Dakota women to action: "To the women voters of North Dakota: Do you know that under the state law you are entitled to vote in all school matters?" After citing the North Dakota Constitution and reprinting Rowe's comments about separate ballot boxes during the constitutional convention debate, Sara Smith urged North Dakota women to seize their rights and exercise their franchise: "Show our appreciation of the privilege extended us by voting in large numbers. . . . Extra ballot boxes should be provided for the women at each polling place. See that your county commissioners are requested to attend to this. If difficulties are thrown in the way, remember that there is the need of effort on our part to claim our just dues."[42]

While some newspapers published GFWSA's announcement, others refused. The *Bismarck Tribune*, which did not believe Eisenhuth qualified for candidacy to statewide office, castigated this effort to inform women of their rights when it singled out Cora E. Smith's attempt to place GFWSA content into the paper: "These documents come from that charming little piece of femininity, Miss Cora Smith of Grand Forks—with the kindest, prettiest little request to publish—the TRIBUNE was almost tempted to do as Cora wished—insert for a number of times and charge to gallantry—but the article is so long—two or three columns—really it is impossible—besides the TRIBUNE doesn't believe Mrs. Eisenhuth is eligible—notwithstanding Cora and all the legal opinions cited."[43] Notably, the *Bismarck Tribune* employed sexist language, dismissing Smith as a "charming little piece of femininity." The *Tribune*'s readers would have recognized the stereotype of the woman who had overstepped her boundaries and made unreasonable demands, even though Smith had only assumed that the newspaper would publish her letter to the editor for free as it did for men who entered the political debate. This example contrasts with press coverage of Smith during the convention, when male delegates and the media appeared open to her conventional femininity and moderate messaging. But perhaps those men were politely receptive because they were ultimately able to push off the larger question of women voting to a later date. When women actually attempted to exercise their

EQUALITY AT THE BALLOT BOX

right to run and vote for statewide school office, men's resistance emerged more forcefully.

Without clear guidance from the state legislature, local election judges individually decided how to handle the women's votes or if they would allow women to vote at all. As the *Grand Forks Herald* cheekily put it on Election Day in November: "This is election, we vote today. Everybody votes today that's of age and a citizen. Ladies can vote today in certain counties—ladies will vote today in certain counties. Some men will not vote today for various reasons."[44] Indeed, many women were denied access to the ballot, including at least one of the Smiths, who may have been singled out by Grand Forks election judges. Following the election, the *Grand Forks Plaindealer* revealed that separate ballot boxes for women—which in some cases were offensively fashioned from "cigar boxes with a hole carved through the lid"— "were provided in all the wards by the judges except the first," which is where the Smiths voted. The *Plaindealer* named eighteen women voters in Grand Forks's six wards; however, it reported without additional comment or clarification that Sarah E. B. Smith and Mrs. H. D. Slater "offered their votes for state superintendent of schools, but the judges refused to receive them."[45] Without the support of women's votes, Ogden defeated Eisenhuth to win the election. This election day, the Smiths and countless other women were bested by men's resistance to even this limited form of woman suffrage. What is more, the effort to prevent them from exercising their hard-won rights appeared to target them for their activism.

Frustratingly for the Smiths, many women in Grand Forks and other municipalities remained prohibited from voting during the half decade that followed the 1890 election. Cora E. Smith intermittently spoke out on the issue and, on the eve of the 1895 legislative session, expressed her desire to see separate ballot boxes for women voters legitimized by law. As she explained to the journal *Western Womanhood*, this issue "has been the quibble raised by the unfriendly state's attorneys. They have thrown out our votes sometimes because there is no law expressly providing for the ballot-boxes for the women."[46] But Smith's statement obscured the fact that the ballot-box issue had been more than a "quibble." Notably, the third North Dakota Legislative Assembly of 1893 passed a woman suffrage bill on the last day of the session. The bill, however, became "lost" on its way to be signed by the governor, and the proceedings were expunged. Though it thus ignored the question of full suffrage, in 1895, the legislature finally established separate ballot boxes for women. Even when North Dakota women achieved full suffrage upon the passage of the Nineteenth Amendment in 1919, continued resistance to women voting resulted in the preservation of separate ballot boxes for women until 1923.[47]

Legitimizing separate ballot boxes for women was a marginal victory in light of the continued failure to achieve full suffrage. Following the fateful fall of 1890, North Dakota's suffrage movement stalled without Cora E. Smith's sustained leadership. After earning her M.D. from Boston University in 1892, Smith returned to Grand Forks to become the first licensed female doctor in North Dakota. In addition, she returned to UND to teach women's physical culture, continued touring as an elocutionist, and married Grand Forks attorney Robert A. Eaton in November 1893. Cora Smith Eaton subsequently focused on building her medical practice, although she found time to revive GFWSA in preparation for the 1894 election and the 1895 legislative session.[48] In the fall of 1894, the reorganized GFWSA elected Smith Eaton president and established a plan of work that included securing "as large a vote as possible from the ladies at the coming election."[49]

While GFWSA's goal seemed lofty, its 1894 election activities closely resembled those undertaken during the election of 1890 and focused on using the press to educate women voters. In her capacity as GFWSA president, Smith Eaton published an announcement in local papers insisting "every woman should use her franchise" to vote for state superintendent of public instruction in the general election.[50] While GFWSA lobbied the fourth legislature in 1895 for separate ballot boxes for women, they failed to secure full woman suffrage and to raise the age of consent for women to eighteen.[51]

Smith Eaton had found the legislative session of 1895 to be particularly fraught, especially regarding the initiative for full woman suffrage. Armed with a deeper understanding of men's resistance to women voting, Smith Eaton and GFWSA sought assistance from lecturers familiar with the Northern Great Plains. They invited Emma Smith DeVoe to help them educate the public and lobby the legislature. Smith Eaton and other members of GFWSA had followed DeVoe's progress in the South Dakota and Kansas campaigns and "concluded that she was the best candidate to lobby the legislature on their behalf."[52] To raise funds for DeVoe's salary, Smith Eaton produced a popular musical that netted more than three hundred dollars. DeVoe and Smith Eaton then joined state superintendent of public instruction Emma F. Bates and WCTU president Elizabeth Preston to work the delegates, with DeVoe's speech to the legislature in support of woman suffrage serving as the centerpiece of their operation.[53]

Writing to DeVoe, Smith Eaton reflected on the session and acknowledged that lobbying and lectures were not enough to secure full suffrage. "We realize that our greatest need is to organize," she admitted. Looking ahead to the 1897 session, she determined, "With two years for organization however, we stand a fair chance."[54] Bates concurred, but offered a much sharper analysis regarding the role of the WCTU and the resulting entanglement of suffrage with prohibition. Bates told DeVoe she believed North Dakota suffragists must "make an aggressive campaign of education among the women of the state in the next two years." She also believed that the National American Woman Suffrage Association (NAWSA) needed to provide North Dakota with significant organizing assistance—and that the WCTU and prohibition should be kept out of the suffrage cause. To support her conclusion, she described a conversation with a supporter who agreed with her and admitted that Preston's work "had probably harmed the cause, though she meant well." In a biting indictment of Preston, Bates concluded, "As Samantha says, some people mean 'awful well,' but they lack judgment."[55]

In noting her expectation that NAWSA would help North Dakota suffragists, Bates referred to the group's new focus on state-level organization. At its annual convention in February 1895, NAWSA emphasized building its membership, observing, "The chief work of [American] suffragists for the past forty years has been education and agitation, and not organization."[56] The following year, NAWSA established and funded an organization committee chaired by Iowan Carrie Chapman Catt that planned to "aid in strengthening and increasing the organization of North Dakota, South Dakota, Montana, Idaho, Nevada, Arizona, New Mexico and Oklahoma." As the committee explained, "These states surround our nucleus of suffrage states, where the greater promise of the early enfranchisement of women is to be found."[57] The organization committee modeled their work on the strategies of large national women's organizations such as the General Federation of Women's Clubs and the WTCU, which focused on establishing a robust membership network that could be employed for organizing and funding local, regional, and national suffrage activities. Reflecting the gender expectations of the day, Catt believed the best organizers were "experienced suffrage lecturers who dressed well, were tactful, had good manners, and were hard workers."[58] With the right strategies and organizers in place, the committee hoped it could overcome longstanding efforts to stigmatize suffrage women and discredit their message.

How NAWSA's organization committee would assist North Dakota was a matter of debate. While Smith Eaton and Bates favored moderate organizers like DeVoe, it seems Catt did not follow her own advice, for in the case of North Dakota, she hoped to employ more radical organizers with established track records. Instead of offering to resend DeVoe, Catt offered a South Dakota organizer who was also a Populist. Bates rejected the offer because she did not want suffrage to be linked to either prohibition or the radicalism of Populism.[59] After the difficulties of the 1895 legislative session, Bates had a clear sense of what kind of organizer best fit North Dakota and appealed to DeVoe for support: "We cannot have anybody but Mrs. DeVoe in this state for organization . . . if you have any other way to impress upon the National Association that they are not going to send any South Dakota 'Pop' woman in here to organize us, if they want to succeed in suffrage work in North Dakota, why, just impress it. It is clearly a political deal which will ruin us in North Dakota if permitted to be carried out."[60] As Bates's letter demonstrates, many

North Dakota suffragists feared that bringing in radical outsiders could jeopardize their work.

In the end, NAWSA sent Kansan Laura M. Johns to organize North Dakota in October 1895. Bates declared her "*All right* (nearly as good as Mrs. DeVoe)" but also acknowledged that Johns "had a very *hard* time."[61] Johns herself noted that suffrage organizing in North Dakota was challenging and declared, "the non-organization of the suffragists of the state has borne bitter fruit in delay and loss from which we might have been saved" if only suffragists could have adequately organized.[62] Suffrage activities in the state vacillated between periods of high and low—or no—activity, and Johns's comments lead one to wonder if Smith Eaton's inability to assume a consistent leadership role in North Dakota's suffrage organizing activities had a negative impact on the forward trajectory of equal suffrage. In addition to the demands of her medical practice, Smith Eaton's personal life had taken a difficult turn. In 1895, her husband, Robert Eaton, was disbarred from practicing law after being found guilty of removing documents from the district court and then lying about it. The Supreme Court of North Dakota later reversed the disbarment, but the presiding judge of the Grand Forks district court refused to allow Eaton to practice, effectively ending his career.[63]

Although she did not name Smith Eaton, Johns's angry missive in *Western Womanhood* about the difficulties of state organizing highlighted North Dakota suffragists' lack of focus and their limited leadership. Johns castigated North Dakota women for being "so very busy with work for others . . . that they have neither time nor strength left to do anything for their own salvation—wearing themselves out with labor for a hundred things, but not willing to let their little fingers ache for this cause—woman's own cause." Continuing her diatribe, Johns declared:

I find that women glory in this self-immolation on the altar of self-sacrifice, and press and pulpit commend them; but the world is waking up to the knowledge of the fact that a day has dawned in which woman's first duty is found to be not self-sacrifice, but self-development. . . . To make the most of herself she must cease to stand in a false position. Her relation to the home, to children and to society will be a nobler one and stronger in its good influences when she sustains a right relation to the government under which she lives. Therefore, in the name of justice and progress and of the National American Woman Suffrage Association which I here represent, I urge the organization of the suffragists of North Dakota in local and state associations.

Concluding her call to action, Johns reiterated, "There is no force like organized force. Therefore, friends, you are called upon to organize."[64]

North Dakota suffragists appear to have responded to Johns's efforts because the *Bismarck Tribune* claimed she had organized twenty suffrage clubs around the state by early November, leading NAWSA to call a state convention in November 1895 for the purpose of establishing a statewide suffrage association. Johns contacted Smith Eaton, the best-known suffragist in North Dakota, to lend her name to the NAWSA appeal.[65] Smith Eaton volunteered Grand Forks as the host city and chaired the local arrangements committee. "Come one! Come all!!" declared the invitation for the state mass meeting, which was "hereby called by the National American Woman Suffrage [A]ssociation . . . for the purpose of organizing a North Dakota Woman's Suffrage association." Signed by NAWSA's president Susan B. Anthony, secretary Rachel Foster Avery, Catt, and Smith Eaton, the call invoked Wyoming's success and asserted: "The progressive spirit of North Dakota will not permit her to lag behind her neighbors in this line of march. The time to act is now."[66]

By all accounts, the convention was well attended. In addition to hearing from speakers that included Smith Eaton, Bates, and Johns (Preston was not on the program), the convention perfected the new North Dakota Equal Suffrage Association (NDESA) by adopting a constitution and crafting a plan of work focused on club organization and suffrage education throughout the state. Convention attendees elected Smith Eaton NDESA's first president and chair of the plan of work committee, while they selected her mother Sara as corresponding secretary. In the months following the convention, however, it appears that only four clubs affiliated with NDESA under Cora Smith Eaton's presidency: GFWSA, the Fargo and Jamestown political equality clubs, and the Bismarck Fortnightly Club—far fewer than the twenty Johns had reportedly organized.[67]

In spite of high expectations, NDESA's work proceeded fitfully. Smith Eaton continued as the most high-profile North Dakota suffragist by serving as the state's delegate to NAWSA's annual convention in Washington, D.C., in January 1896. There, her role as a rising young suffragist from the West led the organization to select her to testify in support of suffrage before the judiciary committee of the United States Congress beside Susan B. Anthony and others she had worked with during North Dakota's constitutional convention. Though entitled to several minutes, her remarks were brief—she only offered about one hundred and fifty words. She emphasized her status as a member of a "Western" state and articulated a platform that unified the sexes, asserting, "I represent the women of North Dakota and the men." She also demonstrated her elocutionist wit, saying, "We Western people are always on the lookout for business, and I would like to prescribe for this committee a favorable report on this resolution for the enfranchisement of woman. . . . The men of that State will stand by us, and, unless you gentlemen get ahead of them, they will enfranchise their women by an amendment to the State Constitution."[68]

Of the experience before Congress, Smith Eaton playfully reported to the journal *Western Womanhood*: "It was delightful to note the attitude of the congressmen and senators from the three [suffrage] star states. They treated the women as fellow citizens and constituents and showed a consideration and practical courtesy worth all the condescension and empty gallantry in the world." Clearly, Cora Smith Eaton still held high hopes for full woman suffrage in North Dakota, tying it to an independent, forward-thinking western identity that unified women and men for a common purpose. At NAWSA's national convention, Smith Eaton also used her newly acquired status in that organization to advocate for additional resources for North Dakota suffrage. She informed NDESA's membership of NAWSA's plan to focus on western states, announcing, "Thus North Dakota will be again helped by having national organizers." She added, "I hope next year North Dakota will have her full number of delegates at the convention."[69] Cora Smith Eaton's wish was not granted, and following the organization of NDESA, the forward progress of North Dakota suffrage came to a stop.

In spring 1896, Smith Eaton abruptly left Grand Forks to accept a position as surgeon at the Minneapolis Maternity Hospital in Minnesota, where Dr. Ella M. S. Marble, an early speaker for GFWSA, also practiced.[70] Still loyal to the cause of North Dakota suffrage, Smith Eaton continued to hold the NDESA presidency and attempted to direct its work from Minneapolis. North Dakota's suffrage work became even more difficult when, despite earlier promises, Catt announced that NAWSA would not send an organizer to the state in 1896 ahead of the next legislative session—a decision *Western Womanhood* reported was made to favor Delaware, California, Idaho, Arizona, and Oklahoma instead. "North Dakota will have her turn sometime," the writer lamented.[71]

By late summer 1896, suffrage activities languished in Smith Eaton's absence. *Western Womanhood* reported: "No word comes to our official E. S. A. department in this paper from any of the state clubs. No reports of attendance or monies raised are sent in. Our treasury is in such a depleted condition that our State President, Dr. Cora Smith Eaton, donated from her own pocket $12.00 for this official space for the last four months."[72] The brutal election of November 1896 did not help the situation. Emma F. Bates, who had served as state superintendent of public instruction for one term, was removed from the Republican ticket, and she subsequently announced her candidacy as an independent. The Democrat-Populist "Fusion" Party nominated Laura J. Eisenhuth, whom Bates succeeded, to oppose her. Eventually the Prohibition Party nominated Bates.[73] Both women lost to Republican John G. Halland, and *Western Womanhood* excoriated the entire process, declaring, "Woman is 'all right' while she keeps her opinions to herself so long as they agree with those of men, but utterance of or difference in them usually constitute her 'all wrong.'" The journal's stark conclusion: "Suffrage dead."[74]

By 1913, Cora Smith King (far right) served as an officer in the
National Council of Women Voters, alongside (right to left)
Emma Smith Devoe, Jane Addams, and Maude Bjorkman.
Washington State Historical Society

Four months later in the spring of 1897, a writer for *Western Womanhood* confirmed the demise of suffrage activity in North Dakota, noting, "It is with regret we realize that organized suffrage work is done in our state, as the last active club has been ordered disbanded."[75] A few months following that announcement, Cora Smith Eaton, who had briefly returned to North Dakota to speak at the woman's day of the North Dakota Chautauqua Association, called an impromptu meeting of NDESA and tendered her resignation in order to focus on her work with the Minnesota Woman Suffrage Association (MWSA). In an act of respect, NDESA listed Cora Smith Eaton as honorary president for several years following her departure. Eventually, the organization disbanded, and no state suffrage association existed until the Votes for Women League of North Dakota was formed in 1912. In 1917, North Dakota passed a limited woman suffrage law, allowing women to vote for presidential electors and municipal officers but not for governor, members of the legislature, or for United States senators or representatives. North Dakota women achieved full suffrage when the legislature ratified the Nineteenth Amendment to the United States Constitution during a special session in December 1919.[76]

Had Cora Smith Eaton remained in North Dakota and focused entirely on leading the state's organization efforts, the state's fortunes may have been different. At the least, NDESA concluded, "Her removal from the state was a great misfortunate [sic] to the state work."[77] North Dakota's loss, however, allowed others to gain. In 1910, Smith Eaton reunited with Emma Smith DeVoe to help bring woman suffrage to Washington State, the fifth star on the national suffrage flag. Following that success, DeVoe and Smith Eaton established the National Council of Women Voters, a nonpartisan union of full suffrage states that supported the Congressional Union for Woman Suffrage in the years preceding the ratification of the Nineteenth Amendment.[78]

Cora Smith Eaton's unconventional life did not easily fit into the usual portrait of the woman suffragist. An independent-thinking western woman, she was a wage-earning professional, a two-time divorcee, and an adventurist who did not shy away from showy activities such as planting a "Votes for Women" banner on the summit of Mount Rainier. She gained renown as a woman's rights activist, elocutionist and orator, university teacher, mountaineer, and well-respected surgeon who was the first licensed female doctor in North Dakota and later served as personal physician to the radical American suffragist Alice Paul of the National Woman's Party.[79] Her suffrage activities in North Dakota allowed her to develop skills as a speaker, writer, collaborator, and political strategist and were foundational to her later activism in Minnesota, Washington State, Washington, D.C., and California, where she was often joined by her mother. Examining Cora Smith Eaton's early suffrage activism helps rebalance the historical narrative and emphasize the importance of suffrage

EQUALITY AT THE BALLOT BOX

campaigns on the Northern Great Plains. Her profound impact on the larger American woman suffrage movement began with her work in North Dakota. Yet, while she achieved many important victories, her efforts were not enough to add North Dakota's star to the suffrage flag.

NOTES

1. *Grand Forks Daily Herald*, 4, 8 Aug. 1890; *Woman's Journal* (Boston, Mass.), 16 Aug 1890, p. 260.

2. For the campaign in South Dakota during the time period under consideration in this article, *see* Cecelia M. Wittmayer, "The 1889–1890 Woman Suffrage Campaign: A Need to Organize," *South Dakota History* 11 (Fall 1981): 199–225; Jennifer Ross–Nazzal, "Emma Smith DeVoe and the South Dakota Suffrage Campaigns," ibid. 33 (Fall 2003): 235–62; Ross–Nazzal, *Winning the West for Women: The Life of Suffragist Emma Smith DeVoe* (Seattle: University of Washington Press, 2011). For the campaign in Nebraska, *see* Kristin Mapel Bloomberg, "'Striving for Equal Rights for All': Woman Suffrage in Nebraska, 1855–1882," *Nebraska History Quarterly* 90 (Summer 2009): 84–103; Carmen Heider, "Suffrage, Self–Determination, and the Women's Christian Temperance Union in Nebraska, 1879–1882," *Rhetoric & Public Affairs* 8, no. 1 (2005): 85–108. For North Dakota, *see* Barbara Handy-Marchello, "'Swashing Around in the Sisterhood of States': Statehood for North Dakota in 1889," *North Dakota History* 79, no. 1 (2014): 4–12; Linda Johnson Wurtz, "Elizabeth Preston Anderson: A Rhetorical Legacy," ibid. 63, no. 2 (1996): 49–58; Jeanne F. Tucker, "The History of the Woman's Suffrage Movement in North Dakota," 1951, folder 12, box 1, Research Papers Written on North Dakota History Collection, OGLMC 263, E. B. Robinson Special Collections, Chester Fritz Library, University of North Dakota (UND), Grand Forks.

3. *Grand Forks Daily Herald*, 24 Jan. 1885; "With Honors," ibid., 14 June 1886; "A Literary Treat," ibid., 6 Oct. 1886; "A Superb Entertainment," ibid., 9 Oct. 1886; "Contract Let," ibid., 8 July 1887; "Annual Contest," *Philadelphia Inquirer*, 9 Jun. 1886; *University of North Dakota Catalogue*, 1884–1885, 1886–1887, 1889–1890, folders 1, 2, and 5, box 1, UND Catalogs, UA 129, UND. The territorial assembly established the University of North Dakota as a coeducational university in 1883, six years before North Dakota statehood. It opened to students the fall of 1884. Cora E. Smith was a member of the first graduating class in 1889, which was made up of six women and two men. This essay uses the name style preferred by Cora Smith Eaton King at different points in her life; as a result, it will primarily use her birth name. I was unable to determine if her middle name was Elizabeth or Eliza, but it is clear that she preferred the use of her middle initial in her early life. North Dakota's

scant suffrage scholarship is the result of a lack of source material. Thus, I primarily employ newspapers, journals, and serials to establish Smith's role in the early history of North Dakota suffrage.

4. "Woman Suffrage," *Grand Forks Daily Herald*, 6 Apr. 1888; "Organized. Woman Suffrage Association," ibid.,13 Apr. 1888; Proceedings, *Twenty-Eighth Annual Convention of the National-American Woman Suffrage Association Held in Washington, D.C., January 23d to 28th, 1896* (Washington, D.C.: By the Association, 1896), p. 151; "Organization in Dakota," *Woman's Journal*, 12 May 1888, p. 150. Greetings from the ASWA included those of Julia Ward Howe, president of the Association for the Advancement of Women, William Dudley Foulke, president of the AWSA, and Lucy Stone, chair of the AWSA executive committee and publisher of the influential woman's rights newspaper, *Woman's Journal*. As in cities across the nation, Grand Forks had embraced the club movement that brought like-minded people together to discuss the issues of the day. For example, Jane Cunningham Croly notes that women established the Grand Forks Pioneer Reading Club in 1884. Croly, *The History of the Woman's Club Movement in America* (New York: Henry G. Allen & Co, 1898), p. 323. Other progressive clubs included the North Dakota Educational Association, which elected Cora E. Smith secretary of the Grand Forks chapter in the fall of 1887 shortly after she began teaching at the university. "Dakota Department," *School Education* 4 (July 1885): 114; "Educational Association," *Grand Forks Daily Herald*, 25 Nov. 1887. The Dakota chapter of the Woman's Relief Corps organized in 1884, and Sara E.B. Smith was an active member and later president of its Dakota Department. Woman's Relief Corps, *Journal of the Sixth Annual Convention of the Woman's Relief Corps . . . Columbus, Ohio, Sept. 12, 13, and 14, 1888* (Boston: By the Association, 1888), p. 6.

5. *Journal of the Sixth Annual Convention of the Woman's Relief Corps*, p. 207. The Grand Forks chapter of the WCTU appears to have been organized several months after the woman suffrage association. Later that fall, Grand Forks hosted the WCTU county convention. Sara E. B. Smith, the delegate from Grand Forks, was elected county superintendent for woman suffrage. "W.C.T.U. Formed," *Grand Forks Daily Herald*, 9 Jul. 1888; "W.C.T.U. Convention," ibid., 11 Oct. 1888.

6. "Organized. Woman Suffrage Association." *See also* "Suffrage Society in Dakota," *Woman's Journal*, 19 May 1888, p. 159.

7. "Organized. Woman Suffrage Association."

8. "Woman Suffrage," *Grand Forks Daily Herald*, 20 July 1888, p. 4; "Ella M. S. Marble," ibid., 23 July 1888; "Local Lay-Out. Address of Mrs. Marble on Woman Suffrage at Methodist Church Last Night," ibid., 25 July 1888; "Personal," ibid., 8 Sept 1888; ibid., 5 Sept. 1888; "Woman Suffrage and Temper-

ance," ibid., 10 Sept. 1888; "Notes of Travel," *Woman's Journal*, 22 Sept. 1888, p. 303. Blake was in Dakota to attend the state WCTU at Fargo, where she also presented the lecture "Is it a Crime to be a Woman?" "Equal Suffrage Meeting," *Bismarck Tribune*, 14 Feb. 1889; "Equal Suffrage," ibid., 22 Feb. 1889.

9. Louis G. Geiger, *University of the Northern Plains: A History of the University of North Dakota, 1883–1958* (Grand Forks: University of North Dakota Press, 1958), p. 81.

10. Both quoted in "Eight Graduates!" *Grand Forks Daily Herald*, 13 Jun. 1889.

11. "Resignation Tendered," ibid., 29 May 1889; "Class of '89," ibid., 12 June 1889. For an analysis of Blackwell's participation in Montana's constitutional convention, *see* Leslie Wheeler, "Woman Suffrage's Gray-Bearded Champion Comes to Montana, 1889," *Montana: The Magazine of Western History* 31 (Summer 1981): 2–13. The National American Woman Suffrage Association (NAWSA) was formed in 1890 through the merger of the American (led by Stone, Blackwell, and Julia Ward Howe) and the National (led by Elizabeth Cady Stanton and Susan B. Anthony). For more than two decades, the rival associations pursued different strategies: AWSA focused on state-by-state campaigns, while NWSA fought for a federal constitutional amendment but also participated in state campaigns.

12. Blackwell to Lucy Stone, 3 July 1889, in *Loving Warriors: Selected Letters of Lucy Stone and Henry B. Blackwell, 1853–1893*, ed. Leslie Wheeler (New York: Dial Press, 1981), p. 316–17.

13. Wheeler, "Woman Suffrage's Gray-Bearded Champion," pp. 2–13.

14. Blackwell to Stone, 3 July 1889 (emphasis in original).

15. "Hon. H. B. Blackwell," *Bismarck Tribune*, 3 Jul. 1889.

16. North Dakota, *Official Report of the Proceedings and Debates of the First Constitutional Convention of North Dakota Assembled in the City of Bismarck, Jul. 4th to Aug. 17th, 1889* (Bismarck, 1889), p. 41 (hereafter cited as *Constitutional Convention*).

17. "Beautiful Harmony," *Bismarck Tribune*, 9 July 1889.

18. Blackwell to Stone, 8 July 1889, in *Loving Warriors*, pp. 317–18 (emphasis in original).

19. Ibid., 9 July 1889, p. 318. For more on the Farmers' Alliance, *see* Larry Remele, "'God Helps Those Who Help Themselves': The Farmers Alliance and Dakota Statehood," *Montana: The Magazine of Western History* 37 (Autumn 1987): 22–33; Donald F. Warner, "The Farmers' Alliance and the Farmers' Union: An American-Canadian Parallelism," *Agricultural History* 23 (Jan. 1949): 9–19. After serving as North Dakota Insurance Commissioner (1894–1897), Frederick Bartlett Fancher became North Dakota's seventh gov-

ernor from 1899 to 1901. It does not appear that Fancher advanced woman suffrage during his term. At its convention in Fargo, the territorial Farmers' Alliance added a plank to its platform endorsing woman suffrage, although it affirmed, "That the constitutional convention be requested to submit separately the question of granting full suffrage to women" ("Alliance Platform," *Grand Forks Daily Herald*, 28 Jun. 1889).

20. "To the Members," *Bismarck Tribune*, 11 July 1889; "The Suffrage Meeting," ibid., 12 July 1889; Blackwell to Stone, 10 July 1889, in *Loving Warriors*, p. 319. The United States census reports the population of Bismarck in 1890 as 2,186. Blackwell's notion of a large audience obviously reflected the size of a typical crowd in Boston. U.S., Department of Commerce, Bureau of the Census, *Twelfth Census of the United States, Census Bulletin No. 40* (23 Jan. 1901), p. 4.

21. Blackwell to Stone, 10 July 1889 (emphasis in original).

22. Susan B. Anthony and Ida Husted Harper, eds., *History of Woman Suffrage*, Vol. 4 (Rochester, N.Y.: Susan B. Anthony, 1902), p. 545.

23. "On the Side," *Jamestown Weekly Alert*, 25 July 1889. An example of popular American humorist Artemus Ward's views on suffrage can be found in Ward, *His Book* (New York: Carleton, 1862), pp. 119–22.

24. North Dakota, *Legislative Manual, 1889–1890*, p. 101 (emphasis added).

25. Anthony and Harper, eds., *History of Woman Suffrage*, p. 546. Janette Hill Knox of Wahpeton, North Dakota, was an active leader of the WCTU and served for a period of time as the secretary of the North Dakota State Woman Suffrage Association. A graduate of Baker University in 1877, she was a faculty member at Red River Valley University, a Methodist Episcopal college in Wahpeton that later merged with UND. Knox's husband, Rev. Martin Van Buren Knox, served as the institution's president from 1891 to 1892. Wallace N. Sterns, *History of the Red River Valley University* (Bismarck: State Historical Society of North Dakota, 1908); *Catalogue of the Officers and Students of Baker University, Baldwin, Kansas, for the Collegiate year 1892–93*, p. 87.

26. "The Ladies Win," *Grand Forks Daily Herald*, 1 Aug. 1889.

27. Blackwell to Stone, 1 Aug. 1889, in *Loving Warriors*, pp. 327–28 (emphasis in original).

28. *Grand Forks Daily Herald*, 1 Aug. 1889. Lawyer, banker, and farmer Henry Foster Miller of Cass County had introduced the suffrage article. "Who They Are," *Bismarck Weekly Tribune*," 12 July 1889.

29. Dakota Territory, *Laws Passed at the Fifteenth Session of the Legislative Assembly of the Territory of Dakota* (Yankton, 1883), p. 92, and *Laws Passed at the Seventeenth Session* (Bismarck, 1887), p. 113.

30. *Legislative Manual*, 1889–1890, p. 101.

EQUALITY AT THE BALLOT BOX

31. *Constitutional Convention*, p. 573 (emphasis added). Rowe, a Republican, was a farmer, journalist, lawyer, and businessman who may later have moved away from North Dakota. "Who They Are"; "State News," *Bismarck Weekly Tribune*, 15 Sept. 1893. Cora E. Smith took credit for writing the amended clause. "Progress in North Dakota," *Woman's Journal*, 6 Sept. 1890, p. 288.

32. *Constitutional Convention*, pp. 573–74. Stevens, then of Lisbon, North Dakota, was a Republican lawyer and farmer who migrated to Dakota in 1882. Elected to the state legislature in 1889 and 1898, he also served as editor of the *Bismarck Tribune* from 1894 to 1896 and of the short–lived *Grand Forks Republican and Northwest News* in 1898. Curt Eriksmoen, "Famous Book has N.D. Ties," *Bismarck Tribune*, 19 July 2008.

33. *Constitutional Convention*, p. 574. Eugene Strong Rolfe was a lawyer and banker who migrated to Dakota in 1884. His sister Ellen May was married to the famous midwestern scholar Thorstein Veblen, whom she divorced in 1911.

34. Ibid., pp. liii, 574–75; *Legislative Manual*, 1901, p. 120.

35. "Yesterday's Election," *Grand Forks Plaindealer*, 5 Aug. 1890; "The Election," *Bismarck Tribune*, 18 Jun. 1890; "Slaughter Items," ibid., 25 Jun. 1890. The *Tribune* printed a long list of Bismarck women voters' names. The *Grand Forks Daily Herald* reported on 20 August 1890 that women voting in the upcoming general election would need "to secure from the judges of election separate boxes for receiving their ballots" because "still the legislature has made no provision for separate ballot boxes for their special use, which certainly will be necessary at a general election."

36. *Grand Forks Daily Herald*, 3 Sept. 1890. Cochrane, a Grand Forks County judge, also served as state's attorney for the county from 1887 to 1890 and as a justice of the state supreme court from 1903 to 1904. "Summons to Noble Man," *Grand Forks Daily Herald*, 21 July 1904.

37. "Progress in North Dakota," *Woman's Journal*, 6 Sept. 1890, p. 288. Smith's letter to the *Journal* is dated 23 August.

38. Anthony and Harper, eds., *History of Woman Suffrage*, p. 551; Tucker, "History of the Woman's Suffrage Movement," pp. 23–25; "No! She Can't Vote," *Grand Forks Daily Herald*, 5 Sept. 1890; "District Attorney Cochrane," *Bismarck Tribune*, 12 Sept. 1890.

39. *Grand Forks Daily Herald*, 10 Sept. 1890; "Women May Vote," ibid., 23 Oct. 1890; "Bismarck in Brief," *Bismarck Tribune*, 11 Oct. 1890; "Proceedings of the Board of County Commissioners of Burleigh County," ibid., 17 Oct. 1890.

40. George F. Goodwin to Hon. C. J. Paul, 21 Oct. 1890, in North Dakota, *Report of the Attorney General to the Governor of North Dakota for the*

Year Ending Oct. 31, 1890 (Bismarck, 1890) pp. 92–93. Eisenhuth was elected North Dakota state superintendent of public instruction in 1892 and thus became the first woman in the United States to win statewide office. *See* Barbara Handy-Marchello, "Quiet Voices in the Prairie Wind: The Politics of Woman Suffrage in North Dakota, 1873–1920," herein.

41. "Suffrage Association," *Grand Forks Daily Herald*, 17 Sept. 1890.

42. Quoted in "Womans' Suffrage," ibid., 29 Sept. 1890.

43. *Bismarck Tribune*, 30 Sept. 1890.

44. "Election," *Grand Forks Daily Herald*, 4 Nov. 1890.

45. "The Ladies Who Voted," *Grand Forks Plaindealer*, 5 Nov. 1890. Mary E. Slater often appeared in Grand Forks WCTU activity notices with Sara E. B. Smith. While the *Plaindealer* named "Mesdame E. Smith" as the other voter in that ward, the fact that the article separates mesdames from misses suggests that the reference is to Sara E. B. Smith and not Cora E. Smith.

46. *Western Womanhood* 2 (Jan. 1895): 3

47. Both the *Grand Forks Daily Herald* and *Bismarck Tribune* covered the dramatic events on 4 Mar. 1893. *See also* Anthony and Harper, eds., *History of Woman Suffrage*, pp. 548–49, 551; North Dakota, *Revised Codes of the State of North Dakota* (Bismarck, 1895), p. 171 (hereafter cited as *Revised Codes*); North Dakota, *Session Laws*, 1923, p. 269.

48. "Our Educational Facilities," *Grand Forks Daily Herald*, 18 Dec. 1892; "Bride and Benedict," ibid., 5 Nov. 1893. Following marriage, she dropped her middle initial and preferred "Cora Smith Eaton."

49. "Local Brevities," ibid., 13 Oct. 1894.

50. "Women Should Vote," ibid., 3 Nov. 1894.

51. "In the Legislature," ibid., 7 Feb. 1895; "North Dakota," *Arena* 15 (Oct. 1895): 208–9; *Western Womanhood* 2 (Jan. 1895): 3; *Revised Codes*, p. 171. The *Revised Codes* established the age of consent for women at thirteen years of age and men at sixteen. Ibid., p. 608.

52. Ross–Nazzal, *Winning the West for* Women, p. 83.

53. Proceedings, *Twenty–Eighth Annual Convention of the National-American Woman Suffrage Association*, p. 152; *Western Womanhood* 2 (Jan. 1895): 3; "Society Notes," *Grand Forks Daily Herald*, 27 Jan 1895. Bates was a Republican from Valley City and an active member of the North Dakota WCTU. She succeeded Laura J. Eisenhuth as state superintendent and served from 1895 to 1896. Elizabeth Preston Anderson was a long-time president of the North Dakota WCTU and its chief state organizer. She was likely the only woman's rights advocate in North Dakota who participated in suffrage activities from statehood to women's achievement of full suffrage. Wurtz, "Elizabeth Preston Anderson," pp. 49–58.

54. Smith Eaton to DeVoe, 2 Mar. 1895, folder 2, box 2, Emma Smith DeVoe Papers, Washington State Library, Tumwater.

55. Bates to DeVoe, 26 Feb. 1895, folder 1, box 3, DeVoe Papers. Bates may refer here to Samantha, the eponymous character of a series of popular satire novels by American humorist Marietta Holley.

56. Proceedings, *Twenty-Seventh Annual Convention of the National-American Woman Suffrage Association Held in Atlanta, GA, January 31st to February 5th, 1895* (Washington, D.C.: By the Association, 1895), p. 21.

57. Proceedings, *Twenty-Eighth Annual Convention of the National-American Woman Suffrage Association*, p. 60. Catt would be elected president of NAWSA twice, from 1900–1904 and 1915–1920.

58. Ross–Nazzal, *Winning the West for Women*, p. 88.

59. Ibid., p. 85.

60. Bates to DeVoe, 21 Mar. 1895, folder 1, box 3, DeVoe Papers.

61. Ibid., 23 Nov. 1895 (emphasis in original).

62. Johns, "Woman Suffrage in North Dakota," *Western Womanhood* 2 (Nov. 1895): 1.

63. *In re Eaton*, 62 N.W. 597 (N.Dak. 1895); *Bismarck Tribune*, 25 Nov. 1895.

64. Johns, "Woman Suffrage in North Dakota," p. 1–2. *See also Bismarck Tribune*, 20 Nov. 1895.

65. "Political Equality Club," *Bismarck Tribune*, 4 Nov. 1895.

66. "Woman Suffrage," *Grand Forks Daily Herald*, 14 Nov. 1895.

67. Ibid., 15, 17 Nov. 1895; "The Suffragists," *Bismarck Tribune*, 18 Nov. 1895; "State Correspondence: North Dakota," *Woman's Journal*, 28 Dec. 1895, p. 416; "Report of North Dakota Equal Suffrage Association," *Western Womanhood* 2 (Dec. 1895): n. p.

68. U.S., Congress, *Hearing of the National American Woman Suffrage Association, Committee on the Judiciary, House of Representatives*, 54th Cong., 1st sess. (28 Jan. 1896), pp. 12–13.

69. "The National Convention," *Western Womanhood* 3 (Mar. 1896): 1.

70. "Hospital Surgeon," *Grand Forks Daily Herald*, 7 Mar. 1896.

71. "Equal Suffrage Association," *Western Womanhood* 3 (May 1896): 9. For more on Marble, *see* Isaac Atwater, ed., *History of the City of Minneapolis, Minnesota*, Vol. 1 (New York: Munsell & Co., 1893), p. 257; "Hospital Surgeon"; "Women Physicians," *Woman's Journal*, 21 Mar. 1896, p. 89.

72. "Equal Suffrage Association," Western Womanhood 3 (Sept. 1896): 11.

73. "An Announcement," *Grand Forks Daily Herald*, 28 Jul. 1896; "Notice of Nominations for Public Office," *Bismarck Tribune*, 26 Oct. 1896.

74. Untitled article, *Western Womanhood* 3 (Nov. 1896): 6–7.

75. Untitled article, ibid. 4 (Mar. 1897): 1.

76. "At the Chautauqua," ibid. (July 1897): 7; "Official Directory," ibid. 5 (Apr. 1898): 10; Ida Husted Harper, ed., *History of Woman Suffrage*, Vol. 6 (New York: National American Woman Suffrage Association, 1922), p. 501.

77. "Equal Suffrage Convention," *Western Womanhood* 4 (Dec. 1897): 8–9.

78. Abigail Scott Dunaway, *Pathbreaking* (Portland, Oreg.: James, Kerns & Abbott Co., 1914), pp. 238–44; Ross–Nazzal, *Winning the West for Women*, pp. 113–55. Alice Paul and Lucy Burns formed the Congressional Union, an American suffrage organization, in 1913, and it was instrumental in creating the National Woman's Party in 1916.

79. Paula Becker, "Suffragists join the Mountaineers outing to Mount Rainier and plant an A–Y–P Exposition flag and a 'Votes for Women' banner at the summit of Columbia Crest on Jul. 30, 1909," HistoryLink.org; "Mountain Climbers Who Have Made New Records," *Seattle Daily Times*, 20 Aug. 1907; "Dr. Cora Eaton a Climber," *Grand Forks Evening Times*, 26 Aug. 1909; "Suffrage Pennant on Snow Peak," *Woman's Journal*, 28 Aug. 1909, p. 137; "State Correspondence," ibid., 3 Sept. 1910, p. 145; "Miss Alice Paul on Hunger Strike," *New York Times*, 7 Nov. 1917, p. 13; "Hunger Striker is Forcibly Fed," ibid., 9 Nov. 1917, p. 13. Cora Smith Eaton won her divorce suit against Robert Eaton in 1906. She married Judson King in 1912 but divorced him in 1925. Smith Eaton was among the first women to climb Mount Olympus and Mount Rainer.

"A RIGHT TO HELP MAKE THE LAWS"

Helen Piotopowaka Clarke, Virginia Billedeaux, and Blackfeet Empowerment

DEE GARCEAU

In September 1914, the *Suffrage Daily News* of Montana interviewed Virginia Billedeaux, asking whether women in Indian country supported suffrage. Billedeaux, a member of the Amskapi Pikuni division of the Blackfeet Confederacy, replied, "Yes, nearly every Indian woman thinks that she ought to have a right to help make the laws as well as the men." Billedeaux also praised the leadership of her senior contemporary Helen Piotopowaka Clarke, the first American Indian woman to hold elected office in Montana Territory. "We all know Helen P. Clark[e]," said Billedeaux. "The Blackfeet Indians know her to be our own dear friend."[1] As a public official, lobbyist, and educator, Helen Clarke represented more fully the possibilities of woman suffrage. And though Clarke would become well known, both women witnessed trauma and injustice that moved them toward a vision of Blackfeet empowerment through women's political action. If Clarke became the public figure while Billedeaux supported suffrage, taken together their lives reveal how the forces driving Blackfeet women's activism differed from those of Euro-American suffragists.

What Clarke and Billedeaux did share with white feminists in Montana was a shrewd and practical opportunism. In an interview with Kristen Inbody, historian Martha Kohl remarked that Montana suffragists "targeted their message in every case to whatever people wanted to hear." They pitched suffrage to church groups as a path toward temperance, to union men as a means of protecting wage-earning women, to parents as a way to prevent child labor and improve education, and to farmers and ranchers as a strategy to reshape the economic playing field.[2] Clarke and Billedeaux were similarly pragmatic. They saw in woman suffrage an opportunity to grow Blackfeet political influence beyond reservation borders. Indeed, they differed from most Montana feminists in that they were more concerned with Blackfeet empowerment than women's rights. Clarke's political career and Billedeaux's support for suffrage emerged from their experiences as Blackfeet women facing colonial regimes that included paternalistic Indian policy, peacetime dispossession, and racist discourse about American Indians and mixed-blood peoples. Clarke and Billedeaux were Blackfeet activists first, and women's rights advocates second.

The Blackfoot Confederacy is composed of three divisions: the Siksika, or Northern Blackfoot; the Kainah, or Bloods; and the Piegans, who claim a northern branch, Apatohsi Pikuni, and a southern branch, Amskapi Pikuni, also known as Montana Blackfeet. Historically, the Siksika, Apatohsi Pikuni, and Kainah lived in what is now western Canada. The Amskapi Pikuni, or Southern Piegans, once lived, harvested, hunted, traded, and raided on the Northern Great Plains, ranging across country known today as southern Alberta, Montana, and the Dakotas, with occasional forays farther south into Shoshone country.[3] After 1873, they were confined to the Blackfeet Indian Reservation, an area spanning northern Montana that shrank precipitously as starving Pikunis made land cessions to the United States in return for rations and annuity payments in 1874, 1888, and 1896. By the early 1900s, the reservation was reduced to one-sixth of its original size, situated just east of present-day Glacier National Park.[4]

There is little in Blackfeet oral tradition and little in the archival record to illuminate Amskapi Pikuni suffrage politics.[5] Nonetheless, as historian Andrew Graybill demonstrates in his three-generation biography of the Clarke family, one can construct the outline of a person's life from fragmentary evidence and then fill in the social, economic, and political milieu in which she lived to shed light on the choices that she made. Clarke and Billedeaux belonged to the first generation of Blackfeet people to endure ward status at the hands of the federal government. The forces that drove their activism reveal not only threats to Black-

EQUALITY AT THE BALLOT BOX

Helen Piotopowaka Clarke, c. 1910.
Montana Historical Society Research Center

feet survival but also the tensions of intersectionality. As mixed-blood women, Clarke and Billedeaux navigated terrain riven with racism and reform like braided streams.[6]

The world in which Helen Clarke grew up was destabilized. Her father, Malcolm Clarke, named Four Bears by the Blackfeet, was a Scottish-American trader; her mother, Coth-co-co-na, was Amskapi Pikuni. Clarke's maternal grandparents, Under Bull and Black Bear, were Amskapi Pikuni. Listed in a 1907 Blackfeet genealogy as "1/2 Piegan," Helen Clarke identified as a mixed-blood Blackfeet woman.[7] And while mixed-blood identity had been advantageous during the fur trade, by the late nineteenth century, it had become a liability in Montana. Graybill allows that "race was not necessarily the intractable issue for the Clarkes" that it had been for other multigenerational mixed-blood families. He cites Clarke family members' impressive accomplishments as proof that they transcended racial divides: Helen earned elective office; her brother Horace prospered in business and served on the Blackfeet tribal council; and her nephew John Clarke became a well-known sculptor. But Graybill also recognizes that the high status accorded mixed-blood people as cultural brokers in fur trade society had not lasted. "The Clarke children," he explains, "inherited a realm in which hybrid peoples were pushed increasingly to the margins by white newcomers, a process laden with physical as well as emotional violence."[8] Indeed, by the time Helen Piotopowaka Clarke came of age, mixed-blood people occupied a tenuous niche on the Northern Great Plains.

In late nineteenth- and early twentieth-century Montana, a discourse asserting white supremacy and patriarchal privilege competed with reformers' efforts to promote Indian citizenship and women's rights, respectively. The results were convoluted state laws regarding voting rights for both women and American Indian residents. In 1889, the new state of Montana declared every male resident age twenty-one or older eligible to vote, provided he was a United States citizen and had lived in Montana for at least one year. Under section twelve of this act, women who were taxpayers could vote as well. To pay taxes, a woman had to own taxable property, such as land, a home, or a business. The exceptions to section twelve were school elections and school offices, for which women could vote or run without property qualifications. In 1891, however, the Montana legislature added a taxpaying requirement for women voting in school elections. By the turn of the century, statewide woman suffrage campaigns gathered force, culminating in a well-organized drive led by Jeannette Rankin. In 1913, the Montana legislature passed a woman suffrage amendment, and in November 1914, voters across the state ratified it.[9] Still, without United States citizenship, neither Blackfeet women nor men could vote in Montana.

In 1887, the federal government opened a path toward United States citizenship for American Indians with the Dawes Severalty Act. The Dawes Act divided tribal lands held in common into individual allotments. To guard against exploitation by real-estate speculators, the federal government would hold each of these parcels in trust for twenty-five years, during which time the allotment was exempt from taxation. The Dawes Act held that if Indians accepted their allotments, lived apart from their tribe, and "adopted the habits of civilized life," they could become United States citizens. However, an allottee had to wait until the end of the twenty-five year trust period to claim title to the land (fee patent). Once an allottee gained legal ownership, his or her land could be taxed. Only then, as a *property holding, tax-paying* United States citizen, would a Blackfeet resident of Montana become eligible to vote. So the Dawes Act created a path to voting, but it was a slow one, and state restrictions created further road blocks to Indian suffrage. In 1895, for example, Montana law prohibited voting precincts within an Indian reservation, agency, or trading post.[10]

The federal government did not begin allotting Blackfeet lands until 1907. By mid-1916, some 2,623 Blackfeet in Montana had been allotted their section of reservation land. Recall, however, that Indian voting rights remained on hold for twenty-five years while allotments were held in trust. Enter the Burke Act, which defined criteria by which an American Indian resident could prove "civic competency" to bypass the waiting period created by the Dawes Act. Markers of competency varied, from boarding-school education, to wage work, to farming one's allotment, to blood quantum, with the racist notion that over one-half white blood conferred civic competency. Beginning in the twentieth century, the United States Census Bureau tracked these criteria on a separate reservation census that recorded the blood quantum of every American Indian, as well as whether they held a wage job, accepted rations, had attended a boarding school, lived in a wood frame house (labeled "civilized") or tipi (labeled "aboriginal"), and whether they had been allotted.[11] Between 1907 and 1924, if a Blackfeet person ran this gauntlet and was judged competent, they could claim their fee patent and, with it, voting rights in Montana. But in practice, many Amskapi Pikuni who proved civic competence and gained ownership of their allotment wound up losing their land because they could not pay the taxes. Once they lost their land, they were stricken from tax rolls and lost their right to vote.[12] Without votes, they could neither initiate referenda nor elect officials who would advance Blackfeet interests.

To make matters worse, from 1907 through 1919, the Interior Department encouraged white settlers to purchase unallotted reservation land and lease "unused" acreage from allottees. Interior officials even allowed land held by "noncompetent" allottees to be sold, interpreting "noncompetency" broadly in order to free up tribal lands for white settlers. By 1920, more than one million acres of tribal lands held in trust for so-called noncompetent Indians had been sold, and 4.5 million acres had been leased to white ranchers and farmers.[13] To fight these forms of dispossession, the Amskapi Pikuni would need the franchise. And the Blackfeet were not alone in this dilemma; as late as 1912, few American Indians on Northern Great Plains reservations could vote in local, state, or national elections.[14] Clarke and Billedeaux must have seen woman suffrage as an alternate path toward political voice for the Blackfeet people.

The Interior Department's management of water and timber on reservations further muddied humanitarian goals with economic exploitation. Ostensibly, the federal government guided resource management for the benefit of American Indian residents. Yet, reservation resources often wound up in the hands of white businessmen and farmers. In 1907, the Interior Department persuaded the Blackfeet to allocate over three hundred thousand dollars for an irrigation project to promote agriculture on the reservation. However, Blackfeet tribal members often lost their water rights through sale or lease of acreage to white farmers, who then established first claim on the water. By 1920, white settlers on reservations controlled almost 50 percent more land along irrigation canals than American Indian residents. Blackfeet who managed to obtain water rights and hold onto their acreage still faced white encroachment. Abundant prairie grasses along the Rocky Mountain front attracted Euro-American cattlemen like Dan Floweree, who turned his vast herds onto rangelands within the Blackfeet reservation. White-owned cattle trespass

EQUALITY AT THE BALLOT BOX

became so pronounced that by 1904 some eight to ten thousand cattle were illegally foraging on Blackfeet range.[15]

Euro-American economic interests also jockeyed for control of timber. In 1908, the federal government turned management of reservation timber over to the United States Forest Service (USFS). The USFS, in turn, leased reservation forest land to logging companies that worked to "yield the full market value of timber cut."[16] Though Blackfeet residents could hire on to logging crews, timber profits rarely found their way into Blackfeet pockets.[17] In short, the first two decades of the twentieth century saw colonial policies that eroded tribal control of reservation land, water, and timber. Having witnessed this dispossession firsthand, Helen Clarke would spend the second half of her life as a political advocate for the Amskapi Pikuni, her mother's people.

The plot thickens. In 1917, Commissioner of Indian Affairs Cato Sells ordered fee patents issued to all allottees—like Helen Clarke—whose ancestry was at least one-half white. Commissioner Sells believed that it was "almost an axiom that an Indian who has a larger proportion of white blood than Indian partakes more of the characteristics of the former than the latter."[18] The Interior Department thus used blood quantum as a shorthand for whiteness, awarding land title and citizenship to those who were at least half white. As a result, some mixed-blood Blackfeet in Montana received fee patents without their knowledge, such as soldiers who were fighting overseas in World War I. When these soldiers failed to pay taxes on the land they did not know they owned, the state of Montana took it over as payment and sold their parcel to non-Indians. Meanwhile, stateside, scores of mixed-blood Blackfeet received title to their allotment between 1917 and 1919. As propertied citizens, they should have become eligible to vote. But many could not afford the tax payments. Once an allottee missed a tax payment, he or she was dropped from state and county voter registration lists. By 1924, fully 95 percent of Blackfeet-owned allotments in Montana had been sold to pay taxes. Blackfeet voting rights were collateral damage.[19]

Clarke and Billedeaux responded not only to dispossession and disfranchisement, they also faced a negative discourse about mixed-blood Indians in Montana newspapers. Reformers in Washington, D.C., may have thought a half-measure of white blood merited United States citizenship and voting rights, but mixed-blood identity carried a stigma in Montana. In 1909, the Montana legislature passed an anti-miscegenation law prohibiting interracial marriage between whites and Asians or African Americans. Marriage between whites and American Indians remained legal, but many looked down their noses at white men who married American Indian women, calling them "squaw men" and their mixed-blood children "breeds," both of which were derogatory terms.[20] Newspapers displayed these prejudices.

In 1902, for example, *Butte Inter Mountain* and *Fergus County Argus* reports on a manslaughter case revealed racial divides being drawn. The case involved two generations of white men who had married outside their race in the ranch country near Fort Belknap. Both reports served up a discourse about race relations in which marriage between white men and mixed-blood American Indian women led to disorder, while endogamous marriages symbolized decency and social order. Briefly, the case involved a young man, Charles Perry, who allegedly shot an acquaintance, William Allen. Reporters characterized key players in this drama as follows: Allen, the victim, was a white man married to the mixed-blood daughter of "Old Man Ball." Old Man Ball was white and married to an American Indian woman. Reporters derisively referred to Allen and Ball as "squaw men" and portrayed them as violent types who picked fights and harbored grudges. One subheadline read, "Allen Had Long Cherished an Intense Hatred, Which Was Cause of Trouble," blaming the victim for provoking the conflict.[21] Another reporter wrote, "the breeds and the squaw men sided with the Allen gang." Linking terms like "breeds" and "squaw men" with the term "gang" implied criminality among the so-called squaw men and their mixed-blood children.[22] In this discourse, white men who married outside their race and their mixed-blood children became violent pariahs.

Further, reporters sketched the perpetrator, Charles Perry, as a sympathetic character because Perry had stayed within racial boundaries. That is, Perry, "an Indian," had married a mixed-

EQUALITY AT THE BALLOT BOX

blood woman, which in Montana racial parlance meant marrying an American Indian woman; thus, Perry had married within his race. Reporters cast Perry favorably, as "a man whose every feature indicates a cheerful and generous disposition. In manner he is quiet and reserved, and in no feature is there any trace of cruelty or thirst for excitement, so often depicted on the faces of his race."[23] White Montanans' contradictory notions of race emerged in this kind of newspaper story. First, if one were a mixed-blood woman, one's American Indian ancestry drew the derogatory term "breed." Second, if one were an American Indian man who stayed within racial boundaries, one could draw praise for this virtue (recall descriptions of Perry as "cheerful," "generous") and be tokenized as the exception rather than the rule (Perry showed none of the "cruelty . . . so often depicted on the faces of his race"). Third, if one were white and married a mixed-blood or American Indian woman, the person had crossed a racial boundary, which rendered the person morally suspect.

Such prejudices played out in action as well as in the press; six years earlier, Allen and another "squaw man" had been tarred and feathered by a white mob "for an offense" that the *Butte Inter Mountain* reporter neither investigated nor explained. Nor did the *Butte Inter Mountain* condemn the mob for acting outside the law. Thus, the *Butte Inter Mountain* tacitly condoned vigilante violence against white men who crossed racial boundaries by marrying mixed-blood American Indian women. By implication, mixed-blood women were a subordinate class within Montana's shifting racial landscape.[24]

If newspapers condemned white men with American Indian wives, implied the criminality of mixed-blood children, and racialized mixed-blood daughters as "Indian," where did that leave Helen Piotopowaka Clarke? Fur trade society a generation earlier had valued marriage to American Indian women for their roles as cultural brokers, producers of expedition supplies, tanners of fine furs, and interpreters, as well as for providing companionship and families to Euro-American trappers and traders. By the late nineteenth and early twentieth centuries, however, acceptance of interracial marriages, American Indian wives, and mixed-blood children was in steep decline. As Andrew Graybill observes, white newcomers to Montana in the latter half of the nineteenth century "had no sense of the relative racial accommodation that had characterized the fur trade era. Instead . . . white emigrants looked with revulsion upon the mixed-blood communities they discovered, seeing in them a combination of the worst elements of both races: white dissipation on the one hand, and native ignorance on the other."[25]

A new discourse appeared around mixed-blood women, somewhat akin to the "tragic mulatto" of black/white racial mythology. Consider how Helen Clarke fared on the marriage market. In late nineteenth-century Helena, Montana, Clarke drew attention from white bachelor businessmen, writers, and politicians. Beautiful, lively, and intelligent, she met eligible white men through her deceased father's contacts, such as the Fisk-Sanders clan, one of Montana's leading white families. But none of the men within the Fisk-Sanders orbit treated Clarke as eligible for marriage. In 1884, a beau named Henry wrote to Clarke while on business in San Francisco. He called her "my darling," referred to himself as "your lover," sent kisses, and waxed romantic about missing her while away from Montana. In the next breath, he referred to two young white women from Helena's elite society who had called on him in San Francisco and described his evenings with them as "delightful." He then insisted he would remain "good and true" to Clarke during his sojourn, though one wonders if he protested too much. Nothing more from Henry appears in the archival record.[26]

In 1901, a Helena journalist wrote unsparingly about the status of mixed-blood women when he said, "Though endowed with much beauty, Miss Clarke was known to be the daughter of a Piegan woman, and this fact caused her to be looked down on socially . . . the gilded doors of Helena's social realm were closed to her by the four hundred."[27] In another version of this story, published in the *San Francisco Chronicle*, the reporter added, "Miss Clarke was proud, and when it was demonstrated to her humiliation that her birth prevented her from taking the place in society her education and refinement warranted, she decided to leave Helena."[28] This story cast Helen Clarke as a tragic figure, rejected by the society in which she would have thrived but for her status as a mixed-blood woman.

The tragic mixed-blood narrative continued in public memory after Clarke's death in 1923. In 1939, a human-interest story about Clarke mused that she had selflessly refused to marry a white man lest her racial identity stigmatize him. "As you study her life," the author wrote, "you feel her poignant tragedy was her Indian blood. . . . More than once the light of romance might have entered her life, but she refused to allow it, feeling always that her Indian ancestry was a bar [to matrimony with a white man]. She went her way alone—the hard way but perhaps the best way."[29] Stunning in its complacency, this comment represented the unexamined racism that infused white sympathy toward mixed-blood and American Indian people. In another posthumous sketch of Clarke's life, a different author sighed, "Sadly . . . her experiences convinced her that as a half-breed she would never find a white man who would neither pity nor patronize her."[30] As late as the mid-twentieth century, then, white Montanans uncritically accepted the social segregation and subordination of mixed-blood women. In such a climate, even if Clarke herself had other reasons for remaining unmarried, the racial boundaries were palpable and likely painful to her and other mixed-blood women. Clarke's intersectionality—her encounters with gendered racial prejudice—created motives for political action that differed from those of Euro-American suffragists in Montana.

Clarke and Billedeaux shared the challenges of mixed-blood status, and both women witnessed the erosion of Blackfeet control over reservation lands and natural resources. But their experiences as children were not the same. While Clarke was a child of economic privilege, the available evidence suggests that Billedeaux's family struggled economically. Born in 1870, Virginia ("Puss") Howard (later Billedeaux) probably knew poverty at an early age. The 1880 census listed Virginia Howard, age ten, as a domestic servant in a middle-class Irish home in Helena.[31] Boarding out children as servants was one strategy that both white and American Indian parents turned to when they could not make ends meet. Making sure one's child had enough to eat took priority, even if it meant placing a daughter as an employee in another household. If this was her parents' reasoning when she began work as a servant, then Virginia Howard's family was struggling on the eve of the Starvation Winter of 1883–1884.

In 1883, the Amskapi Pikuni had been confined to a reservation just ten years. The bison population had been hunted almost to extinction; it is said that a man shot the last buffalo bull in the fall of 1883, alone in a gully near the medicine line (the United States-Canada border). With the bison economy decimated, and off-reservation hunting restricted, Blackfeet families went hungry. In a letter written to Montana territorial governor John S. Crosby in the fall of 1883, a white visitor to the reservation found the Amskapi Pikuni in crisis: "It needs no medical eye to see that their condition is that of a starving people. While all are very gaunt and thin, on the young the situation has told plainly and all of them are shockingly emaciated."[32]

By all accounts the winter that followed was brutal. Deep snow, sub-zero temperatures, and gale winds battered the northern plains for eight months straight. No longer free to follow migrating animals, Blackfeet hunters despaired as animals drifted south to escape the bitter weather. Blackfeet families were unable to fill their larders with game. At the same time, rations owed to the Blackfeet people failed to come through. In Blackfeet oral tradition, 1883–1884 is called the Starvation Winter because fully 25 percent of the Amskapi Pikuni died of starvation.[33]

Virginia Howard was thirteen years old during the Starvation Winter, old enough to understand and remember. Even if she lived in Helena as a domestic servant, she would have known about relatives and friends on the reservation who starved to death. As a young teen, Virginia Howard would have understood that colonial policies of Indian removal and confinement on reservations, combined with bureaucratic ineptitude and racism made a lethal combination that cost Blackfeet people their lives. Virginia Howard never forgot the Starvation Winter.

In 1888, at age eighteen, Virginia Howard married Edward Billedeaux, a twenty-three-year-old, mixed-blood man from Yankton, South Dakota. Their household appeared in the 1900 Glacier County census, which listed Edward Billedeaux as a "Ration Indian" without steady wage work. Soon after, Virginia

EQUALITY AT THE BALLOT BOX

and Edward Billedeaux responded to federal encouragement to try cattle ranching. Cattle herds promised a replacement for the bison economy and required good horsemanship, already a Blackfeet tradition. Billedeaux accepted her allotment on the Blackfeet reservation in 1907, and there she and her husband raised cattle and horses on the Milk River between Burd and Peterson. Extra horses brought cash income or goods in trade, while beef was a hedge against starvation.[34] Virginia and Howard Billedeaux would raise their children to become educated land-owners; they saw literacy and property as paths to greater economic security. Thus it was not surprising that Billedeaux told the *Suffrage Daily News*, "Most of our children are well educated and hold property and must obey the laws—so why not learn to be citizens?" Billedeaux enlisted her twenty-one-year old daughter in the campaign for woman suffrage in Montana. "My daughter Genevieve," she announced, "is a smart girl and will be glad to take charge of the literature you send us."[35] Virginia Billedeaux's endorsement of suffrage reflected her own keen awareness that political voice would be necessary for Blackfeet physical as well as cultural survival.

Helen Piotopowaka Clarke never faced the economic hardships that Billedeaux survived, but she would survive trauma of a different sort. At first glance, her life reads like a series of rewarding accomplishments: Shakespearean actress, schoolteacher, county superintendent of schools, Dawes Allotment Act administrator, lobbyist, and advocate for the Montana Blackfeet. A closer look, however, reveals three significant traumas that shaped Clarke's life, each one arising from colonial practices and systemic racism. The first was her father's murder; the second, a massacre of innocent Blackfeet people; and the third, her encounters with racist discourse about mixed-blood people. Moved by these traumas, Clarke would transform her outrage into politicking for the Montana Blackfeet.

As the daughter of a prominent Scottish trader and his Ams-kapi Pikuni wife, Clarke grew up bilingual and remained fluent in English and Blackfeet. Clarke spent most of her grade school and teen years with a Scottish aunt in Cincinnati, attending Catholic academies where she became well read, and adept at framing an

argument. In 1869, at age twenty, Clarke returned to her parents' ranch in the Prickly Pear Valley. Her Blackfeet name, Piotopowaka, has been translated to "The Bird That Comes Home"
or "Comes Walking from a Distance."[36]

In August 1869, Helen Clarke witnessed the shooting death
of her father, Malcolm Clarke, by a renegade band of Blackfeet.
Though he had earned respect among the Amskapi Pikuni, a
small faction led by Pete Owl Child attacked Malcolm Clarke to
avenge the unjust killing of Owl Child's nephew. The nephew had
been accused of stealing horses from white ranchers and never
got due process; he was executed on trumped-up charges. Later, it
came to light that Owl Child's nephew had been innocent; a band
of Crows had stolen the horses in question. Because Malcolm
Clarke had sided with white authorities seeking the horse thieves
before finding out the full story, Owl Child wreaked vengeance
on him. Owl Child wanted to send a clear message to white settlers that the Blackfeet were formidable adversaries. The murder
reflected tensions between the Amskapi Pikuni and a burgeoning white population on the Rocky Mountain front. Helen Clarke
valued her ties to relatives in both cultures, so Owl Child's attack
on her father provoked deep grief and dismay.[37]

Her father's murder was not the only trauma issuing from
settler colonialism in Blackfeet country. In a tragic disconnect,
the United States military avenged Malcolm Clarke's murder by
attacking an innocent band of Blackfeet. In the winter of 1870,
United States troops shot, beat, and burned members of Heavy
Runner's band, in what is known as the Marias Massacre. Heavy
Runner's band had had nothing to do with the murder of Malcolm
Clarke. Like the hasty execution of Owl Child's wrongly accused
nephew, the Marias Massacre revealed a profound devaluation of
Blackfeet peoples' lives at the hands of American authorities. For
Helen Clarke, staying in Montana became untenable. She fled to
her Scottish relatives in Minnesota.[38]

For five years, Helen Piotopowaka Clarke stayed far away from
Montana. She immersed herself in white society, traveling as far
as New York City, where she trained as an actor and began a career
on the stage. During the early 1870s, Clarke acted with a Shake-

spearean company, performing in New York, London, Paris, and Berlin, where she drew praise from the kaiser for her portrayal of Lady MacBeth. But her father's murder and the Marias Massacre burned in her memory, and Clarke could not forget who she was. "I was too much of self to become great [as an actor]," she said, "I could not forget I was Helen Clarke and become some new being of imagination."[39] In 1875, Clarke returned to Montana. Her family on the Prickly Pear had disbanded after her father's murder. Clark's mother, Coth-co-co-na, never recovered from the shock of seeing her husband murdered and was cared for by Clarke's siblings a hundred miles away in Highwood. Clarke spoke little of her mother thereafter, but one can infer the pain of grieving a mother who was still living yet broken in heart and spirit. Perhaps this, too, moved Helen Clarke toward political advocacy for the Blackfeet people, to prevent future tragedies like her father's murder, her mother's trauma, and the Marias Massacre. Without family in the Prickly Pear Valley, Clarke gravitated to the city of Helena, where she turned to friends of her deceased father, the Fisk-Sanders clan.[40]

The Fisks and Sanders were prominent families of white businessmen and club women, politically influential in Montana. Wilbur Fisk Sanders, a territorial legislator, became one of Clarke's most valuable political contacts, but their bond went deeper than politics. According to Graybill, Sanders and his pro-suffrage wife, Harriet, became surrogate family and mentors to Clarke. Wilbur Sanders did everything he could to establish Helen Clarke among Helena's educated classes. With the Sanderses' patronage, Clarke landed a teaching job in Lewis and Clark County. In 1882, Wilbur Sanders's influence in the state Republican Party helped earn Clarke's nomination for county superintendent of schools. The *Helena Weekly Herald*, owned and operated by the Fisk brothers, promoted her candidacy in editorials. In November, Clarke won a handy victory, becoming the first American Indian woman elected to public office in Montana. She earned reelection for two more terms, running unopposed in 1884 and winning against her Democratic opponent, 1,418 votes to 1,261, in 1886. Each time, Clarke drew unanimous nominations from county Republicans and some support from Democrats as well.[41] In 1884, the *Herald* bragged that Clarke "seems to have the concurrence of all respectable Democrats in her candidacy for a second term."[42]

Despite Republican support and endorsements from the powerful Fisk-Sanders clan, not all voters favored a female or a mixed-blood county superintendent of schools. Another leading Helena newspaper, the *Independent Record*, editorialized against her candidacy. The writer remarked skeptically that state laws governing education implied male leadership only: "The language of the school law does not seem to admit such an innovation [innovation being a female candidate]. It [the law] refers to such an officer throughout as a male, not a female officer. The personal pronouns 'he' and 'his' are used throughout, as will be seen by sections 1,095-96 and 1,139-40 of the Revised Statutes." The writer then quoted select phrases from Montana statutes, such as the superintendent "shall take office on the first Monday after December next succeeding *his* election."[43]

In addition to doubts about the suitability of women to hold public office, some Montana citizens acted out their prejudice against those with American Indian ancestry. Andrew Graybill discovered that when Clarke had been teaching about four years, before her run for school superintendent, Elizabeth Chester Fisk, leading matron and wife of the *Helena Weekly Herald* publisher, announced her disapproval of Clarke, "a half-breed Indian," and removed her children from Clarke's tutelage. Elizabeth Fisk's actions revealed racist currents even within progressive Republican circles. Graybill suggests that Elizabeth Fisk's racism was symptomatic of changing demographics. Indeed, by 1880, whites in Montana Territory outnumbered American Indians and had grown increasingly unwilling to accommodate their presence.[44]

Helen Clarke served as county superintendent of schools from 1882 to 1888, allocating a sixty-thousand-dollar budget to district schools while also serving as principal of the Westside School in Helena for the 1883–1884 school year. During this time, and periodically over the next decade, Clarke would live in boarding houses near Wilbur and Harriet Fisk Sanders in Helena, frequently visiting their household.[45]

In 1890, the Interior Department hired Clarke as a liaison be-

Clarke (seated at left) worked as an allotment agent
among the Otoes in Oklahoma Territory in the early 1890s.
Montana Historical Society Research Center

tween tribes and federal officials to explain the Allotment Act. Perhaps Clarke reasoned that if she helped federal officials navigate tribal cultures, tragedies on the scale of the Marias Massacre could be averted. In 1891, Clarke traveled to Oklahoma Territory, where she was assigned to allot tribal lands among the Tonkawas, Otoes, Missourias, and Poncas. At that time, Clarke supported allotment and saw property ownership as an alternative to migratory seasonal economies and as a path toward citizenship and voting. From 1891 to 1894, Clarke struggled to persuade tribal leaders to accept allotment. While the Tonkawas cooperated with subdividing their lands into individually owned parcels, the Missourias, Otoes, and Poncas bitterly opposed it, preferring to hold their tribal lands in common. Savvy and prescient, they predicted that allotment would lead to further land loss. For her part, Clarke wondered how she would earn a living if her efforts as an allotment agent failed. Indeed, after she left in 1894, the Missourias, Otoes and Poncas undid her efforts, moving back into their own camps and allowing communal land use. But in 1897, the Interior Department sent her back to Oklahoma to reinstate allotment. Finally, in 1899, Piotopowaka turned her face toward home, this time to her brother Horace's homestead in Midvale, known today as East Glacier, on the Blackfeet reservation.⁴⁶

As she reconnected with Blackfeet relatives and friends, Clarke grew increasingly critical of white officials who bungled management of the Blackfeet reservation. Over the next two decades, she emerged as a spirited advocate for the Amskapi Pikuni, trying to make their Montana reservation a safer, more humane, more prosperous place. Time with her mother's people affirmed for Helen Clarke the value of her Blackfeet heritage and mixed-blood identity. In 1903, she publicly refuted a 1901 newspaper article that had cast her as a tragic mixed-blood woman. In an interview with the *Montana Daily Record*, Clarke said, "The story in question did me an injustice in many ways. . . . It declared that I was ashamed of my Indian blood, and that being 'ostracised,' by the best people of Helena, I had moved to California." She added, "I am far from being ashamed of my origin . . . [and] am proud of both my father and mother. . . . Furthermore, I had always numbered the very best people of Helena among my friends, and so the statement that I had been ostracised was ridiculous."⁴⁷ Despite Clarke's insistence on her friendships with Helena's best, she voted with her feet. From 1903 until her death in 1923, Helen Clarke lived on the Blackfeet reservation, with periodic visits to the Fisk-Sanders mansion in Helena. On the reservation, Clarke and her brother Horace raised cattle and horses, while Clarke would increasingly direct her talents toward getting justice for the Amskapi Pikuni.⁴⁸

In 1903 and 1904, for example, Clarke led a drive to remove James Monteath from his post as Indian agent. Monteath had withheld rations from Blackfeet families to extort their cooperation with the allotment program. In a letter to former United States senator Wilbur Fisk Sanders, she exposed Monteath's mismanagement: "The supplies for the Blackfeet in the past two years [have] been almost nothing as rations are not available to the tribe in general."[49] According to Graybill, the Blackfeet "were still on a slow climb back from the abyss of starvation. . . . During his ruinous tenure between 1900 and 1905, Monteath slashed the ration rolls from more than 2,000 names to fewer than 100."[50] By 1906, Clarke's lobbying bore fruit, and Monteath was removed from his post.

In another example of Clarke's activism, she asked Wilbur Sanders to ensure equal pay for Blackfeet workers on the Cutbank irrigation project. In 1904, she wrote, "work on the Cutbank Ditch is just commencing. It is . . . said that Indians complain of not getting full pay or time for their work." Clarke called for an investigation that would include "inspecting the payroll."[51] The record does not show whether her call was heeded, but it is significant that she asserted their right to equal wages.

During the last two decades of her life, Clarke lost patience with the discourse about mixed-blood people as either tragic or morally bankrupt. Her frustration with racist tropes surfaced in a letter to white author Edwin M. Royle of Darien, Connecticut. Royle had penned *The Silent Call*, a work of fiction that Clarke judged respectful toward American Indians. She confided to Royle her exasperation with racism and attributed it to "the ignorant—the poor white trash and the half-civilized westerner who believes that us Indians could be called good only when dead." She pointed out the irony of Euro-Americans romanticizing indigenous people while looking down on mixed-blood persons like herself who were educated and accomplished: "This nation has ever held and does hold in esteem . . . the descendants of Pochahontas [*sic*] and yet . . . this nation looks with eyes askance at the cultured—the intelligent, intellectual half-breed or mixed bloods who reside either off or on the reservation." Clarke added that she began to "wonder if this [negative bias] be a melancholy fact," impervious to education.[52]

In 1909, Clarke applied for her own allotment and expanded her ranch lands. She continued to advocate for the Amskapi Pikuni, and they began to see her as their champion. In 1911, she exposed black market alcohol sales on the reservation. To do so, she composed a document, "The Tragedy of the Blackfeet Reservation," in which she cited nine Blackfeet deaths resulting directly from whiskey consumption in the space of only one year. Clarke's report showed the devastating consequences of traders profiting from selling adulterated whiskey that literally could be poisonous.[53]

Finally, as a former educator, Clarke stressed the importance of literacy for reservation dwellers. She believed that literacy allowed Blackfeet people to meet the white man on equal terms. In an early speech on elocution and literature, Clarke had emphasized that reading comprehension and analysis combined with effective speaking skills would outfit tomorrow's adults with the ability to shape opinion and influence decisions—political skills the Blackfeet could use to protect their interests.[54] Gradually, Clarke's reputation among the Amskapi Pikuni grew. In 1913, Helen Fitzgerald Sanders, Senator Sanders's daughter-in-law, penned a tribute to Piotopowaka: "To her Indians turn in times of trouble and perplexity . . . knowing that in her they have a wise counselor, an unfailing friend, and an intellect of which this nation can be proud."[55]

Like Virginia Billedeaux, Helen Piotopowaka Clarke's journey toward political activism grew out of traumatic experiences resulting from settler colonialism. Clarke survived the traumas of her father's murder, her mother's crippling grief, and the mass murder of Heavy Runner's band, as well as a disparaging discourse about mixed-blood people in Montana. Billedeaux, in turn, witnessed relatives and friends devastated by the Starvation Winter of 1883–1884. Both women, one coming from economic privilege, the other from economic struggle, came to believe that engaging with the American political system was a pragmatic strategy for advancing Blackfeet interests. But it was Clarke who most fully explored political activism, fighting increasing settler control over Blackfeet lands, water, and timber. In her efforts to empower the Amskapi Pikuni, Clarke chose multiple related paths, including United States citizenship, office-holding, lobbying, and—like Virginia Billedeaux—votes for women.[56] Unlike Euro-American suffragists in Montana, Clarke and Billedeaux wanted to outfit Blackfeet people with the political rights and skills necessary to protect themselves from colonial exploitation, racist discourse,

EQUALITY AT THE BALLOT BOX

and economic disaster. And yet, when Montana ratified woman suffrage in 1914, most American Indian women were excluded. Not until 1924 would all American Indians, men and women alike, gain full American citizenship with voting rights. Clarke and Billedeaux's legacy would be felt a century later with the expansion of American Indian representation in both the Montana state legislature and the United States Congress.[57]

NOTES

The author would like to thank Blackfeet elders Marie Gussman and Kenneth Charles Eaglespeaker for sharing their knowledge of Amskapi Pikuni history and culture. They changed the way I see the Northern Great Plains, past and present. Appreciation goes to William Farr as well, my mentor at the University of Montana, whose research inspired me. Archival staff at the Montana Historical Society provided invaluable assistance with the Helen P. Clarke Papers. Lastly, Molly Rozum and Lori Lahlum's probing editorial questions made this essay a better story.

1. "Indian Suffragettes," *Suffrage Daily News* (Helena, Mont.), 24 Sept. 1914.

2. Kristen Inbody, "My Montana: Women's Suffrage," *Great Falls (Mont.) Tribune*, 9 Nov. 2014.

3. Steven Grafe, ed., *Lanterns on the Prairie: The Blackfeet Photographs of Walter McClintock* (Norman: University of Oklahoma Press, 2009), p. xi. Grafe explains that in Canada, the northern divisions of the confederacy, i.e., Siksika, Kainah, and Apatohsi Pikuni, are collectively referred to as "Blackfoot." In the United States, however, the federal government assigned the name "Blackfeet" to Amskapi Pikuni confined to a reservation within Montana. Hence the Amskapi Pikuni became known as the "Montana Blackfeet." Grafe also provides the original translation of these names: *Siksikawa* means "[person having] black feet." *Kaina-wa* translates to "many chiefs." *Aapatohsipikani* refers to "spotted robes," the northern branch, and *Aamskaapipikani* to the southern branch of the "spotted robes" people.

4. William Farr, *The Reservation Blackfeet: A Photographic History of Cultural Survival* (Seattle: University of Washington Press, 1987), pp. 2–8.

5. For example, Blackfeet elder Kenneth Charles Eaglespeaker did not mention woman suffrage in his accounts of early twentieth-century tribal history. Kenny Eaglespeaker interviews with Dee Garceau, Browning, Mont., Apr. 2010, Nov. 2010, July 2011, transcripts in author's possession.

6. Andrew Graybill, *The Red and the White: A Family Saga of the American West* (New York: W.W. Norton, 2013). For Graybill's chapter on Helen

Piotopowaka Clarke, *see* pp. 153–94. For densely contextualized biographies of American Indian women, *see* ethnographer Bunny McBride's narrative of four generations of Abenaki women, *Women of the Dawn* (Lincoln: University of Nebraska Press, 2001). Andrew Graybill's three-generation study of the Clarke family deftly used this approach as well. This essay draws from Graybill, but it focuses on Helen Clarke's career as it relates to the development of her activism, with analysis of gendered contingencies and race relations in late nineteenth and early twentieth-century Montana. In cases where I drew insight directly from Graybill's study, I attributed his work. In other instances, I drew on the same archival sources that Graybill used, and there may be some overlap in our discussion regarding Helen Clarke, but the interpretation is my own.

7. Robert Ege, *Blackfeet Heritage, 1907–1908: Blackfeet Indian Reservation, Browning, Montana* (Great Falls, Mont.: Blackfeet Heritage Program, 1969), p. 67.

8. Graybill, *Red and the White*, pp. 4, 244.

9. Richmond L. Clow, "Crossing the Divide from Citizen to Voter: Tribal Suffrage in Montana, 1880–2016," *Montana: The Magazine of Western History* 60 (Spring 2019): 39; Judith Cole, "A Wide Field for Usefulness: Women's Civil Status and the Evolution of Women's Suffrage," *American Journal of Legal History* 34 (Fall 1990): 289; T. A. Larson, "Montana Women and the Battle for the Ballot," *Montana: The Magazine of Western History* 23 (Winter 1973): 30–39; Inbody, "Key Events in Montana Suffrage Fight Timeline," in "My Montana." Foreign-born men who met the other qualifications could continue to vote as they had under the territorial constitution for five years, at which point only United States citizens could vote.

10. Frederick Hoxie, *A Final Promise: The Campaign to Assimilate the Indians, 1880–1920* (Lincoln: University of Nebraska Press, 2001), pp. 75–77; Wilbur F. Sanders, ed., *Complete Codes and Statutes of the State of Montana in Force July 1, 1895* (Helena: Montana Legislature, 1895), p. 102, cited in Clow, "Crossing the Divide," pp. 40, 93n34. The prohibition on voting precincts within a reservation was not lifted until 1919.

11. Ironically, the Burke Act withheld citizenship until an allottee proved competent, even as it created ways to shorten the trust period. U.S., Congress, *Disposal of Surplus Unallotted Lands in the Blackfeet Reservation, Montana*, 64th Cong., 1st sess., H. Doc. 1041, serial 6905, p. 5; Hoxie, *Final Promise*, pp.166–80; U.S., Department of Commerce, Bureau of the Census, *United States Census for 1910*, Blackfeet reservation.

12. Clow, "Crossing the Divide," p. 48.

13. Hoxie, *Final Promise*, pp. 165–84.

14. Ibid., pp. 231–33. *See also* Clow, "Crossing the Divide," p. 42. By 1919,

only about twenty-five thousand American Indian adults had voted as American citizens in a local, state, or national election.

15. Farr, *Reservation Blackfeet*, pp. 98, 103; Hoxie, *Final Promise*, 169–72, 185.

16. Hoxie, *Final Promise*, pp. 172–73.

17. Farr, *Reservation Blackfeet*, p. 32. Corrupt reservation agents embezzled or misspent monies from leasing reservation land to timber companies. *See* Farr's discussion of Interior Department administrative corruption at the local reservation level, pp. 11, 100.

18. U.S., Bureau of Indian Affairs, *Annual Report of the Commissioner of Indian Affairs for the Year 1917* (Washington, D.C.: Government Printing Office, 1917), pp. 3–4. In Washington, D.C., Indian voting rights were not a priority. Commissioner Sells was anxious to free up Indian lands locked in trust; hence his liberalized fee-patent award system. *See* Hoxie, *Final Promise*, pp. 231–32.

19. Clow, "Crossing the Divide," pp. 46–47.

20. "May Cause Big Indian Fight in the Belknap Reservation," *Butte Inter Mountain*, 1 Apr. 1902; "Story of Chas Perry," *Fergus County Argus* (Lewistown, Mont.), 18 June 1902.

21. "Story of Chas Perry."

22. "May Cause Big Indian Fight." Reinforcing this notion was a statement in the article that the shooter, Perry, "incited the envy of half-breeds and squaw men around the reservation," which "resulted in an attack on Perry."

23. "Story of Chas Perry."

24. "May Cause Big Indian Fight." Nearly two decades later, in 1919, the *Great Falls Daily Tribune* featured a lengthy story headlined, "Indian Morals Need Governor," with a sub-heading, "Shameful Looseness' in Marriage Relations." The reporter called attention to an Interior Department report that decried American Indian marriage practices. Because some tribespeople ended marriages in ways that reflected their own cultural traditions rather than using the American legal system, Indian Affairs commissioners railed against an "increase of immorality . . . husbands leave their wives and wives their husbands to live with other 'husbands' and 'wives' without ever thinking of legal divorce." The reporter called for "departmental regulations or congressional legislation which will secure the adequate punishment of offenders, both whites and Indians, against morality." By including intermarried whites in this jeremiad about American Indian marriage practices, the writer presented both groups as morally inferior. *Great Falls Daily Tribune*, 10 Feb. 1919.

25. Graybill, *Red and the White*, p. 163.

26. Henry to Clarke, 11 Jan. 1884, folder 2, box 5, Helen P. Clarke Papers,

SC1153, Montana Historical Society, Helena. In 1884, the term "lover" meant sweetheart, and "making love to" meant courting. Neither of these terms necessarily meant a sexual liaison, as they would later in the twentieth century.

27. "Montana Society Frowned upon Daughter of Piegan Woman," *Sausalito (Calif.) News*, 28 Dec. 1901, clipping in vertical file, Clarke Papers.

28. Article quoted in "Helen Piotopowaka Clarke and the Persistence of Prejudice," *Women's History Matters*, Montana Historical Society, 2016, montanawomenshistory.org. *See also* Graybill, *Red and the White*, p. 184. Clarke spent two years, 1901–1902, teaching elocution in San Francisco.

29. "Malcolm Clarke's Daughter Was Treasure State Heroine," 11 Dec. 1939, clipping in folder 5, box 2, Clarke Papers.

30. Nancy Mayborn Peterson, *People of the Old Missury: Years of Conflict* (Frederick, Colo.: Renaissance House Publishers, n.d.), p. 83, copy in vertical file, Clarke Papers. *See also* "Color No Barrier: Brains Count Against the Handicap of Dusky Skin," *Print Outfit* (1907), copy ibid., which struck a contradictory note, announcing "Color No Barrier" while perpetuating the cant of white supremacy: "The white man found the dark races in possession when he colonized America. . . . Of course there is a vast amount of discussion about what should be done with them. . . . Recently the talents of individual Chinese, Indians, and Negroes have thrown an entirely new light on the subject and created a hope that the so-called 'inferior races' will work out their own evolution to a higher development."

31. Ege, *Blackfeet Heritage*, p. 34; *United States Census*, 1880, Helena, Mont., James Ryan household. Ryan, age 45, occupation "capitalist," and his wife, Catherine, age 27, listed Virginia Howard as a live-in servant. She probably helped Catherine Ryan with housework and caring for the Ryan's three-year-old daughter, Florence. Virginia's parents were Joe Howard, a white man, and Mary Howard, who was half Amskapi Pikuni and half African American. Billedeaux's maternal grandparents were Charley Woods, Amskapi Pikuni, and an African American woman whose name has disappeared from the record. A 1907 Blackfeet genealogy described Billedeaux as one-quarter Piegan.

32. Author unknown, letter in the possession of Marie Gussman (Amskapi Pikuni), Browning, Mont.

33. Farr, *Reservation Blackfeet*, p. 8. *See also* William Farr, "A Point of Entry: The Blackfeet Adoption of Walter McClintock," in *Lanterns on the Prairie*, ed. Grafe, pp. 43, 52.

34. Ege, *Blackfeet Heritage*, p. 34; *United States Census*, 1900, Glacier County, Mont. *See also* the 1920 census, which lists Edward Billedeaux as "rancher," with wife Virginia and two teenage sons living on and working the ranch with him. Extended kin networks on adjacent land made ranch-

ing more successful, as relatives could help each other with such labor-intensive tasks as round-ups, hay-cutting, or branding. In 1935, a reservation census found Virginia and Edward Billedeaux living adjacent to adult sons Edward and Francis, each of whom headed his own household; neighboring them were Virginia's brothers-in-law Greeley and Merlin Billedeaux with their families, farming their allotments. *See* abbreviated Blackfeet reservation census, 1935, AncestryLibrary.com. Blackfeet elder Kenneth Charles Eaglespeaker remarked that "things become tradition really fast" when the tribe deems something useful. Cattle ranching was added to Blackfeet tradition during the early twentieth century. Eaglespeaker interview, Apr. 2010, available in *Women in Native North America*, a digital archive within the "Women and Social Movements" Collection, Alexander Street Press, 2016. *See also* Farr's discussion of Blackfeet cattle ranching in *Reservation Blackfeet*, pp. 98–103.

35. "Indian Suffragettes."

36. Clarke's letters to legislators, club women, and federal officials, folder 5, Clarke Papers; Graybill, *Red and the White*, pp. 161, 280n25.

37. "Death of Helen Clarke Recalls Tragedy of the Murder of Malcolm Clarke by the Blackfeet Fifty Years Ago," *Grass Range (Mont.) Review*, 1923, clipping in vertical file, Clarke Papers. The article quotes Helen Clarke's own narrative of the incident, in which she explains how the summary execution of two Blackfeet youths for a theft committed by Crows offended Blackfeet honor and led to the murder of her father. *See also* James Welch, *Fools Crow* (New York: Penguin Books, 1990) pp. 209–15. Welch (Amskapi Pikuni and Gros Ventre) drew from Blackfeet oral tradition for his depiction of Owl Child's motives for killing Malcolm Clark.

38. Bear Head (Amskapi Pikuni), "Account of the Massacre on the Marias," in *Our Hearts Fell to the Ground: Plains Indian Views of How the West Was Lost*, ed. Colin Calloway (Boston: St. Martin's Press, 1996), pp. 108–10; Graybill, *Red and the White*, p. 157. Blackfeet oral tradition refers to the massacre of Heavy Runner's band as the "Baker Massacre" or the Marias Massacre.

39. Quoted in Joyce Clark Turvey, "Helen Piotopowaka Clarke," *History of Glacier County*, p. 87, copy in vertical file, Clarke Papers.

40. Graybill, *Red and the White*, p. 160.

41. Ibid.; *Helena Weekly Herald*, 13 Apr. 1882. In the months before the 1882 election, the *Helena Weekly Herald* reported favorably on Clarke's leadership in education, printing the text of her essay on elocution in April and noting her presentation of a paper at the Territorial Teacher's Institute that summer. Clarke had become recognized as a skilled professional in her field. In 1884, the *Herald* editorialized that she deserved, "hearty and active support" in her bid for reelection (6 Nov. 1884), and in 1886 promoted her reelec-

tion, stating, "Noone could more capably or conscientiously have discharged the duties of Superintendent" (14 Oct. 1886).

42. *Helena Weekly Herald*, 30 Oct. 1884.

43. *Independent Record*, 10 Sept. 1882 (emphasis in original).

44. Graybill, *Red and the White*, pp. 161–62.

45. *Helena Weekly Herald*, 12 Apr. 1883, 22 Dec. 1887; *United States Census*, 1880, 1900; Graybill, *Red and the White*, pp. 159–61. In 1880, Clarke had boarded with an unidentified white family in Helena. Clarke was working as a teacher at the time, and the census enumerator listed her as white, which was not unusual; mixed-blood people occasionally entered bureaucratic records as white and, given the hostile racial climate, sometimes said nothing to correct officials. In 1900, Clarke boarded with Bedelia Dickens, a forty-five-year-old white widow, and her twenty-three-year-old daughter, Sadie, on Broadway. Again, Clarke's occupation was "teacher," and she was listed as white.

46. Graybill, *Red and the White*, pp. 167–77.

47. Quoted in "Maligned by Newspaper: Miss Helen P. Clarke Refers to Libelous Story of Years Ago," *Montana Daily Record*, 26 Sept. 1903.

48. Turvey, "Helen Piotopowaka Clarke," p. 87. For registration of Clarke's cattle brand, *see State of Montana, Office of the General Recorder of Brands and Marks*, 28 Dec. 1895, copy in folder 5, box 3, Clarke Papers.

49. Clarke to Sanders, 1903–1904, esp. 2 Apr. 1904, folder 2, box 5, Clarke Papers.

50. Graybill, *Red and the White*, p. 185.

51. Clarke to Sanders, 12 Apr. 1904.

52. Clarke to Royle, 15 Feb. 1911, folder 5, box 4, Clarke Papers.

53. Clarke, "The Tragedy of the Blackfeet Reservation," ibid. Teddy Blue Abbot described "Indian whiskey" as a beverage that early traders sometimes adulterated with water and red pepper to extend the volume. Other additives included tobacco, soap, and even small amounts of strychnine as a "stimulant" (Teddy Blue Abbott, *We Pointed Them North* [New York: Farrer & Rinehart, 1939], p. 124).

54. Clarke's speech on elocution was reprinted in the *Helena Weekly Herald*, 13 Apr. 1882. Although she drafted it before focusing on Blackfeet empowerment, the speech demonstrates her attitude regarding persuasive public speaking skills and effective argumentation. *See also* Turvey, *History of Glacier County*, p. 87, who observes that Clarke saw literacy as an equalizer.

55. Helen Fitzgerald Sanders, draft introduction to *The White Quiver* (a compilation of Blackfeet oral traditions told by chief Little Dog and Bear Head), p. 3, folder 5, box 4, Clarke Papers. Helen Sanders was fond of Clarke

and dedicated *The White Quiver* to Helen Clarke and her brother Horace Clarke.

56. "Indian Suffragettes."

57. *See* Bobby Caina Calvan, "Native Americans Turn Focus Inward for Political Empowerment," *Missoulian*, 26 June 2016, in which state senator Lea Whitford, Amskapi Pikuni, comments that serving in the state legislature offers "opportunity and . . . empowerment" for Blackfeet people. *See also* Nicky Ouellet, "Nine Native Americans Elected to Montana State Legislature," *Montana Public Radio*, 7 Nov. 2018, mtpr.org. In the 2018 midterm elections, two American Indian women won seats in the United States Congress: Deborah Haaland (Laguna Pueblo), D-New Mexico; and Sharice Davids (Ho-Chunk), D-Kansas.

KATE SELBY WILDER
Clubwoman, Suffragist, Temperance Activist, and City Commissioner

ANN W. BRAATEN

In 1914, Kate Selby Wilder criss-crossed eastern North Dakota stumping for the passage of an amendment that would grant non-American Indian women full suffrage rights in North Dakota. Wilder, a suffragist, prohibitionist, and clubwoman in Fargo, regularly campaigned for women's voting rights under the auspices of the Woman's Christian Temperance Union (WCTU). Working tirelessly on issues related directly or indirectly to temperance, Wilder personified the connection between woman suffrage and the "Do-Everything" policy of the WCTU. Wilder became politically active before women in North Dakota, South Dakota, and Montana achieved the right to vote, and her activism continued after women were nationally enfranchised. Her successes during the campaign for woman suffrage demonstrate that linking prohibition and temperance with suffrage often worked in North Dakota, despite movement leaders' skepticism.

The sisterhood of clubwomen to which Wilder belonged profoundly shaped her experiences. These organizations gave agency to women and enabled them to move into the public sphere, which at that time some viewed as the dominion of men. Her participation in women's clubs furthered her education and developed her skills organizing, administering, and communicating. Her work with the National Federation of Women's Clubs helped steer the organization toward support of woman suffrage. When the North Dakota legislature passed an amendment to its state constitution on woman suffrage in 1913 and sent it to voters for ratification, Wilder was in the field campaigning from its passage until the election in November 1914. The referendum's defeat did not diminish her belief that women needed to play a part in governmental affairs. After North Dakota granted partial suffrage to women in 1917, Wilder ran for and won a seat on the Fargo City Commission in 1919, serving one term. She demonstrated that women had the intellectual capacity and administrative ability to govern successfully.[1]

Nineteenth-century ideals and Progressive Era efforts to reshape American life framed Wilder's life. During the nineteenth century, the family was understood to be the basic unit of society, and the ideal of separate spheres for men and women shaped the social order. Men represented the family in the public sphere, which included business and politics. Women directed the private sphere of the home, bearing responsibility for the domestic duties of feeding and clothing the family, child rearing, and housekeeping, as well as for equipping their children with the necessary social skills, ethics, and morality to be responsible citizens. As the twentieth century approached, industrially manufactured products replaced homemade goods. As middle-class women gained more leisure time, women's clubs developed to provide a gendered space for social and literary engagement, expanding women's domain into the public sphere. By the 1890s, many women's clubs began advocating for social reform on issues affecting their homes and families.[2]

Protestants, who prized pious devotion to the duties of ordinary life, considered the home to be a sanctified place where a man and a woman would raise a family. In 1874, Protestant women founded the WCTU and invoked women's moral authority to protect the home and promote individual and community improvements through temperance. At that time, Elizabeth Cady Stanton of the National Woman Suffrage Association (NWSA) encouraged the WCTU to work for woman suffrage, which she argued would give women the power to address a broad array of social issues. Initally, the WCTU was reluctant, but in 1879, when Frances Willard assumed leadership of the organization, she extended its focus beyond temperance to social reform, requiring only that members pay dues and sign a temperance pledge. Her vision and evangelism decentralized the group's power structure, instilled a sense of sisterhood, and fostered the WCTU's expansion across the United States.[3]

Willard worked to convince WCTU members that they had a sacred duty to become political. The WCTU formally endorsed woman suffrage in 1881, authorizing a Franchise Department to advocate for the vote. Susan B. Anthony negotiated an alliance between the WCTU and the NWSA. Anthony was confident that the support of churchwomen would offset the liquor lobby's opposition to suffrage. Other suffragists, including Stanton, believed the alliance would cause the movement to drift towards a more conservative state-by-state approach to suffrage rather than promoting a federal amendment. Other WCTU members feared the alliance would take away from their focus on prohibition. Promoting suffrage was not required, however, as the group's decentralized configuration allowed members to advocate for suffrage if they deemed it appropriate for their communities. As WCTU members worked to address local needs, members increasingly developed their leadership and advocacy skills. Many suffrage activists, including Kate Selby Wilder of North Dakota, Alice Pickler and Irene G. Adams of South Dakota, Emma Smith DeVoe of South Dakota and later Washington state, and Jeannette Rankin of Montana, became committed to suffrage after active membership in the WCTU.[4]

The WCTU's creative titles for its departments and initiatives reflected the organization's long-term goals. For example, the Department for Social Purity focused on domestic violence and strove to end the double standard associated with sexual morality and to halt the exploitation of women and children. It included practical and preventative measures to help women fleeing prostitution, as well as "life-saving stations" staffed by WCTU women to assist young women entering cities for the first time. Through their mothers' associations, the WCTU provided sex education to children. Members also lobbied against pornography and to strengthen rape laws. The Department for Social Purity allowed members to bring social issues once considered outside the realm of polite discussion into the mainstream. The North Dakota WCTU's Department for Social Purity established the Florence Crittenton Home for Unwed Mothers in Fargo in 1893. The home could accommodate twelve to fifteen young women at a time. It prevented young women whose families shunned them for becoming pregnant outside of marriage from becoming destitute. In 1908, the North Dakota WCTU transferred responsibility for maintaining and managing the home to the Florence Crittenton Mission. Wilder represented the WCTU in the transfer and continued to serve on the Florence Crittenton Home's board of directors for many years.[5]

The WCTU's Home Protection initiative supported woman suffrage, arguing that having the ability to vote would allow women to truly protect their families instead of being legally classified with children and the "feeble-minded." Gaining the vote for women became a preeminent issue for the North Dakota WCTU from 1910 to 1920. As women's domestic sphere expanded and young, unmarried women worked outside the home, women's clubs, including the WCTU, became more politically involved in order to control these new influences. Frances Willard realized the potential of the WCTU to change society. As a result, she implemented the Do-Everything policy in 1890 to encourage members to work on social issues of concern regardless of whether they related to temperance. This strategy helped make the WCTU one of the largest and most influential women's organizations in the United States, with 245,229 members by 1911. Middle-class, Protestant, American-born women who were well regarded in their communities became core members. They participated in local charities, missionary work, and church-related campaigns, creating an army of women committed to advancing the WCTU's goals.[6]

Kate Selby was born on 23 January 1876 in Meadville, Pennsylvania, to William A. and Adelia (Watson) Selby. In 1880, the family settled on a soldier's claim in Traill County, Dakota Territory, which her father earned after serving the Union for three years during the Civil War. Her father set up a legal practice in Caledonia, about twenty miles away from their farm. He traveled by pony, leaving Wilder and her mother alone on the homestead for weeks at a time. The sparseness of population and dearth of women during the early years of settlement increased their isolation. Wilder's maternal aunt was their nearest neighbor at three miles away, while a Norwegian woman lived ten miles away. Witnessing these women fight to ensure their family's survival helped Wilder develop empathy with farm women and Scandinavian women because she knew the struggles they faced.[7]

In 1882, after two years on the farm, the Selby family moved to Grand Forks where her father continued to practice law and two more children joined the household. Wilder's mother, a steadfast member of the WCTU, a charter member of the Woman's Relief Corps—an organization that supported Civil War Veterans—in Grand Forks, and an active member of the Congregationalist church, provided an example of civic engagement. Both parents were interested in the politics of the day and held political discussions in their home with friends and acquaintances. Tragedy struck the Selby family, however, as Wilder's father died in 1888. Soon thereafter, Wilder attended high school, which both of her parents had encouraged. She graduated from Grand Forks Central High School as valedictorian after serving as president of her senior class. After graduation, Wilder taught for one year in a Traill Country rural school and then returned to Grand Forks, where she worked for five years in the office of the register of deeds in Grand Forks County, rising to chief clerk.[8] These experiences helped Kate Selby develop her ability to communicate with authority to the public while enabling her to provide support for her family.

In 1901, Kate Selby married Frederick H. ("Frank") Wilder, a lawyer and Tufts College graduate. They relocated to Fargo for her husband's work with the Ancient Order of United Workmen of North Dakota, a fraternal insurance organization. Women's club membership helped the young couple build connections with the city's elite. By 1905, Wilder was a member of Fargo's Fortnightly Club, a civic and literary association focused on sociology that brought women together for study. From 1910 to 1912, Wilder served as the club's president. In her opening remarks as president, she took members to task with what the secretary's report described as a witty but pointed message, asking them to be prepared for meetings and to do their homework. By 1897, the club had joined the General Federation of Women's Clubs (GFWC),

EQUALITY AT THE BALLOT BOX

which first organized in 1895 to bring women's groups together under the umbrella of a national organization with state and local branches. The state federations collaborated with local clubs to avoid duplication of efforts and to coordinate civic projects.[9]

The GFWC's affiliated clubs tended to have membership rosters of high-society women who embraced suffrage slowly. While members of the Fortnightly Club, like many members of GFWC, were among Fargo's elite, they fully supported woman suffrage and provided a nexus for suffrage activism. Its members included Clara D. Darrow, who became president of the North Dakota Votes for Women League; Mrs. Helen deLendrecie, a long-time advocate for woman suffrage whose husband founded the O. J. deLendricie Department Store, by then Fargo's oldest and largest such store; and Christine Pollock, who assumed editorship of the *North Dakota White Ribbon Bulletin*, the official organ of the North Dakota WCTU, in 1904. Pollock's husband Robert was a prominent temperance advocate who drafted and introduced the resolution prohibiting the sale and manufacture of alcohol, which North Dakota voters approved when the state's constitution was adopted in 1889. In 1917, he framed the successful North Dakota woman suffrage law. The Fortnightly Club connected Wilder with women and men of influence who helped broaden her view of the world and inspired her political activity.[10]

Wilder also followed her mother's example of active involvement in the WCTU. In 1906, as president of the Young Woman's Club of Fargo, Wilder recruited young women into the WCTU, hosting receptions and classes in the WCTU Club House. The Young Woman's Club offered "thimble bees" for women working outside the home, with classes in cooking and sewing to be offered if there was interest.[11] These activities provided young working women with the opportunity to improve their domestic skills while developing a community of friends in a safe and respectful environment. In 1909, Wilder was elected president of the Fargo Union, an umbrella organization that included separate English- and Norwegian-speaking clubs. She facilitated a sense of common purpose between the two groups by organizing their joint travel by rail to a WCTU convention in Portland, Oregon. Delegates gathered at the Fargo station and prior to depar-

*This photograph of Kate Selby Wilder appeared in the
January 1913 issue of the* North Dakota White Ribbon Bulletin, *a publication of the state Woman's Christian Temperance Union.*
Institute for Regional Studies, North Dakota State University

ture Wilder gave each small bunches of wheat and white ribbons to symbolize their unity as sisters in the North Dakota WCTU.

Wilder's 1909–1910 WCTU president's report highlights a flurry of activity: she attended eighteen meetings of the Fargo Union, coordinated committees face-to-face and via telephone, wrote 27 letters and made 23 telephone calls for the Union, presented 110 bouquets to hospital wards and to the sick, and distributed 4,202 pages of literature. She praised members who helped the Fargo Union achieve its goals, singling out Christine Pollock for her work organizing public meetings and soliciting money for comfort bags that were shared with needy women and families. Wilder also described how the telephone helped her to organize efficiently and motivate the group's members. Telephone or no, Wilder's participation in women's clubs served to further her education and build her organization, administration, and communication skills.[12]

Wilder rose to leadership in the North Dakota WCTU with her appointment as superintendent for press work in 1909. Her first report promoted South Dakota WCTU organizer Esther Thomas, who lectured in English and Norwegian, encouraged members to use their limited suffrage to vote for school officials and school boards, and urged voters to support men running for office regardless of party affiliation who were known to favor WCTU goals of providing pure water, good schools, clean alleys, and improved sanitation. This approach presaged the tactics of the Nonpartisan League (NPL), which was founded in North Dakota in 1915. Wilder further implored members to communicate with their local press, which the WTCU believed was the best way of educating the public. Wilder's efforts to spur members to action served to implement the Do-Everything policy of the national WCTU on the local level.[13]

Wilder's work as a suffragist began in earnest in February 1912 when a separate group focused on acheiving woman suffrage in North Dakota organized in conjunction with militant British suffragette Sylvia Pankhurst's visit to Fargo. Pankhurst spoke to a standing-room-only crowd at a Sunday lecture at the Grand Theatre, announcing afterwards that the North Dakota Votes for Women League (VFWL) had been formed. At Pankhurst's suggestion, the League admitted men as associate members but not as voting members. The local papers reported Wilder and other Fortnightly Club members as among the well-known women of the city who affixed their names to the VFWL's membership list. Members elected Wilder to serve the VFWL as recording secretary.[14]

Women in Grand Forks organized a VFWL Club on 1 March 1912, with an initial membership of fifty. Fargo's club had fifty-two members at its start. The Fargo VFWL reported receiving letters from women in Rugby, Osnabrock, and Courtney, North Dakota, interested in starting affiliate chapters. Miss Candis Nelson, on faculty at Valley City Normal School and state superintendent of franchise for the North Dakota WCTU, wrote that the WCTU would be glad to cooperate with the VFWL. The *White Ribbon Bulletin* also announced the formation of the VFWL, encouraging women to join by pledging to work for the cause and paying twenty-five cents to the treasurer. Wilder was listed as the contact for more information.[15]

In August of 1912, Progressive Party presidential candidate Theodore Roosevelt generated additional energy for the VFWL when he included woman suffrage in the party's platform. Jane Addams, head resident of the Hull House settlement of Chicago and board member of the National American Woman Suffrage Association (NAWSA), seconded his nomination for president. The Progressive Party platform meshed with Wilder's beliefs, and she took on the role of chairperson of an organization called Women for the Progressive Party. This role required her to invite and host speakers to address party-sponsored events in North Dakota. In October 1912, she secured Jane Addams for lectures in Fargo and Grand Forks. Wilder reserved a block of seats so North Dakota VFWL members could attend en masse. Excited by this opportunity to hear Addams and to promote woman suffrage, the league ordered and sold Votes-for-Women badges for members to wear at the talk and afterwards.[16]

Wilder's work in the Progressive Party, the North Dakota VFWL, the Federation of Women's Clubs, and the WCTU provided networks through which she could act on her beliefs and implement societal change. This involvement expanded in 1913, when the North Dakota legislature passed a woman suffrage referendum that required putting the proposed constitutional change to the voters the following year. Using her networks, Wilder went all out to win support for the referendum, organizing public lectures featuring notable suffrage advocates, setting up booths offering water, toilets, and suffrage information at county fairs, holding street meetings, hosting teas, and going door-to-door to promote the cause. During the strenuous campaign in support of the woman suffrage amendment to the North Dakota Constitution,

EQUALITY AT THE BALLOT BOX

Wilder would be in the field from 1 February 1913 until Election Day on 3 November 1914.[17]

On 16 July 1914, Wilder traveled to Grand Forks with Jane Thompson, field organizer for NAWSA, to lay plans for street meetings and a debate. Their first street meeting occurred on an automobile parked in front of the Dakota Hotel; later, a second street meeting was held in the city's Central Park. The VFWL used automobiles, still a relative novelty in 1914, to their advantage. Suffrage supporters volunteered an automobile and drove speakers to busy areas in the cities and towns they visited. Curious people gathered around the car, which speakers then used as a dais from which to address the crowd. When the lecture and exchange among attendees and suffragists ended, the automobile quickly conveyed suffragists to their next location. Like the VFWL, the NPL used automobiles to aid its work when it organized in 1915. For both organizations, automobiles symbolized modernity, and epitomized the possibility of change, whether political or technological.[18]

Wilder ensured that suffrage remained on the front page of the newspapers by bringing a continual stream of renowned speakers to North Dakota. The 31 July suffrage debate was well-attended, with Jane Thompson arguing for suffrage and Marjorie Dorman, a leading anti-suffragist from New York, speaking in opposition. In September, Dr. Anna Howard Shaw, president of NAWSA, and Annie Kenney, a militant suffragist from England, spoke eleven days apart. In October, Wilder and Menza Burke of Idaho spoke on the question of suffrage at the Congregational church in Grand Forks. Wilder asked her WCTU sisters to come to the church fifteen minutes early to make their entry more conspicuous. Later, Burke and Wilder traveled by car to give short presentations in the lobbies of four hotels in Grand Forks.[19]

Despite the suffragists' well-coordinated efforts, North Dakotans did not vote to amend their constitution. The referendum required a majority of all those voting at the election, including those who declined to vote on the suffrage issue, to pass. The referendum was defeated with 49,348 (55 percent) votes against and 40,209 (45 percent) votes supporting full voting rights for women. A suffrage amendment also lost in South Dakota in 1914, suggesting regional reluctance to support woman suffrage. That same year, however, non-American Indian women in Montana received full suffrage.[20]

North Dakota suffragists remembered the words of caution that Sylvia Pankhurst had offered in 1912: reforms come gradually, but each man and woman should do their share. Women continued their campaign, lobbying the legislature and rallying the citizens of North Dakota to support women's issues, such as financial support from counties for mothers with dependent children under fourteen years of age living at home. In 1915, the North Dakota legislature passed the Mothers' Pension Law, but it failed to bring a woman suffrage amendment back to the voters. In 1915 and 1916, the VFWL teamed with a Grand Forks theater to sponsor a movie about suffrage and staffed booths at county fairs to sell postcards and women's journals. The money earned helped sponsor lectures and programs, send mailings to voters, and defray travel costs of delegates attending state and national meetings. The network of women's clubs and suffrage organizations allowed North Dakota women to be involved as delegates to meetings of the NAWSA, WCTU, and National Council on Women of the United States. Delegates brought local issues forward to the national stage and carried national issues and decisions back to local members.[21]

Wilder had begun attending national WCTU meetings annually in 1912, and while in Washington, D.C., for a national WCTU convention in 1913, she met with the North Dakota congressional delegation and watched the United States Senate debate the proposed Kenyon-Sheppard bill, which would regulate interstate liquor shipments. In 1916 and 1917, Wilder served as North Dakota VFWL delegate to the National Council on Women of the United States. Upon her return, she gave updates on congressional action relating to the status of woman suffrage, prohibition, and other issues important to women. The North Dakota WCTU appointed her state lecturer in 1916, making her responsible for disseminating news statewide. One of Wilder's speaking circuits included engagements in Mandan, Glen Ullin, and Hebron, culminating in a three-day institute to train WCTU members in Dickinson. She informed women about political issues from all levels of government and motivated women to improve conditions for families as politically active citizens.[22]

Wilder's lectures across North Dakota occurred as the Non-partisan League (NPL) organized against the control that "old Republican stand-patters," who favored railroads and out-of-state businesses over the economic needs of farmers, had on state politics.[23] The NPL gained control of the Republican Party in 1916, won on election day, and began work transforming the state in early 1917. On 23 January 1917, the North Dakota legislature passed a limited woman suffrage bill that NPL governor Lynn J. Frazier signed into law. North Dakota women could now vote and run for any office not listed in the state's constitution, including presidential electors, county surveyors, and county constables; and for all officers of cities, villages, and towns except police magistrates and city justices of the peace; and upon all questions or propositions submitted to a vote of the electors of their municipalities or other political divisions of a state. Women could not vote for governor, members of the legislature, senators, or representatives to Congress. With new voting responsibilities, the North Dakota VFWL offered programs for its members to clarify the offices and questions on which women could vote.[24]

The entry of the United States into World War I on 6 April 1917 changed the focus of the women's organizations to which Wilder belonged. The General Federation of Women's Clubs organized members across the country to support the government's war effort. The North Dakota branch of the federation worked with the North Dakota WCTU and VFWL to implement Red Cross programs for clothing and bandage production for soldiers, to increase food production at home through gardening and food conservation, and to encourage women to invest in the Liberty Loan program. Wilder was appointed chief of the Women's Bureau of Speakers in North Dakota for the four Liberty Loan campaigns conducted between 1917 and 1918. Wilder tapped into her women's club community to meet the goals set for North Dakota in each of the campaigns. The North Dakota WCTU contributed to the effort by purchasing two five-hundred-dollar bonds.[25]

The North Dakota VFWL continued meeting during the war, but as NAWSA leaders suggested, limited public suffrage activities. Members stayed informed of developments relating to Alice Paul's National Woman's Party (NWP) in part through Fortnightly Club member and NWP field worker Beulah Amidon and through a visit from Mabel Vernon of the Congressional Union and NWP. The NWP criticized President Woodrow Wilson and the Democratic Party for failing to support a federal woman suffrage amendment. Following Wilson's reelection in 1916, the NWP picketed the White House starting 1 January 1917. After the United States entered the war in Europe that April, protesters held banners that chastised Wilson for saying the United States was fighting for democracy abroad while denying it to women at home. That June, picketers were arrested, part of a wartime crackdown on dissent. During their imprisonment they conducted hunger strikes and endured forced feedings. The brutality inflicted upon the imprisoned protesters horrified the public. The North Dakota VFWL sent telegrams to President Wilson protesting the treatment of suffragists and the injustice of their arrests. The government yielded to the public outrage and released the imprisoned picketers on 27 and 28 November 1917.[26]

President Wilson publicly declared support for woman suffrage on 9 January 1918. The Nineteenth Amendment to the United States Constitution passed the Senate and House on 4 June 1919 and went to state legislatures for ratification. North Dakota's legislature voted to support ratification of the amendment on 1 December 1919, the twentieth state to do so. Tennessee became the thirty-sixth state to ratify on 18 August 1920, and the amendement became law when the secretary of state certified its ratification on 26 August.[27]

On 13 May 1918, Wilder led a roundtable discussion sponsored by the Fortnightly Club where several Fargo city officials shared their positions on issues of concern to citizens. Wilder's confidence in her ability to affect government had grown stronger, and she threw her hat in the ring for a seat on the Fargo City Commission in early 1919. She was the only candidate who promoted the building of a city-owned municipal power plant, which gained her the support of tradesmen. Voters approved the power plant on 2 April 1919 and elected Wilder to the commission by seven votes. She became the first woman in North Dakota elected to a city-wide office. Clubwomen in Fargo successfully lobbied for Wilder to be issued the police portfolio, and she was likely the first woman in the nation to serve as police commissioner. After meeting with the police force, she reappointed police chief Louis H. Dahlgren, who had served for over twenty years, reappointed Alice Duffy as policewoman, and selected several other officers. In her efforts to modernize, the City Commission authorized her to trade in an old Excelsior motorcycle and spend an additional two-hundred dollars to purchase a Harley Davidson for police use. Wilder gained celebrity as a woman police commissioner and received invitations to visit police headquarters in many American cities, including Chicago. After two years, Wilder moved to the health commission, an assignment which more closely fitted her interests. Her success working with the city commission defied those who believed women were not fit to govern.[28]

Wilder ran again for city commission in 1922, but lost her bid for re-election. She continued her advocacy through the WCTU, the Fortnightly Club, the Business and Professional Women's Club, and the League of Women Voters (LWV), established in 1919 after the Votes for Woman League dissolved. The LWV succeeded in lobbying the North Dakota legislature to have the word "male" struck from the state statute describing eligibility for jury service starting 1 July 1921. Wilder used the experience gained during the suffrage campaign and in city government to improve the lives of women and families for a quarter century after woman suffrage was won.[29]

Wilder deepened her involvement in WCTU activities at the state and national levels, serving on the Child Welfare Committee to provide clothing, food, and other resources to needy children at the state level. She also coordinated speakers' circuits in North Dakota for the Field Work Committee, and arranged workshops devoted to WCTU issues in North Dakota and on the national level for the Institutes Committee.[30] After her death on 12 April 1946, North Dakota WCTU president Elizabeth Preston Anderson wrote an "In Memoria" for Wilder that paid tribute to her involvement in the organization:

An active clubwoman throughout her life, Kate Selby Wilder (back row, fourth from left) posed with members of the Fortnightly Club in 1940. Institute for Regional Studies, North Dakota State University

Kate Selby Wilder had the honor of filling more important positions in the Woman's Christian Temperance Union of this state than any other one person in its history. When by changing conditions, a state office of a certain department of work assumed special importance, and it was difficult to find the right one to fill the place, we often turned to her, and she never disappointed us.

She used to say that the "S" in her name stood for "Substitute." Her first experience in public speaking was substituting for an outside speaker who failed to fill the engagements made for her. At different periods she served as director of a number of important departments and was director of Legislation at the time of her death. . . . She left no loose ends in her work—she finished her task.

EQUALITY AT THE BALLOT BOX

Her personality was enriched by her vivacity, her love of life, her interest in young people and her keen sense of humor. As a writer, she was clear and concise and as a speaker she was entertaining and convincing.[31]

Kate Selby Wilder successfully combined her support for temperance and prohibition with advocacy for woman suffrage. In North Dakota, that linkage resonated with many.

Wilder's involvement with the WCTU lasted throughout her adult life. She took the WCTU's Do-Everything directive to heart and became the embodiment of that policy through her efforts to protect home and family, to combat the double standard of sexual morality, and to work towards equal rights for women. Further, Wilder's leadership in the Fargo District of the WCTU moved Norwegian-speaking women from the margins to the core of the North Dakota WCTU and facilitated their integration into its governing structure. Wilder used networks created through women's clubs at the local, state, and national levels to advocate for and to enact political change. Her direct involvement with the North Dakota Votes for Women League, the General Federation of Women's Clubs, the Progressive Party, and the WCTU helped suffragists coordinate efforts, thus amplifying their message and expanding their reach. Wilder adopted nonpartisan strategies and modern campaign strategies as she spoke on behalf of the WCTU and woman suffrage. Indeed, her activities demonstrate the significance of the WCTU not only in North Dakota, but throughout the Northern Great Plains states and the nation during the early 1900s. WCTU members helped secure passage of two federal amendments to the United States Constitution: the Eighteenth Amendment (prohibition) and the Nineteenth Amendment (woman suffrage). Wilder motivated women and trained them as activists to achieve a stronger political voice. In the process, Kate Selby Wilder created women of considerable influence.

NOTES

I am grateful for the work of H. Elaine Lindgren whose research notes on Kate Selby Wilder were invaluable for this essay.

1. Edith Moriarty, "With the Women of Today," *Grand Forks (N.Dak.) Herald*, 25 Apr. 1922; "W.C.T.U. Notes," *Hope (N.Dak.) Pioneer*, 30 Apr. 1914.

2. Aileen S. Kraditor, *The Ideas of the Woman Suffrage Movement, 1890–1920* (New York: W. W. Norton & Co., 1981), p. 20; Elise Boulding, *The Underside of History: A View of Women through Time* (Boulder, Colo.: Westview Press, 1976), pp. 663–71.

3. "Women's Suffrage," Frances Willard House Museum and Archive, Francis Willard Historical Association (2015), franciswillardhouse.org.

4. Ibid.; June O. Underwood, "Western Women and True Womanhood: Culture and Symbol in History and Literature," *Great Plains Quarterly* 4 (Spring 1985): 95–96; Eleanor Flexner, *Century of Struggle: Women's History and the Women's Movement* (Cambridge, Mass.: Belknap Press of Harvard University Press, 1959), pp. 174–76; Kathleen Barry, *Susan B. Anthony: A Biography of a Singular Feminist* (New York: Ballentine Books, 1988), pp. 288–95; Carrie Chapman Catt to the Officers of the WCTU, 20 May 1899, folder 6, box 16, collection no. 2, Papers of Frances Willard, Frances Willard Memorial Library, Evanston, Ill.; Jennifer M. Ross-Nazzal,*Winning the West for Women: The Life of Suffragist Emma Smith DeVoe* (Seattle: University of Washington Press, 2011), pp. 26–28; "Honorable Jeannette C. Rankin, First Woman Elected to United States Congress a White Ribboner and Suffrage Worker from Montana," *North Dakota White Ribbon Bulletin* 21 (Oct. 1917): 2, copy in folder 7, box 2, Elizabeth Preston Anderson Papers, Mss 653, Institute for Regional Studies, North Dakota State University, Fargo.

5. Erin M. Masson, "The Woman's Christian Temperance Union 1874-1898: Combating Domestic Violence," *William & Mary Journal of Women and the Law* 3, no. 1 (1997): 185; "Kate Selby Wilder," *Woman's Who's Who in America: A Biographical Dictionary of Contemporary Women of the United States and Canada, 1914-15*, ed. John W. Leonard (New York: Commonwealth Co., 1914), p. 883; H. Elaine Lindgren, "Kate S. Wilder Research Notes," p. 5, folder 28, box 5, Subject File Series, Mss 0292, Institute for Regional Studies; "Mrs. Wilder Made First Money Selling Books," *Fargo Forum*, 19 Nov. 1921.

6. Karen J. Blair, *The Clubwoman as Feminist: True Womanhood Redefined, 1868-1914* (New York: Holmes & Meier Publishers, 1980), p. 104; "Social Reform," Frances Willard House and Musem Archive; Nancy Burkhalter, "Women's Magazines and the Suffrage Movement: Did They Help or Hinder the Cause?" *Journal of American Culture* 19 (Summer 1996): 343, 346; Boulding, *Underside of History*, pp. 663–71.

7. "Adelia Watson Selby," roll 1, North Dakota Federation of Women's Clubs, Indexes and Biographies, Pioneer Mother Project Records, Institute

for Regional Studies, microfilm. Civil War veterans could deduct up to four years from the five years the Homestead Act required to live on the land and make improvements before receiving the deed to the land.

8. Ibid.; "Mrs. Wilder Made First Money Selling Books."

9. Lewis F. Crawford, "Frederick Henry Wilder," in *History of North Dakota*, Vol. 2 (Chicago and New York: American Historical Society, 1931), pp. 346–47. *The Fortnightly Women's Club Annual Program Booklet, 1905–1906*, p. 4, *1910–1911*, p. 6, *1912–1913*, p. 6, all folder 8, box 2, Fortnightly Club Papers, MS 35, Institute for Regional Studies.

10. North Dakota, Insurance Department, "Market Conduct Examination Report–Pioneer Mutual Life Insurance Co." (Bismarck, 2001), pp. 2–3. The Ancient Order of United Workmen of North Dakota was a fraternal insurance organization that built its assets by absorbing the Grand Lodges of other states. Fargo became its headquarters in 1916. In 1947 it became the Pioneer Mutual Life Company. *Fornightly Women's Club Annual Program Booklets*; Blair, *Clubwoman as Feminist*, p. 104; *North Dakota White Ribbon Bulletin* 6 (Oct. 1904): 2; Bill G. Reid, "Elizabeth Preston Anderson and the Politics of Social Reform," *The North Dakota Political Tradition* (Ames: Iowa State University Press, 1981), pp. 183–202; "Equal Suffrage Warmly Defended by Noted Speaker," *Fargo Daily Courier News*, 5 Feb. 1912.

11. *Grand Forks Evening Times*, 17 Feb. 1906.

12. Kate S. Wilder, "Fargo Union President's Report, 1910 and 1911," *North Dakota White Ribbon Bulletin* 14 (Oct. 1910): 2; "Scandinavian W.C.T.U. Meet," *Devils Lake Weekly World*, 11 Oct. 1912.

13. Wilder, "Press Work," *North Dakota White Ribbon Bulletin* 14 (Mar. 1909): 4; Michael J. Lansing, *Insurgent Democracy: The Nonpartisan League in North American Politics* (Chicago: University of Chicago Press, 2015), p. x.

14. "Equal Suffrage Warmly Defended by Noted Speaker," pp. 1, 6; Meeting Minutes, 4 Feb. 1912, folder 3, box 1, Votes for Women League of North Dakota, Fargo Branch Records, Mss 49, Institute for Regional Studies (hereafter Fargo VWL Minutes).

15. Meeting Minutes, 1 Mar. 1912, folder 1, box 1, Votes for Women Club Records, OGLMC 80, Elwyn B. Robinson Department of Special Collections, Chester Fritz Library, University of North Dakota, Grand Forks (hereafter VWC Minutes); Fargo VWL Minutes, 4 Mar. 1912, 1 Apr. 1912; *North Dakota White Ribbon Bulletin* 16 (March 1912): 2.

16. Leslie Leighninger, ed., "From the Archives: Jane Addams and the Campaign of Theodore Roosevelt," *Journal of Progressive Human Services* 15 (Oct. 2004): 57–60; "Mrs. Wilder Made First Money Selling Books"; Fargo VWL Minutes, 20 Oct. 1912; VWC Minutes, 22 Oct. 1912.

17. VWC Minutes, 19, 27 Jan. 1913, 16, 31 July, 1914; Edith Moriarty, "With the Women of Today," *Grand Forks Daily Herald*, 25 Apr. 1922.

18. Lansing, *Insurgent Democracy*, pp. 62–63; *Grand Forks Herald*, 25 Apr. 1922; VWC Minutes, 16, 31 July 1914.

19. VWC Minutes, 10, 28 Sept. 1914; *Grand Forks Daily Herald*, 31 Oct. 1914.

20. North Dakota, Secretary of State, "General Election 11–03–1914, Archived Election Results," vip.sos.nd.gov; Jeanne F. Tucker, "The History of the Woman's Suffrage Movement in North Dakota," 1951, pp. 33–34, folder 12, box 1, Research Papers Written on North Dakota History Collection, OGLMC 263, UND.

21. "Equal Suffrage Warmly Defended by Noted Speaker"; "Mothers' Pensions," Ch. 185, H.B. No. 119 in N.Dak., *Laws Passed at the Fourteenth Session of the Legislative Assembly of the State of North Dakota* (Bismarck, 1915), p. 295. VWC Minutes, 12 Feb. 1915, (n.d.) July 1915, 12 Apr. 1916, 24 July 1916, 3 Oct. 1916; Fargo VWL Minutes, 2 Mar. 1916.

22. "Letter from Mrs. Wilder," *North Dakota White Ribbon* 16 (Jan. 1912): 2; ibid. 17 (Jan. 1913): 4; ibid. 21 (Oct. 1917): 2; "W.C.T.U. Notes: Mrs. Wilder of Fargo, Visited Hope Union," *Hope Pioneer*, 30 Apr. 1914; "Will Attend National W.C.T.U. Convention," *Valley City Weekly Times-Record*, 7 Oct. 1915; "Local News," *Dickinson Press*, 27 May 1916; Fargo VWL Minutes, 26 Oct. 1917.

23. Lansing, *Insurgent Democracy*, p. 2.

24. Ibid.; Emma S. Pierce, "North Dakota," in *History of Woman Suffrage*, Vol. 6, ed. Ida Husted Harper (New York: National American Woman Suffrage Association, 1922), p. 506; VWC Minutes, 13 Feb. 1917; VWL Minutes, 3 Feb. 1917.

25. Richard Sutch, "Liberty Bonds, April 1917–September 1918," Federal Reserve History, federalreservehistory.org; Ruth Roberts Haggart Diary 1917, folder 12, box 1, J. Roberts Haggart Papers, Mss 247, Institute for Regional Studies; "Mrs. Wilder Made First Money Selling Books"; "North Dakota Woman's Christian Temperance Union," p. 3, folder 11, box 1, Anderson Papers.

26. VWC Minutes, 13 Feb. 1917, 23 Oct. 1917; Fargo VWL Minutes, 19 Apr. 1917; J. D. Zahniser and Amelia R. Fry, *Alice Paul: Claiming Power* (New York: Oxford University Press, 2014), p. 292; "Women of Protest: Photographs from the Records of the National Woman's Party," Detailed Chronology National Woman's Party History, pp. 16–17, *American Memory*, Library of Congress, loc.gov/collections.

27. "Women of Protest," p. 22.

28. "Municipal Power Plan Discussed at Union Meeting," *Cooperstown (N.Dak.) Courier-News*, 27 Mar. 1919; "Mrs. F. H. Wilder Is Elected City Commissioner Over J.H. Dahl," *Fargo Forum*, 2 Apr. 1919; "Mrs. F.H. Wilder Is Elected City Commissioner," *Cooperstown Courier-News*, Apr. 15, 1919; Lindgren, "Kate S. Wilder Research Notes," pp. 5–7; Fargo VWL Minutes, 15 Mar., 11 Apr. 1919.

29. Edith Moriarty, "With the Women of Today," *Grand Forks Herald*, 18 Apr. 1919; Pierce, "North Dakota," p. 507; "North Dakota Action Praised," *Nonpartisan Leader* (Fargo, N.Dak.), 4 April 1921; Fargo VWL Minutes, 11 Apr. 1919.

30. "Child Welfare Department," in *Report of the Thirty-Third Annual Meeting North Dakota WCTU, Park River, North Dakota, 21–25 Sept. 1922*, pp. 45–46; "Minutes of the Woman's Christian Temperance Union," in *Report of the Thirty-Sixth Annual Meeting North Dakota WCTU, Bismarck, North Dakota, 24–27 Sept. 1925*, p. 38; *National Woman's Christian Temperance Union Department of Institutes Plan of Work, 1944–1945* (Evanston, Ill.: National WCTU Publishing House, 1945), p. 38, all in "Kate S. Wilder Research Notes," folder 28, box 5, H. Elaine Lindgren Research Papers, Mss 0292, Institute for Regional Studies.

31. Anderson, "In Memoriam," in *Report of the Fifty-Seventh Annual Meeting of the North Dakota WCTU, Bismarck, North Dakota, 1–3 Oct. 1946*, p. 29.

CONTRIBUTORS

Kristin Mapel Bloomberg is professor of women's studies at Hamline University in Saint Paul, Minnesota, where she also holds the Hamline University Endowed Chair in the Humanities. Her research interests focus on the history, culture, and literature of American women of the nineteenth century in the Trans-Mississippi West. She has published on such topics as women's social and civic organizations, woman suffrage, women and early co-education, and women-authored journals and novels. She is working on a biography of Nebraska woman's rights advocate Clara Bewick Colby.

Ann W. Braaten, Ph.D., is an associate professor of practice in the Department of Apparel, Design and Hospitality Management and curator of the Emily Reynolds Historic Costume Collection at North Dakota State University, Fargo. She studies the material culture of women to reveal their contributions to their families, business, and society.

Sara Egge is an associate professor of history at Centre College in Kentucky. Her book *Woman Suffrage and Citizenship in the Midwest, 1870–1920* examines how the woman suffrage movement emerged in rural communities in Iowa, Minnesota, and South Dakota. She received her Ph.D. from Iowa State University and undergraduate degrees from North Dakota State University.

Cody Dodge Ewert is associate editor at the South Dakota Historical Society Press. Raised near Power, Montana, he earned his B.A. and M.A. from the University of Montana before receiving a Ph.D. in history from New York University. His work on education and nationalism in the Progressive Era United States has appeared in the *Journal of the Gilded Age and Progressive Era* and *Montana: The Magazine of Western History.*

Dee Garceau is a historian and documentary filmmaker who specializes in American Indian history of the Northern Great Plains as well as selected topics in western gender history. After twenty-two years at Rhodes College in Memphis, Tennessee, where she earned the rank of full professor, Garceau now works as an adjunct professor at the University of Montana, Missoula. Her award-winning documentaries include *We Sing*, a film about powwow cultures of the intermountain West. Broadcast on Montana PBS, *We Sing* was filmed in collaboration with elders from the Confederated Salish and Kootenai Tribes and from the Blackfeet Nation.

Barbara Handy-Marchello, associate professor emerita, University of North Dakota, earned an M.A. at North Dakota State University and a Ph.D. at the University of Iowa. She is author of *Women of the Northern Plains: Gender and Settlement on the Homestead Frontier, 1870–1930*; *Traces: Early Peoples of North Dakota* with Fern Swenson; and *North Dakota: People Living on the Land*, as well as several articles on North Dakota history.

Jennifer Helton is assistant professor of history at Ohlone College in Fremont, California. A native of Wyoming, Helton first became interested in woman suffrage in her fourth-grade Wyoming history class. She holds undergraduate and master's degrees from Stanford University. She recently published an essay on woman suffrage in the West for a National Park Service website commemorating the 100th anniversary of the Nineteenth Amendment.

Jennifer J. Hill teaches, researches, and writes in the field of American Studies with an emphasis on reproductive history, women's history, and museology. Her lifelong interest in interdisciplinary scholarship drives her research projects, which are focused on the culture and history of the American West. She is currently an assistant teaching professor at Montana State University in Bozeman, Montana.

Ruth Page Jones received her M.A. in history from the University of Wisconsin-Milwaukee in 2015, completing a thesis on rural women in South Dakota in the early settlement years. She earned her B.A. in German and political science at the University of South Dakota, followed by a B.S. in applied computer science at the University of Wisconsin-Parkside. Following careers in computer technology, political advocacy, and charitable nonprofit work, she is now pursuing her interest in the histories of communities and women in South Dakota.

Kelly Kirk is an instructor of history and the director of the University Honors Program at Black Hills State University in Spearfish, South

Dakota. She also directs the National Cemetery Administration's Veterans Legacy Program on campus, which seeks to tell the stories of those interred in veterans' cemeteries through public history materials. While her specialization is gender and politics in western American history, Kirk is focusing on topics in state and regional history.

Renée M. Laegreid, Ph.D., is professor of history, United States West, at the University of Wyoming. Her area of specialty is women and gender in the twentieth-century West with publications that include *Riding Pretty: Rodeo Royalty in the American West* and a co-edited volume of essays, *Women on the North American Plains*. A longtime member of the Coalition for Western Women's History, she actively encourages scholarship in all areas of women, gender, and sexuality in the American West.

Lori Ann Lahlum is professor of history at Minnesota State University, Mankato, where she teaches courses on the American West, environmental history, Minnesota history, western women's and gender history, and political history in the northern grasslands. With Betty Bergland, she edited *Norwegian American Women: Migration, Communities, and Identities*. She hopes to complete her book on Norwegian immigrant women in the northern grasslands soon so she can begin a biography of South Dakotan Richard Olsen Richards. Lahlum grew up on a farm in the Griswold community, which no longer appears on North Dakota maps.

Amy L. McKinney is an associate professor of history at Northwest College in Powell, Wyoming. She teaches a variety of courses including women in the West, history of the North American West, Wyoming history, and Montana history. She received her Ph.D. from the University of Calgary, specializing in rural and western women's history, North American western history, and the United States–Canadian borderlands.

Paula M. Nelson is professor emerita in the Department of History at the University of Wisconsin-Platteville, where she taught for twenty-six years. Her research interests include agricultural settlement in the Great Plains and upper Midwest, rural life and culture, rural women's history, and small towns. Nelson is the author of *After the West Was Won* and *The Prairie Winnows Out Its Own*, books about West River South Dakota; the editor of *Sunshine Always*, courtship letters from Dakota Territory; and co-editor of *The Plains Political Tradition*, vol. 3, essays on the political culture of South Dakota.

Kelly O'Dea is an M.A. student in the University of South Dakota's Department of History. Her thesis, "Eastern Bloc Response to the 1973 Wounded Knee Occupation: A Study of Cultural Phenomena in Political Activism," focuses on the connections between indigenous activists in North America and Eastern Bloc residents.

Molly P. Rozum, a native of Mitchell, South Dakota, is associate professor and Ronald M. Nelson Chair of Great Plains and South Dakota History at the University of South Dakota in Vermillion. She teaches courses on United States women, the Great Plains, the American West, and South Dakota. She earned a Ph.D. from the University of North Carolina at Chapel Hill and a B.A. from the University of Notre Dame. Her research interests center on comparative United States-Canadian northern grasslands and her book, *Grasslands Grown: Sense of Place and Regional Identity on North America's Canadian Prairies and American Plains*, 1870–1950, is forthcoming.

INDEX

Abbot, Teddy Blue, 366n53
Aberdeen, S.Dak., 105n52, 135, 141–42,
163n55, 182, 209, 229
Aberdeen Daily News, 223
Aberdeen News, 140, 201
Aberdeen Pioneer, 240
abolitionist movement, 37, 39, 44, 48,
253. *See also* slavery
Adams, Irene, 132
Addams, Jane, 299n4, 302, 331, 376
African Americans: interracial
marriage and, 248, 364n31;
migration to Northern Great Plains,
27n31; as research topic, 20; suffrage
efforts in Montana, 10, 27n33; voting
rights and, 4–5, 15, 28n39, 39–42,
47–48, 51, 55, 148, 246–47. *See also*
slavery
Alaska Territory, 193
Albany County (Wyo.), 60
alcohol, 86, 359–60, 366n53. *See also*
prohibition
Alderson, Mary Long, 12, 18, 108–9,
115–23, 124n26, 126n45, 127n54
alien suffrage, 15, 155–56, 175, 219, 221,
227–28, 234
allotments. *See* Dawes Severalty Act of
1887
American Indians: assimilation, 39,
243–44, 255, 263n64, 318; Burke
Act of 1906, 258n9, 345, 362n11;
citizenship and suffrage, 99, 262n61,
341–61; decline in land ownership,
258n10; empowerment of, 341–61;

encroachment of white settlement
on, 4, 40–41; Fort Laramie treaties,
35, 38, 40–41, 52; Ghost Dance
movement, 254–55; interracial
marriage and, 347–49; land cessions,
244–45, 342; Marias Massacre/
Baker Massacre, 354, 360, 365n38;
mixed-blood prejudice, 342–44,
347–53, 356, 358–60, 366n45; Peace
Policy, 52; restrictions on voting,
15, 18–19, 62, 98, 240–47, 252–53,
256, 345, 347–48; South Dakota
enfranchisement of, 240–56; women
excluded from voting, 15; Wounded
Knee Massacre, 255. *See also* Dawes
Severalty Act of 1887
American Society of Equity, 92
American Woman Suffrage Association
(AWSA): NWSA merger, 26n27,
259n23, 314, 335n11, 370; NWSA
split, 252; and state campaigns, 111,
310–11, 313–16, 334n4; strategy of,
193
Amidon, Beulah, 380
Ancient Order of United Workmen of
North Dakota, 372, 385n10
Anderson, Elizabeth Preston, 12, 17, 82,
89, 92–95, 99, 338n53, 381
Anderson, John, 89
Anthony, Susan B.: at Democratic
convention, 49; denigration of
Indians, 250; Do-Everything
policy, 223; and *History of Woman
Suffrage*, 16–17, 124n12; merger

[393]

Index

EQUALITY AT THE BALLOT BOX

North Dakota, 89, 325-33, 377-80; on prohibition and ethnicity, 219-34; in South Dakota, 61, 138-43, 146, 219, 237n31; state campaigns, 8, 10-11, 303; and suffrage anniversary, 266, 278n5; and WCTU, 9; in Wyoming, 61

National Association Opposed to Woman Suffrage (NAOWS), 146

National Council of Women Voters, 310

National Education Association, 209

National Federation of Women's Clubs, 368

National Woman's Party, 152, 340n78

National Woman Suffrage Association (NWSA): and AWSA merger, 26n27, 259n23, 314, 335n11, 370; in Dakota Territory, 78, 313; and state campaigns, 7-8; strategy of, 193, 335n11; and WCTU, 369

National Woman Wage Earners' League Opposed to Suffrage, 90

National Women's Rights Association, 61

Nebraska, 4, 38; early suffrage campaign in, 2; prohibition of slavery in, 38; restricts Indian voting, 262n61; statehood, 23n11, 63n7

Neil, Caroline, 56, 68n92

Nelson, Candis, 376

Nelson, Julia B., 224-26, 229-31, 233

Nelson, Paula M., 18, 128-58, 391-92

Nevada, 38, 63n7, 125n30, 326

New England Anti-Suffrage League, 146

New Hampshire, 146

New Jersey, 68n98, 120

New Mexico, 326, 367n57

New Ulm, Minn., 185

New York, 43-45, 50, 66n54, 126n45, 128, 140, 142-43, 145, 156, 285, 297, 354-55, 377

New York Call, 156

New York State Association Opposed to Woman Suffrage, 138-39

New York State Woman Suffrage Association, 311

New York Times, 285-86, 292

New York Tribune, 266

Nez Perce Indians, 35

Nichols, Clarina Howard, 194

Nickerson, H. G., 268-69

Nielson, Minnie J., 96-98

Nineteenth Amendment, 3, 13-16, 19, 28n40, 34, 60, 100, 131-32, 187n15, 192-93, 264-78, 324, 332, 380, 383

Nonpartisan Leader, 105n64, 274

Nonpartisan League (NPL), 13, 17, 81, 93-97, 274, 297, 375, 379

nonpartisanship, 131, 137, 165n93, 332, 383

Norbeck, Peter, 155, 271, 275, 303-4

Norlin, Dennis A., 176

North Dakota: resistance to woman suffrage in, 310; enfranchisement of women, 1-4, 10, 16, 21n4, 27n36, 192, 379; and Indian citizenship, 99; and Nineteenth Amendment, 273-78, 380; politics of woman suffrage in, 71-100; prohibition, 80-81, 83-85; statehood, 1, 75-77

North Dakota Association Opposed to Woman Suffrage (NDAOWS), 90-91

North Dakota Chautauqua Association, 331

North Dakota Educational Association, 334n4

North Dakota State Nurses' Association, 89

North Dakota State Sunday School Association, 89

EQUALITY AT THE BALLOT BOX

Dakota, 80–81, 83–85, 104n46; South Dakota, 137–38, 174–78, 199, 219; Wyoming, 112. See also *Woman's Christian Temperance Union*

prostitution, 7, 25n26, 148, 154, 157, 211n4, 370

Prucha, Francis Paul, 243–44, 258n9

Puerto Rico, citizenship and suffrage, 28n40

Pyle, Mary Shields ("Mamie"), 9, 13–14, 17, 146, 154, 274–75, 301, 303

Queen City Mail, 245

race/racism, 19, 51–52, 240–56, 342–44, 347–53, 356, 358–60, 364n30, 366n45

railroads: on Great Plains, 37–38, 43; and suffrage, 81, 85–86; in Wyoming, 63n8, 287

Ramsey, Alexander, 72–73

Rankin, Jeannette, 9, 12, 17–18, 20, 89, 120–21, 126n45, 126n47, 294–99

Rankin, Wellington D., 300n15, 344, 370

Ransom County (N.Dak.), 205, 318

Rapid City, S.Dak., 163n55, 191, 197, 201–2, 204

Rapid City Republican, 205, 211n4

Rawlins, Wyo., 43

Reconstruction, 4–5, 17, 22n11, 35, 41–43, 47, 51–52, 58, 62, 247, 249–50, 252–53, 279n17, 371–72

Red Cloud War of 1866–1868, 40

Red Cross, 135, 301, 303, 379

Redfield, S.Dak., 154

Red River Valley University, 336n25

Reed, Dorinda Riessen, 28n44, 145, 151, 212n6, 304

Reel, Estelle, 60, 210

religion. See churches/Christianity

Remonstrance, 128–30

Remonstrants (anti-suffrage group), 9, 133, 142, 152. See also anti-suffrage movement

Revised Codes, 338n51

Revolution, 45, 55

Rewman, Mabel Fontron, 14, 20, 301–4

Rewman, Paul, 302

Rhode Island, 146

Rickards, J. E., 112

Roberts County (S.Dak.), 245–46

Robinson, Doane, 102n12

Rock Creek County (Wyo.), 60

Rock Springs, Wyo., 43

Rockwell, William S., 50

Rogers, Elwin, 178n3

Rolfe, Eugene Strong, 319, 337n33

Roosevelt, Theodore, 376

Rossteuscher, Charles, 5

Rowe, William H., 318–19, 322, 337n31

Royle, Edwin M., 359

Rozum, Molly P., 240–56, 392

Ruble, S. S., Mrs., 163n55

Rugby, N.Dak., 376

Saint James African Methodist Episcopal Church (Helena), 27n33

Saint Louis World's Fair of 1904, 150

Samantha (fictional character), 325, 339n55

Sanborn, Alice, 205

Sanders, Harriet Fisk, 355

Sanders, Helen Fitzgerald, 360

Sanders, Wilbur Fisk, 355, 358–59

Sanders, William Fisk, 355

San Francisco Chronicle, 350

Sargent County (N.Dak.), 151, 205

Sauve, Jeff, xii, 178n

Scandinavians. See Danish immigrants; Norwegian immigrants; Swedish immigrants

Schell, Herbert S., 304

Schlicting, Henry, 151

Schofield, John, 41, 46

school suffrage: campaign for, 69n98, 102n11, 134, 192–211; Dakota Territory, 2, 6, 10, 73–77, 80, 102n12, 191–96, 212n6, 215nn12–14, 234n3; early approval of, 192–93; Montana Territory, 2, 6, 10, 112, 121, 192, 205, 344–45, 356; North Dakota, 2, 83, 88, 205, 309–33; as research topic, 18, 211n, 212n6; South Dakota, 2, 11, 130, 138, 161n24, 196–211, 216n55, 216n57, 227–29, 303, 375; Wyoming, 60, 205

school superintendents, county/state, 2, 6, 11, 57, 59–60, 69n105, 71, 82–83, 96–98, 112–13, 161n24, 196–99, 319–21, 323–25, 330, 337n40, 338n55

Schroeder, John, 184

Scotland, S.Dak., 201

Scott, John W., 79

Seawell, Molly Elliot, 148, 164n60

Sells, Cato, 347

separate spheres, ideology defined, 133–36, 159n14, 369

sexism, 138, 161n22, 194, 292, 296, 316–18, 322–23, 326, 330. *See also* feminism; gender/gender roles

Shaw, Anna Howard, 8, 89, 151–52, 228, 249–52, 254–55, 263n64, 266, 377

Sheeks, Ben, 51, 53–54, 58

Sheldon, Emily K., 93–94

Sheridan, Wyo., 59

Sheridan County (Wyo.), 276

Sheridan Enterprise, 276

Shortridge, Eli, 84

Shoshoni Indians, 23n15, 35

Shuler, Marjorie, 274

Silent Call (Royle), 359

Simmons, Anna R., 145–46, 199

Simpson, Josephine Sarles, 93

Sioux Agreement of 1889, 244

Sioux Falls, S.Dak., 136, 138, 141, 152, 184, 213n12

Sioux Falls Argus-Leader, 138, 162n45, 245

Sioux Falls Brewing and Malting Company, 151

Sioux Valley News, 163n47

Slack, Artemus, 44

Slack, Edward Archibald ("E. A."), 43–44, 46, 54–56, 170, 268

Slack, Robert, 44

Slater, H. D., Mrs., 323

Slaughter, Benjamin F. ("Frank"), 75, 102n16

Slaughter, Linda Warfel, 17, 71, 73, 75–76, 78, 81, 100 & n1, 102n16, 103n35, 205

slavery, 22n11, 38–39, 44–45, 253. *See also* African Americans

Smith, Cora E. *See* Eaton, Cora Smith

Smith, Goldwin, 128

Smith, John G., Mrs., 274

Smith, Lizzie W., 60

Smith, Sara Emma Barnes, 309–33, 334nn4–5, 338n45

Sneider, Allison L., 243

socialism/socialists, 93–94, 96–97, 142, 155–56

Socialist Party, 92–93

Sonnesberger, Delilah, 59

South Dakota: anti-suffrage efforts in, 128–58; enfranchisement of women in, 1–4, 10, 16, 25n24, 27n37, 28n39, 156–57; and Nineteenth Amendment, 273–78; Norwegian immigrants in, 174–78; post-statehood suffrage referendum, 240–56; statehood, 1, 77, 203; suffrage efforts in ethnic communities, 218–34

EQUALITY AT THE BALLOT BOX

True Womanhood (Cult of
Domesticity), 71, 100. *See also*
gender/gender roles
Tucker, Jeanne F., 28n44, 101n1,
103n27, 105n57
Turner, Ezra, 80
Turner County (S.Dak.), 229, 231–32,
234
Turner County Herald, 199–200, 215n51

Uncle Tom's Cabin (Stowe), 45
Under Bull (Blackfeet), 343
*Unexpurgated Case Against Woman
Suffrage* (Wright), 147
Union Pacific Railroad, 287
Union Signal, 199–200
Unita County (Wyo.), 60, 169, 171
Universal Franchise League, 154
universal suffrage, 183, 242–43, 260n33,
310
University of North Dakota, 28n44,
101n1, 310, 313, 315, 324, 333n3,
334n4, 336n25
University of South Dakota, 304
University of Washington, 296
University of Wisconsin, 113
University of Wyoming, 265, 269, 272
United States Congress: and African
Americans, 4–5, 51; Burke Act,
258n9, 345, 362n11; creates
Northern Great Plains territories,
4, 24n14, 37, 40–41, 71–72; Dawes
Severalty Act, 243, 263n61;
Expatriation Act, 28n40; first
woman elected to, 120, 298–99;
Fort Laramie Treaty of 1851, 36,
38; Homestead Act, 39; and Indian
citizenship, 98; Indian women
elected to, 361, 367n57; Kenyon-
Sheppard bill, 378; Nineteenth
Amendment, 98, 131–32, 264,
277–78, 380; Reconstruction,
38–39, 252–53; statehood petitions/
approvals, 1, 4, 6, 21n2, 77, 131, 170–
72; and woman suffrage, 40, 43, 61,
72, 187n15, 250, 252, 329
United States Constitution. *See* specific
amendments to
United States Forest Service, 347
United States Supreme Court:
citizenship and suffrage rulings,
28nn39–40, 247, 262n61
Utah/Utah Territory, 23n12, 35, 68n98,
138, 148, 193
Ute Indians, 35

Valley City, N.Dak., 93, 97, 338n53, 376
Vanderhule, Adena, 228–34
Vanderhule, Clarence, 229
Vanderhule, George, 228
Vanderhule, Matilda, 228–34
Vanderhule, Ross, 229
Van West, Carroll, 110
Veblen, Ellen May Rolfe, 337n33
Vermillion (S.Dak.) Equal Suffrage
Association, 142
Vermont, 49, 146, 194, 212n6
Vernon, Mabel, 380
Villard, Henry, 77
Virginia, 41, 148, 212n8
Volin, S.Dak., 218
Votes for Women (slogan), 140, 153, 298,
332, 340n79, 376
Votes for Women League (VWL),
12, 88, 91, 93–96, 332, 373–80, 383
voting rights: admission of Northern
Great Plains states and, 1–4, 192;
African Americans and, 4–5, 39, 42,
47–48; citizenship and, 15, 249, 361;
ethnic prejudice and, 234; Fifteenth
Amendment and, 39, 252; land
ownership and, 242, 249, 252, 256,

258n10; limited to white men, 4, 24n14; Montana women, 7, 298, 344; Nineteenth Amendment and, 13, 15, 270; non-citizen immigrants, 25n25, 253–54; North Dakota women, 12–13, 74; restrictions on Indians, 15, 18–19, 62, 98, 240–47, 252–53, 256, 345, 347–48; South Dakota women, 131; voting as privilege, 89, 249; voting as duty, 183; voting as right, 74–77, 80; women and, 5–7, 39–40, 58, 377–78; Wyoming women, 5–6, 33–62, 169–72, 267–69. *See also* school suffrage

Wade, Benjamin, 47
Wadsworth, Alice, 156
Wage-Earning Women and the State (Bronson), 150
Wahpeton, N.Dak., 336n25
Waite, Davis, 193
Waldron, Jane Van Meter, 247–48
Walsh, George H., 84
Walshtown, S.Dak., 230
Walworth County (S.Dak.), 205–6
Ward, Doris Buck, 28n44, 125n43
Wardrope, Victor, 88–89
Warren, Francis E., 1, 169, 267
Washington (state), 11–12, 22n11, 78, 111, 125n30, 126n45, 162n33, 162n44, 296–97, 310, 313, 332, 370
Washington, D.C., 41, 60–61, 121, 146, 252, 270, 297–98, 299n5, 300n12, 302, 329, 332, 348, 378
Washington Evening Star, 297
Washington State Equal Suffrage Association, 301
Watertown, S.Dak., 61, 153–54, 162n45
Webb, Walter Prescott, 15–16, 22n7
Webster, S.Dak., 132, 140
Weed, M. I., Mrs., 206–8

Weekly Rocky Mountain Star, 42
Weible, Mary Darrow, 88
Wessington Springs Herald, 200–1, 203–4
Western Womanhood, 323, 327, 329–31
Whedon, Mary Ann, 88
Wheeler, Mary, 113
Wheeler, Roy McMillan, Mrs., 163n55
Whitford, Lea (Blackfeet), 367n57
Wickster, Marion, 94
Wilcox, Hamilton, 5
Wilder, Frederick H. ("Frank"), 372
Wilder, Kate Selby, 19–20, 88, 290–92, 368–83
Wilder, Laura Ingalls, 157
Wilkinson, Jean, 153
Willard, Frances, 61, 223, 369–71
Williams, Clare, 142–43, 162n45
Wilson, Woodrow, 121, 185, 299n5, 380
Wisconsin, 151, 270, 287, 297
Woman's Anti-Suffrage Association of South Dakota, 180, 184
Woman's Column (newsletter), 193
Woman's Journal (newspaper), 2, 111, 154, 227, 313, 320, 334n4
Woman's Protest (journal), 147, 149, 151
Woman's Relief Corps, 334n4
Woman Suffrage Society of Toledo, Ohio, 40
Women Against General Women's Voting, 184
Women and Politics (Catt), 152
Women on the North American Plains (Laegreid and Mathews), 15–16
Women's Anti-Suffrage Association of South Dakota, 180, 184
Woman's Christian Temperance Union (WCTU): Do-Everything policy, 19, 223, 228, 368, 371, 375; founding of, 369–71; Grand Forks chapter, 334n5, 338n45; Minneapolis chapter, 311;

North Dakota chapter, 81; petitions for woman suffrage, 6–7; supports state suffrage campaigns, 10–11; and suffrage politics, 9, 136–37, 175, 368; Wyoming chapter, 61

women's clubs: activities of, 134, 368–69, 371–73; anti-suffrage clubs, 135–36, 144, 162n45; and immigrant groups, 224; Montana, 10, 118; and networking, 228, 326, 372, 376, 378, 383; North Dakota, 12, 78, 87–90, 328–31, 334n4, 368–83; political role of, 94–97, 144, 149–50, 301, 376–78, 381, 383; South Dakota, 61, 138, 143–44, 218; and WWI, 379; Wyoming, 264–65, 275

Wood, Francis B., 93

Wood, Howard R., 95

Woods, Charley (Blackfeet), 364n31

Woolege, W. A., Mrs., 137

Woolege, William A., 161n20

Woonsocket, S.Dak., 162n45, 201

Woonsocket Times, 240, 245

Working Women's Home (Chicago), 45

World's Columbian Exposition of 1893, 114–16, 122–23

World's Congress of Representative Women, 116

World War I, 97, 131, 135, 151, 155–56, 182, 185, 233, 298–99, 347, 379

Wounded Knee Massacre, 255

Wovoka (Paiute prophet), 254

Wright, Almroth, 147

Wynn, C. H., 262n61

Wyoming: African American voting rights in, 47–48, 51–52; anti-suffrage efforts in, 139, 169–72; as first suffrage state, 4, 16, 43, 169, 264, 266–67; and Indian lands, 40–41; and Nineteenth Amendment, 264–73, 275–78; railroads, 43, 63n8; statehood, 1, 21n2, 69n104, 138, 172; and suffrage anniversary, 19, 266, 268–69, 272–73, 278n5; suffrage movement in, 1–5, 16, 33–35, 101n4, 138, 192; as territory, 4, 37–38, 40–41, 101n4; women run for office in, 57, 68n98; women's early voting in, 68n98; women's political rights in, 33–62; women's property rights in, 50

Wyoming Blue Book, 69n105

Wyoming Day, 272–73, 278

Wyoming State Journal, 268

Yankton, S.Dak., 5, 37, 61, 72, 81, 101n3, 141, 154, 156, 182, 213n12

Yankton County (S.Dak.), 205–6, 218, 221, 223–34

Yankton Indians/Indian Reservation, 250

Yankton Press and Dakotan, 128

Yates, Richard, 39–40

Young, Ida Clarke, 90, 135

Young, Newton C., 90, 105n57

EQUALITY AT THE BALLOT BOX